SMALL FRUIT CULTURE
FIFTH EDITION

SMALL FRUIT CULTURE
Fifth Edition

James S. Shoemaker

Horticulturist Emeritus,
University of Florida
Agricultural Experiment
Station, Gainesville, Florida

THE AVI PUBLISHING COMPANY, INC.
Westport, Connecticut

Library of Congress Cataloging in Publication Data

Shoemaker, James Sheldon, 1898-
    Small fruit culture.

    Bibliography: p.
    Includes index.
    1.   Berries—United States.   2.   Viticulture—United
States.   3.   Berries—Canada.   4.   Viticulture—Canada.
I.   Title.
SB381.S53   1977   634′.7′0973   77-15469
ISBN 0-87055-248-1

Printed in the United States of America

Preface To
The Fifth Edition

The continuing demand for *Small Fruit Culture* by instructors, students, growers, extension services, vocational groups, foreign markets, libraries and others, for over more than a 40-year period since its first publication in 1934, has been most encouraging.

An impressive amount of new information for the Fifth Edition has appeared since publication of the Fourth Edition in 1975. Some important new illustrations have also been included. The fruits discussed in the six chapters are grapes, strawberries, various bramble fruits, currants and gooseberries, blueberries, and cranberries.

The objectives in the Fifth Edition, as in earlier editions, have been to retain basically sound information and to update the text with new practical and technical developments.

Since use of the metric system is increasing in the United States and Canada, and is mandatory in some cases, the notations for weights and measures have been converted from the formerly dominant British system. Notations for the British system appear parenthetically, immediately following the metric system, throughout the text. The corresponding Celsius (Centigrade) and Fahrenheit notations have been listed in a similar manner.

Each fruit is discussed in considerable detail, from propagation through harvesting and marketing, including topics such as site, soil, planting, fertilization, cultivars, pruning, irrigation, and other cultural practices. Diseases and insects are also discussed.

Extensive references have been presented for the various fruits. The listings broaden the scope of the text by including results of research in widespread areas.

It is again hoped that the material presented, and the manner in which it is presented, will continue to prove useful as a text and reference work, and as a guide to field practice.

JAMES S. SHOEMAKER

Gainesville, Florida
June 1977

Preface To
The Fourth Edition

Small Fruit Culture in its three previous editions, including substantial reprintings, dating back to first publication in 1934, has definitely proved to have a place in its field throughout a 40-year period of time. The steady and continuing demand for the book by instructors, students, growers, extension personnel, vocational groups, and others has been most encouraging. A complete Russian translation of the Third Edition appeared in 1958.

The book had a role in the development of a correspondence course made available by the Canadian Legion and Department of Veterans Affairs, during and after World War II, for study and rehabilitation by men in the services. The course was also taken by a number of United States service men who supplied only the same central address for forwarding to their location.

The objective in the Fourth Edition, as in earlier editions, consistently has been to retain basically sound information and to update the material by adding new practical and technical developments. The production of the crop of each fruit is dealt with from propagation through harvesting.

To support the usefulness of the book, and to broaden its scope, an extensive bibliography has been included for the fruits discussed. The revision of the reference lists indicates, in one way, the progress which has been made and that a large number of investigators are actively engaged in the field of small fruits.

One of the most pleasing experiences in writing the book has again been the splendid spirit of cooperation on the part of all from whom favors were asked. Hence, much more useful information has been included than otherwise would have been possible.

The author is greatly indebted to the following men who directly supplied useful information for the development of this edition: E.T. Andersen and O. A. Bradt, Horticultural Institute of Ontario, Vineland Station; J. F. Brooks, North Carolina State University, Raleigh; M. N. Dana, University of Wisconsin, Madison; E.L. Denisen, Iowa State University, Ames; A. Duncan and L. B Hertz, University of Minnesota, St. Paul; G. W. Eaton, University of British Columbia, Vancouver; R. G. Hill, Ohio Agricultural and Development Center, Wooster; G. S. Howell, Michigan State University, East Lansing; R. H. Sharpe and S. J. Locascio, University of Florida, Gainesville; H. J. Sefick, Clemson University, Clemson; B. J. E. Teskey, University of Guelph, Guelph; C. C. Zych, University of Illinois, Urbana.

Instead of indicating the references by a code number as in earlier editions, the name of the person and date of publication are given, usually at the end of a paragraph. This enables the reader to more easily relate the subject material to the source of the contribution.

A few of the new features include the Geneva Double Curtain system of training grapes; mechanical aid and machine-harvesting; disease-tested bramble fruits and strawberries; French Hybrid grapes; use of plastic mulch for southern grown strawberries; solid beds for high yields in strawberries; crumbliness in raspberries; improved handling methods for harvested berries; avoiding troubles with overbearing grapes by balanced pruning and suitable fertilizer, and in French Hybrids and vinifera, by bunch thinning; enlargement of some particular portions of the text; technical explanation of certain production troubles; pick-your-own berry harvesting; and new illustrations.

It is again hoped that the material presented, and the way in which it is presented, will continue to prove useful as a text and reference work, and as a guide to field practice.

JAMES S. SHOEMAKER

August 1974

Contents

Chapter 1

Grapes

Botanically the fruit of the grape is a berry. It is a simple fleshy fruit derived from a superior ovary and originating from a simple or compound pistil, with all parts of the ovary wall (except possibly the exocarp or external portion) remaining fleshy. Grapes are borne in clusters or bunches which vary greatly in size and number of berries. Grapevines often outlive the persons who set them. Many growers estimate the profitable usefulness to be 40 to 50 years.

Grape growing in North America is divided as follows: (1) European type (*Vitis vinifera*, as in California and Arizona). (2) American bunch type (*V. labrusca* and its derivatives), as in (a) the Great Lakes section —New York (including the Finger Lakes and other districts), Pennsylvania, Michigan and Ohio in the United States, and Ontario in Canada; (b) the Pacific Northwest—Washington and Oregon in the United States, and British Columbia in Canada; (c) the Midwest section— Arkansas, Missouri, Iowa, Illinois, Indiana, Kansas and Nebraska; (d) other areas, such as New Jersey and the Carolinas. (3) Muscadine *(V. rotundifolia)*, as in the South Atlantic and Gulf States. (See also French Hybrids).

Total production of all grapes in North America is about 3,723,540 metric tons (4,104,500 tons) a year. It is roughly divided as follows: (1) European type in California and Arizona 3,175,147 metric tons (3,500,000 tons); (2) American bunch grape in (a) Great Lakes section 453,592 metric tons (500,000 tons), (b) Pacific Northwest 77,000 metric tons (85,000 tons), (c) Midwest 12,000 metric tons (13,000 tons), (d) other states 3175 metric tons (3500 tons); (3) Muscadine 2722 metric tons (3000 tons). There is presently a great expansion in grapes produced for wine.

1

PART 1

VINIFERA (European or California Type)

In the vinifera type the skin adheres firmly to the flesh. Types in which the skin does not adhere, especially the American bunch, are often called "slip skin" grapes.

PRODUCTION REGIONS

Vinifera in the East

The many European-type cultivars[1], which have been tested in the East for several centuries, have required a longer and warmer summer, have not been winter-hardy, or have otherwise failed (e.g., from disease).

In spite of the difficulties encountered in growing vinifera cultivars in the East, there are growers who are willing to try. To give these grapes the best possible chance, consider the following points (Bradt 1972).

Select a site with above-average air and soil drainage. Avoid over-cropping by bunch thinning. Maintain moderate vine size and avoid late growth by ceasing cultivation in early summer. Use double trunks and delay pruning until just before growth starts. Maintain a thorough spray program to prevent mildew. Select only those cultivars that have had at least some limited success, e.g., Pinot Chardonay, White Reisling, Gamay Beaujolais, Pinot Noir and Gewurtytraminer.

California

California has over 202,350 ha (½ million acres) of vineyards, or about 45% of the total world acreage. It produces about 5% of the wine, 15% of the table grapes, and 40% of the raisins of the world. About 90% of the bunch grapes grown in North America are produced in California.

As in other grape areas of the country, there recently has been a tremendous boom in production for wine, due in part to the advent of machine-harvesting.

Grape Areas in California.—California contains a Great Interior Valley over 64 km (400 mi.) long and 80 to 137 km (50 to 85 mi.) wide, stretching from Redding to Bakersfield with these sections: the central part, Central Valley; the southern part, San Joaquin Valley; and

---

[1] According to the *International Code of Nomenclature for Cultural Plants*, "cultivar" has replaced "variety" for a designating a cultural variety, e.g., Concord grape.

the northern part, Sacramento Valley. All three parts are protected against adverse weather from the east by the 3050 m (10,000 ft) rampart of the Sierra Nevadas, from the wintry blasts of the north by the Siskiyous, and from ocean fogs by the coast ranges that parallel the shore.

The intermediate Central Valley is its coolest part, with 30.5 to 45.7 cm (12 to 18 in.) of rain and an effective temperature summation at Lodi of about 1943 C degree-days (3530 F degree-days) from April 1 to October 31. The accumulated daily mean temperature is over 10°C (50° F) (see Heat Summation). It owes its relative coolness to sea breezes that pass through the gap in the coast ranges near the Golden Gate.

Proceeding south through the San Joaquin Valley, the average temperature increases until it reaches, near the center of the south section at Fresno, a heat summation of 2588 C degree-days (4690 F degree-days). Annual rainfall decreases gradually from 27.9 cm (11 in.) at Modesto to 15.2 cm (6 in.) at Bakersfield, where irrigation is necessary. This is the main raisin-producing region, but large quantities of table and wine grapes are also grown.

Proceeding north from the Central Valley through the Sacramento Valley, the influence of the sea breezes gradually diminishes. Seasonal temperature increases until it reaches about 2527 C degree-days (4690 F degree-days) at Chico in the north section, or nearly the same as at Fresno. Unlike the San Joaquin, however, rainfall increases also, until it is 61 cm (24 in.) at Chico and 94 cm (37 in.) at Redding. Less irrigation is needed than farther south, except in Sutter County and parts of Yuba where Thompson Seedless covers a considerable area.

The Salinas Valley ("Salad Bowl of the World") is a narrow 129 km (80 mi.) long. The wine industry is moving into southern Salinas Valley at a rate which has led to the prediction that the value of the wine grapes will exceed that of the immense lettuce crop. The number of vineyards is rapidly increasing as the wineries move out of the increasingly congested San Francisco Bay area to the cleaner air and lower costs of the Salinas Valley.

Southern California.—This area includes counties south of the Tahachapi Mountains. The Colorado Desert region of the Imperial and Coachella valleys is the hottest grape growing area and produces the earliest grapes. About 80% of the United States grapes harvested in May, June and July are from the southeastern section of California.

Central Coast.—This area has two subdivisions: (1) North Bay, including Humboldt, Mendocino, Lake Sonoma, Napa and Marin counties; (2) South Bay, including Contra Costa, Alameda, Santa Clara, San Benito, San Francisco, San Mateo, Santa Cruz, Monterey and San Luis Obispo counties.

Arizona

Some of the larger river valleys and mesas at elevations of 1219 m (4000 ft) are suited for very early Thompson Seedless. Harvest in the Salt River Valley usually is 7 to 10 days earlier than in the San Joaquin Valley of California.

Washington State

This is primarily an area where the *labrusca* grape predominates. However, even with the possibility of critical sub-zero temperatures occurring on the average of every three years it is possible for growers to avoid cold damage to the more sensitive European cultivars. This is achieved by the control management under semi-arid conditions. By obtaining full maturity of grapes and vines at this latitude, prior to the occurrence of low temperatures, not only can fine wines be produced, but also cold damage to the vines is minimized (Clore 1976).

MAIN USES OF GRAPES

Wine

Table or dry wines require grapes of high acidity and moderate sugar content; dessert or sweet wines require grapes with high sugar content and moderately low acidity. Quality wines that are outstanding in bouquet, flavor and general balance require grapes with special characteristics. Texture of skin and pulp does not affect wine quality, but thick skin and firm pulp may reduce quantity.

In California, grapes with low pH and high acidity at maturity are generally desired for table wines. Therefore, breeding new cultivars for warm growing regions such as the interior valleys will probably necessitate the selection of fruits with high tartrate/malate ratios in order to ensure high acidity at maturity (Kliewer 1971 A).

Table

Grapes eaten fresh are called table grapes. They have an attractive appearance and good eating, carrying and keeping qualities.

Raisins

Raisins are essentially dried grapes. But different cultivars and drying methods may yield unlike products; hence there is a distinction between raisins and dried grapes. Desirable characteristics of a raisin cultivar include soft texture of the dried product, lack of tendency of the raisins to stick together when stored, seedlessness, early ripening, pleasing flavor, ease of drying, large or very small size, and high yield. Leading raisin cultivars are Thompson Seedless and Muscat of Alexandria. Dried "currants" are made from Corinth (Zante currant).

Unfermented Juice

Grapes for making sweet, unfermented juice should retain their natural fresh-fruit flavor throughout processing. The desirable strong, "foxy" flavor of Concord comes through processing almost unchanged; hence most American grape juice is made of Concord grapes. California is not an important producer of Concord.

Canning

Canning grapes are those seedless kinds, usually Thompson Seedless, used primarily in combination with other fruits for canned fruit salad and cocktail.

VINIFERA CULTIVARS

The "Big Five" cultivars in California are Thompson Seedless, Emperor, Zinfandel, Carignane and Tokay.

Cabernet Sauvignon.—Small black berries. Basis of the famous claret wines of the Gironde district of France. Makes a fine dry-wine grape when grown in the coastal regions of California. Origin: France.

Calmeria.—White to amber. Perfect-flowered and replacing the imperfect-flowered Almeria. High sugar content. California.

Cardinal.—Medium to dark red, large, early. "Shot" berries have been a weakness. Grown in the desert regions and in the warm interior valleys. California.

Carignane.—Black. Useful for making bulk red wine.

Carmine, Centurion, and Carnelion.—These are recent introductions as red, table wine cultivars.

Corinth.—Black. Berry very small, high in sugar and acid, mostly seedless. Dried to make "currant" raisins. Greece.

Emperor.—Deep rose to purplish. A leading shipping and storage table grape. Origin unknown.

Malaga.—Yellowish to light amber. Once California's leading grape. Most of the crop is now used for distilling material for wine. Spain.

Mission.—Berry black, small to medium. Used for making sweet wines, such as Angelica. Spain.

Muscat of Alexandria.—Yellowish-green. Ranks second in California for raisins (10%). Extensively used for muscatel, a dessert wine. Deficient in appearance for table grape shipment. North Africa.

Courtesy of Ontario Ministry of Agriculture and Food

FIG. 1.1.   TOP — TOKAY (RED), LEFT — THOMPSON SEEDLESS (WHITE),
RIGHT — RIBIER (BLACK)

Perlette.—White. Clusters compact, require thinning. Ripens 18 days before Thompson Seedless; 33% larger. Sugar content rather low. Retains its appearance well. California.

Petite Sirah.—Black, medium small. Red table wine. France.

Pinot Noir.—Black, medium small. Red table wine. France.

Queen.—Dark red. Midseason. Berries large, uniform. Although flesh texture is not as firm as in Tokay, the cluster is better and full color is more easily attained. Shipping quality fair. California.

Red Malaga.—Reddish-purple. Very large clusters. Earlier than Tokay. Shipping quality fair. Spain.

Ribier *(Alphonse Lavallee)*.—Berry very large. Chief black table grape in California. France.

Semillon.—Golden yellow. Chief sauterne cultivar of France. In California it is best suited to the North Coast region. France.

Thompson Seedless (Sultanina, Sultana, Oval Kismish).—White. Bunch large, heavily shouldered; berry oval, seedless; early. Leading table and raisin grape. Provides over 50% of the world's raisins and about 90% of California's. Annual ringing is practiced to improve berry size and adherence of the berries to the cluster for shipping. From it are made large quantities of white dessert wines and much distilling material to furnish alcohol for arresting the fermentation of other dessert wines. It constitutes 33% of California's grape acreage. Persia.

Tokay.—Flame-red. Bunch large and compact; berry large and ob-long. Formerly California's premier table cultivar, but now surpassed by several others. Grown in an intermediate region with moderately warm day weather and cool nights. Spain.

Zinfandel.—Black. Leading red wine grape in California. Compact cluster. Origin unknown.

Propagation

A grape cultivar is not reproduced to name from seed. The seedlings differ greatly, even though there has been no cross-pollination. New cultivars originate from seed, but it may be necessary to plant thousands of seeds and wait for a long period of time and testing before anything better than, or as good as the parent is found.

Cuttings.—Vinifera cuttings for own-roots are made a little longer than for labrusca cultivars which are discussed in Part 2.

Grafted Rootstocks.—Grafting on special rootstocks is standard practice where nematodes and phylloxera would otherwise cause serious damage.

For bench grafting use dormant, disbudded cuttings. Fit each of these with a 5.1 cm (2 in.) long scion and tie tightly. A knife-type grafting machine, which makes the cuts for stock and scion, promotes rapid work. Callus the grafts at 27°C (80°F) for 3 weeks or at 21°C (70°F) for a longer time. Pack them in a mixture of such as 3 parts sawdust and 1 part "chick" charcoal until planted.

Nematode-resistant stocks are such as Dog Ridge, Salt Creek, Solonis × *riparia* 1616, Solonis × Othello 1613, and *berlandieri* × *riparia*. Many vineyards in the San Joaquin Valley may be infested with nematodes. In general, grapes are seriously injured by nematodes only when grown in light or sandy soil, or sandy loams.

Phylloxera-resistant stocks are such as *rupestris* St. George (on shallow soils) and Aramon × *rupestris* Ganzin (on highly fertile soils). Phylloxera infestations are more severe in the coastal valleys than in the dry, irrigated interior vineyards.

Harmony is a new nematode- and phylloxera-resistant rootstock (Weinberger and Harmon 1966).

Bench grafting done at the ground level on the trunk of established vines is much like the grafting of fruit trees.

Yield

Yields of more than 22.4 metric tons per ha (10 tons per acre) are not uncommon with vinifera grapes. This is higher than that for the American type.

Heat Summation

Vinifera grapes begin growth in spring after the daily mean temperature reaches 10°C (50°F). A winter rest of 2 to 3 months while the average daily mean is below 10°C (50°F) is desirable, with some freezing but with no cold below –17.8°C (0°F). Daily means of at least 18°C (65° F) are needed for some.

Time from bloom to ripening is largely determined for each cultivar by the effective heat summation which, for a given place, is calculated by subtracting 10°C (50°F) from the mean temperature for each day and adding together algebraically the quantities thus obtained. For whole months, the same result or degree-days is obtained by multiplying the monthly mean (less 10°C or 50°F) by the number of days in the month.

Earliest cultivars need 871 C degree-days (1600 F degree-days); the latest need at least 1927 C degree-days (3500 F degree-days).

Thompson Seedless is ripe for table use at 18° Balling, and fully ripe for raisins at 25° Balling when the heat summation above 10°C (50°F), beginning at full bloom, reaches 1093 and 1649 C degree-days (200 and 3000 F degree-days), respectively. Tokay is ripe for table use at 1231 C degree-days (2250 F degree-days), and Emperor at 1816 C degree-days (3300 F degree-days) (Jacob and Winkler 1950).

Heat unit accumulation and mean monthly temperatures from April to October fall within a reasonably similar range for the British Columbia interior, Germany, northern France, and Ontario. California, New York and Washington state are somewhat higher, largely because of higher September and October temperatures. Vinifera cultivars mature well in Germany and France with as low or lower heat-unit accumulations than in British Columbia, where the same cultivars rarely ripen. This may be related to lower yield per vine, less fertile soil, and smaller day/night temperature fluctuations in the European areas (Fisher and Vielvoye 1968).

Winter minimums are sharply limiting to the cultivars that can be grown in many areas. California winters present little or no problem.

Day and Night Temperatures

Pinot Noir and Cabernet Sauvignon are mostly restricted to the coolest regions along the California coast. Tokay is grown in the intermediate region with moderately warm and cool nights. Cardinal is grown in the desert regions and in the warm interior valleys of California.

The levels of malate in the berries is inversely related to temperature. Degree Brix of Tokay fruits ripened at 32°C (90°F) phototemp was less than that of fruits ripened at 15°C (60°F). But nyctotemp had little effect on the concentration of sugars in Tokay and Cabernet Sauvignon. Temperature during maturation had no effect on berry weight or on level of arginine (Kliewer 1973).

Heat and Pigmentation

Formation of red pigments is reduced by high temperature to a greater extent in Tokay than in some other cultivars. Tokay ripened at cool day and night temperatures has better coloration than fruit ripened at hot-day and cool-night temperatures or cool-day and warm-night temperatures. The relatively low amounts of sugars and anthocyanins in Tokay grapes ripened at high phototemp may be due to either a reduction in synthesis or to degradation of these compounds, or a combination of both (Kliewer 1973).

Low light intensity markedly reduces the levels of sugars and starch in root and trunk compared with levels in vines grown at high temperatures (Kliewer 1972).

Planting

Growth of unwanted scion roots sometimes is a problem in growing vinifera grapes on nematode- and phylloxera-resistant stocks. Place the graft union above soil level; remove scion roots where they develop at other planting levels.

In the interior valleys and desert areas of California most vigorous wine grapes and practically all table grapes do well at 2.4 × 3.7 m (8 × 12 ft). In the cooler coastal areas, space moderate-growing cultivars 1.5 to 1.8 × 3.7 m (5 to 6 × 12 ft) and vigorous ones 1.8 to 2.4 × 3.7 m (6 to 8 × 12 ft).

Wide row spacing reduces harvesting labor in four ways: (1) the grapes can be hauled out from between the rows rather than carried to the avenue by hand; (2) pruning brush can be disked or shredded instead of hauled away; (3) more machine equipment can be used; and (4) more space is provided for handling irrigation water.

Generous spacing in the row further improves efficient operation. About the only point in favor of close spacing is that it usually results in larger crops while the vines are young. But unless wide spacing is carried to extremes, the influence on yield is minor.

Machine harvesters vary and spacing may need to be altered accordingly.

Fertilizer

Soil and leaf (petiole) analyses have become increasingly efficient and available to growers. Growers should avail themselves of these services in their locality.

Nitrogen (N).—N fertilizer may increase yield about 10% in California. Total N, in foliar analysis, is high at bloom and then declines rapidly to a fairly constant level in midsummer. Nitrate levels also decrease sharply during rapid growth, but partially recover before harvest. Fertilized and check vines may differ more in nitrate content than in total N. Bloom-time nitrate content of petioles is inversely correlated with yield after two years of N application; the lower the initial nitrate level, the greater the yield response. On sites already high in nitrates, fertilizer may depress yields below the checks (Cook and Kishaba 1957).

Arginine is the main form of storage N in the grapevine, accounting for 50 to 70% of the soluble N in roots, trunk and canes just prior to budbreak. Arginine, and to a lesser extent other free amino acids, largely supply the vine with its N requirements during the spring flush of new growth. Total soluble free amino acids or arginine may be better indicators of the N status of grapevines than is total N (Kliewer and Cook 1971).

Total soluble solids, total acidity, and tartrate in grape berries is not significantly affected in Thompson Seedless by N treatment (Kliewer 1971 B).

Potassium (K).—K deficiency is not extensive enough to warrant general fertilization of California's 404,700 ha (½ million acres) of grapes. K content, especially of leaf petioles, seems more reliable than soil analysis for exchangeable K as an indication of K needs. Until conclusive correlation is developed between K and yield response, restrict heavy potassium sulfate treatments necessary for uptake by the vines to localized areas that show visual deficiency. In San Joaquin vineyard K-deficiency is corrected better by infrequent massive doses, 1120 to 1681 kg per ha (1000 to 1500 lb per acre), of potassium sulfate than by smaller annual rates (Cook and Carlson 1961).

Zinc (Zn).—Probably the most prevalent visual symptoms of mineral deficiency in California vineyards are associated with low levels of Zn. They include stunted growth, midsummer development of small, cholorotic leaves with a wide petiole sinus, a poor set of fruit resulting in shot-berry clusters, and a light crop. Yields are reduced on vines that are only slightly affected by Zn deficiency; they are low on badly affected vines.

Other Elements.—See introductory statement under Fertilizer.

Salt

Excess chloride causes leaf burn, defoliation and dieback so that even moderate chloride salinities may be lethal. With low chloride accumulation, moderate salinity may cause a small reduction in vegetative vigor.

Thompson Seedless, Dog Ridge, 1613-3 and Salt Creek roots may accumulate only ½, ⅓, ¹⁄₁₀ and ¹⁄₁₆ as much chloride (dry weight), respectively, as do scions on Cardinal roots. Because of very low chloride accumulation by vines of 1613-3 and Salt Creek roots, the salt tolerance on these vine roots probably is limited by osmotic effects long before chloride reaches toxic levels (Bernstein 1969).

Irrigation

Early in the season rapidly elongating shoot tips normally have a soft, yellow-green look. This condition persists almost until ripening starts if some of the soil below cultivation depth loses its readily available moisture.[2] If increasingly large portions of the soil become dry,

---

[2] Readily available moisture is that fraction of soil moisture between the field capacity and the permanent wilting percentage.

the growth rate diminishes and the tips gradually become harder, darker, or the gray-green of mature leaves. When most of the soil is depleted of its available moisture, growth ceases; leaf curling results and the older leaves become dry, die and fall (Jacob and Winkler 1950).

When to Irrigate.—During the dormant season the root zone should be filled to field capacity[3] by rain or by irrigation. Apply enough water to wet the areas that require most water or that are slowest to take the water.

After growth starts, apply no further water until some of the soil in the root zone dries out almost to the permanent wilting percentage (PWP).[4] Change in appearance of the vines, caused by slower growth, indicates when much of the soil has reached the PWP. On deep soils no great damage may occur for several weeks after the water shortage symptoms appear.

Amount of Water Needed.—Insufficient water during berry enlargement keeps the fruit from reaching full size; later irrigation does not enable undersized ones to become normal size. Severe shortage of readily available water during ripening causes delayed maturity, dull fruit color and possibly sunburn. A slight shortage just before and during this period may hasten ripening, because it limits shoot growth.

After the fruit is ripe, and especially after harvest, the vines become adjusted to a limited water supply. They retain their leaves and their canes ripen, even though the soil throughout most of the root zone is at the permanent wilting percentage. No further shoot growth occurs. In hot, dry regions, however, only early cultivars are grown for table grapes; they ripen and are picked in early summer. Neglect of the vine for the rest of the season causes damage; irrigate at least once and often several times after harvest.

Effect on Fruit.—Storage qualities of Thompson Seedless, Tokay and Emperor table grapes are not affected by irrigation soon before harvest. No visible differences occur in either Thompson Seedless or Muscat raisins produced under dry treatments. Wines of grapes from both wet and dry treatments differ little if the fruit reaches maturity. A continuously moist soil sometimes slightly delays maturity. But berry size is smaller, and the wine darker, if the soil moisture in the main root zone area is reduced to the permanent wilting percentage and remains there for a considerable time while the fruit is growing (Hendrickson and Veihmeyer 1951).

When readily available moisture is continuously present, fruit size

---

[3] Field capacity is the amount of moisture a drained soil can hold 2 to 3 days after a rain or irrigation.

[4] Permanent wilting percentage is the soil moisture condition, measured in percentage, at which the leaves wilt and the plants cannot obtain enough moisture to grow normally.

is not affected by irrigation. The water requirements are served if the moisture content of the soil in contact with the roots does not reach the permanent wilting percentage and remain there long.

Suckering, Pinching, Topping and Removing Leaves

In California, sucker carefully and thoroughly in young vineyards and at least once every year in old ones. Crown suckering (removing growths from the branches and arms) opens the head of the vine to improve fruit quality or to better concentrate growth; but constant and complete removal of all suckers from large branches and arms may promote sunburn.

Pinching (removing the growing shoot tip) may be useful to check the elongation of too vigorous shoots. It lessens wind damage and aids in developing young vines. It seldom stimulates the formation of laterals.

Topping, removing 30.5 to 61 cm (1 to 2 ft) from the end of a growing shoot, in early summer may reduce wind damage. Severe late topping may seriously depress the next crop.

Removal of some leaves may help certain cultivars (e.g., Emperor) to color. But remove only those in the head of staked vines and those on the lower part of the north or east side of trellised vines. To promote fine table grapes one may remove, soon after the berries set, any leaves that rub the clusters and any tendrils that may intertwine the cluster.

Pruning and Training

Three general classes of vinifera pruning and training are head, cordon and cane. The first two classes, on which the retained annual growth is usually reduced to spurs, are featured by the form given to the more or less permanent parts of the vine. The third class is named from the bearing unit—the fruit cane (Jacob and Winkler 1950).

Head Pruning.—In the head system the mature vine has a short, upright trunk, which bears at its summit a ring of arms or short branches. At the end of these arms, at each winter pruning, leave spurs to produce the shoots that bear the next crop and to furnish canes for the next year's spurs. Thus this system consists of head training and spur pruning. The point or region at which the trunk divides into or bears the arm is the head.

Usual support for head-pruned vines is 5.1 × 5.1 cm (2 × 2 in.) split coast redwood reduced to stakes 1.2 to 1.8 m (4 to 6 ft) long, 1 stake per vine. A tractor-drawn stake driver or press is economical for large plantings. The vines become self-supporting when the trunks are 7.6 to 10.2 cm (3 to 4 in.) thick.

This type of training is often called vase or goblet. The vase-form arrangement of the arms, though usual, is not universal or essential. Hence the term head pruning is preferable. In hot regions with low humidity the head may be sunburned in the vase arrangement; hence sufficient growth should be maintained directly above it for shade.

Retain one bud on spurs as thick as a lead pencil; two on spurs as large as the little finger; three on those as thick as the middle finger; and four on spurs as large as the thumb. Medium-sized canes (those proper for 2 to 3 buds) are best.

Headed vines are the easiest to establish (trunk short and upright) and the cost of supports is comparatively low; cross-cultivation is possible. Objections are the depressing effect of severe pruning on growth and yield and massing of the fruit within a small area. Head pruning suits most cultivars that bear well on short spurs, but must be severe in order to avoid over-bearing. Other systems are better adapted to machine-harvesting.

Cordon Pruning.—Cordon-pruned vines have no definite head. In the horizontal bilateral form the trunk arises vertically to 15.2 to 25.4 cm (6 to 10 in.) below the supporting trellis wire. At this point it divides into equal branches, which rise to the wire in a gentle bend and extend in opposite directions along the wire to near the cordons of adjacent vines on either side. The bearing units are spurs on small arms located at regular intervals on horizontal parts of the branches. They should be on the upper side of the branches or should extend upward if they originate elsewhere.

The usual support for wine grapes is a two-wire trellis. The cordon is on the lower wire. The upper wire protects the shoots from wind damage and provides a place to tie shoots in young vineyards to prevent the cordon from turning over. The top wire of the two-wire trellis may be replaced by a horizontal cross-arm (61.0 × 76.2 cm, or 24 × 30 in.) with a wire near each end. For table grapes, make the flat-topped trellis with 88.9 cm (36 in.) cross-arms and a 2.1 m (7 ft) stake to elevate the fruiting surface to permit thinning and picking from both sides of the row. Cordon-pruned table grapes may also be supported by a sloping wide-top trellis. However, one wire is dropped down to support the cordons, thus leaving three wires, equally spaced, on the sloping cross-arms. This allows picking from one side of the row (Winkler and Kasimatis 1959).

Higher training systems for grapevines should support large shoots which are more exposed to the sun than are those on lower systems.

Cross-arms tend to spread shoots so that the leaves are not as likely to shade each other.

Thompson Seedless vines were trained to heights of 1.4, 1.7 and 2.0 m (4.6, 5.6 and 6.6 ft) with and without cross-arms. Analysis of combined results over a period of three years revealed that the highest trellis resulted in most yield, most clusters and most berry sugar per vine. Vines on the lowest trellis had the least pruning brush weight. Vines with cross-arms had higher weight per berry, soluble sugar and brush weight per vine than did vines without cross-arms.

On horizontal cordon-pruned vines all clusters are at about the same level for uniform development and maturation. Some cultivars that need long spurs with head training bear fair crops on spurs of normal length when cordon-pruned. The cordon is laborious and expensive to establish; the workmen must be skillful, and a trellis or other permanent support is essential. Cordon pruning is well adapted for table cultivars and for vigorous wine cultivars that produce very large clusters.

Cane Pruning.—Establish two arms on each side of a trunk (see Kniffin system in Part 2). At each annual pruning of mature vines, retain 4 canes 8 to 12 buds long (60.9 to 152.4 cm) (2 to 5 ft) for the crop. The next year's canes arise from two bud renewal spurs near the base of each cane.

Cane pruning is suitable for cultivars with mostly unfruitful basal buds, (e.g., Thompson Seedless and small-cluster cultivars). Combined with thinning, the fruit may be distributed over a large area, and the tendency of certain cultivars (e.g., Muscat) to produce small, undeveloped seedless berries and straggly clusters may be reduced. Since more clusters appear than are needed, thin off the least desirable ones to improve the quality.

For raisin and wine grapes use either a 1-wire or 2-wire trellis. For table grapes, in which quality and appearance are very important, use a multiple-wire wide-top trellis. Many Thompson Seedless vines for raisins or wine are supported on a 1-wire trellis 106.7 cm (42 in.) high; the vines are headed just above tie wire. Small cluster wine grapes may be supported on a single wire 91.4 to 106.7 cm (36 to 42 in.) above ground.

For a wide-topped trellis for large-growing table grapes attach a cross-arm 5.1 × 5.1 × 106.7 cm (2 × 2 × 42 in.) to the top of each stake or alternate stakes. Brace the lower end to hold the cross-arm at a 30° angle. The lower part is 30.5 cm (12 in.) long and the upper part is 76.2 cm (30 in.). Fasten a wire to the stake and just below the cross-arms; use a No. 12 wire on each side. Drive a nail through the cross-arms into the stake. Then with a cross-arm in a horizontal position, take a 91.4 cm (3 ft) length of No. 14 wire doubled over the long part, around the stake, and under the short part, and twist its ends together until the wire is taut. The head is just below the wire nearest the stake. Tie the canes on the middle two wires, equally divided in each direction along the trellis. In most Thompson Seedless raisin vineyards, use shorter cross-arms and two wires. To avoid shading raisin trays during drying, have the high side of the trellis toward the south (Winkler and Kasimatis 1959).

Training for Machine-harvesting.—Several kinds of harvesting machines are in use, particularly for wine grapes. The trellis should be arranged accordingly.

The Geneva Double Curtain system is discussed in Part 2 of this chapter.

Girdling

Girdling of vinifera vines consists in removing a complete ring of bark 3 to 6 mm (⅛ to ¼ in.) wide from the trunk, arm, or cane below the fruit to be affected. Food materials elaborated in the leaves accumulate in the parts above the wound, including the clusters of flowers or fruit, and influence their development.

In girdling remove only the bark, i.e., the tissue outside the cambium layer. For girdling canes use special pliers that have double blades on each side. Use double-bladed knives to girdle trunks.

Callus bridges form across girdle wound, often within two weeks. Phloem connections are re-established across such wounds within a few days following bridging by callus pads. Callus development is faster and more extensive from the upper than from the lower edge of girdle wounds (Sidowski et al. 1971).

To Increase Berry Set.—Girdling during bloom increases the number of seedless berries that set, and sometimes the number of seeded berries.

Use of 4-chlorophenoxyacetic acid (2½ to 10 ppm) has largely replaced girdling of Black Corinth in California. Vines sprayed with CPA produce a good set, and usually the berries are larger than those on girdled vines (Weaver and Nelson 1959).

To Increase Berry Size.—A complete girdle that is open and effective during rapid berry growth (a few weeks after bloom) may increase the size of seedless berries 30 to 100%, but of seeded berries usually less than 20%. Girdling immediately after normal berry drop causes the greatest increase in berry size, with little or no influence on the number.

For table grapes, girdle Thompson Seedless soon after normal berry drop. Girdling too early causes the clusters to become too compact. Less increase in berry size results from a delay of more than a few days. After a delay of three weeks or more, little increase in berry size results.

Thinning is necessary with girdled Thompson Seedless. Increase in total crop, without thinning, is roughly proportional to increase in berry size. Vines that are girdled but not thinned are overloaded, weakened and produce poor-quality fruit.

In cluster thinning, eliminate clusters that are too large, misshapen or otherwise defective, and leave the required number of the best. Berry thin those that are too compact. Cut off the forked-tip ends of all retained clusters. Girdling to enlarge the berries of seeded cultivars is of doubtful economic value.

To Improve Color and Hasten Ripening.—For these purposes the girdles must be open and effective when the first traces of color appear in the fruit. Girdling often improves the coloring and speeds the ripening of most seeded cultivars, particularly on vigorous vines bearing a light crop. In very early districts it may mean a few days advance in maturity and a price sufficient to compensate for the added expense and risk of failure.

Weakening Effect.—Since girdling checks the downward movement of organic food materials past the wound until after healing, the lower parts of the vine, particularly the roots, may be undernourished while the wounds are open. The longer the wounds are open, the greater is the weakening effect. Trunk girdles that do not heal during the growing season may cause the vines to die; cane girdles that fail to heal are less serious. Girdles made during or soon after bloom, and not more than 13 mm (½ in.) wide, usually heal in 3 to 6 weeks. Those made later, wider or reopened to influence ripening heal more slowly and are more weakening.

Care in irrigation and in thinning to regulate the crop makes the girdle less weakening. Increase irrigation while the wounds are open. If properly thinned and well cared for, Thompson Seedless may be girdled year after year.

Thinning

Overcropping is probably the single factor most harmful to vine and fruit quality in grapes in California. Damage from nematodes, unfavorable environment and other factors may be compounded in overcropped vines. Overcropping weakens the vines; the fruit matures late, with more danger of decay, especially after heavy rain; fails to color well; and may develop a flat taste. Thinned fruit is less likely to be decayed, and any decay present is less likely to be overlooked in packing. Properly thinned fruit requires less time in selection, rejection and trimming.

Crop level and vine capacity may be increased by thinning after pruning, since the vines may be pruned longer (more leaf surface) than when the crop level is adjusted by pruning alone.

Flower-cluster Thinning.—The cluster of rudimentary flowers appears with leaves in early spring. Individual flower parts continue to develop until bloom. Removal of some of them soon after emergence, with no removal of leaves, improves the nutrition of those remaining; a better set of normal berries may result. Flower-cluster thinning is useful on cultivars having loose or straggly clusters, or on those that set many shot berries with usual pruning. Except with compact-cluster cultivars, prune to longer spurs (to leave more buds). More than one thinning per vine is necessary, because the first berries have set before the last clusters appear. Thinning does not improve the set on vines infected with virus diseases or deficient in zinc.

Flower-cluster thinning can be done for half the cost of fruit-cluster thinning, since there is little vine growth at the early thinning. But this advantage is offset somewhat by more difficulty in selecting the best potential clusters. Also, as late-developing clusters may be missed, the crop may be heavier than planned.

Cluster Thinning.—Removal of entire clusters soon after berry set is a widely used means of reducing an overload on vines of wine and raisin cultivars to ensure that the remainder develop and mature properly. Leaving enough fruiting wood in pruning for a good crop in a poor year and then reducing the overload in a good year by cluster thinning promotes large crops annually.

By improving the nutrition of the fruit that is left, cluster thinning enhances the size or weight of berry and hastens maturity. The average quality of table grapes is further improved in some cultivars by retaining only the best clusters. At thinning time, to avoid damage to many fine clusters during harvest, disentangle the clusters of table cultivars from one another or from shoots on wires around which they have formed.

Market quality sometimes is improved by clipping off 10 mm (⅜ in.) or less from the apex of the inflorescence immediately before bloom. The bunches ripen earlier, have more uniform color, improved shape, and more normal seeded berries (especially on the shoulders). Total yield may be slightly reduced. Associated with grade improvement is a slight increase in berry size, and fewer shot berries in early-ripening bunches. Two possible explanations are: removal of an inhibitor of the pollination or fertilization mechanism, which is located in the inflorescence apex, permits the set and development of more normal seeded berries; and better distribution of nutrients throughout the inflorescence stimulates embryo growth and therefore inhibits excessive flower abscission (Sharples *et al.* 1961).

Berry Thinning.—Removing parts of the bunch of developing berries has merit when the berries are so numerous as to make the bunches too compact for high quality or when over-large bunch parts interfere with proper coloring and maturing. Cut off the ends of the main stem and several branches of the bunch, or enough to leave only the desired number of berries. This alters the shape of the bunch. In certain cultivars (e.g., Malaga) it decreases bunch size and percentage of sugar; in certain others (e.g., Thompson Seedless) it increases berry size.

Berry thinning is done at the fruit-set stage. When it is delayed 8 to 10 days, gain in berry size is usually about 33%; when it is delayed 15 to 20 days it is 66% less.

Berry-thinned Thompson Seedless clusters ripen faster than unthinned clusters on the same vine. Berries of the basal portions of clusters approach maturity more rapidly and berries on the apical portion the slowest. Rate of ripening of Red Malaga berries is inversely related to the number of seeds in a berry (Weaver and Ibrahim 1968).

The final rapid rate of growth of the berries may be a result of increased osmotic intake of water resulting from increased concentrations of sugar (Coombe 1969).

Gibberellin (GA).—Loose clusters reduce the possibility of rot. Packing of bunches in shipping boxes is also facilitated. Some compact cultivars are sprayed with 10 to 20 ppm GA 2 to 3 weeks before bloom to obtain a loose cluster. Such clusters are elongated and fruit set is decreased. Similar treatment of seeded table grapes may be unsuccessful because of the formation of shot berries which detract from the appearance of the cluster (Weaver and Pool 1971B).

GA was applied at bloom to the seeded Zinfandel and Tokay. With Zinfandel, concentrations of 5 to 20 ppm caused increasing reduction in weight of fruits per vine. In Tokay GA at 10 and 20 ppm reduced fruit set. GA applications successfully thinned the compact clusters. Formation of unsightly shot berries was not a serious problem in Tokay. With Zinfandel, applications at the end of bloom were more effective than those at initiation of bloom. Comparison of objective methods of measuring cluster compactness revealed that both number and weight of berries per centimeter of branches are adequate indicators of compactness (Weaver and Pool 1971B).

Harvesting

Hand Picking.—Grapes for table use require more careful handling than those for juice or wine. Hand picking requires a large supply of labor and is slower than machine picking. Most picking of vinifera grapes is done by migrant labor.

The Balling hydrometer reading divided by the acidity, in grams per 100 cc, gives the Balling acid ratio. Minimum desirable Balling acid ratio varies with different cultivars. For example, it is about 25 parts sugar to 1 part acid for Thompson Seedless and Ribier, 30 to 1 for Muscat and Emperor, and 35 to 1 for Tokay and Malaga. Most cultivars, except notably Ribier, Red Malaga and Emperor, should have a Balling of 17° or higher. These cultivars should test at least 16° Balling (Jacob and Winkler 1950).

If the weather is very hot during ripening, the Balling acid ratio will be high and the grapes palatable at a relatively low sugar level. If the weather is cool, the acid will be higher and more sugar will be required for equal palatability. A refractometer may be used for a quick test of sugar.

Storage

Store only good fruit. Vinifera grapes sometimes are precooled before storage, but most of the table-type volume goes directly into storage. Best storage quality results in a year with dry weather before and during harvest. Largely because of their high sugar content, grapes have lower freezing points than most other fruits. An increasing quantity or percentage of vinifera grapes, chiefly Thompson Seedless, is stored each year and for longer periods.

Modern cold storage techniques, combined with the use of SO_2, make it possible to market California grapes over much of the year.

Packing and Marketing

Chests.—For many years grapes for foreign markets have been shipped in chests. Sawdust is used to fill slack space, cushion the fruit, and absorb moisture that might come from crushed berries. To hold high quality over long storage requires cooling both grapes and sawdust before packing. Cooling sawdust by stacking packs in cold storage requires two weeks and ties up valuable space. For a more rapid method a fan is used to force air through the sawdust which has been moistened.

Display Boxes.—For a long time California grapes have been shipped to eastern markets in lug boxes that measure 14.6 × 34.3 × 41.0 cm (5¾ × 13½ × 16⅛ in.) inside and hold 9 kg (20 lb) net weight. Total depth of the lug is 14.6 cm (5¾ in.) and it is made up of two parts—the lower part 11.43 cm (4½ in.) and the upper part 3.1 cm (1¼ in.). The lid is nailed on the box with no cleats other than the 3.1 cm (1¼ in.) top section. When the lid is removed the entire top part comes off, leaving the box 11.43 cm (4½ in.) deep. The box is filled by hand as compactly as possible without damaging the fruit. Grapes settle during transit, but removal of the top 3.1 cm (1¼ in.) section with the lid leaves the remainder of the box completely filled and therefore suitable for display.

A shift seems to be occurring from the display lug to "tight fill" cartons. The basic idea of the tight fill is that the fruit is vibrated for a short controlled period to settle the individual fruits into a compact unit that will resist the pressures and frictions that normally develop in transportation and handling. Fruit so packed will arrive in better condition than the conventional "place-packed" fruit (Rogers 1973). The vibrator can be mounted on a trailer for convenience in hauling, or on a pick-up truck for field packing. Stationary equipment is installed in packinghouses. When the fruit settles in the container, it is held in place by some tension on the cover (e.g., by stapling the cover under pressure).

Some eastern supermarkets receive and sell preweighed plastic-covered "boats" of grapes.

Machine-harvesting

Several different kinds of machines, particularly for wine, juice and raisins, are now widely used in large vineyards. See also Machine-harvesting in Part 2 of this chapter.

Vibrating Fingers.—One self-propelled row-straddling machine uses the vertical-shake principle and operates from a single engine, with a hydraulic system carrying power to the shakes. As the harvester moves down the rows, "fingers" reach into the vine and shake the trellis wires up and down, causing the grapes to fall onto the harvester's catching frame. A blast of air blows trash out into the vineyard as grapes are dropped onto the conveyor which carries them into a tractor-drawn gondola running alongside.

Originally designed for "T" trellised vineyards, the harvester may be modified for use on cane-pruned grapes grown on standard two wire trellises. Growers must wrap and tie canes to run parallel with the row, and also de-bud and de-florate the cane between the crown and the trellis so that bunches are formed at a relatively uniform height.

The unit requires three workers (a harvester operator plus two gondola tractor drivers).

Shaker Arms or Paddle.—A harvester designed for Concord has been used successfully on vinifera cultivars. One model is best for conventional vineyards, another for Geneva Double Curtain trellised vineyards. The self-propelled harvester features a high clearance frame and has a Ford diesel power unit with 10-speed transmission for speeds up to 27.3 km per hr (17 mph). Side shaker arms, conveyors, elevators and cleaning fans are hydraulically powered. Fruit to be harvested should be at least 76.2 cm (30 in.) from the vineyard floor or ground level. The machine straddles the row, removing berries by a side-shaking action of the shaker arms. Berries fall on overlapping movable plates which transfer them to conveyors, are dropped through an air current cleaner, then are raised in bucket elevators to conveyors which run along the top of the harvester to a swinging conveyor from which they are discharged into a portable bin. Under favorable conditions a harvester covers about 0.4 ha (1 acre) per hour.

Grapes are removed from the vines by an impactor which strikes the underside of the trellis wire. The impact separates most fruit from the cane immediately ahead of the impactor rod. With cultivars having large, compact clusters and weak stems (e.g., Thompson Seedless) removal is largely in whole clusters. Cultivars with small, loose clusters or fibrous stems are subject to a high percentage of cluster breakup. Cluster breakup also increases with maturity.

Pruning and trellising are important for all types of grape harvesters. The best trellis for the impactor is the general shape of a T with a single wire supported at each end of the cross-bar. The wire is supported in a vertical slot so that the motion imparted by the impactor will not damage the trellis. The Duplex system places the canes so that essentially all fruit is produced along the wire.

Chemical Loosening.—Many cultivars do not detach readily from the vine for machine-harvesting. This can often be overcome by the use of an agent which enhances drop of mature berries. In Thompson Seedless, for example, there is a second abscission zone, about five cells wide, between the distal end of the pedicel and the berry. This zone sometimes facilitates the drop of mature berries and abscission agents may enhance activity.

Ethephon (Ethrel) is a thinning agent. Proper timing and concentration must be determined for each cultivar to avoid over- or under-thinning. Ethephon may cause an increase in anthocyanin in Tokay. It seems to initiate responses usually associated with senescence, e.g., loss of acidity and increase in pigments. But it does not usually affect the concentration of sugar in the berries. The color increase could be of benefit to growers, especially when grapes such as Tokay, which tend to be deficient in color, are grown in areas where color development is restricted. Differential applications of Ethephon might be used to change the levels of acidity and thus spread the harvest season in any one area. In some of the colder areas, where acidities are often excessive for optimum wine quality, use of Ethephon might initiate and minimize loss of acids at an early date (Weaver and Pool 1969).

PART 2

AMERICAN-TYPE BUNCH GRAPES

Unlike the vinifera type, in which the skin is firmly attached to the flesh, in the American-type grape (*Vitis labrusca* and its derivatives) the skin slips readily from the flesh.

PRODUCTION REGIONS

Great Lakes

The Great Lakes region comprises districts in New York, Pennsylvania, Ohio and Michigan in the United States, and Ontario in Canada. The crop is: in New York 180,500 metric tons (200,000 tons); in Michigan 62,600 metric tons (69,000 tons); in Pennsylvania 51,700 metric tons (57,000 tons); in Ohio 20,000 metric tons (22,000 tons); and in Ontario 73,000 metric tons (80,000 tons) or more. New plantings have mostly been for wine.

Chautauqua-Erie Belt.—This is a narrow strip, 104.6 km (65 mi.) long and 1.6 to 8.0 km (1 to 5 mi.) wide, along the south shore of Lake Erie. The New York section is 64.4 km (40 mi.) long. The land gradually rises from the shore for 4 mi. to a high hill or escarpment. New York plantings center at Portland, Westfield, Ripley, Silver Creek, Sheridan, Dunkirk and Fredonia. The belt's western end extends into Erie County, Pa., where Northeast and Girard account for 98% of Pennsylvania's crop. In most of this belt the lake moderates the climate, and the slope from the hills ensures adequate soil and air drainage. About 85% of the crop goes into wine or juice and 15% is sold as fresh fruit.

Finger Lakes.—This district in New York centers at Keuka, Canandaigua and Seneca lakes. Leading points are: Jerusalem town on Bluff Point, Yates County; across the west branch of Keuka Lake from Bluff Point, at Pultenay, in Steuben County; Naples, in Ontario County; north of Watkins Glen along the east shore of Seneca Lake about Burdett and Hector, in Schuyler County; and at Kendaia near Seneca Lake. The Keuka area in Yates and Steuben counties is the largest. Hammondsport is a leading center.

The Finger Lakes are deep. The grapes are grown along the steep slopes abutting the lakes. Cultivars that ripen latest are planted on the lower levels or nearest the lakes; earlier ones are higher on the slope. At least one or more of these lakes is divided into two strips. That nearest the lake brings Catawba through to maturity; just above this line Catawba does not ripen, but Concord will. Grapes rarely ripen well on the elevated benches that separate these lakes.

Hudson River.—This grape area in New York centers in Columbia, Dutchess, Orange and Ulster counties. The tempering effect of the river and a lower altitude than in the Finger Lakes area favor good maturity in most years.

Niagara River.—This area is east of the Niagara River and south of Lake Ontario. The vineyards are located farther from the lake than those of the Lake Erie basin, but the ridge or escarpment is high and the fruit ripens 7 to 10 days later.

Michigan.—Berrien and Van Buren counties, with centers at Benton Harbor and Paw Paw, are the leaders. Kalamazoo, Ottawa and Kent counties produce grapes in quantity, but their combined acreage is not more than 10% of the state total.

Ohio.—At one time the area along the Ohio River, near Cincinnati, with 600 ha (1500 acres) of grapes was called the "Rhine of America," and Nicholas Longworth of Cincinnati was called the "Father of American Grape Culture." Renewed interest is occurring in grape production in southern Ohio. The main commercial production stretches along the southern shore of Lake Erie, chiefly in Ashtabula, Lorain, Lake, Cuyahoga, Erie, Geuga and Ottawa counties. Most vineyards are located on the lake plains and on gravel ridges paralleling the lake shore.

Concord comprises 77% of Ohio's grapes, being highest east of Cleveland. In Ottawa and Erie counties, west of Cleveland, and on Kelley's and Middle Bass Islands, Catawba comprises about 13% of the acreage. A miscellaneous group of cultivars makes up the remainder.

Ontario.—Over 95% of Canada's grape acreage is in Ontario. It is concentrated in Lincoln, Welland and Wentworth counties in the Niagara Peninsula, with Halton, Peel, Norfolk, Essex and Kent counties growing some of the total crop. Because of high real estate values resulting from urban expansion, new plantings have been made above the escarpment from St. Catharines west to Hamilton.

The grape acreage (1971) in Ontario is about 9713 ha (25,000 acres) and the total crop 73,000 metric tons (80,000 tons), most of which is purchased by processors, and the farm value of which is $12,000,000. An additional 809 ha (2000 acres) were planted in 1971.

In the Niagara Peninsula the general aspect is north, facing Lake Ontario, with the escarpment in the rear. The crop varies from year to year, but is rarely a complete failure. Most-favored locations are back from the lake shore, just below and on the first rise of the escarpment where, depending somewhat on the direction and force of air currents, spring and summer temperatures often are several degrees higher than nearer the lake. Concord matures about mid-October in this district.

Many new plantings of grapes have been made above and on the first ledge of the escarpment, owing to high real estate values in the Niagara Peninsula, and to the fact that non-agricultural developments make less land available for grapes below the escarpment.

West Central Region

Annual production in this region is about 10,900 metric tons (12,-000 tons).

Arkansas.—The grape acreage is chiefly in Benton and Washington counties.

Missouri.—In 1870 Missouri produced more wine than any other state except California, centering near St. Louis, Hermann and other river towns; but from 1875 on the acreage steadily declined. New plantings have been chiefly in the southwestern part.

Iowa.—Chief acreage is near Council Bluffs. There the average date of harvest is August 25.

Illinois.—The Nauvoo section is the largest in the state. It is near the junction of Illinois, Iowa and Missouri.

Kansas.—Chief acreage is in the southwest where, extending along the Missouri River, it adjoins the areas in northwestern Missouri and southwestern Nebraska. It centers at Wathena. An area also extends westward along the Kansas River from Kansas City to near Topeka. A smaller area is in south-central Kansas, near Wichita.

Nebraska.—Chief acreage is near Omaha and on the west side across from the Council Bluffs district in Iowa. It centers at Florence. The Nebraska area extends farther southward along the river than the area in Iowa, and in fact is a continuation of areas in Missouri and Kansas.

Pacific Coast Region

Washington.—For years this state has ranked third in vineyard acreage and sometimes second in production (70,000 metric tons, or 80,000 tons). A survey in 1972 showed more than 7285 ha (18,000 acres) in grapes. Concord made up 6637 ha (16,400 acres) of those with 40% nonbearing. About 10 to 15% of the juice goes to wineries in California for blending purposes. The acreage is expanding because of the warm, dry summer with long, cloudless days and moderate fall temperature, and the high yield per acre. Water is inexpensive and plentiful when needed.

Largest production is in the south-central Yakima and Columbia River valleys. The central Wenatchee area production for juice is substantial. The western and southwestern acreage in Mason, King and Clark counties is smaller than east of the Cascades. The biggest new development is east of the Columbia River, near its junction with the Snake.

Oregon.—Clackamas and Washington counties lead in the Willamette Valley; Josephine leads in the south region. Annual production is about 1360 metric tons (1500 tons).

British Columbia.—The potential for grapes is 9072 metric tons (10,000 tons) a year from 1214 ha (3000 acres). There are four climatic grape areas: (1) cool summer and mild winter (lower mainland and south Vancouver Island; (2) cool summer and cold winter (Creston and Salmon Arm); (3) warm summer and cold winter (Okanagan Center to Ocoyoos, Lower Similkameen, Lytton); and (4) warm summer and very cold winter (Kamloops, Grand Forks). Winter protection is required in region (4), and with some cultivars in regions (2) and (3) Fisher and Vielvoye 1968).

British Columbia can grow a wide range of cultivars, including some of the better late-maturing kinds in the warm districts of Oliver-Ocoyoos and Keremos-Cawton, early and midseason cultivars throughout the interior fruit zone, and early cultivars only on Vancouver Island and the lower mainland.

Other Areas

In New Jersey, production is mostly in Atlantic, Gloucester and Camden counties, and near Vineland in Cumberland County. Some early Concord is produced in Kent County, Delaware. In Kentucky, small areas occur near Louisville. North and South Carolina have 607 ha (1500 acres) of Concord, mostly in the Piedmont. Several other states have small plantings. Most grapes in Arizona are vinifera, but some American types are grown at elevations above 1372 m (4500 ft).

CULTIVARS

Before planting a vineyard for wine purposes consult wineries with respect to acceptable cultivars.

26 to 24 Days Before Concord

Seneca.—White. Bunch medium size, somewhat straggly. Berry firm, tender. It has some vinifera eating quality. Attractive to birds. New York origin.

Himrod.—White. Seedless. Stem rather brittle. Only moderately hardy. Good quality. New York.

24 to 20 Days Before Concord

Ontario.—White. The fruit does not handle too well. Only moderately hardy and productive. Good quality. New York.

Buffalo.—Black. Bunch somewhat loose. Often overbears (bunch thin in heavy crop year). May be sensitive to K deficiency. Good quality. New York.

Schuyler.—Black. Somewhat tender to cold. Bunch and berry large. New York.

Van Buren.—Bunch and berry smaller than Concord. Good table quality. New York.

20 to 10 Days Before Concord

Romulus.—White. Seedless. Bunch large, compact. Berry small, sweet, skin somewhat tough. Bunch thinning might help. New York.

10 to 8 Days Before Concord

Fredonia.—Black. To partially avoid straggly bunches and a light crop, leave more buds than for Concord. New York.

8 to 6 Days Before Concord

Campbell Early.—Black. Needs highly favorable conditions (e.g., light deep soils). Red "brush" left when a berry is picked, instead of a whitish one as in Moore Early and Concord. Ohio.

6 to 4 Days Before Concord

Moore Early.—Black. The berries tend to crack and shell and the bunches may be loose. Less productive than Concord. Massachusetts.

4 to 2 Days Before Concord

Alden.—Reddish black. Bunch large, somewhat straggly. Berry large. Vine tends to overbear. Mild quality (low in sugar and acid). New York.

Veeport.—Black. Good for dessert and wine. Somewhat susceptible to powdery mildew. Ontario.

Concord Season

Concord.—Black. The chief cultivar. Productive over a wide range of conditions. Berries attractively covered with bloom, ripens evenly, foxy. The desirable flavor is carried through, better than with other cultivars, to unfermented grape juice. Massachusetts.

Steuben.—Black. Bunch attractive, long, tapering. Berry sweet, free from foxiness, and with a spicy tang. New York.

2 to 3 Days After Concord

Bath.—Black. Bunch fairly compact. Tends to overbear. New York.

Delaware.—Red. Bunch and berry small, compact. High quality for table use and esteemed for Delaware wine and for blending in making other wines. Rather subject to mildew. Resistant to black rot. New Jersey.

Dutchess.—White. Vine somewhat tender to cold. Used for champagne and for a high-quality wine. Out-yields Delaware on good soil. New York.

Vincent.—Black. Bunch compact. Berries medium size. Juice very dark. Excellent for wine. Ontario.

Canada Muscat.—Best of the white muscats in Ontario. Vigorous grower, but crop often only medium. Subject to powdery mildew. New York.

4 to 5 Days After Concord

Sheridan.—Black. Bunch large, compact. Berry large. Good keeping quality. New York.

Agawam.—Red. Berries large, sweet, foxy; skin thick. Pulp coarse. Subject to mildew. Stores well. Massachusetts.

Catawba.—Red. Needs a long growing season. Bunch thinning may hasten maturity and improve quality. Makes a light-colored, high-grade wine. North Carolina.

Ventura.—Fruit smaller than Concord. Bunch larger than Elvira.

Does not split during wet weather. Resistant to mildews; susceptible to dead arm. A wine grape. Higher in sugar and lower in acid than Elvira. Ontario, 1976.

POLLINATION AND FRUIT SET

Most commercial cultivars (e.g., Concord) are self-fruited and bear well in large isolated vineyards. But a few cultivars (e.g., Lindley, Herbert and Brighton) are self-unfruitful and are improved by inter-planting pollinators such as the self-fruitful Concord. Brighton is easily cross-pollinated and sets good crops of large, well-filled bunch-es. But even when ample provision has been made for cross-pollina-tion of Lindley and Herbert, the bunches are often straggly and the yield light. Straggly bunches in Campbell Early may largely involve the pruning and site.

In Concord, a hermaphrodite, self-fertilized and seeded grape cul-tivar, development of pollen and the growth of pollen tubes in the style are adequate for fertilization. Seed formation is limited by: (1) the arrested development of many ovules before bloom; and (2) the post-bloom dropping of many ovules containing one or more fertiliz-ed but retarded ovules. The abscission zone at the base of the pedicel was distinct during drop. An average of two seeds per berry was neces-sary for berry adherence (Pratt 1975). (See also "Shot" Berries.)

Self-fruitful grapes have upright stamens. But pollen of cultivars with reflexed or recurved stamens is worthless for pollination. Do not plant large isolated blocks of cultivars having reflexed stamens.

"SHOT" BERRIES, SEEDLESS BERRIES, AND SHELLING

Small berries, especially spherical "shot" berries, on clusters of nor-mal seeded cultivars are not necessarily parthenocarpic and the result of vegetative development.

Seeded-cultivar clusters may have three types of berries: (1) seeded; (2) stenospermacarpic (seeds begin to develop after pollination); and (3) parthenocarpic. Stenospermacarpic berries, the poor set of seeded berries, and the many small "seedless" berries may be due to inade-quate pollination or none at all. These fruits are not entirely seedless but have at least one rudimentary seed. The berries may be tiny, but even this small amount of seed development promotes berry enlarge-ment and its retention on the vine (Stout 1936).

Gibberellin (GA).—The Japanese have developed techniques of handling and treating Delaware on an overhead trellis and claim prac-tically 100% seedlessness. In order to be seedless, the color from GA treatment has to be deeper than normal and test more than 20% soluble solids (sugar). (Kishi and Amamiya 1961; Kajura 1962).

In Washington state, GA treatment tends to make the berries too tart for good eating even though they have 18 to 20% soluble solids (Clore 1965).

Little-leaf.—Shelling of berries soon after bloom and the development of shot berries may be symptoms of little-leaf disease, which in most cultivars is also associated with small, chlorotic and deformed berries. Zn may promote recovery from little-leaf and overcome shelling.

Pruning Effect on Fredonia.—Pollen from severely pruned vines may be less effective than that from lighter pruned vines in setting fruit in Fredonia (Shaulis 1948).

Hot Drying Winds.—Hot drying winds at bloom may cause a poor set and smaller, more straggly clusters.

Ovule Abortion.—The frequency of nonfunctional ovules varies from year to year and may be important in fluctuating cluster size. Results of ovule abortion without parthenocarpy may be seen in the increased drop, and consequently poor set, and few seeds per berry; cluster size is lower than in normal fruit (Pratt and Einset 1961). (See also Pollination.)

Alar.—Alar tends to reduce berry size while increasing cluster size in Concord. When applied to Himrod it has the opposite effect, presumably related to seedlessness. It is possible to enhance fruit set with Alar so that the vine has a greater load than it can mature. Under such conditions fruit solids may be reduced, maturity delayed, and winter hardiness of the vine reduced. To avoid these problems, make a vineyard evaluation as to cluster number, vigor and so forth, before applying Alar. Combining Alar and GA may nullify berry size decreases over that from either Alar or GA alone, especially with Himrod (Cahoon and Pathak 1972).

FRUITING HABIT AND FRUIT-BUD FORMATION

Buds

On a young shoot two buds develop in the axil of each leaf. On growth extension they separate and one gives rise to a short side shoot that usually falls with the leaves in autumn. The other bud develops several accessory buds. Since these, as well as the one giving rise to the short side shoot, are enclosed in common scales they appear as one large bud (a group of buds or a compound bud or "eye"). The side buds seldom develop further; the central bud constitutes the main unit. The compound bud is dormant in winter.

Inflorescence

The inflorescence is a racemose panicle. Its main axis bears lateral axes of the first order, and these, in turn, bear lateral axes of several later orders.

Fruit-bud Formation

Fruit-bud initiation occurs in midsummer and continues in newly forming buds during the growing season. Cluster primordia appear as blunt outgrowths of the growing point of the bud. The leaf primordium, however, appears as a pointed outgrowth from the growing point. Primordial clusters in basal and apical buds of the canes do not become as large as those in mid-cane buds.

Fruiting Cluster

Clusters occur with "shoulders" or a large secondary cluster on one side, without a shoulder, and with a tendril instead of a shoulder, and tendrils may occur with a few buds on their sides. Usual position of flower clusters is opposite the leaves at nodes 3, 4, 5 and 6 of spring shoots of Concord.

Influence of Nutrition on the Cluster

A large primordium in the dormant bud depends on adequate food at the node. The number of flowers that develop in a cluster largely depends on growing conditions in spring, which determines how the stored food is to be used and also the amount of carbohydrates that may be produced in the young leaves.

Fruiting of a cane is related also to external characteristics of dormant canes (the manner in which shoot growth took place in the preceding year). This relation extends to both weight and number of bunches per shoot. Shoots with most bunches usually produce bunches of good size. Thus, as pointed out by N.L. Partridge in Michigan 50 years ago, a cane tends to maintain the favorable or unfavorable nutritional conditions of the shoot the preceding year. If growth conditions are favorable for primordia development, a larger store of carbohydrates is laid down near the nodes, which are therefore more likely to produce well. This food is not only available to supply the developing primordia and to aid in cane maturity but also gives the young shoot a good supply in early spring for vigorous growth.

Vigor or length of shoot affects the number of flower buds differentiated in the cluster. Unless conditions in spring permit full development of the primordium, flower clusters will not reach full size.

The number of bunches is more closely associated with cane than with shoot features; the reverse is true of the size of the flower cluster. Both the number and size of bunches affect total yield. Number of bunches is more important in small-bunch cultivars, and size of bunch in large-bunch cultivars.

PROPAGATION

Hardwood Cuttings

American-type bunch grapes are usually propagated by hardwood cuttings made from the dormant new wood. Therefore, the cultivars are on their own roots. Canes of medium size are preferable to large or spindly ones. The length of cutting is usually 20.3 to 25.4 cm (8 to 10 in.) or 3 buds.

Cuttings from middle and basal parts of the cane produce the most vigorous vines. Percentage of reserve carbohydrates and N differs little in canes of different vigor, but differs from base to tip of a cane. The highest percentage is near the base.

Cuttings are often taken from the prunings before they have dried out. With cuttings taken in late fall, danger of winter injury is minimized. Discard cuttings damaged by cold. In preparing cuttings make the cuts close below the basal bud (either straight or slanting) and 2.54 cm (1 in.) above the top bud to make it easy to tell the top and bottom in future handling, and to avoid cracking of the wood on the node, which might let the top dry out and injure the bud. Tie the cuttings in bundles (e.g., 50) with the butts turned in one direction. Store in moist sand, sawdust, peat moss, polyethylene bags or other material in a cool place; or bury the cuttings in a well-drained sandy site and press at least 7.6 cm (3 in.) of sand or sandy soil firmly around them. In cold areas a heavy straw mulch may be placed over the cutting bed.

In spring firmly plant the stored cuttings 15.28 to 20.3 cm (6 to 8 in.) apart in nursery rows. A furrow may be made deep enough so that most of the cuttings can be set in a vertical position with the top bud just at the normal soil level; cuttings that are too long may be slanted slightly.

Cuttings are best grown in the nursery for only one year; if not sold by then, they may be cut back and kept another year.

FIG. 1.2.   GRAPE CUTTING SHOWING LEAFY GROWTH FROM THE TOP
BUD AND ROOT GROWTH FROM THE LOWEST BUD

Grafting on Rootstocks

Some 50 years ago F.E. Gladwin in New York showed that both Concord and Niagara may yield less on their own roots than on Clinton, St. George or Riparia Gloire rootstocks. However, plants grown from cuttings have continued to be used by most growers. Often thinning, moisture stress, trellis spacing and other factors may affect the results as much as does the rootstock (Shaulis and Steel 1969).

In Ontario, cultivars such as New York Muscat and Delaware, which normally lack vigor, may benefit from a rootstock other than their own. In general, however, phylloxera, nematodes or high Ca do not seem to limit the yield. To compensate for the extra cost of grafted vines, better rootstocks than the 42 tested still need to be found (Bradt and Hutchinson 1971).

FIG. 1.3. 100,000 ONE-YEAR-OLD GRAPE CUTTINGS

Layering

Layering is useful to refill vacancies in established vineyards, since young vines when used for this purpose often grow poorly. Fasten down and bury a portion of a vigorous cane, with the top 2 to 3 buds protruding, in a hole dug 15.2 to 20.3 cm (6 to 8 in.) deep at the vacancy. As the shoots develop from the cane remove them to where the new plant is developing. Leave the cane connected to the mother plant for 2 to 3 years, when the new vine should be well established.

FIG. 1.4.   LAYERING IS USEFUL TO FILL VACANCIES IN AN ESTABLISHED VINEYARD

YIELDS AND COSTS

Yield

With American-type bunch grapes set 2.4 × 3 m (8 × 10 ft), 1346 vines per ha (545 vines per acre) and no plants missing, a yield of 6.8 kg (15 lb) per vine is about 8.96 metric tons per ha (4 tons per acre).

At the above spacing, increasing the yield from 6.8 to 9.1 kg (15 to 20 lb) per vine would increase the yield from 9 to 12.3 metric tons per ha (4 to 5½ tons per acre). Some of the better growers of Concord obtain yields of 13.4 metric tons or more per ha (6 tons or more per acre). Improved cultural practices, pest control and vine-training technique now make possible higher grape yields than some years ago.

However, too high a yield (over-bearing) in a given year may have a serious detrimental effect. This is considered later in relation to pruning (Table 1.1).

Yields of Delaware and Catawba are usually lower than with Concord, but the price per ton is higher.

Costs (Hand-picked Vineyards)

The economy of the country markedly influences the cost of materials, labor and overhead. Some costs may be spread over a period of years. All the fixed costs and some of the variables continue in a vineyard in which some vines are missing; these vines should be replaced.

In establishing a vineyard the period involved is commonly the first three years. During this period, and especially in the first year, cost of materials is at its highest. Plants, posts, wire and other items may be about 41% of the cost. Labor charges include preparing the soil, planting, placing posts and wiring, cultivating, fertilizing, pruning and tying. These labor charges may amount to about 43% of the cost. Interest, taxes, and prorated payments for machinery, and so forth, may be about 16%.

Annual production costs may be considered as beginning in the fourth year after planting and continuing for the life of the vineyard. Labor costs may be 70% of this.

Harvesting and containers are usually the chief cost in a mature hand-picked vineyard and may be 30% of the labor cost. The third largest charge is usually sprays and spraying. Other labor costs include weed control, positioning shoots in the Geneva Double Curtain system, applying fertilizer and sowing cover crops. Other costs include overhead and taxes.

Pruning and machine-harvesting costs for large wine and juice vineyards vary depending on whether the grower owns the equipment, leases it, or uses equipment owned by the processor.

LOCATION AND SITE

Length of Growing Season, Temperature and Sunshine

Concord generally succeeds in Michigan when the growing season averages 270 days, is of doubtful success at 157 days, and generally is unsuccessful at 145 days. An average mean temperature for May to September (inclusive) of at least 18.6°C (65.5°F), with a growing season longer than 160 days, is essential commercially. A commercial vineyard succeeds only with a season long enough to allow the fruit to attain high quality nearly every year, plus a margin of at least two weeks for picking. In areas where Catawba succeeds, the required growing season approaches 200 days.

Regions and years in which the temperature is comparatively low in the growing months of May, June and July, and high with much sun in the maturing months of August, September and October, result in the best grapes in New York. An average of 12.8° to 18.3°C

(55° to 65°F) for the former period and 18.3° to 23.9°C (65° to 75°F) for the latter is ideal. Most cultivars fail to produce good crops if rain averages about 15.2 cm (6 in.) for the three growing months and 12.7 cm (5 in.) for the maturing months. It seems best if the rainfall is as low as 10.2 cm (4 in.) for the former period and 5.1 cm (2 in.) for the latter.

The amount of sun from March to September (inclusive) influences the quality of the crop. The content of sugar, acid and astringent substances in the juice of fully ripe grapes from normally loaded vines is determined largely by the sun during this period.

In the Yakima and Columbia valleys of Washington state the frost-free growing season is 160 to 200 days. The meager amount of rain, 17.8 cm (7 in.) per year, occurs mostly in late fall and early spring. There is much sunshine during the growing season; as few as 10% of the days may be cloudy. Daytime temperatures are high, up to 32.9° to 40.6°C (90° to 105°F). Night temperatures may be 15.6°C (60° F). Humidity is low (25 to 35%). Irrigation is done when needed. Average yield of good growers is 17.9 metric tons per ha (8 tons per acre).

SOIL

Grapes thrive on many soil types. A virtue of Concord is its adaptability to a wide range of soils. Light soils are more easily worked, are prepared for planting earlier in spring, are tilled at less expense, and are better for propagation (at a nursery) than clay soils. Clays, however, are usually higher in organic matter, more retentive of moisture, and naturally more fertile, but often less well drained, than sandy soils. A good soil for grapes is a well-drained, deep, naturally fertile, gravelly or sandy loam, easily tilled, with a subsoil which is not so heavy that it holds the water. Sugar content and fruit quality usually are highest on clay loams.

Soil Properties

Soil organic matter and total N content, available moisture capacity, capillary porosity, clay and silt content, and total exchange capacity may all be related to vine vigor and yield. Soil erosion is often responsible for differences in surface soil. None of the soil properties closely related to production can be changed easily enough to immediately improve growth and yield. But since these soil properties are closely interrelated, it is impossible to alter one without in some way altering the others. Cover cropping, manuring, and the use of plant residues (such as straw and waste hay) as soil amendments, especially on heavy-textured areas where soil structure and drainage are problems, are applicable in vineyard soil management.

Soil Structure

Soil particles cling together in groups or aggregates whose sizes and shapes and resistance to breaking down constitute the structure of the soil. This in turn determines the ease of root penetration, rate of absorption, movement of water and aeration. A good granular soil structure may be as important as proper balance of nutrients. In fact nutritional deficiencies are, in general, easily remedied; but basic soil characteristics, once disturbed, are hard to restore.

Soil structure affects growth in several ways: (1) Good structure permits rapid and deep penetration of incident precipitation and prevents or reduces runoff and surface evaporation. With a given amount of rain, this provides the maximum amount possible in the root zone of plants in that soil. It also reduces soil erosion. (2) A porous well-aggregated soil ensures ample soil aeration and supplies adequate O_2 for chemical and microbiological reactions that are essential for a high level of soil fertility. (3) A well-aggregated soil is conducive to extensive root development (Forshey 1955).

Grapes may occupy the soil for 50 years or more. Long-time continuous cultivation may result in almost complete breakdown of the natural soil structure. Poor soil structure contributes to the decline in yields in certain vineyards. The relation between yield and air space porosity increases as the season advances. Since the water requirement increases as the fruit develops and approaches maturity, this is indirect evidence that the effect of soil structure on water relations of the soil is a chief influence exerted by this soil characteristic (see also Tillage and Fertilizer).

Soil Type

The two major groups of soils in the Niagara region of Ontario are the poorly drained clays and clay loams below the escarpment, and the moderately well and imperfectly drained clays and clay loams above and on the first ledge of the escarpment.

The large area of soil classified as Jeddo clay loam is an example of a poorly drained soil. Root development of the vine is largely restricted to the surface layer, normally 15.2 to 22.9 cm (6 to 9 in.) deep. Such soils must be well supplied with organic matter for good yields. A high organic matter content compensates to some extent for the restricted rooting area by holding moisture and nutrients in forms available to the vine (Bradt 1968).

The Smithville, Oneida, Chinguacousy and Haldimand soils on the first ledge of, and just above, the escarpment are, in general, better drained than those previously mentioned. More vigorous vine and root growth can be expected on these soils. In recent years large acreages of such soils have been planted to grapes in the area above the escarpment, from St. Catharines west to Hamilton. Here again, organic matter maintenance is important. Also, vineyards set on these soils have responded well to N and K. There may be more extensive planting on these desirable soils.

Besides these two major soil groupings grapes are grown successfully on sandy-loam soils both below the excarpment and in the Fonthill area. The higher acre-return from other crops in the past has usually resulted in the poorer soils being used for grapes. This is not because grapes prefer such soils, but because they will withstand these conditions better than any other fruit grown in the district.

Grapes grown on light soils usually ripen earliest. But grapes on some sandy soils fail to mature properly and even in a favorable year fail to develop as much sugar as on heavier soils. In Ontario, fruit was secured from every area between Burlington and the Niagara River and from the various soil types. Grapes on the heavier soils matured earlier than on the lighter soils, especially in a year when all grapes matured late. Only on the heavier soils were grapes really fit for market when early frosts came.

Soil type may be subordinate to other related factors. For example, grapes may be immature on weak vines in infertile sand because of pest injury, but they may be fully mature on more vigorous vines with a larger leaf surface per berry in more fertile loam soil in spite of an equal or perhaps heavier infestation.

Extent of Root Growth

In a fertile, deep silt loam, roots of 5- to 7-year-old Concord vines may extend 4.6 m (15 ft) vertically and 9.75 m (32 ft) radially, with greatest concentrations within a 1.8 m (6 ft) radius of the trunk and 2.4 m (8 ft) deep. In a less fertile silt loam, root growth may be 3 m (10 ft) vertically and 7.3 m (24 ft) radially. Usually it is less than these distances.

Air Drainage

Good air circulation aids in control of mildew and rot. Danger of frost injury in spring and fall depends much on the site. Cold air tends to settle on low-lying land, flowing down from higher ground.

Poor Water Drainage

Poor water drainage for any length of time may cause damage, even though the grape is somewhat more tolerant in this respect than some other fruits. Usually the heavier the soil the poorer the natural drainage, particularly where the subsoil is heavy.

Grapes grown on poorly drained soils may not respond well to fertilizer unless the organic matter is kept at a high level, but this is not true on well-drained soils. On poorly drained soils, no response to N may occur, and sometimes application of N in the absence of adequate K depresses yield.

Cool soils usually delay ripening. Also, when the soil is so wet that it cannot be worked until late, the effective growing period is shortened. Good cultural care fails to give desired results in fields where drainage is the limiting factor unless the drainage is improved.

Most vineyards in the Chautauqua belt possess an excellent site. However, grapes have been set on the flat between the old bench gravel ridge and the lake shore, where the soil often is poorly drained.

A high water table may cause root killing due to lack of air. The result is equivalent to cutting off the roots. Growth of above-ground parts also is dwarfed. Vines set on poorly drained soils suffer from drought when the water table falls faster than the roots can follow the receding moisture.

The site should slope enough and be free from pockets or basins so that surface drainage takes care of surplus water, particularly in late winter or early spring when snow is melting. Sloping land is not always well drained; sometimes impervious rock layers form basins for rain falling some distance away.

A slight slope is sufficient to carry off surface water. Too great a slope may result in severe soil erosion.

Before setting a vineyard, poorly drained land may need tile drainage. Later, if the soil is still wet, surface drainage may be provided to make the best of the situation by ridging the rows. However, a sufficient area of well-drained soil exists in most grape regions to supply all demand for the fruit. Hence it may be economically inexpedient to set vines on a soil that must be tiled at large expense. Subsoiling in late fall before planting helps to break up the subsoil and to improve drainage.

EROSION

When erosion removes soil, the roots may be injured in tillage and in other ways. This reduces the vigor of the vine and its ability to produce superior fruit. Rapid erosion is very harmful. With slight erosion, especially on rich soil, the vines may be able to renew their roots in the lower part of the soil rapidly enough to offset the loss of the upper roots.

Water Erosion

On gravelly light-textured soils, water erosion is a selective process in which the organic matter, silt and clay are sorted from the surface soil and transported to depressions on level areas where they are deposited. The eroded areas tend to have low contents of these finer particles and areas of deposition tend to have higher contents of these same constituents.

Water erosion may be reduced in part by placing the rows across the slope, thus permitting level tillage; by increasing the capacity of the soil to absorb water rapidly by adding organic matter; and by protecting the ground during the dormant period with a cover crop.

Sheet Erosion

This is a slow, persistent wearing away of the soil that may go on for years without giving any warning until a grayish patch appears on a knoll. By this time the field has lost several inches of valuable topsoil. In vineyards subject to sheet erosion, the crop on the upper slope may mature before that farther down, and growth may be weaker.

Rill Erosion

The water causes small channels a few inches deep as it moves along sloping land. If rill erosion is unchecked, gullies may eventually develop. Growers often rub out the rills by plowing and harrowing and forget about them. Without some control the problem becomes worse. Gullying occurs on steep slopes. Gullies are formed in sloping cultivated land by concentration of water in a small channel. Once a channel has formed both velocity and volume increase, enabling the water to loosen, scour and carry away soil.

Steep slopes that wash cannot be worked as well as land more nearly level. In certain areas, after clearing the land, field crops are grown until the hillsides become so badly eroded that such crops can no longer be produced, then grapes are set. These lands lose their most fertile soil. Terracing and soil building are too expensive when the fruit from such an overcapitalized vineyard must be sold in competition with fruit grown on naturally fertile soil. However, vinifera grapes, particularly in Europe, are often grown on a trellised site.

Wind Erosion

This occurs mainly on light soils and mostly on bare ground, and is reduced by cover crops. Avoid adverse conditions by selecting a good site.

WINTER INJURY, FROST INJURY AND EXPOSURE

Winter Injury

Grapes do not succeed in areas with very cold winters. Covering the plants with soil during the winter and selecting very early cultivars is the best hope. In a year when many buds have been winter-killed in commercial grape areas, the injury may be traced to immaturity of tissue owing to a sudden termination of the maturing period by unseasonable cold. Killing of a few buds may have a thinning effect and promote larger clusters from the sound buds. There may be injury when none is suspected, and relatively unproductive shoots from secondary buds may give the vine an appearance of normal growth.

Spring Frost

In certain vineyards yield over a five year period may be reduced 50% or more by frost while other vineyards within a few miles lose less than 1%. Low, flat sites or others that prevent circulation of air are not conducive to control of mildew and rot.

The grape is one of the last fruits to bloom; often strawberry picking starts before nearby grapes bloom. Because of the late bloom it might be thought that the grape is less subject to frost damage than other fruits, but this is not necessarily so. The new shoots start early in spring, for several weeks are succulent and tender, and are often damaged by cold before their flowers open.

Grape buds are compound, and when the first growth is removed after severe frost, secondary buds may develop and produce a partial crop.

Fall Frost

Light frosts in autumn may injure the foliage, and heavy frosts injure both fruit and foliage. Poor air drainage occurs in low spots in hilly sections. Sometimes, however, particularly in areas that are not the best for grapes and with late cultivars, a southern or eastern exposure provides opportunity for maturing the fruit.

Effect of Lakes on Temperature

A large deep body of water modifies the temperature near it. The expanse of melting ice retards the starting of buds until the season is far enough advanced to preclude injury from late frosts. During May Lake Erie is only 3.8°C (7°F) above freezing a foot below the surface. In late July it gradually rises to air temperature, and from August until late fall the water is several degrees warmer than the air. In September it is 1.6° to 2.2°C (3° to 4°F) warmer, and in October it is often 3.3°C (6°F) warmer. The influences vary from year to year. In mild winters little ice forms and retardation of buds is at a minimum.

But if the ice forms over much of Lake Erie, buds are rarely injured by late frosts in the Chautauqua-Erie belt. The ridge paralleling the lake on the south wards off early fall frosts and thus several more growing days occur in places somewhat farther south. As the ridge approaches the lake shore, or the area between lake and ridge becomes narrower, fall frosts are delayed. For example, ice may form at one place, but 25 mi. to the west and at the same elevation freezing temperatures may not occur until several days later. Without excessive humidity and with few days during the growing season when the air is not in motion, this region is comparatively free from disease.

The most favorable sites in Ontario are those where winter temperatures are moderated by the influence of Lake Ontario and the growing season is long. In the Niagara Peninsula the general aspect is north, facing Lake Ontario, with the escarpment or "mountain" in the rear. Here the crop varies from year to year, but is never a complete failure. The most favored locations are back from the lake shore, just below and on the first rise of the escarpment where, depending somewhat on the direction and force of air currents, spring and summer temperatures are often several degrees higher than close to the lake. In some years fruit fails to mature fully in lakeshore vineyards, where the cooling effect of the water delays start of sorting growth and tempers the summer heat.

PLANTING

It is important that grape roots be kept moist before and during planting. Heeling-in is a useful practice to hold plants for a short time, but is makeshift for planting directly. Select a shady spot protected from wind and closely arrange the plants there in a furrow or trench so that the roots of each plant are in direct contact with a covering of soil.

Choice of Plants

Plants of one year growth, with well-developed roots and a good top, are usually the best to plant. But if one-year-olds are not available, thriving two-year-olds may be preferable since they have a larger root system and produce more vigorous growth in the first year. As a rule, discard weak plants.

Often two-year-olds are culls of the preceding year. If growing conditions are favorable, good cuttings usually make top-grade vines the first year in the nursery. The weak cuttings furnish the No. 2's and culls. Hence, desirable two-year-olds are not the No. 2's and culls of the previous year but are those that were graded top quality and transplanted to the nursery for another year.

When cuttings are used the cultivar becomes established on its own roots. In grafts, the cultivar scion is of one kind and the root another.

Marking the Field

Unless the plants are set in straight rows, difficulty is encountered in aligning the trellis and in various operations on flat land.

Digging individual holes for the plants is a dependable planting method. For large vineyards a plow is commonly used to mark a straight row; by returning in the row, a furrow 2.54 to 30.5 cm (1 to 12 in.) deep is prepared for planting.

A rod cut to a length equal to the distance between vines is convenient for marking, but be sure to line up the vines crosswise. In large plantings, measure in a row of stakes at the proper distance for individual vines, a few feet from the first row, where they can remain undisturbed. Measure in other rows of stakes every tenth row. With these stakes as guides, stretch a wire or cord attached to heavy stakes across the furrows and pull it tight. The position of each vine in each furrow is then quickly marked. Strike out several furrows before starting to plant. In very large plantings a surveyor's help may be needed.

Setting the Plants

At or before planting remove all but one cane and shorten it to two buds. Besides the single two-bud cane, leave a short stub as a convenient place for tying when the vines are to be trained to the trellis in the planting year. Tying to the stub rather than the cane avoids girdling as the cane increases in size. Cut back long roots to facilitate planting. Set the vines, except grafts, a little deeper than they stood in the nursery. Spread the roots carefully and tramp earth around them. Planting machines speed planting.

Direction of Rows

On level land probably the best exposure to sun is when the rows run north and south. However, where there is more than a slight slope, run the rows across the slope to reduce erosion to a minimum. A little wider spacing than usual may be wise when the rows run east and west. Least damage to the vines occurs if strong winds blow between the rows rather than across them.

Number of Plants

To determine the number of plants required to set a hectare, multiply the distance between rows by the distance within rows in meters and divide the product into 10,000, the number of m² in a hectare; or, in feet, divide the product into 43,560 (the number of ft² in an acre).

The number of vines per hectare, unless some die and are not replaced, is a permanent feature. Spacing cannot be changed from year to year in the vineyard. The width of modern equipment often limits the minimum spacing between rows of 3 to 3.7 m (10 to 12 ft). Spacing 2.4 m (8 ft) apart in the row is a general guide for Concord.

Some other factors involved in the planting distance are: provision of ample space for optimum training of the vines; reservation of sufficient soil area so that the roots have proper opportunity to forage; convenience and efficiency in spraying, machine-harvesting and other operations; soil fertility; cultivar habits; alleys; size and shape of vineyard; training system; and influence on yield and quality.

Any cultivar grown on well-drained deep soil will produce longer shoots and more foliage than when it is grown on poorly drained soil. Adjust spacings to cultivar, soil type, and method of training. With low-vigor types on clay, use the closest practical between-row and in-row spacings; with a vigorous cultivar on good soil, both spacings must be greater.

The main competition in a trellised vineyard is between adjacent rows and is not serious until the rows are very close together. Very high Concord yields have been obtained when rows were 1.4 m (4.5 ft) apart and vines 2.7 m (9 ft) apart in the row. This is not a practical distance until suitable equipment is developed to work in such rows. But it shows that gains in yield are possible by increasing vine population and yet not excessively increasing competition along the row.

When the vineyard is large, provide alleys crosswise to the rows to facilitate such operations as spraying and harvesting. Leave alleys wide enough to permit easy turning with tractor equipment, and a headland to permit easy turning with tractors and machine harvesters.

TILLAGE

Cultivation

For many years it was customary to cultivate frequently during the growing season, sometimes once a week. Stress was placed on clean appearance of the vineyard, on sanitation which may accompany a clean vineyard, and on making available more plant nutrients to stimulate growth. Vineyards are now cultivated less frequently and less deeply than formerly. The care of a vineyard is a long-time matter.

Today more importance is attached to the conservation of organic matter in the soil (which is not easily increased), to preventing soil erosion from water or wind, and to saving moisture and nutrients in the soil.

Frequent cultivation gradually reduces the size of the soil aggregates until finally the surface of the soil is reduced to a fine, loose, single-grain condition. Such soil tends to puddle badly when wet, surface runoff becomes excessive, and soil erosion is more severe. The fine soil particles tend to clog the large water conduction pores of the soil and thus prevent rapid and deep penetration of rain. Under such circumstances loss of water from surface evaporation may be excessive. Good soil structure permits efficient usage of rain.

The detrimental effects of deep cultivation have long been known, but not always heeded. Soil compaction by the increasing use of heavy machinery in large vineyards may have some adverse effect on soil structure.

Cultivation has been resorted to as a method of preventing competition for moisture by other vegetation. Although the value of cultivation in moisture conservation has in many cases been publicized, even greater moisture, soil and nutrient losses were overlooked. Even though cultivation has been advocated for the maintenance of a dust mulch as a protection against moisture losses, the operation usually liberates moisture and may make the soil susceptible to crusting after heavy rains, resulting in less penetration and more runoff. A less uniform seasonal supply of moisture may result.

The release of available N by cultivation may result in some stimulation of the vines. But it is also wise to add N and to retain the organic matter in the soil for controlling erosion, maintaining soil porosity, and improving the general physical structure of the soil.

Considerable cultivation is practiced in commercial vineyards. Make the first cultivation as soon as the soil is in good workable condition, since early cultivation encourages the new growth to develop earlier in the season. If, however, the soil is not in good workable condition, soil structure may be impaired and slow to recover. In midsummer and early fall, depending on the location, cease cultivation and sow a green manure or cover crop to aid in maturing of the vine and fruit.

Trash cultivation is a good practice. In this system, done in the fall, hay or straw is applied and a disk or other implement is used to break, disorganize and partly cover the material with soil.

Grape Hoe

The grape hoe is a useful implement with vines up to 3 to 4 years old. Tractor-mounted grape hoes greatly reduce the labor required for control of weeds under the trellis. Even careful operators, however, cause some injury and vines are lost. The operation, especially in old vineyards, is sometimes described as "snap, crack, and pop" in reference to the cutting of the shallow roots.

Grape hoe damage can be reduced by more careful operation, straight trunks to reduce mechanical injury, cover crop seeding only in the middle of the row, and by running the blade parallel to the soil surface.

In an old practice the grape-hoe was used as a means of grape berry moth control, but has been largely replaced for this purpose by insecticides.

On light well-drained soils a ridge under the trellis is seldom needed. On heavier, poorly drained soils it may be desirable to throw up a ridge 10.2 to 17.8 cm (4 to 7 in.) high on each side of the trunks in the fall, and take it down in spring.

Many herbicides are useful to control weeds in vineyards, to reduce the amount of cultivation required, and as a replacement for grape hoeing. The kinds of weeds vary greatly in different regions. Simazine, caeseron, diuron and Paraquat are a few examples of herbicides. 2-4D should not be used in or near a vineyard.

ORGANIC MATTER, MANURES AND COVER CROPS

Physical and Chemical

Study of soils in Ohio vineyards reveals these facts (Wander 1946):

(1) A favorable surface soil granulation or good state of aggregation often has been destroyed by excessive cultivation and lack of cover crops or manure over a long period of time.

(2) Organic matter and total N, which are closely related to aggregation, have often been seriously depleted. Organic matter losses have been 20 to 80%, and losses of N as high as 85%.

(3) Decrease in total exchangeable bases may be 18 to 76% of the original amount assumed to have been present.

(4) Losses of Ca, K, and P are not as pronounced as loss of organic matter and N, but sometimes become limiting, especially when enough organic matter and N are not restored to the soil.

(5) Only two vineyard soils showed a loss of exchangeable Ca. Amount of exchangeable Ca depends largely on the soil origin.

(6) There is usually no consistent change of exchange K. Some soils originally have more than others.

(7) Except where there has been serious erosion and loss of organic matter, readily available P in the vineyard may be equal to or higher than that in adjacent undisturbed soil.

(8) No great change occurs in soil reaction.

(9) Less intensive cultivation and the use of manure or fertilizer with cover crops can restore and maintain grape soils in a more productive condition.

Purposes and Functions

Manure (farm or green) or cover crops turned under help maintain the organic matter necessary for good physical condition and moisture-holding capacity of the soil and in supporting desirable soil organisms. Unless organic matter is maintained, the soil eventually declines in fertility. Grapes outlive the organic matter content of many soils, and its content in most vineyards is too low.

The recommended rate of manure or straw is intended as a maintenance application only. Higher rates are advised where the organic matter is low. Fertilizer application for the green-manure or cover crop is probably the cheapest means available of maintaining soil organic matter by increasing the amount of cover to be retained in the soil. Fertilizer used for green-manure crops returns to the soil in a desirable state.

Some further functions of green-manure crops are: to check late growth, thus aiding the vine to mature fruit and wood; to utilize N available in the soil after the vines have ceased growth and reduce its loss by leaching; and to hold snow and thus avoid root freezing. A green-manure crop checks washing of the topsoil and thus avoids root freezing. If it is left standing over the winter it helps prevent erosion, and holds many of the grape leaves which add organic matter to the soil.

Thickness of humus layer may influence growth and yield more than any other soil factor. Yield of humus layers 7.6 to 10.2 cm (3 to 4 in.) or more thick may be twice that on thinner layers.

Experiments in Ontario indicate that more response might have been obtained from a cover crop or fertilizer if more buds than the orthodox number had been left (Archibald and Bradt 1963).

Sow the green-manure or cover crop soon after cultivation ceases. If the space between rows permits, sow with a grain drill rather than a cyclone seeder since no seed will be sown under the vines where it might interfere with air circulation. A green-manure crop is difficult to turn under when sown close to the wires.

Selecting the Cover Crop

Crops that live through the winter, unless turned under early in the spring, may reduce the early season growth of the vines, as well as the later growth. A somewhat similar result may follow from an attempt to increase the humus supply by sowing a cover crop in spring in the vineyard. Where the vine growth is checked too early, the adverse effect also shows in the fruit. Unfortunately many growers do not start cultivation early enough when an overwintering crop is making a vigorous spring growth. The cover crop should not prevent the covering of the berry-moth pupae where this pest is present.

Oats (170 liters per ha, or 2 bu per acre) is a fairly good cover crop if it can get a good start, but it may not be the best to use on sandy soils lacking in humus. Millet, like oats, winter-kills. On moderately fertile soils, millet (22.4 to 33.6 kg per ha, or 20 to 30 lb per acre) may make more growth than oats. Oats and some millets may make strong growth in the fall and so may be objectionable at harvest time, though they can be knocked down with a stone boat or disk. Since oats and millet are killed by frost there is no temptation to delay spring cultivation as in the case of rye, which makes its heavy growth in spring.

Rye (30 liters per ha, or 1.5 bu per acre) is one of the most common cover crops. Letting rye grow tall in spring gives more material to turn under, but owing to its more mature condition it may break down slowly, causing drying of the soil and reducing its nitrate content, thus adversely affecting growth.

Buckwheat (44.8 kg per ha, or 40 lb per acre) will succeed on soil too poor for many other cover crops and grows rapidly in the fall, thus tending to check vine growth. Some growers use a mixture of oats and buckwheat. Soybeans also winter-kill and, when inoculated and sown soon after the grapes begin to bloom, may make a good cover crop on soil that is too poor for oats.

Vetch overwinters, makes a good early growth, and is a legume. It needs inoculation at the outset, the seed may be expensive, and sometimes the seed does not germinate well. Rye and hairy vetch make a good combination in some cases, as do barley and winter wheat. Most clovers start too late in spring to give good growth by the time spring tillage should be done.

Domestic ryegrass or Italian ryegrass is often a good choice of cover crop. Ryegrass is difficult to control in the vineyard if allowed to grow more than 30.5 cm (1 ft) high in spring, but if seeded in August in northern areas, it may develop beneath a canopy of weeds and afford good winter and spring soil protection.

In using humus-supplying crops it may be wise to seed alternate rows from year to year. This avoids wet conditions when picking.

In Erie County, Pa., vineyards on the lighter soils that were seeded with a cover crop have yielded 13% better than have those that were not seeded. Only a part of this increase has been due to cover crops, however, because more fertilizer was applied.

Residues

Grape stems, or pomace, applied on the dry weight equivalent of 13.4 metric tons per ha (6 tons per acre) of barn manure, may increase yield 1120 kg per ha (½ ton per acre) on eroded Chenango soil in Pennsylvania as well as greater growth (weight one-year prunings). Besides adding some nutrients, soil organic matter is maintained or increased; it decreases in untreated soil. On non-eroded Chenango soil these materials have little effect on yield or growth, despite an increase in soil organic matter. Annual returns of prunings to eroded Chenango soil tends to give higher yield, but no improvement in growth (Fleming and Alderfer 1955).

FERTILIZER

General fertilizer recommendations for grapes may serve as a rough guide. As a more accurate guide to determining specific fertilizer needs for a given area, make use of petiole and soil analysis services available in most areas. Results of such analyses give an accurate measure of the ability to extract the needed nutrients from the soil, and thus indicate fertilizer needs.

The petiole is used in analysis with Concord because its heavily pubescent leaves make leaf-blade analysis difficult. Soil tests provide general information such as soil texture, organic matter levels, pH, and relative levels of major and minor elements which are useful in establishing a fertility management program.

Fertilizer used for green-manure crops returns to the soil in a desirable form.

NPK (Nitrogen-phosphorous-potassium)

N, P, and K are the three main elements in a "complete" fertilizer. For a more complete fertilizer, specified minor elements may be mixed in with the NPK and carrier. The different fertilizer elements should be in balance, not in actual amounts or percentage, but in relation to each other.

Nitrogen (N)

N-deficient foliage is light green, vine growth is weak, cane and shoot elongation stops early, and the internodes are comparatively short.

N is often the chief limiting factor in vine growth and production. N fertilizer is highly soluble and quickly translocated in the vine. A noticeable response to N is stimulated vegetative growth and dark green leaves.

Too much N may promote a hazard that the vines will become over-vegetative and hence less fruitful. Neither the current crop nor the canes for the next year mature well when excessive growth occurs in autumn.

Sources.—N fertilizers differ in cost, analysis, and the carrier employed, e.g., calcium cyanamide (20% N and 70% Ca), sodium nitrate (16% N), and urea (38.5% N). Any one of them may be best suited for a particular set of conditions, e.g., if the pH of the soil is high, ammonium sulfate (20% N) may be best, to make more Mg available to the roots.

Treatment.—Apply N at least 2 to 3 weeks before new growth begins in spring. A critical growth stage is during bloom and fruit setting. When spring growth is weak, the leaves on main shoots are small, few laterals develop, and the flower clusters and ripe bunches are small. Within limits, the greater the vigor and leaf area, the larger are the flower clusters. If growth during bloom is too rapid, the bunches may be loose and straggly. The flowers under such conditions do not receive enough food material to develop normally, probably because the rapidly growing tips of shoots and laterals use these materials.

Rate.—The amount of N to supply varies with many factors. Many vineyards should receive 44.8 to 67.2 kg per ha (40 to 60 lb per acre) actual N annually, broadcast over the entire vineyard. Leaf and soil analyses may indicate that half the above amount is adequate for a specific vineyard.

High rates of N may stimulate excessive growth and result in undesirable late growth and possibly a deficiency of K and Mg. Adverse effect of late growth is due to loss of materials which support unwanted growth instead of being used for maturing wood and buds.

Range.—A range of 0.85 to 1.3% N in the leaf petioles of Concord during early July often represents a level of N nutrition for a desirable balance between vegetative vigor and yield of high-quality fruit. Within this range, N content of the petioles and yield are positively correlated; the soluble solids-acid ratios are highest. But the nearer the upper limit of this N range is approached the more likely is the possibility of a reduced level of soluble solids. Also, the N range in tannin content of finished juices coincides within those limits which impart desirable body and character to juice (Beattie and Baldauf 1960).

Phosphorus (P)

P may not move very far from the point of application because of the rapid fixation with the hydrated oxides of aluminum and iron to form relatively insoluble compounds in acid soil, or as calcium phosphate in highly alkaline soils. A soil may have abundant P and yet have little available to the vines. Lack of response to P is often the result of surface rather than deeper placement. Mg helps plants absorb P.

Green-manure crops benefit from P, and this fact may make it more available for grapes. Farm manure applications, especially poultry manure, can supply some P to vineyard soils. Mulches of straw or hay release P to the soil as a product of decomposition.

Grapes seem unable to absorb adequate P from soils with strong P-fixation tendencies, soil in which other plants could not be grown without liming or heavy fertilization, or both.

P-deficiency symptoms are not common in the vineyard. Severe P-deficiency may result in weak growth, small leaves, delayed start of spring growth, and dull, dark foliage that becomes bronzed at the midrib. Low temperatures accentuate P deficiencies by reduced root growth and reduced rate of absorption.

Three commonly used sources of P are superphosphate (20% P), ammonium phosphate, and rock phosphate.

A basic "complete" fertilizer usually supplies adequate P.

Potassium (K)

K is deficient in many vineyards, despite a high level in many soils. It is essential in the manufacture and translocation of sugars and starches, and is a factor in the uptake and loss of water by the vine. It may slightly increase resistance to disease and cold.

Sources.—Supplemental K can be applied in a complete fertilizer, in combination with P, or as potassium sulfate (50% K_2O or potash), potassium chloride (muriate of potash, 60% K_2O), and potassium nitrate (46% K_2O). Organic matter may supply some K. Because of possible detrimental effect from repeated applications of muriate of potash, due to the high chloride content, the more expensive sulfate form may be best.

Deficiency Symptoms.—Severe K deficiency may reduce vine vigor, berry and bunch size, and yield. Moderate K deficiency may result in poor root development and in fruit of poor color and quality. Probably the two most useful diagnostic means of identifying K deficiency are purplish-black areas between the leaf blades and marginal scorch.

By the time the vines show K deficiency, yields may already have been reduced. Therefore the K level in the vines or soil should not be allowed to be depleted to the point at which this condition exists.

Level.—In late summer and early fall a minimum petiole sample level of 1% may be good as a basis for advice on K fertilization (Boynton et al. 1958).

Treatment.—K may be applied at any time during the year, depending on the area. However, since potassium nitrate contains N, do not apply it in late summer.

K compounds tend to be fixed in the soil surface, although to a lesser extent than P. This fixation, which renders K unavailable to the roots, is generally greater in a clay loam near pH 7.0 than in a sandy soil near pH 5.0. The K rate may need to be greater and more frequent on clay than on sandy loams, especially if the soil pH is above 6.

A large application of K every two years seems more effective than smaller applications annually. Heavy rates of K may not give desired results until after the second year. This period of time between responses often seems to be due to a slow rate of K movement through certain soils, e.g., silt loam, when the fertilizer is placed in the bottom of irrigated rills.

Response to K fertilizer may be greatest if most of it is applied in a band 0.61 m (2 ft) wide beneath the trellis. Base the rate on soil and petiole analysis.

Balance.—The greater the supply of available N up to a point, the greater is the rate of vine growth and the greater the demand on all essential elements, especially K. Thus N applications alone can readily lead to K deficiency. The amount of K required is governed more or less by the amount of available N in the soil.

Excess K in the soil does not generally do any harm, but in soils low in Mg excessive K may cause Mg deficiency in the plants.

K deficiency sometimes occurs as the result of an excess of P. The uptake of K and P increases in the leaf tissue with increased moisture and with increased K and P levels. There is a direct interrelation between K and P intake.

Too much Ca and Mg in the soil may interfere with the uptake of K.

Foliar Spray.—Soil applications of K have a more lasting effect than foliar spray. However, foliar sprays of potassium sulfate or potassium nitrate can be effective in temporarily alleviating severe K deficiency. Use a solution containing 2.7 to 4.5 kg (6 to 10 lb) of either carrier in 378.5 liters (100 gal.); apply 458 liters per ha (300 gal. per acre) of mature vineyard.

Magnesium (Mg)

Mg is the only mineral found in chlorophyll. Mg helps plants absorb P, an element which is difficult to absorb.

Deficiency Symptoms.—Mg-deficient leaves are pale green or have creamy white interveinal veins. At first, the center of the blade shows more marked symptoms than the margin. In acute cases, chlorosis may be followed by necrosis of the center or even the entire leaf blade. Leaf symptoms rarely occur until midsummer and may become more acute until late fall. In early stages Mg and K deficiencies may be confused. Consistent occurrence of most severe Mg-deficiency symptoms on basal leaves aids in diagnosis. Mg deficiency is most likely to occur in vineyards where large amounts of K have been applied (Shaulis 1957).

Treatment.—Dolomitic limestone (contains Mg), 907 to 1814 kg per 0.4 ha (1 to 2 tons per acre), usually corrects Mg deficiency on soils below pH 5.5, but it may take a few months to 2 years. If the soil pH is above 5.5 and no liming is needed, then correction may be best achieved by foliage application of Mg sulfate, 7.3 kg in 378.5 liters (16 lb in 100 gal.) of water. Make one application soon after bloom and a second a week later. Thoroughly wet the vines.

Manganese (Mn)

Mn and Mg deficiency symptoms are much alike, but are usually first apparent in young leaves for Mn and in older leaves for Mg. A Mn chelate (EDTA), applied according to the product label, may give long-season control.

Concord may show visual Mn deficiency when the Mn petiole content in midsummer is less than 30 ppm of dry matter. Treat for two consecutive years with 0.45 kg (1 lb) per vine of Mn sulfate, either in autumn or in early spring, in a band 0.6 to 0.9 m (2 to 3 ft) wide along the row. Do not apply this heavy dosage, unless the symptoms show, or continue it for more than two years, because of possible toxicity (Beattie 1955A).

Iron (Fe)

Fe deficiency is associated with "lime-induced chlorosis" and usually occurs on soils high in lime. Certain Fe chelates, applied on the soil in early spring, may overcome this chlorosis. Moisture helps bring the chelates in contact with the roots. The chelates are broken down in the soil by too much water and the Fe can then be tied up.

Zinc (Zn)

Zn deficiency is characterized by a rosetting of the leaves ("little leaf"), interveinal chlorosis, and a widened angle formed by the basal lobes of the leaf blade where the stem is attached. The fruit clusters are small and may have shot berries. Where Zn deficiency is serious the fertilizer should contain 1 to 2% Zn oxide equivalent. Foliar application of 0.91 kg (2 lb) neutral Zn per 378.5 liters (100 gal.) of water may be helpful.

Boron (B)

B deficiency may occur on sandy soils in a dry year. Lack of boron may result in a light set of fruit, with many flower clusters "burning" off entirely; a set with a high percentage of shot berries; or an apparently normal set that shatters severely about midsummer. These fruiting symptoms may be accompanied by a leaf chlorosis occurring first on the terminal leaves. The terminal shoot tips may die back in early summer.

Borax contains 11.34% boron or 17.9% boric acid. B fertilizers should be broadcast to avoid toxicity; B can cause severe injury, e.g., speckling, cupping and puckering of leaves. Vinifera cultivars have a higher requirement than labrusca cultivars (Ashby 1968).

GRAPE TRELLIS AND ITS CONSTRUCTION

The standard systems still widely used are discussed first. The newer Geneva Double Curtain is discussed later.

The trellis for American-type bunch grapes is often erected in spring of the second year; the vines are allowed to trail on the ground the first year. However, if posts are set and wired before planting, training the vines can start immediately. The young vines will be out of the way of implements and weeds are more easily controlled. These advantages may outweigh the cost of planting and posting over two years.

Tying the shoots to temporary stakes encourages a straight trunk (in systems that require it), aids in establishing the vine to the top wire, avoids "stringing up," and may shorten the nonbearing period.

In one method tightly tie grape twine from the short stub (see Setting Plants) to the wires above the vine. Usually both buds on the two-bud stub cane start growth. Remove the weaker one when it is 2.5 to 5.1 cm (1 to 2 in.) long along with any surplus shoots. As the cane grows longer, twist it loosely around the twine several times during the season, and when it reaches the top wire (Kniffin systems), which may take two years, cut it off just above the wire and tie it tightly. If the cane is too short to reach the top wire after a year's growth, cut it off just above the last good bud. Tie below the bud, draw the cane up straight, and then tie to the top wire.

The trellis is a large item of expense, but it is usually cheaper in the end to erect a substantial trellis than to have to replace a poor one frequently.

Posts

Kind of Post.—Erect strong, durable posts. White cedar and oak posts last about 15 years, red cedar slightly longer, and locust for 25 years or more. Soak wooden posts, both below-ground and above-ground parts, in a preservative such as creosote for 24 hr or in pentachlorophenol in an oil base, to prolong their life and make it possible to use somewhat lighter ones. The preservative should dry for a month or more. Wooden posts are commonly 12.7 to 20.3 cm (5 to 8 in.) thick and 2.4 to 3 m (8 to 10 ft) long for the end posts, and 7.6 to 10.2 cm (3 to 4 in.) thick and 2.4 m (8 ft) long for interior posts, with allowance for driving into the ground.

FIG. 1.5. ONE METHOD OF BRAC-
ING END POSTS

Steel posts are easily driven into the ground. They also have advantages over wooden posts in durability, greater freedom from frost
heaving, convenience in raising and lowering wires, and in avoiding
lightning damage to the vines (they are conductors). But every 3 or 4
posts should be wooden; otherwise a strong wind when the vines are
heavy with fruit may bend the entire row.

Height of Posts.—The best length of post depends, in part, on the
system of training. Drooping systems require longer posts and higher
top wires than upright systems. It probably is not economical to
raise the trellis on low-vigor vineyards where prunings are under 0.45
kg (1 lb) per vine. But for vigorous Concord vineyards, yield, cluster
size, and juice quality are likely to be highest on a Kniffin trellis 1.7 to
1.8 m (5½ to 6 ft) high.

Spacing of Posts.—Optimum spacing of posts depends largely on
the spacing of the vines. Generally, 2, 3 or 4 vines occur between posts.
If, therefore, vines are set 2.4 m (8 ft) apart in the row the spacing of
posts is 4.9, 7.3 or 9.75 m (16, 24 or 32 ft) apart. In general, with 3
or 4 vines between posts, firmer posts and heavier wires are needed
than with 2 vines between posts.

Bracing End Posts.—In one method the post is set at a slight angle.
Guy it with strong galvanized wire, one end of which is fastened to the
post 60.9 cm (2 ft) from the top and the other end to an anchor or

"dead man" 91.4 cm (3 ft) from the post. For a good anchor that lasts the life of the vineyard, place a 91.4 cm (3 ft) iron bar, with a slight bend, at the bottom, and a 2.5 cm (1 in.) eye at the top, in a post hole, leaving the eye slightly above ground. Pour in 11.4 liters (3 gal.) of concrete around the bar as it is held in the center of the hole.

Certain anchor disks are easy to install. They screw into the ground and come in various sizes, e.g., 10.2 cm (4 in.).

Wires and Wiring

Size.—Sizes of wire in common use in vineyards are No. 9, 10, 11 and 12. No. 9 is the heaviest. The number of ft per lb of galvanized wire is: No. 9, 17.9; No. 10, 22.3; No. 11, 27.3; No. 12, 34.3. No. 9 is used for the top wire. A lighter wire gives way too soon. The lower wire, especially on short runs, often is No. 10. In upright systems, such as the Fan, the lower wires commonly are No. 10 or 11. (One ft is 0.3 m.)

Crimped wire (No. 11, 29 ft per lb) is very strong and hard and requires special cutters and stretchers. It stretches like a spring, returning to its normal position as loads are reduced or removed. It does not require loosening and tightening in fall and spring. The wire ties do not slide as they do on smooth galvanized wire. For long runs it may be worth considering because of its strength and possible long maintenance-free life.

Spacing of Wires.—See Training Systems.

How to Wire.—Bore 6.4 mm (¼ in.) holes in the wooden posts in the same direction as the wire is to be strung, at the heights the wire is to be above ground. When the wire is stretched along the row, pass the ends through the holes in each post and make fast to the wire-tightener. A wire-tightener with block and pulley is favored, but many simple devices may be used. One device is a 3.8 × 3.8 cm (1½ × 1½ in.) block of hardwood 20.3 to 22.9 cm (8 to 9 in.) long with a 6.4 mm (¼ in.) hole bored through the center. Pass the wire through the hole and make fast; then tighten it by turning the block with a monkey wrench. Its shape and the tautness of the wire keep the block in place. In another method, use a small iron reel on which to wind the wire after it passes through the hole in the end post. A good wire-tightener is a small, slightly curved iron bar about 13 cm (½ in.) thick. Like the wood block, it can be wound up tight. Fasten the wire on the windward side of the interior wooden posts by means of 2.5 to 3.8 cm (1 to 1½ in.) staples. About 7.8 to 9 kg per ha (7 to 8 lb per acre) of staples are needed for a two-wire trellis. In stapling, leave space for free passage of the wire in fall and spring.

Unless the wires are slack during winter they may break and the end posts loosen. After pruning and cutting the old ties, one may proceed as follows: Against the end post set a stay post that is 1.8 m (6 ft) long and extends from the ground to a point about 1.2 m (4 ft) high on the end post. Attach this stay post temporarily; loosening it merely requires raising the end of the stay post next to the end post, which can then sag and slacken the wires. In late winter or early spring, but before the new ties have been made, tighten the wires by replacing the stay post on the end post and by using a wire-tightener.

TRAINING AND PRUNING

There are several systems for training grapes. The purposes of training are to establish the framework of the vine and to ensure systematic distribution of parts on wires so that the vines can be conveniently managed in cultural practices. Proper pruning regulates and encourages good annual yield, size, and quality of the fruit. To the uninformed, grape pruning seems drastic because a high percentage of the growth of the previous season is cut off.

Usual practice is to gather up and remove the prunings from the vineyard and then burn them. Machines are available for chopping, breaking or macerating pruned canes right in the vineyard.

The parts of a vine, in relation to training and pruning, are the following:

Trunk: Main stem of the vine.

Arms: Main branches arising from the trunk.

Old Wood: Any part of the vine older than one year.

Shoots: New leafy growths developing from buds. They are called shoots during the growing season. After the leaves fall they become canes.

Laterals: Secondary shoots arising from the main shoots.

Canes: Dormant shoots grown the past year.

Spur: Basal portion of a cane cut back to 1 to 4 buds or nodes in length.

Fruit Spur: A spur that is primarily intended to bear fruit.

Renewal Spur: A cane cut back to a short stub usually two buds long to produce next year's fruiting wood at a desired location.

Nodes: Joints on shoots or canes where leaves or buds are attached.

Internodes: The part between the nodes.

Eye: The compound bud at each node on a cane.

Primary Bud: Largest and strongest bud of an eye.

Secondary Bud: The smaller bud of an eye.

Suckers: Shoots arising from below or just above ground level.

Bull Wood: Canes of large diameter with long internodes and many laterals.

Dormant Pruning

The chief pruning, and usually the only pruning, of grapes each year is commonly done while the canes are dormant.

"**Bleeding.**"—Bleeding of grape vines may occur after early spring pruning. This causes many growers, particularly novices, great but usually undue concern. Actually, the exudating sap consists almost entirely of water. When pruning has been delayed, it is generally better to prune in late spring, even though the vines bleed, than to leave them unpruned. When the leaves appear, bleeding usually stops. No great amount of nutrients is lost by bleeding.

Fall Pruning.—Good yields may result when a mild winter follows fall pruning. But if pruning is done soon after leaf fall, the canes may kill back several buds in cold winters.

Concord vines trained to the 4-cane Kniffin system in New York were pruned in November; unpruned checks were left. The following February, cane samples were cut for freezing tests. Fall-pruned vines, particularly the portion of the canes near the cuts, showed more injury after freezing at $-30°C$ ($-22°F$) than the checks. Parts of the canes near the trunk (2 ft or more from the pruning cuts) showed less injury than samples near the cuts. Also, more bud injury occurred on fall-pruned canes (Edgerton and Shaulis 1953).

In Ohio, after $-24°C$ ($-11°F$) on the night of March 12, the most severe injury to dormant buds and canes usually occurred, irrespective of time of pruning, on low, poorly drained sites.

In Ontario, pruning can begin any time after the first hard frost $-7°C$ ($20°F$) or below. The important consideration is that the vines be completely dormant (Bradt 1968).

Canes are brittle on cold days; while brittle, they may be damaged in pulling out brush. It is often wise to delay pruning until after the low winter temperatures, especially after a year unfavorable for maturing buds and wood. But with large acreages this is impossible unless adequate help is available.

Dormant pruning is not likely to be comfortable or efficient when done on quite cold days.

Summer Pruning

Summer pruning is seldom good practice, except to remove suckers. Sometimes 0.6 m (2 ft) or more of the growth is removed from the end of shoots in late summer to admit light to the fruit and to control mildew by permitting better circulation of air through the vine. Objections are that the vine is weakened, undesirable laterals are produced, maturing of wood is delayed, best flavor and color may fail to develop owing to reduction in leaf surface, sunscalding of berries may result, and some of the best fruiting wood for the next year may be interfered with. Spraying to maintain healthy foliage, and summer pruning to remove part of it, are opposite procedures. Carbohydrates and other materials that are produced and used by the plant in the development of roots, tops and fruit occur in the leaves. Reduction of the leaf surface, whether by summer pruning or pests, adversely affects both plant and fruit.

Topping is justified, if at all, only in years of excessive growth and after mildew is seen to be developing. In the most severe topping, no fewer than 7 to 8 leaves should be left beyond the outermost bunch. Growers can better avoid excessive growth and maintain reasonable vigor by balanced pruning and other practices, as outlined elsewhere in the text.

Suckering

Suckering is the removal of all shoots produced low on the vine or from the roots. These suckers bear little or no fruit, and hence grow vigorously, appropriating food materials that should go to the vine; or, if grafted plants, they may bear unmarketable fruit. Careful suckering during the first 4 to 5 years saves time and expense later. After the fifth year few shoots appear on vines that were properly suckered while young, but vines carelessly handled may sucker every year.

Suckering is best done in early summer before the shoots become hard and woody. Woody suckers are more difficult to remove than young shoots and, if imperfectly removed, the remaining part becomes a perennial source of trouble. (See also Renewing Old Trunks.)

TRAINING SYSTEMS
(LONG-TIME CONVENTIONAL SYSTEMS)

Systems with Shoots Trained Upright

In the upright system arms are laid off to the right and left and carried along a horizontal wire, or they are carried obliquely across one or more wires. As the shoots grow upward they are tied to wires above. This system has been used mostly with cultivars such as Catawba and Delaware, where vines are not as vigorous as Concord and Niagara.

Fan System.—Usually the trunk is carried up to or above the height of the lowest wire. The trellis consists of 3 wires, the lowest 45.7 to 50.8 cm (18 to 20 in.) high and the upper at 50.8 cm (20 in.)

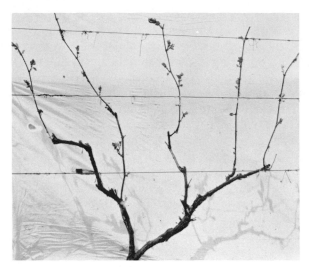

FIG. 1.6.   FAN SYSTEM OF TRAINING

intervals. Prune 5 to 6 canes to 5 to 8 buds each and tie them, fan-shaped, to the top wire. Leave renewal spurs at the base of some of the surplus canes.

This system suits certain cultivars, and relatively short posts are used. Objections are: summer tying is needed and is slow work; the best canes often develop at extremities where they cannot be used most effectively; some fruit is produced near the ground and becomes dirty; yield of vigorous cultivars is lower than with drooping systems; canes for fruiting often are too short for best results; low shoots are injured in tillage and interfere with tillage; canes are often blown down in summer and require re-tying; "stringing up" is often necessary.

The advantages of the 4-cane Kniffin system, such as one less wire per row, less tying, and greater efficiency of machine-harvesting, may offset the slight decrease in yield in moderately vigorous cultivars such as Catawba (Bradt and Wiebe 1971).

Chautauqua.—In training a young vine, cut back a cane (future trunk) and tie it at its top to the lowest wire. Buds just below this wire produce large shoots in the second growing season. For the third year, prune two of these shoots as bearing canes and tie horizontally to the right and left of the trunk to become arms. Tie canes arising from them vertically to the top wire. Leave two-bud spurs at intervals along the arms for fruiting canes the next year. Establish new arms, as needed, from two-year wood. The objections are the same as for the Fan system.

FIG. 1.7.   CHAUTAUQUA SYSTEM

Systems with Drooping Shoots

In the drooping method the growing shoots hang down during the growing season. Since these shoots need not be tied, labor is saved.

Single-trunk, 4-Cane Kniffin.—Train a permanent trunk to the upper of two wires. Select 4 canes, 2 to the right and 2 to the left of the trunk, and tie to the wires. The lower wire is 0.76 to 1.07 m (2½ to 3½ ft) above ground, and the upper is 0.6 to 0.76 m (2 to 2½ ft) higher.

Extend and tie a stem or trunk to the top wire at the first opportunity. Arrange canes along the wires as illustrated. Leave several more buds on each top cane than on the lower canes. The canes should arise each year from spurs left near the trunk; otherwise crowding with adjacent vines occurs. The usual number of canes per vine is four, but if more are needed for proper bud number, put the extra one or more canes on the upper wire.

The merits are: it is well adapted to vigorous cultivars with a natural drooping habit, such as Concord and Niagara; training and pruning are simple; summer tying is not necessary and thus labor is saved; tillage is done with little injury to the shoots; the drooping foliage prevents sunscalding of the fruit; only two wires are needed; air circulation in the vines is good; the foliage and developing clusters are well disposed for spraying; the fruit is fairly easily picked. Most of our information on best cane diameter, internodal length, and so forth is based on this system.

The objections are: it is not well suited to cultivars or conditions in

FIG. 1.8.   SINGLE-TRUNK, 4-CANE KNIFFIN SYSTEM

which growth is slow or the canes short; often, many bunches become entangled with the wires and canes, thus decreasing the ease of picking; heavier wire is needed than for some other systems; tall posts are needed (which may be a good investment).

6-Cane Kniffin.—Train a cane to the right and left of the trunk along three wires; the first wire is 61 to 66 cm (24 to 26 in.) above ground and the other two at 71 cm (28 in.) intervals higher. The growth is spread over a large area, thus making pruning, spraying and picking somewhat easier, and in unfavorable seasons more of the vine is exposed to wind and sun, thus lessening disease and hastening maturity. Also, the higher trellis may have merit compared with wider spacing of vines. In yield a slight difference occurs in favor of three wires, but usually not enough to condemn a two-wire system on this account.

Some objections are: more pruning cuts and more ties are needed than with other Kniffin systems; three wires and tall posts are needed; the crop and growth on the lowest wire are not always good. The lowest wire may detract from the efficiency of machine-harvesting.

In a three year study in Ontario, widening the foliage canopy by spreading the shoots, or narrowing the canopy by shoot tip removal, did not affect yield, cluster weight, or berry set of mature, moderately vigorous DeChaunac vines trained to the 6-cane Kniffin system. Widening the canopy by training shoots horizontally and away from the row widened the zone of light interception and tended to increase fruit soluble solids. Shoot tip removal narrowed the zone of light interception and resulted in a lower fruit soluble solids content than the check. Shoot tip removal reduced vigor by a reduced weight of two year wood removed at dormant pruning.

The plants were 3.5 m (14.5 ft) apart with vines 2.15 m (7 ft) in the row. Before bloom, each thinning was done to leave one cluster per shoot. Pruning was balanced to vine vigor by leaving 30 buds for the first lb (454 gm) and 8 buds for each subsequent pound of pruning wood weight. The 6 to 8 leaves acropetal to a fruit cluster supply the bulk of photosynthate to the trunk and root system (Wiebe 1975).

Umbrella.—Establish a trunk with its head 10.2 to 20.3 cm (4 to 8 in.) below the top wire. From this head bend 1 to 6 canes over the top wire and down to the lower wires. Formation of a Y-terminal of the trunk permits the canes to be more rapidly bent over this wire without breakage. Bend the canes over the top wire so that the outer bark cracks.

Bending stretches and tears the vascular system in the canes, which tends to temporarily obstruct the movement of sap; it is done to promote the growth of fruiting canes for the next year. It also reduces vine vigor, which results in large bunch size. Weak vines do not respond well to this treatment.

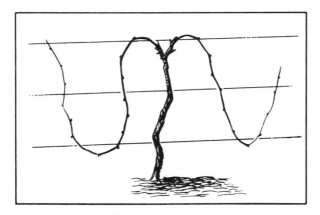

FIG. 1.9.   UMBRELLA SYSTEM

In this system, the crop is somewhat superior in size of bunch and berry, compactness of bunch, and maturity; summer tying is not necessary; the vine is quickly and easily pruned; good air circulation is possible; tying, spraying, and picking are facilitated. Some objections are: yield is often slightly less than with some other systems; breakage of one cane if only 1 to 3 canes are left after the pruning, as practiced in some areas, reduces the crop per vine. (See also Shoot Positioning.)

Munson System.—Pass two wires over 2 × 4 cross-arms about 61 cm (2 ft) long, set at right angles to the row on posts 1.2 to 1.4 m (4 to 4½ ft) high. String a third or central wire about 15 cm (6 in.) lower than the others. Train a trunk, supported at first by a stake and later by tying, to the central wire, where a head with short arms is established. Tie a cane to the right and one to the left of the trunk on the central wire. The two outside wires support the growing shoots. A modification of this system is to dispense with the central wire and string four canes along the top of a four-wire horizontal trellis.

The merits are: the pendant clusters, which can be plainly seen, appeal to the grape fancier; a person can pass from row to row under the vines; no summer tying; air circulation is good; fruit and foliage are out of the way of tillage tools; the fruit is not near the ground, and thus dirty fruit is avoided. The trellis is expensive to construct, and the cross-arms interfere with cultural operations.

PRUNING FOR EARLY BEARING

Vigorous vines can be brought to full bearing the third year by forming a trunk (Kniffin and adapted systems) to the top wire at the end of the first year. A growth cannot always be found that will reach the top wire the first year, but when such growth is present, severe pruning may delay production without any compensating gain. Aim to form the framework of the vine as quickly as possible.

Bearing a full crop of vigorous Concord in the third year does not reduce the yield or vigor in later years. Vines pruned lightly at the start and established to the 4-cane Kniffin system 1 to 2 years before vines that were severely headed back continue to be as productive, with as strong trunks and as much vigor, as those pruned to two buds for the first two years.

Plants with the most top growth have the largest root system. Diameter and length of the single cane are greater than in vines with two canes.

Relation of Growth to Yield

The more fruit produced by a vine, the smaller is the amount of shoot growth during that year. A vine that overbears makes less growth during that year than in the preceding year. Over-bearing weakens a vine. Growth of the shoots is made stronger by over-pruning, but is too costly because it reduces yield.

Proper maturity of fruit and canes depends considerably on the ratio of effective leaf surface to pounds of fruit on the vine. A vine that is over-bearing and has made weak growth with small leaves will not mature the fruit and canes as well as if it were carrying a smaller crop. Practice proper fertilization, tillage, drainage and pest control. If they are neglected, a vine cannot mature as good a crop as the well-cared-for vine. Correct amount of pruning varies with individual vines.

PRUNING ESTABLISHED VINES

Cane Diameter

The median portion of a cane is usually the region of greatest productivity. Spindly canes and those that taper rapidly are undesirable, as are very large or "bull canes." Canes the thickness of a lead pencil or slightly larger are best.

"Canes of moderate size" may be a misleading expression. In vines of low vigor the best-yielding wood might be discarded to save smaller canes. In very vigorous vines the moderate-size canes may be too large for highest yield. Fredonia canes are larger and Delaware canes smaller than Concord.

Internodes

Examine canes selected for fruiting for both internodal length and diameter, rather than for one alone. When measured between nodes 4 and 6, highest yields occur where the internodal length is 12.7 to 17.8 cm (5 to 7 in.). An internodal length may be so great as to be undesirable, and it is harder to find room to train very long canes on the trellis.

Renewal Spurs

Besides the desirable number of canes, leave several two-bud spurs that are wood of the same age as the canes. These renewal spurs provide a desirable place of origin for fruiting canes the next year and tend to make new canes arise near the trunk instead of relatively far out and intermingled with adjacent canes.

Number of Buds

The term "balanced pruning" means that the number of buds left at pruning time is varied according to the amount of wood removed, which depends on the vigor of the vine. If too many buds are left, over-cropping results; the grapes may not ripen properly, and the vines may

be weakened for the next year. If too few are left, the crop may be reduced. Experienced growers have learned the number of buds required to give a proper balance. But many growers are inclined to
leave the same number of buds on each vine in the vineyard, irrespective of vigor. When this is done, weak vines may become weaker and
vigorous ones over-vegetative.

N. L. Partridge in 1925 in Michigan was the first to publish a pruning scale which related severity of pruning to vigor with Concord. In
his scale 30 buds are left for each increase of 0.45 kg (1 lb) of one-
year-old prunings. The number of buds increases progressively for
each increase of 0.11 kg (¼ lb) of prunings.

N. J. Shaulis in 1948 in New York proposed a "30 plus 10" scale
for Concord, in which 30 buds are left per vine for each 0.45 kg (1
lb) of prunings, and 10 buds for each additional 0.45 kg (1 lb), not
counting the basal buds. In each class it is 10 buds more for Fredonia
and 5 less for Catawba than for Concord.

Under irrigation in Washington state, the vines are more vigorous
than they are in the East. Where growers have left 60 buds for the
first pound of prunings and 20 buds for each additional pound, yield
in the Yakima Valley tends toward biennial bearing, compared with a
50 plus 10 scale. This variation is probably due to overcropping in
the "on" year, which reduces the number of buds developed for the
next year's crop. Vines spaced 2.4 × 2.7 m (8 × 9 ft) and 6-cane Knif-

TABLE 1.1

WEIGHT OF PRUNINGS AS A GUIDE TO NUMBER OF BUDS TO BE LEFT, ONTARIO

Lb of Prunings[1]	Fredonia 40 - 10 No. of Buds Left per Vine	Concord, Niagara, Agawam, Elvira 30 - 10 No. of Buds Left per Vine	Delaware, Catawba, French Hybrids 25 - 5 No. of Buds Left per Vine
Under ½	20	15	10
½	25	20	18
1	40	30	25
1½	45	35	27
2	50	40	30
2½	55	45	32
3	60	50	35
3½	65	55	37
4	70	60	40
4½	75	65	42
5	80	70	45

Source: Bradt (1972).
[1] One lb is equal to 0.45 kg.

fin-trained to 50 plus 10 buds on a 1.8 m (6 ft) trellis attain a maximum production with a vine size of 90 buds retained when the prunings' weight is 2.3 kg (5 lb or more) (Clore and Brummond 1961).

In the grape areas of southern British Columbia, seasonal heat unit accumulations from May 11 to October 11, in an average location, total 1093° C (2000 ° F) but vary from 760° to 1427° C (1400° to 2600° F). Heat accumulations are normally only 15% lower in northern areas and 15% higher in southern areas. Blossom records of four cultivars showed differences of up to 3.5 days between full bloom dates of the first and fourth flower clusters on a node. More crop was produced on the ninth node than on the first node and more on the fifth node than on the first node for 13 out of 14 cultivars trained to the 4-cane Kniffin system. There were fewer fruit clusters on the first and second than on the fourth to ninth nodes on a 10-node cane (Fisher *et al.* 1971).

The scales in Table 1.1 are useful guides in pruning. Actually, leaving the exact number of buds may not be critical, but it is important to vary the number of buds according to vigor and cultivar.

RENEWING TRUNKS

Many cultivars, including Concord, are subject to dead arm, a fungus disease that damages the trunk and arms (see Diseases). Other injuries that make it necessary to renew trunks are cold, lightning, tillage tools, and machine-harvesting.

Remove the old trunk at once if it is badly diseased. If it is in reasonably good condition, the trunk can be completely renewed with a sucker from below ground or near ground level. As the canes are produced and increase in size and vigor, allow the new vine to carry more of the crop. Remove the old trunk as soon as the renewal can carry a full crop, which is usually in about three years.

TYING ON THE TRELLIS

Tying is done after the dormant pruning and tightening of the trellis wires. It is also done in summer with upright training systems. Dormant vines are tied to assure that the trunk, arms and canes are desirably arranged on the trellis, to protect the vines against wind and implement injury, and to avoid sagging, crooked trunks which interfere with vineyard operations. With drooping training systems, tying soon after dormant pruning is all that is needed.

Tying Materials

Girdling may result if wire is used to tie the trunk and main arms. Use material for winter tying of canes that is strong enough to last for the year. Two-ply twine is better than single-ply for winter tying. Binder twine is difficult to remove the next year. Plastic twines are available but some of them are hard to tie securely. Mechanical grape ties may be worth trying.

Improper Tying

Good pruning and training may be ruined by improper tying. It is false economy to use material that is not strong and durable. This results in much retying and often in injured arms.

Skillful pruners are often hired to prune the vines. Later, less skillfull persons do the tying and may make one or more of these mistakes: break the canes by rough handling; make excessive ties per cane; use wire ties or tie too tightly on the young trunk or renewal; fail to recognize canes left for layering or trunk renewal; fail to give trellis space to all the buds the pruner has left; fail to properly bend the canes of Umbrella-trained vines (Shaulis 1950).

MACHINE PRUNING

Grape pruning has long been done by hand. Doing some of the work by machine is now practiced in some large vineyards. Two basic types of pruning machines are available: one has only a more or less vertical cutter bar; the other has both a vertical cutter bar and a horizontal cutter bar that can be moved hydraulically in and out, as well as raised and lowered as needed.

Machine pruning is best adapted to short-cane or spur type pruning. It is most efficient when the vines are combed during the growing season so that they hang down, e.g., shoot positioning in the Geneva Double Curtain system.

A machine can remove much of the wood and thus reduce the hand pruning needed. One problem is that a machine cannot distinguish the vigorous top-quality canes that are deep red in color from the straw-colored smaller canes with less potential.

GENEVA DOUBLE CURTAIN (GDC) SYSTEM

The GDC system of training was developed about 1960 by N. J. Shaulis, Agr. Expt. Station, Geneva, N. Y. It is now the chief method

Courtesy of O. A. Bradt, Hort. Res. Inst. Ont.,
Vineland Station, Ontario, Canada

FIG. 1.10.   GENEVA DOUBLE CURTAIN SYSTEM. UNPRUNED (TOP) AND PRUNED (BOTTOM)

Courtesy of O. A. Bradt, Hort. Res. Inst. Ont.,
Vineland Station, Ontario, Canada

FIG. 1.11.   UNPRUNED (LEFT) AND PRUNED (RIGHT) DOUBLE TRUNK AND
CENTRAL PORTION TRAINED TO GENEVA DOUBLE CURTAIN SYSTEM

of training for machine-harvesting of grapes in the East, particularly
for juice and wine.

Advantages

Compared with other systems the advantages are better exposure
to light, which gives increased yield, increased sugar content of the
fruit, and earlier maturity of the wood, resulting in less winter injury.
Tying of dormant canes is not necessary. (See Shoot Positioning.)

Short-pruned Canes

The vines are pruned to short (five buds) instead of to longer canes,
as described for older systems, and are trained to a bilateral or double
cordon. It may be thought from earlier discussion of Kniffin systems
that the first five nodes do not represent a highly productive portion of
the cane. However, the yield of the 5-node canes on a vigorous vine
arranged on a GDC may exceed that from 10-node canes on a Kniffin-
trained Concord vine. The superiority of GDC probably results from
a greater light exposure of the leaves in the previous season. Light
intensity may be only 100 ft-candles for interior leaves. For maximum

photosynthesis, 2000 ft-candles is adequate; 500 ft-candles is not adequate (Shaulis *et al.* 1966).

Posts and Wires

End posts should be extra sturdy and well-anchored because of the extra stress (a minimum of 2.4 m (8 ft) long, and set at an angle). Used railroad ties make good end posts when available. The posts may have to be set at least 0.9 m (3 ft) deep to enable them to withstand heaving.

The following suggestions are for the 2.7 m (9 ft) row and 122 cm (48 in.) between trellis wires:

For line posts use pressure-treated posts with a minimum diameter of 7.6 cm (3 in.), a minimum height of 1.7 m (5 ft), and a maximum height of 1.8 m (6 ft).

For cordon-wire supports and support wire have the attachment height 137 cm (54 in.) above ground, preferably use white oak, and use No. 11 or No. 12 galvanized wire between post and support. The strongest design is with wire running horizontally from support to post. Staple loosely to the side of the post.

Cordon wire height is about 178 cm (70 in.). A 5.1 × 5.1 cm (2 × 2 in.) spreader near the end post will keep the wires spread near the end of the row. Cordon-wire spacing and row widths should remain uniform in any one row and preferably throughout the vineyard.

FIG. 1.12.   SLANTING END POST FOR GENEVA DOUBLE CURTAIN SYSTEM

Curtains

The elongated trunks are secured to a hori)ontal cordon-wire 1.7 to 1.8 m (5½ to 6 ft) above the ground.

Vines in the row are alternated to the right and left on the cordon wires to give the double curtain effect. These wires are held in place by wood or metal supports attached to sturdy posts 7.3 m (24 ft) apart in the row.

Curtain Formation (Shoot Positioning)

Annual shoot positioning is essential, otherwise there is little advantage in using GDC training. The curtain is necessary to expose more leaves to sunlight. To obtain this exposure, the long horizontal shoots must be placed in a vertically downward position to expose the basal leaves. This positioning is done by hand and requires 40 hr of labor per 0.4 ha (1 acre). First shoot positioning is done during the four week period starting immediately after bloom. The area between the two cordon wires must be kept open to allow light between the two curtains.

Number of Buds

The danger of leaving too many buds on vines trained to the GDC is much greater than in the Kniffin systems. Leave 5-bud canes evenly spaced along the cordon. For a vine with 1.36 kg (3 lb) of prunings, leave 4 of these canes on each side of the 2 cordons, along with 5 one-bud renewal spurs, making a total of 50 buds left. Using the 30 plus scale, the number of 5-bud canes will vary according to amount of wood removed.

Converting Other Systems to the GDC

Unless growth is very vigorous, it is preferable to operate an Umbrella Kniffin system vineyard for the first 4 to 5 years. If shading occurs, it can be converted to the GDC. When in doubt about potential vigor, plant in such a way as to have the option of changing over if vines become overly vigorous. Establishing two trunks and using the Umbrella Kniffin system makes it relatively easy to convert to the GDC.

When it has been determined after 4 to 5 years that there is sufficient vigor to warrant the GDC system, commence the changeover. As the cordon is being established, maintain balanced pruning at the 20 plus 10 level to prevent overcropping. Once the pruning weight reaches 1.36 kg (3 lb), use a 30 plus 10 level.

In the conversion year select three canes. One cane from each trunk starts the cordon. The length is determined by the number of buds required for balanced pruning. The third cane fills the distance between the trunks. In the first year, if more buds are required they may be left on canes trained along the trunk-training wire.

When rows are 2.7 m (9 ft) apart, GDC training has the curtains with a row 1.2 m (4 ft) apart and those of adjacent rows 1.5 m (5 ft) apart. Thus there are twice as many curtains as there are wide canopies with Umbrella training. These curtains, suspended from the cordon wire at 178 cm (70 in.) can be moved toward a row by means of shielding on the tractor, to allow passage of vineyard equipment.

THINNING

When black cultivars ripen unevenly, green, pink and blue berries may occur in the same bunch at harvest. Such bunches may not be marketable. If only a few off-color berries occur in a bunch, some trimming or picking out by hand may be advisable.

Uneven ripening is partly associated with a ratio of fruit to leaf surface. Removing undersized clusters at or near bloom limits the load of fruit without reducing the leaf surface.

The effects of two pruning levels, 20 + 8 versus 30 + 8 for Buffalo, and 15 + 4 versus 30 + 8 for Catawba, plus bunch-thinning of the flower clusters, were studied in Ontario. The vines were thinned in June when the shoots had elongated enough to permit removal of the clusters without injuring the terminals. Thinning was completed before the blossoms opened. The cluster closest to the vine was left, leaving only one cluster per shoot. Treatments involving bunch-thinning of the flower clusters were included with the low level of pruning.

The vigor of Buffalo and Catawba was improved at the heavier pruning rate. The heavier pruning reduced the yield of Catawba but not of Buffalo. Bunch-thinning improved the quality of both cultivars, but resulted in a reduction of cumulative yield of Buffalo; the yield of Catawba was not affected. Catawba benefited more than Buffalo from bunch-thinning. Vine vigor was increased and fruit quality improved without any reduction in yield (Bradt 1968).

HARVESTING AND MARKETING AMERCAN-TYPE BUNCH GRAPES

Stage of Maturity

Proper maturity for harvesting needs stressing. The picking period is fairly long, but grapes are not at their best unless harvested at the right time.

Most cultivars reach full size and have good color several days before they are satisfactorily edible. They are not mature in the sense of full development of sugar content. Ripening processes stop as soon as the grape is cut. Grapes should not be cut even if well-colored until sugar development is sufficient to ensure good quality. Picking for table use usually starts somewhat earlier than for wine or juice.

Familiarity with the different cultivars aids in determining the proper stage for picking. Some guides to proper stage of ripeness for picking are: total soluble solids or sugar; taste (test the least mature grapes of a cluster, those near the apex); aroma; changing of the stems from green to brown; shriveling of the stems; softening in texture of the pulp; thickening of the juice; ease with which the berries separate from their stems; brown seeds; and freedom of seeds from the pulp.

Sugar (Total Solids).—The refractometer (laboratory and field types), now widely used, gives a quick sugar test for maturity. Within reasonable limits, the longer grapes are left on the vine the higher is the sugar content. Although sucrose is the only form of sugar rapidly translocated in the phloem of the canes, the sugar of the berries consists of the invert sugars glucose and fructose (components of sucrose). Sugar content varies with many conditions. It is commonly 17 to 20% in ripe Concord.

Some processors pay according to the sugar content. Since a high sugar content makes both a better quality and quantity of finished product, growers who deliver better than average grapes should receive the highest return.

Soluble solids vary from year to year, but some vineyards tend to remain relatively high or low regardless of seasonal variation. However, there are "permanent" factors within vineyards which influence soluble solids. Delayed maturity of large crops is partly due to inadequate exposure of the leaf surface to light.

The reason some vineyards are consistently low or high in soluble solids probably can be explained by the constancy of the foliage density. Variation of average soluble solids from year to year is probably a response to differences in temperature and/or light intensity.

Acidity.—Chief acids of the grape are tartaric, malic, phosphoric and citric; the first two constitute over 90% of the total. Acidity is determined by titration.

Sugar-acid Ratio.—The sugar-acid ratio gives a better measurement of quality than either sugar content or acidity alone. For example, a cultivar may taste sweet not because the sugar content is particularly high, but because the acid content is relatively low. The sugar content divided by the acid content gives the sugar-acid ratio. Minimum desirable ratios vary among cultivars.

Rate of Maturity.—Under best conditions, all the following seven factors may operate to delay maturity (Shaulis and Robinson 1953).

(1) Vines with 0.9, 2.3 and 3.6 kg (2, 5 and 8 lb) of prunings may bear 9, 24 and 31.4 metric tons of grapes per ha (4, 11 and 14 tons per acre), respectively, and have a sugar content of 18, 16 and 15.5%, respectively. This does not prove that big vines are of inferior quality. Rather it indicates that crop adjustment by pruning is not completely satisfactory for the larger vines.

(2) Pruning severity is important but difficult to evaluate as a direct one-year effect. In general, when a vine with 0.9 kg (2 lb) of prunings and 30 buds is compared with a vine having 0.9 kg (2 lb) of prunings and 50 buds, fruit from the first vine may have over 1% more sugar. Often in vineyards the number of buds retained for fruiting ranges from too few to too many.

(3) Bunch size variation is a major cause for between-years variation in yield of balanced-pruned vines, which reduces the crop and hence the ratio of fruit weight to leaf area.

(4) High-N vines mature their crops more slowly than low-N vines.

(5) Bordeaux mixture may delay maturity more than milder fungicides or no fungicides.

(6) On a 1.6 m (5¼ ft) trellis, Concord matures five days earlier than on a 1.2 m (4 ft) trellis.

(7) K deficiency over 25% of the leaf area affected retards fruit maturity.

Effect on Yield.—First picking of Concord may be, for example, in October. Some Concord from the vineyard may be offered for sale September 23 to 30. Patience in waiting until grapes are ripe permits a full development of sugar, color and flavor.

In a four year test in Ontario, as a result of cutting two weeks ahead of proper maturity, 11.4% less crop was picked of Niagara and 9.6% less crop of Concord.

Pectin.—During the period of commercial harvest in Washington state after September 20, pectic substances decrease only slightly. For jam-making there should be little difference, with respect to pectin, between grapes from early and late portions of commercial harvest (Carter 1971).

Uneven Ripening and GA.—In southern Illinois uneven-ripening grapes were treated with GA_3 about two weeks prior to harvest. "Green berries" (lightest shade before inception of color) responded with increased rate of ripening compared with untreated "green berries" as measured by soluble solids and anthocyanin content. The treated berries also developed a callus-like layer between the pedicel and skin which delayed drop and also resulted in more evenly ripened clusters. In uneven-ripening clusters, "green" in contrast to "colored" berries had fewer seeds, and many of these seeds had aborted (Skirvin and Hull 1972).

Hand Picking

Hand pickers make more in piece work per hour in high- than in low-yielding vineyards, if a uniform rate per unit is paid. Grape shears or clippers are commonly used. Handle the bunches carefully, especially with table grapes, so that the skins of individual berries are not broken. Remove green, cracked or damaged berries. Grapes picked when wet may decay sooner than those picked dry. Do not leave baskets of grapes in the sun. Juice manufacturers may refuse to accept grapes picked during very hot weather.

An experienced picker, able to select good grapes can pick 40 to 50 lugs, 6.8 to 9.1 kg (15 to 20 lb) each, or 273 to 455 kg (600 to 1000 lb), per day for processing purposes.

In large commercial plantings, a forklift mounted on the front or back of a tractor can be efficiently used to move and assemble filled containers.

Packing

When American-type bunch grapes are to be packed, let them wilt 4 to 6 hr first. This reduces shattering and splitting during packing and the berries shrink less in transportation. Start the pack at the lower end of the basket. Then carefully and snugly fill it to about 2.5 cm (1 in.) above the top and level it. Conceal all stems and fill openings between large bunches with smaller bunches. Do not put the lid on until the stems wilt and the bunches settle. Avoid the need of repacking, for each time the bunches are handled there is danger of bruising and cracking the berries and destroying the attractive bloom. Crushing results if the grapes project too far over the top. If grapes are crushed in hot weather, mold may soon develop.

Storing

Most American-type bunch grapes do not store well for more than 10 days to two weeks; then they lose flavor and decay if the temperature is not kept near 0° C (32° F). Catawba and Agawam can be stored for a longer period. Relative humidity below 85% causes shriveling, especially of the stems. Handle grapes intended for storage carefully to avoid cracking of the berries or loosening of the capstems. Such injuries allow juice to exude and this promotes decay.

Machine-harvesting

Machine harvesters for vinifera grapes, discussed earlier, are often adapted to American bunch grapes grown for wine and juice, and to the French Hybrids grown for wine, and vice versa. In fact, as has been mentioned, the self-propelled, over-the-row, paddle type was originally designed for Concord.

Tractor-drawn Over-the-row Harvester.—To operate this two-wheel harvester the tractor should be over 45 hp. The fruit is collected by a bucket elevator system with overlapping lipped baskets. The bottom fruit catcher is composed of spring-loaded, movable "fish-scale" plates which shift around and make a nearly impenetrable platform under the fruit to avoid losses on the ground. The picking fingers are inexpensive and seldom need replacing.

An adjustable-height mechanism allows picking as close as 38 cm (15 in.) from the ground. It is adjustable to hilly areas and can be levelled to follow contours.

Planning in Machine-harvesting.—Plan for machine-harvesting well in advance. Machines speed the harvesting operation; 5.4 metric tons (6 tons) or more an hour can be obtained. Posts should be straight. Remove all materials that could fall in and damage the machine. Allow a minimum of 6.1 m (20 ft) headland. Rows of over 80 vines speed the harvest. Some cultivars (e.g., Foch and Dutchess) are difficult to harvest by machine. A good cover crop and tile drainage, if required, are definite assets at harvest time.

Keep the machine clean; a dirty machine can cause buildup of mold and bacteria and reduce fruit quality. A dirty machine may also reduce the ease of operation, cause belts to stick, and result in breakdown.

Scheduling is very important. Do not harvest the grapes unless the processor is ready to receive them with an 8-hr limit for quality. There must be close communication by all concerned (Bradt 1972).

Chemical Looseners

Ethephon (Ethrel) sprays were applied to Concord in September in Washington state. Daytime temperatures of 17.1° C (63° F) or higher prior to normal harvest seemed necessary to activate berry abscission in six days or fewer. Concentrations of 250 ppm or higher induced leaf yellowing and accelerated leaf senescence. Ethrel resulted in no differ-

Courtesy of E. T. Andersen, Hort. Res. Inst. Ont.,
Vineland Station, Ontario, Canada

FIG. 1.13.   OVER-THE-ROW MACHINE HARVESTER

ence in fruit soluble solids, titratable acidity, pH and color. A −12° C (11° F) temperature on December 30 caused serious bud damage on vines sprayed on September 4 compared with non-sprayed vines (Clore and Fay 1970). (See also Looseners in Part 1 of this chapter.)

Marketing.—Make a thorough consideration of the potential market, including cultivars, prior to establishing a vineyard. This is better than growing the crop and then attempting to find a market. When planting grapes for commercial processing, the grower should first establish an agreement with the processor.

Various types of containers are used in marketing fresh grapes, both in retail stores and in farm markets. Among the more popular is the cardboard carton, which holds 2 to 4 qt and has a handle. Of increasing importance are boats or trays filled with grapes and over-wrapped with transparent film. This type of container protects the grapes from drying out and helps to maintain their fresh appearance. If grapes on display in stores or farm markets can be kept cool, their fresh, attractive appearance is maintained longer than if held at room temperature.

In some areas the grower can legally make a certain number of gallons of wine for private use.

PART 3
FRENCH HYBRID GRAPES

A great interest in French Hybrid grapes has developed, particularly concerning wine. These grapes have commanded premium prices for blending in wines and certain wine-containing cocktails.

The French Hybrids are a group of cultivars originated in France by crossing *V. vinifera* cultivars with certain wild American species, mainly *lincecumii* (post-oak or turkey grape) and *rupestris* (sand, sugar or rock grape), rather than *labrusca*. Several French breeders have been carrying on this work for 75 years with the object of obtaining cultivars bearing fruit resembling European cultivars but possessing the hardy, disease-resistant vine characteristics of the wild American species.

The New York Agricultural Experiment Station, Geneva, has tested some 250 French Hybrids as well as an appreciable acreage of seedlings.

In 1946 the Horticultural Experiment Station, Vineland, Ontario, obtained from France 35 of the earliest-maturing hybrids which by their descriptions seemed to warrant trial. One row of each cultivar, 150 vines, was planted, part of the row on a sandy soil and the rest on a stiff clay.

Some of them proved to be too late and others susceptible to mildew. In some years aerial gall has been a problem, particularly where the vines have over-produced, causing winter injury. When grown too quickly during the first 2 years, many of them winter-killed to ground level.

Plantings of French Hybrids have already attained an important status in New York, Ontario and British Columbia. In Ontario, for example, from small beginnings in the early 1950s, over 4536 metric tons (5000 tons) of blue cultivars and 272 metric tons (300 tons) of white ones were processed in 1970, and the tonnage is rapidly increasing.

Before planting any French Hybrids, growers, among other considerations, should consult their winery outlet, as various wineries may have different requirements.

FRENCH HYBRID CULTIVARS

Blue-black

Baco No. 1 (Baco Noir).—Produces rather small, compact clusters and small berries. Yields well and seldom overbears. It produces long shoots that make management difficult. Sulfur sensitive.

Foch.—Very early. Clusters and berries of medium size. Very attractive to birds. Use grafted vines.

Chancellor (Seibel 7053).—Vines vigorous and have produced good crops in spite of mildew in most years. Ripens ahead of Concord.

Seibel 8357.—Vigorous. Somewhat difficult to establish. High acidity, but the highly colored juice may be useful for blending. Concord season.

DeChaunac (Cameo, Seibel 9549).—Vigorous and productive. One of the best from a vineyard standpoint, and heavily planted in Ontario. Bunch medium to large, but a little loose. Should be cluster-thinned to avoid over-bearing.

Chelois (Seibel 10878).—Very vigorous and productive, but subject to dead arm and winter injury. Bunch medium to large; varies in compactness, depending on the thinning. Readily propagated from cuttings but requires good drainage and better than average growing conditions.

Seibel 13053.—Very early. Attractive to birds. Vigorous and productive.

Bertille-Seyve 1962.—Vines of medium vigor and very productive.

Courtesy of O. A. Bradt, Hort. Res. Inst. Ont.,
Vineland Station, Ontario, Canada

FIG. 1.14.   DeCHAUNAC FRENCH HYBRID

Bunch-thinning advisable. Bunch large, compact. Shows wine possibilities. Concord season or slightly later.

White

Aurora (Seibel 5279).—Very early. Vine vigorous on sand but weak on clay. Moderately productive. Small bunch and berries. Tends to overbear, subject to black rot. Subject to phylloxera in areas where this pest is a problem; a resistant rootstock should be considered there.

Seibel 8229.—Vines vigorous and productive. Grows better than other white Seibels on heavy clay. In some years powdery mildew develops on canes late in the season but the fruit is free. Concord season.

Seibel 13047.—Early. Bunches medium size. Berries small to medium. Good quality.

Joannes-Seyve 23-416.—Bunches large, attractive, turn pink when exposed to the sun. Resistant to powdery mildew and has wintered well.

Seyve-Villard 12-375.—Produces very large bunches of good-sized berries. The all-around vigor, yield and growth characteristics make it one of the best for wine in southern Ohio.

Seyve-Villard 172.—Late. Vines of medium vigor with large tapering bunches. Weakens itself if allowed to overbear. Wineries have shown interest in it.

Seyve-Villard 5276.—Bunches large and compact. Good where downy mildew is controlled.

PROPAGATION

Cuttings are used in propagation of the stronger cultivars (e.g., Seibel 9549). Many others (e.g., Foch and Seibel 9110) should be grafted for most soil types. Grafted plants should be set with the graft union several inches above ground to prevent scion rooting.

SPACING

Since most French Hybrids are wine grapes, long rows should have the vines spaced to accommodate the type of machine harvester to be used.

For hand picking about as good a plan as any is to space vigorous French Hybrids as for Concord, and weaker ones, such as Foch, as for Delaware.

CROP CONTROL PROGRAM

Soon after the introduction of French Hybrids it became apparent that some form of crop control is necessary to maintain vigor and quality. Early efforts on removing shoots, various pruning levels, and even spur pruning failed to give the desired results. As with the American bunch grape cultivars, balanced pruning and a scale are required, leaving fewer buds per vine.

PRUNING

French Hybrids are short-jointed and produce fruit close to the main trunk; the buds right next to the trunk are fruit-bearing. In Concord and similar labrusca-type cultivars the first 1 to 2 buds are low- or non-fruiting. The French Hybrids even produce fruiting shoots from the main trunk. Heavy pruning is not enough to prevent these cultivars from over-bearing in some cases, resulting in winter injury. Bunch-thinning these cultivars is necessary even on severely pruned vines (Bradt 1972).

For the first 2 to 3 years, prune back to the main trunk, leaving 2 to 3 bud canes on the lower wire when the canes are strong. In later years using the French Hybrid scale and bunch-thinning will give a more vigorous vine than severe pruning with or without thinning, as there will be more leaf surface for the fruit produced.

BUNCH-THINNING

Remove all bunches the first two years in the vineyard, thus allowing the vine to become well established. In the third year and later leave one bunch (flower cluster) on the stronger shoots of vigorous vines. If more buds are left, the vine may be weakened and suffer winter injury. Over-loaded vines produce fruit of poor quality with small straggly bunches.

It is important to remove the flower clusters before the blossoms

Courtesy of O. A. Bradt, Hort. Res. Inst. Ont.,
Vineland Station, Ontario, Canada

FIG. 1.15.   SEIBEL 9110: THINNED (LEFT) AND UNTHINNED (RIGHT)

open. At this time the clusters are easily pinched off. Leaving one cluster per shoot, with two on a few of the stronger vines, is usually about the right degree of thinning. In some cases it is wise to remove all clusters from the weaker and secondary shoots. If thinning is left until after the fruit is set, many of the benefits are lost and the operation is more time-consuming. But it may still be necessary to thin to save the vine from winter injury.

In Ontario, yields have not been reduced and average yield has been increased from bunch-thinning. Thinned vines have also been more vigorous than unthinned ones. Pruning severity did not have as much effect on vigor as bunch-thinning. Often yields of unthinned vines were greater in the early years but gradually the thinned ones caught up and surpassed them (Bradt 1972).

Pruning weights and yield fail to show one of the most important differences in favor of bunch-thinning. Size and compactness of bunch and quality of fruit from the thinned vines are markedly better. Since the yield is similar and increases as the vines grow older, the importance of thinning cannot be over-emphasized.

PART 4

MUSCADINE GRAPES

Muscadine grapes *(Vitis rotundifolia)* are commonly harvested off the stems instead of as bunches. The individual berries tend to shell from the cluster when ripe. The clusters are small.

Muscadines succeed in the Southeastern and Gulf states, and generally are limited to areas where winter temperatures seldom fall below $-12.2°$ C (10° F). Total annual production of muscadines is about 2722 metric tons (3000 tons), almost entirely in North Carolina, South Carolina, Georgia, Mississippi, Alabama, Tennessee and Florida.

Most muscadines grown commercially are processed into wine. Wineries have developed specialty products from these grapes and generally label them as "scuppernong" (wine made from light-colored grapes) or "muscadine" (wine made from dark-colored cultivars). These commercial wines are generally too low in alcohol to be classified as true dessert wines and too sweet to be properly called table wines. For lack of a better descriptive term, some have referred to scuppernong and muscadine wines as special appetizer wines to be served before meals (Brooks 1972).

The total solids content of mature fruits of muscadines is comparatively low, e.g., 10 to 18%. The acidity also is low.

Muscadine grapes make excellent and distinctive jellies, jams and juices. Most of the leading cultivars develop an exceptionally fruity flavor different from the "foxy" flavor of some of the labrusca type. They are in demand in areas where they are known. Many growers have developed a substantial pick-your-own trade.

Courtesy of J. F. Brooks, North Carolina Agr. Ext. Service

FIG. 1.16.   MUSCADINE GRAPES

Individual and total sugar and organic acid concentration averages in the juice of 12 muscadine cultivars was determined in each of 3 years as follows: fructose, 5.51%; glucose, 5.16%; sucrose, 1.89%; soluble solids, 13.1%; malate, 0.50%; tartrate, 0.26%; citrate, 0.04%; total titratable acidity, 0.839% (Carroll *et al.* 1971).

When total titratable value for 12 cultivars was pooled for each season, the yearly differences were primarily due to differences in malate levels, since tartrate levels were similar in each of the three years.

MUSCADINE CULTIVARS

Young tendrils of black muscadine cultivars are purplish; those of green or bronze cultivars are green.

Until 1948, when Tarheel was introduced, all available fruit-bearing muscadine cultivars were pistillate (female), with collapsed, infertile pollen. Perfect flowers have both a fully developed pistil and a ring of erect stamens. Both perfect and male types are effective pollinators, but strictly male plants do not bear fruit. Breeding work now places emphasis on improving the perfect-flowered type. Pistillate cultivars, when pollinated, usually have larger berries, thicker skins and fewer seeds per berry than perfect-flowered ones (Mortensen and Balerdi 1973).

Pollination

The perfect-flowered cultivars are self-pollinating, but the imperfect-flowered cultivars need a pollinator near them, one which overlaps them in bloom.

One production plan is to arrange eight imperfect plants in a square with a pollinator in the center, i.e., a pollinator vine at every third place in every third row. If only perfect-flowered pollinators are planted, there is no pollination problem.

Black fruit, perfect flowers: Burgaw, Dulcet, Tarheel, Magoon, Noble, Pride.

Black fruit, pistillate flowers: Creek, Eden, Flowers, James, Hunt, Mish, Thomas.

Green or bronze fruit, perfect flowers: Wallace, Willard, Dearing, Carlos, Magnolia, Yuga.

Green or bronze fruit, pistillate flowers: Topsail, Higgins, Yuga.

RADIATION

Doubling the chromosome number has been induced by treating vigorous, growing lateral buds with gamma rays emitted from a cobalt-60 source (Fry 1963).

PROPAGATION

Cuttings

Muscadine hardwood cuttings root only fairly easily. The percentage of success is not very high.

Succulent summer cuttings 3 to 4 nodes long root readily under mist. Keep them moist to avoid wilting and then place them 7.6×10.2 cm (3×4 in.) apart, in a well-drained propagation bed that contains equal parts of coarse sand and peat, and some perlite. Block out about 50% of the direct sunlight with shade cloth or lath. Maintain humidity close to 100% by mist nozzles.

After the cuttings have rooted, gradually reduce misting and remove the shade. Meanwhile fertilize once a week with a solution of one tablespoonful of 20-20-20 soluble fertilizer per gallon of water; use 3.8 liters per 2.3 sq m (1 gal. per 25 sq ft) of plant bed.

In one way of handling, before cold weather occurs, remove the rooted cuttings from the bed. Gently shake the rooting material from the roots, remove any leaves that are still on the plants, bundle the plants, and immediately seal them in plastic. Store at 2° to 4° C (35° to 40° F) in the sealed plastic until spring; then plant in a nursery for a year before planting in the permanent location.

Layering

Layering in summer has long been a method of propagating muscadines. Select canes of the current season's growth and long enough to extend 60.9 cm (2 ft) beyond the point of touching the ground. Beginning 30.5 cm (1 ft) from the cane tip, remove leaves from the next 30.5 cm (1 ft) inward.

Dig a narrow trench 20.3 cm (8 in.) deep and just over 30.5 cm (1 ft) long. Place the stripped section of the cane in the trench; refill the trench with soil but do not cover the leafy tip. If the cane may be disturbed, peg the stripped section with a heavy wire. Leave the layer undisturbed and attached to the mother plant until fall or early winter, then dig and cut it into rooted plants. If the plants are large enough, transplant them directly to the vineyard; if they are small, place them in a nursery for a year.

TRAINING AND PRUNING

Training and pruning cuts are made during the dormant season. If done too late in the dormant season the vines may "bleed." This causes a messy but not serious condition. The bleeding usually stops when the leaves appear.

System of Training

Overhead System.—Train the vine to a trunk developed alongside a tall permanent post. When the vine reaches the top of the post cut it back or bend it over, so that it spreads from this head on the arbor. Posts can be set 4.6 to 6.1 m (15 to 20 ft) apart, and 4 strong wires strung lengthwise, crosswise, and diagonally so that they radiate from the top of each post in 8 directions like spokes of a wheel at a height of 2.1 m (7 ft).

Horizontal—1 or 2 Wires.—Elongated arms are developed on wires in both directions from the trunk along the row.

Yield Comparisons.—One-wire, two-wire, and overhead trellis systems were compared (cv Hunt) for 20 bearing years. Initially, plants trained to two wires had the highest yield; but for the next 18 years, highest yield was obtained from the overhead trellis. All training sys-

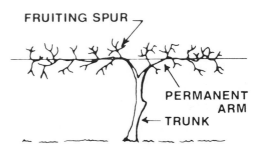

FIG. 1.17.   OVERHEAD SYSTEM
OF TRAINING

Courtesy of J. F. Brooks,
North Carolina Agr. Ext. Service

Courtesy of J. F. Brooks,
North Carolina Agr. Ext. Service

FIG. 1.18.   HORIZONTAL TRAINING

tems exhibited alternate bearing after the seventh crop year. The alternate bearing pattern was the same as for the state pecan production (Brightwell and Austin 1975).

Plants of the Hunt cultivar set 6.1 m (20 ft), 6.4 m (21 ft) and 6.7 m (22 ft) apart in rows 3.0 m (10 ft), 3.7 m (12 ft) and 4.4 m (14 ft) apart were compared. Highest plant density, 477 plants per 0.4 ha (1 acre) gave highest yield per m² almost consistently for 25 years. Highest yields per plant were obtained from the wider-in-the-row spacings (Brightwell and Austin 1975).

Pruning Young Vines

When one stem is long enough cut it back to 10.1 cm (4 in.) below the top wire and place enough tension on the string to straighten the trunk and encourage branching where desired.

Train an arm to stretch along one side on the wire, and another arm to do likewise on the other side of the trunk. Tie it loosely but strongly. Allow the arms to eventually meet halfway between the vines. Retain them indefinitely. If the need arises, allow a new arm to grow from a shoot arising near, or at, the original trunk.

Pruning Established Vines

After the framework is established, pruning is simple. It is essentially the same for all muscadine trellis systems. Only the arrangement of the arms is different.

During the dormant season each year cut back all cane growth to fruiting spurs 2.54 to 10.2 cm (1 to 4 in.) long. Some tendrils may girdle the trunk or arms and kill them. Promptly remove all such tendrils.

The soil in most muscadine vineyards is cultivated like that for other types of grapes.

A non-tillage method with herbicides used in the vine rows and a close-mowed sod maintained between rows has been adopted in some muscadine production areas. Besides better weed control, the herbicide-sod method reduces soil erosion, soil compaction, and labor requirements.

Continued use of a single herbicide may increase the number of persistent weeds. Better results may be obtained with a system using other herbicides in turn.

HARVESTING

Good yields per acre of muscadines are 675 to 1080 kg per 0.4 ha (25 to 40 bu per acre) from 4-year vines, 1080 to 2025 kg (40 to 75 bu) from 5-year vines, and 2700 to 4050 kg (100 to 150 bu) from full-bearing vines of high-yielding cultivars.

Most or all the fruit is harvested at one peak time if commercial processing is the purpose. Traditionally, fruit has been jarred or shaken from the vines onto sheets or burlap spread on the ground under the vines. Machine harvesters can be used efficiently in large plantings. They may accomplish a once-over harvest at the rate of 0.4 ha (1 acre) per hr.

Some growers have built their own harvesting devices that range from picking aids to self-propelled, over-the-row harvesters. Bulk bins with forklifts are also in use, completing the mechanization process. Fruit harvested by machines or by shaking is bruised and spoils quickly.

All the berries do not ripen at the same time; uneven ripening often occurs within individual clusters. Ripe berries shatter more readily on some cultivars than on others. Thus if picking is delayed until most of the crop is ripe, many berries drop and are lost if not caught on sheets etc. Much of this fruit is of high quality and if it is saved it must be picked when ripe, especially on freely shattering cultivars.

One method of doing this is to place a cloth frame, 76 × 243 cm (2½ × 8 ft) under the vines to catch shattered berries while picking. Often a light jarring drops fully-ripe fruit without loosening other berries prematurely or shattering fruit on the next vine. If the berries or clusters are not clipped off with sharp-pointed shears, pick them with a twisting motion or the skins will break and tear. Each broken berry wets many others with juice and renders them unfit for sale as dessert fruit.

To prolong shelf-life use plastic overwraps on containers and hold the fruit at 4° C (40 ° F) until it is sold. Some growers allow customers to pick their own fruit and market some or all the crop in this way.

OXIDANT STIPPLE

Oxidant stipple is a manifestation of photochemical ozone (O_3) phytotoxicity. Initial symptoms are small, dark brown, interveinal flecks on the upper surfaces of mature leaves. In advanced stages, prior to harvest, these leaves may become completely necrotic and abscise prematurely. The amount of oxidant injury to Concord leaves is strongly affected by the vine's management, primarily in relation to its water and N status.

N at 56 and 112 kg per ha (56 and 100 lb per acre), on own-rooted vines, and flower cluster thinning reduced the incidence of oxidant stipple compared to no N, vines grafted on Courderc 3309 rootstock, and no thinning. In a dry growing season, vines in clean-cultivated plots showed less oxidant stipple injury than vines in sod plots. Pruning severity and training system had no influence on oxidant stipple development. Total concentration of tissue was negatively correlated to oxidant stipple severity. The interaction between flower cluster thinning and weed control, rootstock, and N fertilization were significant; thinning moderated the deleterious effects of these factors. Treatments which minimize oxidant stipple are not in contradiction to vine management for high yields of mature grapes (Kender and Shaulis 1976).

GRAPE DISEASES AND INSECTS

Fungus Diseases

Anthracnose (bird's-eye rot) seldom occurs on Concord. In susceptible cultivars young shoots may be girdled; badly spotted leaves curl downward, become distorted, ragged, and some areas drop out. Fruit spots are circular, sunken, and ashy gray, surrounded by a dark margin.

Black rot attracts little attention until nearly half-grown berries begin to rot. Light-brown, soft, circular spots appear on the fruit, increase rapidly in size, and in 2 to 3 days the entire berry may be discolored. By the next day, small black spots may begin to appear on the vines and supply the primary source of spring spores. When rains occur, numerous spores are discharged and carried to the young, tender leaves, where they germinate, cause leaf spotting, and spread to the fruit. Decaying berries soon shrivel, and within 7 to 10 days may become hard, black mummies, which overwinter on the ground or cling to the discolored berries.

Dead arm enters young shoots, trunk or branches through wounds or winter-injured parts. Early shoot growth is delayed, stunted, weak and with short internodes. The shoots are more erect than normal, and the leaves are small, cupped upward, and yellowish. If an arm or the trunk is only partially girdled, shoots that survive the season usually die the next winter. More seriously girdled vines never recover and eventually die.

Downy mildew usually does greatest damage in late summer or early fall, in wet seasons, and in low, poorly drained sites. It winters over on the ground in dead leaves as spores. Infection first appears as light-yellow spots on the upper leaf surface. Later a white moldy growth (fungus threads and spores) forms on the underside of the leaves, which may become dry and crumpled and fall, thus exposing the fruit to sunscald. The fruit does not ripen normally, and is of poor quality. The first wave of infection causes pea-size berries to become soft, to shatter easily and to be covered with white downy growth. During summer heat, rot is less evident, but when cool nights occur a second wave of injury may appear. Later-infected grapes seldom soften and show the downy growth, but become brownish and wither and shatter easily.

Powdery mildew is probably the chief fungus disease of vinifera grapes. White spots form on leaves and canes, making them look as if dusted with flour. Leaves are retarded in growth and odd-shaped; berries have a rusty surface, and may shell.

Bacterial Diseases

Crown gall may cause swellings on the trunk just below or above the soil line, especially in the year immediately following unusually low winter temperatures which rupture the bark and provide points of entry for the organism. Avoid cutting into the galls with the pruning tools or tillage implements.

Virus Diseases

A program is under way in New York and elsewhere to make virus-tested stocks available.

Leaf-curl viruses do not seem to spread in the vineyard. They spread primarily in propagation material, both cuttings and grafts.

Fanleaf viruses cause leaf malformations, and short internodes or double nodes in many vinifera cultivars. These symptoms are essentially absent or very mild in American-type bunch grapes and most French Hybrids. But these viruses can reduce vine vigor and seriously affect fruit yield. Many berries on infected vines may abort, and the bunches may ripen unevenly.

Because of the virtual absence of obvious foliar and wood symptoms in the American-type bunch grapes and most French Hybrids, vines infected with fanleaf viruses often cannot be detected until the vines are several years old, when low vigor and reduced yields are apparent.

Pierce's disease virus is spread by large sharpshooter leafhoppers which penetrate the xylem tissues, chiefly of vinifera and its derivatives and French Hybrids grown in the South. Most hosts are symptomless carriers. Symptoms are browning of the leaves, usually from the margin toward the petiole; delayed foliation of some of the vine; interveinal chlorotic mottling; dwarfing of shoots; uneven maturing of canes; browning of the xylem by tyloses and gumming; gradual dying of roots; and eventual death of the vine. Presence of *alfalfa dwarf* (caused by the same virus) nearby often suggests Pierce's disease. Obtain cuttings free of the disease.

"White Emperor" disease causes yellowish or pinkish berries instead of the normal red. The early leaves are dark red and thick, wrinkled, and curl down at the margins; later they turn reddish-bronze along the main veins and yellowish between the veins. Affected berries are low in sugar.

INSECTS

Bees cannot break the skin of sound grapes with their mouth parts. When the skin has been broken by some means, bees may quickly make the fruit worthless.

Cutworms may destroy grape buds as they begin to swell in spring, or eat holes in the buds, usually at night. They can also damage young plantings.

Grape aphid (tiny, dark brown) may appear in large numbers on young shoots and leaves in dry weather and disappear after a heavy rain. It may infest the fruit clusters, causing some of the grapes to drop.

Grape berry moth first brood larvae web together and feed in the flowers and young berries; later larvae injure more developed berries. After feeding, first brood greenish caterpillars (10 mm or ⅜ in. long when fullgrown) leave the berries, and each cuts out a piece of leaf, folds it over, and makes a cocoon within the fold in early summer. Those of the second brood attack the developing fruit; tying the berries together with silken threads, they bore from one berry to another and feed on the buds. Infested bunches become discolored, have shriveled berries, and are worthless. Larvae of the second brood usually fall to the ground and form cocoons on pieces of leaves under the trellis.

The use of traps baited with synthetic sex pheromones to capture the moths is useful for monitoring insect populations to determine the best time to spray.

Grape cane girdler, a small, black, snout beetle, causes single or double rows of small punctures; the shoot tips break over and hang before dropping.

Grape curculio adults become active when grapes are in bloom. Eggs are placed singly in small cavities. The insect cuts into berries in late summer. Larvae develop inside the berries and feed on the flesh and seeds.

Grape erinium mite causes an injury known as erinose. Early in the summer infested young leaves show raised reddish blotches on the upper surface and concave, densely covered masses of grayish hairs on the under surface.

Lecanium scale (large, brown) may weaken infested parts of the plant.

Grape leafhoppers (several kinds) may be numerous in summer. Both adults and nymphs feed on the leaves, causing them to become blotched with white and later to turn brown and drop prematurely. The injury interferes with growth and fruit ripening. There may be 2 to 3 generations each year.

Grape rootworm larvae devour small roots and rootlets and eat pits and burrow into the outer portion of the large roots. Foliage feeding (chain-like patches or holes) by the adult is minor compared with the root injury.

Japanese beetle, a shiny metallic-green beetle less than 13 mm (½ in.) long, with coppery-brown wing covers, may appear on grapes in early summer and for 4 to 6 weeks feed on the foliage, giving it a lace-like appearance, particularly the part exposed to the sun. Badly injured leaves soon drop. This pest seems to attack thinner-leaved cultivars like French Hybrids more than the thicker-leaved ones like Concord.

Nematode (worm-like, microscopic animal) infestations may result in declining vine vigor, reduces yield, and causes various degrees of root destruction. Larvae of the root knot nematode infest the soft tissue of young roots and feed and reproduce within them. They cause knots, often resembling a string of beads, on the roots around their feeding sites. The dagger nematode transmits virus diseases such as fanleaf and mosaic. Control methods are resistant stocks, soil fumigation, and avoiding infested sites.

Phylloxera, an aphid-like insect (louse) causes galls on both roots and foliage. Root damage is especially serious on vinifera, unless grafted on resistant stocks. The life cycle in California consists of the parthenogenetically reproduced root-inhabiting form, but not of the winged female or fall forms found elsewhere. Lateral movement is therefore confined to crawling of the root-inhabiting larvae on the soil or through subterranean passages or cracks. Once established, it can also be spread by such means as vehicles, tillage implements, picking boxes, vine supports, irrigation water, and planting stock.

Rose chafer adults are fawn-colored, long-legged, awkward, slender, and 10 mm (⅜ in.) long. They may fly into vineyards in large numbers early in the season and eat foliage, leaving only the larger veins.

REFERENCES

ABDALLA, D.A., and SEFICK, H.J. 1965. Influence of nitrogen, phosphorus, and potassium levels on yield, petiole nutrient composition and juice quality of newly established Concord in South Carolina. Proc. Am. Soc. Hort. Sci. *87*, 253-58.

ANDISON, H. 1968. Guyot method of pruning. *Cited by* D.V. Fisher and J. Vielvoye. Grape growing in British Columbia. Brit. Columbia Dept. Agr. Spec. Circ. *45*.

ARCHIBALD, J.A., and BRADT, O.A. 1963. Effect of length of cultivation period, cover crop, and fertilizer on growth and yield of grapes. 1962 Rpt. Ont. Hort. Exp. Sta. 53-56.

ASHBY, D.L. 1968. Fertilizer requirements for grapes. *Cited by* D.V. Fisher and J. Vielvoye. Grape growing in British Columbia. Brit. Columbia Dept. Agr. Spec. Circ. *45*.

BAGBY, J., and HAGLER, T.B. 1955. Muscadine grapes. Ala. Agr. Expt. Sta. Circ. *478*.

BARRITT, B.H., and EINSET, O. 1969. Inheritance of three major fruit colors in grapes. J. Am. Soc. Hort. Sci *94*, No. 2, 82-89.

BEATTIE, J.M. 1955A. Deficiencies of potassium and manganese reduce yields. Ohio Farm Res., Nov-Dec.

BEATTIE, J.M. 1955B. Mulch as a management system for grapes. Ohio Agr. Expt. Sta. Circ. *28*.

BEATTIE, J.M., and BALDAUF, M.P. 1960. Effect of soil management system and differential nitrogen fertilization on yield and on quality of Concord grape juice. Ohio Agr. Expt. Sta. Res. Bull. *868*.

BEATTIE, J.M., and FORSHEY, C.G. 1954. Survey of nutrient element status of Concord grape in Ohio. Proc. Am. Soc. Hort. Sci. *64*, 21-28.

BENSON, N.R. *et al.* 1957. Response of Concord grapes to cultural treatments and fertilizers. Proc. Am. Soc. Hort. Sci. *69*, 235-39.

BERNSTEIN, L. *et al.* 1969. Effects of grape rootstocks on chloride accumulation in leaves. J. Am. Soc. Hort. Sci. *94*, 584-90.

BERTRAND, D.E., and WEAVER, R.J. 1972. Effect of potassium gibberellate on growth and development of Black Corinth grapes. J. Am. Soc. Hort. Sci. *97*, 659-62.

BOYNTON, D. *et al.* 1958. Sampling leaves and soil in vineyards and interpretation of potassium needs. Proc. Am. Soc. Hort. Sci. *72*, 139-48.

BRADT, O.A. 1965. Effect of pruning severity and bunch thinning on yield and vigor of Seibel 9549 grape. 1964 Rpt. Res. Inst. Ont., 44-49.

BRADT, O.A. 1967. Fruit varieties. Ont. Dept. Agr. Bull. *430*.

BRADT, O.A. 1968. Effect of pruning severity and bunch thinning on yield and vigor of Buffalo and Catawba grapes. 1967 Rpt. Hort. Res. Inst. Ont. 22-27.

BRADT, O.A. 1971. Grape breeding and selections in advanced trials. 1970 Rpt. Res. Inst. Ont., 37-45.

BRADT, O.A. 1972. The grape in Ontario. Publ. 487, 1-44.

BRADT, O.A. 1973. Bunch-thinning and suckering grapes. Ont. Min. Agr. AGD *231*, 24.

BRADT, O.A., and CLINE, R.A. 1970. Interrelated effects of pruning severity, growth, and nutrition on yield of Concord. 1969 Rpt. Hort. Res. Inst. Ont., 53-56.

BRADT, O.A., and HUTCHINSON, A. 1971. Grape rootstocks at Vineland. 1970 Rpt. Hort. Res. Inst. Ont., 28-36.

BRADT, O.A., and WIEBE, J. 1971. Comparison of four-arm and six-arm Kniffin training systems for Catawba grape. 1970 Rpt. Res. Inst. Ont., 46-48.

BRIGHTWELL, W.T., and AUSTIN, M.E. 1975. Influence of plant spacing on yield of muscadine grapes. J. Am. Soc. Hort. Sci. *100*, 374-76.

BROOKS, J.F. 1972. Muscadine grape production guide. N. Carolina Circ. *535*.

CAHOON, G.A. 1969. Potassium fertilization of grapes. Ohio Agr. Res. Develop. Center, Res. Sum. *38*, 16-18.

CAHOON, G.A., and PATHAK, S.P. 1972. Response of selected grape cultivars to Alar and gibberellic acid. Ohio Agr. Res. Develop. Center, Res. Sum. *60*, 27-34.

CAMPBELL, E., and GROSDEL, M. 1960. Hardiness of selected grape varieties. Proc. Am Soc. Hort. Sci. *70*, 761-64.

CAMPBELL, E.E., and HODGE, F.B. 1960. Winter injury to peaches and grapes. Proc. Am Soc. Hort. Sci *76*, 332-37.

CARROLL, D.E. *et al.* 1971. Sugar and organic acid concentrations in cultivars of muscadine grapes. J. Am. Soc. Hort. Sci. *96*, 737-40.

CARTER, G.H. 1971. Pectic substances in Concord grapes with relation to maturation. Proc. Am. Soc. Hort. Sci. *92*, 319-22.

CHRISTODOULOV, A.J. *et al.* 1968. Relation of gibberellin treatment to fruit set, berry development and cluster compactness in vinifera grapes. Proc. Am. Soc. Hort. Sci. *92*, 301.

CLINE, R.A. *et al.* 1969. Effect of fertilizer at planting on growth and leaf nutrient composition of fruit trees and grape vines. 1968 Rpt. Hort. Res. Inst. Ont., 149.

CLORE, W.J. 1965. Responses of Delaware grapes to gibberellin. Proc. Am. Soc. Hort. Sci. *97*, 259-63.

CLORE, W.J. 1976. Western situation differs. Am. Fruit Grower, May.

CLORE, W.J., and BRUMMOND, V.R. 1961. Effect of vine size on production of Concord grapes balanced pruned. J. Am. Soc. Hort. Sci. *78*, 239-44.

CLORE, W.J., and FAY, R.D. 1970. Effect of pre-harvest applications of Ethrel on Concord grapes. HortScience *5*, 21-23.

COOK, J.A., and CARLSON, C.V. 1961. California vineyards respond to potash when needed. Better Crops, May-June.

COOK, J.A., and KISHABE, T. 1957. Petiole nitrate analysis as a criterion of nitrogen needs in California vineyards. Proc. Am. Soc. Hort. Sci. *68*, 131-40.

COOK, J.A., and MITCHELL, F.G. 1958. Screening trials of chelated zinc material toward correction of zinc deficiency in vinifera grapevines. Proc. Am. Soc. Hort. Sci. *72*, 149-57.

COOMBE, B.G. 1969. Growth and development of changes in sugars, auxins, and gibberellins in fruit of seeded and seedless *V. vinifera.* Plant Physiol. *35*, 241-50.

COUVILLON, G.A., and NAKAYAMA, T. 1970. Effect of modified Munson training system on uneven ripening, soluble solids and yield of Concord grapes. J. Am. Soc. Hor. Sci. *95*, 158-62.

CROWTHER, R.F., and BRADT, O.A. 1971. Evaluation of grape cultivars for production of wine. 1970 Rpt. Res. Inst. Ont., 121-28.

CROWTHER, R.F., and CLARK, A.P. 1969. Composition of Ontario wines. 1968 Rpt. Hort. Res. Inst. Ont. 75, 121-28.

EATON, G.W. et al. 1970. Embryo sac development in relation to poor fruit set in Agawam grape. 1969 Rpt. Res. Inst. Ont., 52-59.

EDGERTON, L.J., and SHAULIS, N.J. 1953. Effect of time of pruning on cold hardiness of Concord grape vines. Proc. Am. Soc. Hort. Sci. 62, 209-13.

EHLIG, C.G. 1957. Effects of salinity on four varieties of grapes. Proc. Am. Soc. Hort. Sci. 76, 323-31.

EINSET, O. 1930. Pollination of pollen-sterile grapes. N.Y. Agr. Expt. Sta. Bull. 162.

FISHER, D.V., and VIELVOYE, J. 1968. Grape growing in British Columbia. Brit. Columbia Dept. Agr. Spec. Circ. 45.

FISHER, D.V. et al. 1971. Location of fruit on grapevines in relation to cluster size and chemical composition. J. Am. Soc. Hort. Sci. 96, 741-44.

FLEMING, F.K., and ALDERFER, R.B. 1955. Manure and grape residues as organic supplement in soil management program of a Concord vineyard. Proc. Am. Soc. Hort. Sci. 76, 323-31.

FLEMING, L.D. 1970. Relation of temperature and succinic acid 2,2-dimethylhydrazide on berry size in Concord. HortScience 5, 481.

FORSHEY, C.G. 1955. Excessive cultivation can reduce grape yields. Down to Earth (Dow Chemical Co.) 10, 19-21.

FORSHEY, C.G. 1969. Potassium nutrition of deciduous plants. HortScience 4, 39-41.

FRIEDMAN, I.E. 1971. Industrial application of bulk storage in a Concord grape juice industry. HortScience 6, 228-29.

FRY, B.O. 1963. Production of tetraploid muscadine grapes by gamma radiation. Proc. Am. Soc. Hort. Sci. 83, 388-94.

HARMON, F.N., and WEINBERGER, J.H. 1967. Studies to improve the bench grafting of vinifera grapes. Proc. Am. Soc. Hort. Sci. 90, 149-52.

HENDRICKSON, A.H., and VEIHMEYER, F.J. 1951. Grape irrigation experiments. Calif. Agr. Expt. Sta. Bull. 728.

JACOB, H.E., and WINKLER, A.J. 1950. Grape growing. Calif. Agr. Expt. Sta. Circ. 116.

JONES, B.M. 1972. Virus diseases of grapes: a threat to the Ohio grape industry. Proc. Ohio Grape-Wine Short Course, Ohio Agr. Res. Develop. Ser. 383, 50-52.

KAJURA, M. 1962. Gibberellin application for seedless Delaware production in commercial vineyards in Japan. XVI Internat. Hort. Cong. 3, No. 2, Fruit Growing, 495-500.

KENDER, W.J., and SHAULIS, N.J. 1976. Vineyard management practices influencing oxidant injury in Concord grapevines J. Am. Soc. Hort. Sci. 101, 129-32.

KISHI, M., and AMAMIYA, T. 1961. Technique of gibberellin application on Delaware grape. Takada Pharmaceutical Co., Osaka.

KLIEWER, W.M. 1970. Effect of day temperature and light intensity on coloration of V. vinifera grapes. J. Am. Soc. Hort. Sci. 95, 693-97.

KLIEWER, W.M. 1971A. Effect of day temperature and light intensity on concentration of malic and tartaric acids in V. vinifera grapes. J. Am. Soc. Hort. Sci. 96, 372-77.

KLIEWER, W.M. 1971B. Effect of nitrogen on composition of fruits from Thompson Seedless grapevines. J. Am. Soc. Hort. Sci. 96, 816-19.

KLIEWER, W.M. 1972. Effect of controlled temperature and light intensity on growth and carbohydrate levels of Thompson Seedless grapevines. J. Am. Soc. Hort. Sci. *97*, 185-88.

KLIEWER, W.M. 1973. Berry composition of *V. vinifera* cultivars as influenced by photo- and nycto-temperatures during maturation. J. Am. Soc. Hort. Sci. *98*, 153-57.

KLIEWER, W.M., and COOK, J.A. 1971. Arginine and total free amino acids as indicators of nitrogen status of grapevines. J. Am. Soc. Hort. Sci. *96*, 581-87.

KUYKENDALL, J.R. 1970. Berry set of Thompson Seedless grapes to prebloom and bloom gibberellic acid treatment. J. Am. Soc. Hort. Sci. *95*, 697-99.

LOOMIS, N.H. 1965. Further trials of grape rootstocks in Mississippi. Proc. Am. Soc. Hort. Sci. *86*, 326-28.

McGREW, J.R. *et al.* 1961. Control of grape diseases and insects in the Eastern United States. U.S. Dept. Agr. Farm. Bull. *1893*.

MOORE, J.N. 1970. Cytokinin-induced sex conversion in male clones of *Vitis* species. J. Am. Soc. Hort. Sci. *95*, 387-93.

MORTENSEN, J.A. 1968. Stover, an early bunch grape for central Florida. Fla. Agr. Expt. Sta. Circ. *S-195*.

MORTENSEN, J.A., and BALERDI, C.F. 1973. Muscadine grapes for Florida. Proc. Fla. State Hort. Soc., 338-41.

MORTENSEN, J.A., and STOVER, L.H. 1969. Norris, a new bunch grape. Fla. Agr. Expt. Sta. Circ. *S-177*.

NELSON, K.C., and TOMLINSON, F.E. 1958. Factors affecting bleaching and wetness of Emperor and Tokay grapes. Proc. Am. Soc. Hort. Sci. *71*, 290-98.

NESBITT, W.B., and KIRK, H.J. 1972. Effect of size and number of replications upon the efficiency of muscadine grape cultivar trials. J. Am. Soc. Hort. Sci. *97*, 639-41.

POOL, R.M., and WEAVER, R.J. 1970. Internal browning of Thompson Seedless grapes. J. Am. Soc. Hort. Sci. *95*, 631-34.

POOL, R.M. *et al.* 1972. Effect of growth regulators on changes in fruits of Thompson Seedless grapes during cold storage. J. Am. Soc. Hort. Sci. *97*, 67-70.

POWELL, D., and BARRETT, H.C. Black rot of grapes. Ill. Agr. Ext. Serv. Lft. *703*, 1972.

PRATT, C. 1975. Reproductive system of Concord and two sports. J. Am. Soc. Hort. Sci. *98*, No. 5, 489-96.

ROBINSON, W.B. *et al.* 1949. Composition of ripe Concord grapes. N.Y. Agr. Expt. Sta. Bull. *385*.

ROGERS, H.T. 1973. Tight fill for grapes. Am. Fruit Grower, Aug., 11.

SCOTT, L.E., and SCOTT, D.H. 1952. Response of grape vines to magnesium sulfate. Proc. Am. Soc. Hort. Sci. *60*, 117-21.

SEFICK, H.J. 1960. Bunch grape survival in upper South Carolina. Fruit Varieties and Hort. Dig. *15*, 17-18.

SEFICK, H.J. 1969. The vinifera grape: eastern United States. S. Carolina Res. Ser. *125*.

SHARPE, R.H. 1954. Rooting of muscadine grape under mist. Proc. Am. Soc. Hort. Sci. *63*, 88-90.

SHARPE, R.H., and SHOEMAKER, J.S. 1962. Development of temperate-climate fruits for Florida. Fla. State Hort. Soc. *71*, 184-200.

SHARPLES, G.C. *et al.* 1961. Improvement of market quality of Cardinal grape by inflorescence apex removal. Proc. Am. Soc. Hort. Sci. 77, 316-21.

SHAULIS, N.J. 1948. Balanced pruning aids grapes. N.Y. Farm Res. (July).

SHAULIS, N.J. 1950. Cultural practices for New York vineyards. Cornell Bull. *805.*

SHAULIS, N.J. 1954. Spacing for Concord vines. N.Y. Farm Res. (October).

SHAULIS, N.J. 1956. Effect of plant spacing on growth and yield of Concord grapes. Proc. Am. Soc. Hort. Sci. *66,* 192-200.

SHAULIS, N.J. 1957. Association of Concord petiole composition with deficiency symptoms, growth, and yield. Proc. Am. Soc. Hort. Sci. *68,* 141-56.

SHAULIS, N.J., and ROBINSON, W.B. 1953. Effect of season, pruning severity, and trellising on chemical characteristics of Concord and Fredonia grape juice. Proc. Am. Soc. Hort. Sci. *62,* 214-20.

SHAULIS, N.J., and STEEL, R.G. 1969. Interaction of rootstock to the nitrogen, weed control, pruning, and thinning effects on the productivity of Concord grape vines. J. Am. Soc. Hort. Sci. *93,* 422-28.

SHAULIS, N.J. *et al.* 1953. Effect of trellis height and training systems on growth and yield of Concord grapes under a controlled pruning severity. Proc. Am. Soc. Hort. Sci. *62,* 221-27.

SHAULIS, N.J. *et al.* 1966. Response of Concord grapes to light exposure and Geneva Double Curtain training. Proc. Am. Soc. Hort. Sci. *89,* 268-80.

SIDOWSKI, J.J. *et al.* 1971. Phloem regeneration across girdles of grape vines. J. Am. Soc. Hort. Sci. *96,* 97-102.

SKIRVIN, R.M., and HULL, J.W. 1972. Gibberellic acid, seed number, and rate of maturation as related to uneven-ripening Concord grapes. HortScience 7, 391-92.

SMITH, C.J., and COUVILLON, G.A. 1971. Effect of the modified Munson and 4-arm Kniffin training systems on changes in pectic substances of Concord grapes. J. Am. Soc. Hort. Sci. *96,* 547-49.

STEWART, W.I. *et al.* 1953. Effect of potassium salt of gibberellic acid on fruit of Thompson Seedless grape. Proc. Am. Soc. Hort. Sci. *72,* 165-69.

STOUT, A.B. 1936. "Seedlessness" in grapes. N.Y. Tech. Bull. *238.*

SWANSON, C.A., and EL-SHISHENY, E.D. 1958. Translocation of sugars in grapes. Plant Physiol. *33,* 33-37.

TESKEY, B.E.J., and SHOEMAKER, J.S. 1972. Tree Fruit Production. AVI Publishing Co., Westport, Conn.

TUKEY, L.D. 1957. Effects of controlled atmosphere following bloom on berry development of Concord grape. Proc. Am. Soc. Hort. Sci. *69,* 25-33.

TUKEY, L.D., and FLEMING, H.K. 1967A. Alar, a new fruit-setting chemical for grapes. Pa. Fruit. News *46,* 12-31.

TUKEY, L.D., and FLEMING, H.K. 1967B. Fruiting and vegetative effects of N-dimethylaminosuccinic acid on Concord grapes. Proc. Am. Soc. Hort. Sci. *93,* 300-10.

VANATARATNAM, L. 1964. Effect of gibberellic acid on Arab-E-Shah grape. Proc. Am. Soc. Hort. Sci. *85,* 255-62.

WANDER, I. 1946. Physical and chemical studies of soils. Ohio Agr. Expt. Sta. Bull. *663.*

WANDER, I., and GOURLEY, J.H. 1945. Increasing available potassium to greater depths under orchard soil by adding potash fertilizer on a mulch. Proc. Am. Soc. Hort. Sci. *46,* 21-24.

WEAVER, R.J.   1952.   Thinning and girdling of Red Malaga grapes in relation to size of berry, color, and percentage of total solids of fruit. Proc. Am. Soc. Hort. Sci. *60*, 132-40.

WEAVER, R.J.   1953.   Further studies of effects of 4-chlorophenoxyacetic acid. Proc. Am. Soc. Hort. Sci. *61*, 135-43.

WEAVER, R.J.   1954.   Thinning grapes with chemical sprays. Proc. Am. Soc. Hort. Sci. *63*, 194-200.

WEAVER, R.J.   1955.   Relation of time of girdling to ripening of fruit of Red Malaga and Ribier grapes. Proc. Am. Soc. Hort. Sci. *65*, 183-86.

WEAVER, R.J.   1958.   Use of gibberellins in grape production. Blue Anchor *35*, No. 4, 26-41.

WEAVER, R.J., and IBRAHIM, I.M.   1968.   Effect of thinning and seedlessness on maturation of *V. vinifera* grapes. Proc. Am. Soc. Hort. Sci. *92*, 316-18.

WEAVER, R.J., and KASIMATIS, A.N.   1975.   Effect of trellis with and without crossarms on yield of Thompson Seedless grapes.   J. Am. Soc. Hort. Sci. *100*, 252-253.

WEAVER, R.J., and NELSON, K. E.   1959.   Thinning, girdling, plant regulators. Calif. Agr. Expt. Sta. Lft. *1959*.

WEAVER, R.J., and POOL, R.M.   1969.   Effect of Ethrel, abscisic acid, and morphacin on flower and berry abscission and shoot growth in *V. vinifera*. J. Am. Soc. Hort. Sci. *94*, 474-78.

WEAVER, R.J., and POOL, R.M.   1971A.   Effect of 2-chloroethyl phosphonic acid (ethephon) on maturation of *V. vinifera*. J. Am. Soc. Hort. Sci. *96*, 725-27.

WEAVER, R.J., and POOL, R.M.   1971B.   Berry response of Thompson Seedless to application of gibberellic acid. J. Am. Soc. Hort. Sci. *96*, 162-66.

WEINBERGER, J.H., and HARMON, F.N.   1964.   Seedlessness in vinifera grapes. Proc. Am. Soc. Hort. Sci. *85*, 270-74.

WEINBERGER, J.H., and HARMON, F.N.   1966.   Harmony, a new nematode and phylloxera-resistant rootstock for vinifera grape. Fruit Varieties and Hort. Dig. *20*, 63-65.

WEINBERGER, J.H., and POOL, R.M.   1971.   Berry response of Thompson Seedless and Perlette grapes to application of gibberellic acid. J. Am. Soc. Hort. Sci. *96*, 162-66.

WIEBE, J.   1975.   Effect of canopy widening and shoot tip removal on the French Hybrid DeChaunac. J. Am. Soc. Hort. Sci. *100*, 349-51.

WINKLER, A.J.   1962.   General Viticulture.   Univ. of California Press, Berkeley.

WINKLER, A.J. and KASIMATIS, A.N.   1959.   Supports for grapevines. Calif. Agr. Expt. Sta. Lft. *119*.

Chapter 2

Strawberries

Botanically the strawberry *(Fragaria ananassa)* is an aggregate fruit formed by the ripening together of several ovaries, all belonging to a single flower and adhering as a unit on a common receptacle. Each fruitlet is an achene (a dry, small, hard indehiscent fruit which bears only one seed).

THE INDUSTRY

The commercial acreage of strawberries in the United States and Canada is about 10,129 ha (25,000 acres) on a normal yearly level.

Mexico freezer and California fresh strawberries have had a major impact on the production and marketing of this fruit, particularly in the Midwest and East (Antle 1972).

Impact of Mexico Berries

In 1951 the first frozen strawberries arrived from Mexico. By 1953 shipments reached 9 million kg (20 million lb). This did not seriously hurt frozen-fruit markets in the East and Midwest until 1960, when volume jumped from 7.26 million kg (16 million lb) of frozen berries from Mexico to 16.8 million kg (37 million lb). By 1969 the volume of frozen berries from Mexico had increased to 46.7 million kg (103 million lb). At this point many U.S. markets for frozen berries were demoralized. Frozen berries from Mexico were shipped into Midwestern and Eastern markets for a lower price than U.S. local growers could afford to deliver the product to the freezer, and they were priced out of the market.

After the deep price cuts of the 1969–70 winter for frozen berries, Mexico agreed to limit yearly volume to about 36.3 million kg (80 million lb). Mexico was willing to do so since this volume gave them a profitable market and was expected to stabilize the frozen price at about 33 to 48¢ per kg (20 to 22¢ per lb), when an unknown volume that could exceed 45.4 million kg (100 million lb) was expected.

Much of the Mexican crop is produced cheaply in the states of Guanajuste and Michoacan, chiefly near Irapuato City.

Impact of California Berries

Shortly after World War II California berries became a strong factor in most markets in the United States. At about that time, Michigan growers, for example, sold 33% or more of their strawberries to freezers. This put a floor under fresh market prices. The freezer price levels attracted more and more growers. They could pick the largest early berries for fresh sales, when prices were usually best. They could then make a clean-up of late berries that were smaller, more highly colored, and better liked by processors. This was an ideal combination, but it did not last.

Air shipments put precooled and refrigerated California strawberries into Midwest and Eastern wholesale markets about as quickly as from a nearer source by usual methods.

In the late 1940s California produced less than 20% of the total United States volume. About 85% of this volume was frozen. The fresh sales were usually west of the Rockies. In the early 1950s, certain new cultivars (University Series) were introduced, giving California about a 4 to 6 month season with yields several times the former one; second and third generations further increased yields and improved quality. The Driscol cultivars also appeared.

In 1971 California produced 144 million kg (318 million lb) of strawberries, or 61.5% of the 234 million kg (516 million lb) United States total. More than ¾ of this volume was sold fresh. As evidenced by buyer performance in prices paid at terminal markets, both size and shelf-life are generally greater for California berries than for those of the Midwest and East. Precooling within one hour or less after picking is one big factor; another is constant refrigeration.

The $60,000,000 annual California strawberry business accounts for more than 58% of the nation's strawberry production, although it has only 16% of the U.S. strawberry acreage. In 1970 California produced 136 million kg (300 million lb) of strawberries on 3400 ha (8400 acres) with an average yield of 48 MT per ha (17 tons per acre).

Successful strawberry growing in California is built around the relationship of photoperiod, growing temperatures, and chilling under planting systems designed to give sufficient vegetative growth to support high total production and large, high-quality fruit, but not enough to drive them to runner production (Voth 1972).

In the Salinas Valley (see vinifera grape regions), the strawberry, once a minor crop, now is worth $10 million a year.

In the chief California growing areas, strawberry production is a specialized one crop enterprise. Shipping is a primary marketing concern for over six months each year. Each shipper or growers' shipping association either owns a freezing plant or else has a working agreement with such an alternative outlet.

Fresh consumption of California strawberries reached 77% in 1973, compared with 36% in 1956. Average yield increased from 5.8 metric tons (6.4 tons) from 7891 ha (19,500 acres) in 1956 to 13.6 to 16.3 metric tons from 3157 ha (15 to 18 tons from 7800 acres) in 1973.

New cultivars, palletized shipping, a consumer unit package, in-transit controlled atmosphere, air freight transportation, annual summer and winter planting, soil fumigation, use of clear plastic mulch for soil heating and cleaner harvesting, and increased fruit size, shelf-life, and total solids in the berries, have all added to the success of California's strawberry production and marketing.

South, East and Midwest

The previous discussion does not mean that strawberries cannot be grown profitably in the South, East and Midwest. It does imply that adjustments in marketing, labor saving, and higher yields are essential. Discussion bearing on these factors and others related to success are included in this chapter.

A succession of harvesting continues from the South northward for roughly 1600 km (1000 mi.), both *within* and *between* the states.

Earliest Crop.—Picking begins about mid-December in southern Florida.

Early Crop.—Picking begins about April 1 or earlier; included are Louisiana, Mississippi, Alabama and Texas.

Second Early Crop.—Picking begins about mid-April; included here are North and South Carolina, Oklahoma, Tennessee and Arkansas.

Intermediate Crop.—Picking begins about May 1–15 in the Del-Mar-Va Peninsula (Virginia, Maryland and Delaware), New Jersey, Massachusetts, Kentucky, Missouri, Kansas, Indiana, Illinois and Ohio.

Late Crop.—Picking begins about early June to July 1. Includes Michigan, New York, Pennsylvania, Minnesota, Wisconsin, New Hampshire, Vermont, Maine, Ontario and Quebec.

West and Pacific Northwest

Colorado.—Most of the production is near Denver. Irrigation is essential.

Idaho.—Strawberries are grown both under irrigated and dry land conditions. The Boise and Payette valleys are leading areas.

Washington.—The southwestern area is in Clark County and the northwestern district is in the counties which form a tier between Puget Sound and the Cascade Mountains. In eastern Washington, late ripening in the Spokane area avoids main-season competition. Winter-killing of the plants in northwestern Washington, as in southwestern British Columbia, is often a serious problem and has been accentuated by susceptibility of the Northwest cultivar to this damage. Mulching is seldom practiced because of the high autumn and winter rainfall and associated crown diseases.

Oregon.—About 90% of the Washington and Oregon production is processed. The main strawberry area is in the Willamette Valley. It extends south 240 km (150 mi.) and is bounded on the north by the Columbia River, on the east by the Cascades, and on the west by the coast range. The valley floor is about 40 km (25 mi.) wide. Average rainfall is about 107 cm (42 in.) and occurs mostly in fall, winter and spring. July and August are dry months; the rainfall in this period is usually less than 5 cm (2 in.).

Canada.—Annual production of strawberries in Canada is about 27.5 million liters (25 million qt), with Ontario 9.9 million (9 million qt); British Columbia 8.8 million (8 million qt); Quebec 5.5 million (5 million qt); Nova Scotia and New Brunswick 1.1 million (1 million qt) each.

Ontario.—Production has become more decentralized in recent years. The proportion of the total crop produced in the two main producing areas of Niagara and Norfolk County has decreased. Production has increased in other areas, especially those near centers of high population. This change is the result of an increase in PYO (Pick-Your-Own) operations near centers of population. Few Ontario berries are processed commercially.

British Columbia.—The southern end of Vancouver Island is one of the oldest districts. The lower mainland area along both the north and south sides of the Fraser River, from its mouth on the west to Agassiz and Chilliwack on the east, is the largest producer. Other districts occur at Salmon Arm and the Kootenay center at Wynndel. The Okanagan Valley is primarily a tree-fruit area.

Quebec.—Much of the acreage is near Montreal. The 32 km (20 mi.) long Island of Orleans in the St. Lawrence River is noted for its berries.

Eastern Maritimes.—The Kentville area in Nova Scotia and the Fredericton area in New Brunswick are the leaders.

CULTIVARS

Purposeful breeding has played a leading role in the development of modern cultivars, and introductions from government institutions are now much more numerous than from private individuals. The cultivar picture is a rapidly changing one, probably more so than with any other fruit. Great stress is now placed on disease-tested plants.

Because the picture changes so rapidly it is recommended that local sources such as current extension circulars be used as the source for making selections.

POLLINATION

No imperfect or pistillate cultivar which requires cross-pollination to develop berries now ranks among the leaders; stamens are lacking or abortive. The strawberry flower contains many pistils and if a high percentage is not pollinated, a poorly shaped berry and a poor crop result. Without the developing seeds the berry does not swell. Cat-facing (misshapen berries) occurs when a group of seeds in one area of the berry fails to develop. An old custom was to plant a row of a perfect-flowered cultivar to every three rows of the imperfect.

Bees, which normally are effective pollinators, do not work much in very dry, hot weather or during strong wind. Scarcity or inactivity of bees during bloom may be a drawback. One hive of honeybees throughout the bloom period should suffice for a hectare (acre). Maximum yields and desirable fruit size and shape occur only under conditions of adequate pollination.

Captan, if used to control gray mold rot, may inhibit pollen germination, decrease achene set and berry development, and increase the proportion of misshapen fruits when sprayed on anthers after dehiscence. Sprays applied to pistils either just before or just after pollination may decrease achene set. Achene set is not affected by spraying one day after pollination (Eaton and Chen 1969A,B).

FLOWER AND FRUIT CLUSTERS

More than 50 years ago W.D. Valleau found that there is a definite order of blossoming in strawberry clusters. The cluster has two main branches, at the crotch of which one flower is produced; this primary flower blooms first. Each branch is similarly made up of two other branches, at the crotches of which are single flowers; these are the second to bloom. Each of these four branches again divides and at the crotches occurs the third group of flowers to bloom; later flowers may occur on large clusters. Fruits that result from primary flowers are only half as numerous as those from secondary flowers; but more berries are produced on the tertiary flowers, since they are twice as numerous as the secondary and four times as numerous as the primary flowers.

The largest berries are usually produced in the first good picking; the crop increases in later pickings, but the berries are smaller. Fruit size is a function of blossom position, fruit competition, number of developed achenes, and plant vigor. Removal of secondary blossoms has little effect on weight of primary fruit; removal of primary blossoms, however, increases the weight of secondary fruit. Promotion of uniform ripening for machine harvest by selective thinning, or otherwise reducing the number of flowers by inflorescence, may deserve consideration.

A high incidence of aborted flowers may indicate a relation between natural fruit thinning and concentrated ripening, with accelerated development and increased ripening rates in fruit which develops to maturity. High plant populations increase natural thinning. A high abortion rate and/or arrested development in late-blooming flowers may be characteristic of concentrated ripening selections. Inflorescence-branching variations may be related to the photoperiodic adaptation to a specific latitude (Janick and Eggert 1968; Sherman and Janick 1967; Stang and Denisen 1971).

FIG. 2.1.   FLOWER AND FRUIT CLUSTER

FRUIT-BUD FORMATION

In the South Atlantic and Gulf regions fruit buds in standard cultivars are formed in fall, winter and spring. Flower clusters appear shortly after flower buds form, since there is little rest period. Farther north, fruit buds form only in autumn. Low temperatures of late fall and early winter stop fruit-bud formation, and when spring comes day length is too long.

With fall bearers, fruit that ripens in May and early June develops from buds formed in the previous fall. The July crop is from buds formed late in May and in June. Because of little or no differentiation in April, production of fruit in June and early July is virtually nil. Runner formation becomes less and yield increases as summer advances. Absence of developing flower stems for 3 to 4 weeks immediately after the spring crop, plus favorable temperatures and long days, could account for the unusual activity of fall bearers in promoting runners, new branches, and differentiating fruit buds at this time.

ROOTS

The strawberry plant is shallow-rooted, and it "feeds" from a rather small area. The fibrous root system arises from the short, thick stems near the surface. Just beneath the surface, horizontal roots extend about a foot on all sides of the base of the plant. The surface foot of soil is fully ramified by obliquely as well as more or less vertically descending roots. The latter especially may also ramify and penetrate beyond 46 cm (18 in.). Branches are mostly short and usually more profuse and moisture is drawn chiefly from 15 to 31 cm (6 to 12 in.); lateral spread may be 31 to 51 cm (12 to 20 in.).

New main roots of a normal strawberry plant are pliable and whitish. After several months they become woody and dark brown on the surface. When this dark surface is scraped away, a yellowish-white core can be seen. Small feeder roots that branch out from the main roots are white as long as they are active. Cultivars with poor tops usually have poor to fair root systems. The root system may also be poor because of shallowness, limited spread, many dead roots, dead tips, lack of branching and root hairs, few light-colored roots, and root disease.

RUNNERS (STOLONS)

The runner is a true stem with tissue specialized to conduct water and nutrients. Rooted runners can support the parent plant from which the roots have been severed, demonstrating bidirectional movement of water and possibly nutrients. Movement of Ca and P occurs more readily from parent to daughter plant than in the reverse direction (Norton and Wittwer 1963).

There are three phases of runner rooting: (1) Primary roots enter the soil in rather constant numbers during early rooting. Initial penetration and number of primaries extended is independent of soil moisture for the first week. Growth in length increases as soil moisture increases. Rate of new root emergence decreases after three weeks. New primaries are produced throughout the growing season. (2) A sudden increase in branching of primaries starts two weeks after "pegging down" of a runner; sudden branching occurs a week later. Branching is greatly inhibited by a soil moisture below the wilting percentage, and to a lesser degree at contents above 50% available soil moisture, the latter probably because of poor aeration. (3) The runner plant can function on its own root system shortly after the formation of branch roots (Rom and Dana 1960).

CROWNS

Crowns of healthy plants have a lower percentage of ash and a higher percentage of Ca than other parts. The root has the highest Fe content, which is lowest in the petiole and crown. Roots of diseased plants have abnormally low Ca contents and the main part of the leaf is higher in Ca than the serrated edges (Lanning and Garabedian 1963).

In the crown the vascular cylinder consists of a network of short, anastomosing bundles that provide an efficient means of rapid transfer of water and solutes across the stem. Also, these bundles, instead of having long vessels, are composed of short tracheids with many large lateral and terminal pores that further increase the efficiency of both cross and longitudinal transfer of water.

Reduction of any part of the root system affects the whole plant, rather than just one side. Marked differences in arrangement, development, and structure of the vascular tissues of the large adventive roots that arise from the crown, compared with the small fibrous ones, together with the paucity of root hairs, account for their comparative inefficiency as absorbing organs. Hence the difficulty in transplanting plants that possess many large roots, but no fibrous ones.

PROPAGATION

Propagation is accomplished by means of slender runners. These take root at a node (commonly the third node) and form new plants.

Buying Versus Own-grown Plants

Most growers find it better to buy plants, as indicated by the large nursery trade, than to propagate their own. Nurserymen are experienced in preparing plants for shipment; but sometimes plants are damaged in shipment. Pests may be introduced from one section to another on shipped plants.

Most if not all states require inspection of plants sold. Disease-tested plants are highly recommended. Growers should not continue for too many years to set from their disease-tested plants but should obtain a new supply periodically.

A supply of plants should be conveniently on hand to avoid delay in planting, since there is usually a rush of spring work at planting time. Some growers can afford the time to dig and clean their own plants, but others cannot. It is annoying to begin planting and then have to stop until more plants are dug and cleaned.

At times, sale of plants is a profitable sideline to sale of berries. When digging plants from a fruiting or prospective fruiting bed, take them from the edges of the rows.

Desirable degree of chilling for the Deep South and California results either naturally in plants obtained from northern nurseries or by placing them in cold storage.

Thrifty Plants

Plants well-cleaned and with evenly bunched, straight roots make setting easier, quicker and better. It is often difficult to grow top-grade plants in heavy soil. Plants on soil that is reasonably rich in humus or to which organic fertilizer is applied may produce more runners than plants treated with chemical fertilizer. Irrigation encourages prolific plant production.

Plant Selection

Proper selection of plants for propagation helps to safeguard the vitality of a cultivar. Formerly, extra-careful selection was not necessary because most pest disorders were easily seen and usually could be controlled. Many cultivars are virus-infected and often the symptoms are apparent, but many cultivars do not show the color symptoms normally associated with virus diseases and are symptomless carriers. Although no color symptoms are shown, many cultivars, when virus-infected, show reduced vigor and yield and decreased runnering, which are signs of "running out."

Digging and Shipping Plants

A machine digger has a blade that cuts under the row and lifts and conveys the plants to crates, all in one operation. Where many plants are handled, this labor-saving device can greatly reduce costs. In contrast, hand-digging requires a crew slowly picking up plants. In both methods the plants are cleaned by hand.

Strawberry plants are shipped in many kinds of containers and packages. Moss and similar moisture-holding material has commonly been placed around the roots to avoid drying out. A more recent development is to place the plants in polyethylene-lined cartons or in polyethylene bags. It is as important to avoid heating as it is drying out.

Rate of Increase

For spring planting, mother plants that have not fruited usually are set one spring and the new plants dug the next spring. Average increase is about 10 to 1, but ratios vary between cultivars, soils and years. In plantings solely for propagation, more than 40,000 plants per ha (100,000 per acre) can be obtained, depending on many factors.

In Ohio, records were kept of 37,252 runners of early spring-planted

TABLE 2.1

EARLIEST ROOTING RUNNERS IN RELATION TO RATE OF INCREASE OF PLANTS
(PREMIER, PLANTED IN APRIL, OHIO)

Number of Runners Rooted per 15-Plant Row Rooted in June			Runners per Parent Plant	
	October 15	Season[1]	October 15	Season[1]
1	152	328	10	22
3	172	358	11	24
5	227	397	15	26
7	238	403	16	27
9	255	418	17	28
12	274	427	18	29

Source: Shoemaker (1929).
[1] These columns include runners which did not root after October 15.

Premier in a year characterized by drought during parts of May, August, September, and October and by abundant moisture in April, June and July. Of this total, 1% rooted in June; 17.6% in July; 27% in August; 6% between September 1 and October 15; 46.6% formed, but only a small part rooted after October 15 (Shoemaker 1929).

Rows of 15 plants in which only 1 runner had rooted in June averaged 10 rooted plants from each parent plant. In rows with 12 plants rooted in June the ratio was 18:1, i.e., the more plants rooted in June, the more runners per year. These data emphasize the importance of a good early start for the plants.

COLD-STORED PLANTS

Some merits of cold storage of dormant plants are that shipments can be made earlier, or later, than with spring-dug plants; fall digging reduces the labor problem in spring; adequate chilling can be provided for plants to be set in areas with mild winters.

Plants may be placed in storage in polyethylene bags and quickly cooled to $-0.6°$ to $1.1°C$ ($31°$ to $34°F$); this temperature is maintained in storage. The freezing point of the crowns may vary somewhat with the cultivar, but averages about $-1.4°C$ ($30°F$). Freezing of exposed roots may occur at $-1.8°C$ ($28.7°F$). Long storage temperature of $0°C$ ($32°F$) allows development of mold, resulting in breakdown and decay. Some of the leaves may be removed before storing to avoid decay. At $-1.1°$ to $-0.6°C$ ($30°$ to $31°F$) plants can be kept 8 to 10 months.

Between 200 and 250 million strawberry plants are stored annually in California. Of these, 50 to 75 million are grown at high-elevation nurseries for winter planting. These plants are dug in October and stored at $1.1°C$ ($34°F$) for 10 to 15 days. Polyethylene two mil ($\frac{1}{1000}$ in.) liner boxes serve as an adequate moisture barrier and permit adequate gas exchange in cold storage. The remaining 150 to 200 million plants are grown at low-elevation nurseries, dug from late December through January, and stored at $-2.2°C$ ($28°F$) for summer planting (Voth 1972).

CROWN DIVISION

Fall bearers are seldom prolific runner-producers, because the buds that form in the leaf axils often develop into flower clusters and sometimes into branch crowns. Cultivars producing many flower clusters in summer produce few runners. Hence a method of propagation other than by runners is often desirable (see also use of GA and Removing Flower Stems).

Vigorous fall bearers that produce runners usually develop several crowns per plant by winter; some cultivars may produce 10 to 15 crowns. Crown division is simple. Plants from which planting stock is to be made generally should not be more than one year old or have fruited more than once.

First cut or break the plant in half for a better view of the crowns and their roots. Separate each individual crown so that roots remain attached to it; the more roots left the better, though if care is taken in handling and planting, plants with 5 to 10 roots may be satisfactory. Use only crowns that are 1.3 cm (½ in.) or more in diameter and at least 1.3 cm (½ in.) long.

LIFE OF PLANTING, YIELDS AND COSTS

Life of Planting

In southern Florida, the Gulf Coast region, and southern California the strawberry is grown like an annual.

In northern regions many growers crop the planting only once and then turn it under. New plants are set each year, entailing the expense of the plants, setting, and care for every crop obtained, and two-year use of the land for only one crop. Much too often with a second crop, the yield is low, the berries decrease rapidly in size and appearance, picking is slow, and pests and drought cause much damage. But if the planting has been well cared for and is in good healthy condition when the first crop is harvested, it may be wise to continue the planting for a second crop. Success with a second or even a third crop reduces production costs and promotes earlier berries. (See Renewing Plantings.)

Plantings in the East and Midwest are often continued after 1 or 2 crops, since the grower reasons that any fruit picked thereafter is produced with little expense and hence is so much gained; the berries are early.

Yield

Many growers, without increasing their acreage, could more than double their present yield by wise selection of cultivars, use of disease-tested plants, and better culture. With a good site, proper culture, and suitable cultivars, yields of 2150 to 4300 liters per ha (5000 to 10,000 qt per acre) may result in a favorable year. A quart of berries per foot of matted row is not unusual for the total picking in a good year, but in many plantings the yield is only half this amount. A row 30.5 m (100 ft) long should average 3 liters (3 qt) of berries a day for 2 to 3 weeks.

Where top yields are around 23,366 liters per ha (10,000 qt per acre), those less than 1892 liters (2000 qt) return little profit. In the Pacific Northwest at least 6.7 to 9 metric tons per ha (3 to 4 tons per acre) is the minimum profitable yield. Florida yields average 8903 kg per ha (8000 lb per acre) for the winter crop and bring high prices. In California yields may be 33.6 to 38 metric tons per ha (15 to 17 tons per acre).

Costs

In a study by the Ontario Department of Agriculture and Food in 1967 the average yield for 36 growers was 5696 qt per acre. The average cost per acre was $1,511 per acre, or 26.5¢ per qt. The average net returns per acre were $210. Costs per quart up to harvesting were 12¢. Strawberry production costs are high, largely as a result of labor costs. There are a number of different systems of growing and marketing strawberries and the costs of production are not the same for all of them. Within a given production system, most costs up to harvesting, and even some of the harvesting and marketing costs, remain essentially the same regardless of yield.

Costs vary greatly with the economic condition of the country, the methods of production, the efficiency of management, and various other factors. However, the main feature is that high production is essential for a profitable strawberry enterprise.

SOME CLIMATE AND WEATHER FACTORS

Photoperiod

The days are longer in the South in winter than in the North; the reverse is true in summer. Daylight periods of 12 hr or less and moderate temperatures are important in flower bud formation. Each cultivar may have a different day-length and temperature requirement. Tioga is adapted to the warmest temperatures, Headliner to slightly lower temperatures, and Albritton to still lower temperatures. Of these, Tioga can make many flower buds under the longest day-length; Headliner has a shorter, and Albritton a still shorter day-length requirement (Scott and Darrow 1972).

Runner formation is a long-day response; in general, the longer the day the more runners. Northern cultivars are short-day plants; they form their fruit buds chiefly when the days become short.

Fall bearers initiate more inflorescences under long photoperiods.

But with at least the Geneva cultivar, the length-of-light period is more important than the length-of-dark period; hence the response is not a true photoperiodic one. Runner production, on the other hand, is not markedly affected by varying the photoperiod between 12 and 18 hr (Dennis *et al.* 1970).

Although cultivars grown in California may produce fruit throughout the summer in the chief growing areas, they are not everbearers. Some cultivars require the short days of spring or fall before flower buds develop. They cease to produce flower buds and fruit during the long days of summer and become entirely vegetative, producing many runners. This is the way some cultivars behave in the Sacramento and San Joaquin Valleys (see Summer Temperature). But in the Central Coast area they interact with prevailing climatic conditions in such a way that they initiate flower buds through the long days of summer, when only a vegetative response would normally be expected.

Rest Period and Winter Chilling

The rest period is caused by a short-day low-temperature complex and is broken to a degree in some cultivars by additional daily light exposures and in all cultivars by cold. Cultivars adapted to the Deep South require little chilling, grow vigorously, form fruit buds during the short days of late fall and late winter, and can endure the hot summers.

In early fall in Massachusetts a marked and rapid change may occur in response to a relatively small increase in hours of chilling below 7°C (45°F). This response shows as an increase in petiole length, an increase in leaf size, and a short period of increase followed by a decrease in leaf number. Petiole length and leaf index are positively correlated with number of hours below 7°C (45°F). It takes much more chilling to start runner development than leaf development (Bailey and Rossi 1965).

In California freshly dug plants set in November, December, or early January bear 33 to 67% of a full crop the first season in the Central Coast area and in certain other southern areas, where they receive a minimum of chilling. When planted later they do not ordinarily yield a good crop, since they soon go to runners. This is probably a chilling factor, since cold storage also has this effect. Nurseries in California are located in colder areas than fruit production plantings, hence chilling is accumulated there. The reproductive responses can be manipulated in field plantings from almost completely sexual to almost completely asexual. Generally the degree of vegetative response, measured by runner production, is associated with the amount of chilling received by the plants, regardless of whether the chilling was in the nursery, in cold storage, or at the site after planting. In contrast, the degree of floral response as expressed by semi-continuous summer fruiting decreases with increasing chilling (Bringhurst 1955, 1956, 1960).

Summer Temperature

In California certain cultivars initiate flower buds under 15.6°C (60°F) even though they are growing under long days; only leaves and runners develop on them at 21°C (70°F) under the same long days. The relatively low average temperatures of the Central Coast during the long summer days are related to the continuous-bearing behavior there. Certain cultivars produce both the usual spring crop and further crops during summer and fall in the Central Coast area, but 100 mi. to the east in the Sacramento and San Joaquin valleys they bear only in spring. Day lengths in the Central Coast and Interior Valley are the same, but the summer temperatures are different 17.1°C (62.7°F) average at Watsonville on the coast during July and 23.3°C (73.9°F) in the Interior Valley (Bringhurst 1955, 1956, 1960).

Spring Frost

Because the strawberry grows close to the ground where the coldest air settles, especially on clear, cold, calm nights in early spring, the flowers are subject to injury by spring frosts. Unmulched plants, plants on a southern exposure, and early bloomers are often the most susceptible. Straw-mulched plants bloom later and so may escape frost more than they would otherwise. Injury from spring frost is reduced by regulating the time of removing the mulch and by planting on a site with good air drainage.

A range of 3°C (5.4°F) was observed in flower frost tolerance in 21 cultivars. Fruits were more susceptible than flowers or buds (Ourecky 1976).

Rarely does a total loss of crop occur from frost, because the flowers do not all appear at once. In much of the South, frost causes more loss than in other strawberry regions. Loss of an average of 6 to 7 flowers per plant is not unusual in spaced plantings. Some of the nubbin condition which is attributed to frost damage is caused by feeding of plant bugs on the flowers and young berries.

Only occasionally is heating profitable on strawberries. Straw mulch is a fire hazard. Large power-driven fans are sometimes used in large plantings for frost protection. Burning tires, straw, and so forth,

Courtesy of E. T. Andersen, Hort. Res. Inst. Ont.,
Vineland Station, Ontario, Canada

FIG. 2.2.   FROST PROTECTION BY MEANS OF FOAM

is almost a waste of time when frost is predicted. A simple method of protection is to take straw mulch from between the rows and spread it over the plants. Do this when the temperature approaches 1.1°C (34°F).

It is important to select a good open site higher than other areas and where air movement is not stopped by woods or by a windbreak.

Water—1 mm per ha per hour (1/10 in. per acre per hour)—applied with low volume sprinklers is often effective. Start sprinkling when the temperature drops to 1.1°C (34°F) at the lowest place in the field. Continue sprinkling even though the temperature drops to the low 20s. Stop sprinkling when all the ice has melted from the plants (Brooks et al. 1971).

A blanket of foam, applied about 3.8 cm (1½ in.) thick over the plants, is capable of keeping the temperature around 1.6°C (35°F) when applied shortly in advance of an all-night −8°C (18°F) freeze. The foam, with nonphytotoxic chicken feathers as the main ingredient, lasts about two days before it starts to disintegrate. The foam will withstand light to moderate winds when properly applied.

The system consists of a mobile pressurized generator which forces foam through large tubes and nozzles by compressed air. Nozzle sizes and shape can be changed to cover different crops, e.g., some vegetables. The foam concentrate is added to water at the ratio of 5 parts of concentrate to 95 parts of water to form a 5% solution. Cost of the foam may be about 1¢ per gallon.

The foam technique has not become an established practice in any area known to the author, but it has been shown that effective protection can be obtained through this method, especially if there is some warmth in the soil before application. The reason for its not becoming established may be the cost (which could be a good investment in large plantings) and the relatively difficult requirement for rapid application.

LOCATION AND SITE

Though a good site is not a guarantee of success, continued success is seldom obtained without it.

A new planting of Registered or Certified plants, espcially in northern regions, should not be located within 305 m (1000 ft) of older plantings of strawberries or specific disease-susceptible vegetables or flowers.

Slope and Soil

A level site is good if both surface and subsoil are well drained. A 2 to 3% slope promotes water and air drainage. Erosion may occur on a steep site, since the plants are extensively cultivated the first year. On a slope that is likely to wash, set the plants on a contour system.

On a level or nearly level area, a windbreak may cause a frost pocket behind it by lifting what little wind there is. Strawberry flowers may be killed in the still air behind a solid windbreak but be uninjured in the rest of the field.

A southern slope encourages early berries, but there is more danger of frost than on a northern or eastern slope. A northern slope may retard ripening by several days, and a clay loam on the north slope may retard ripening a few days more than a sandy loam on the same slope. Early-ripening cultivars bloom before midseason or later ones and therefore are generally more subject to frost damage.

There is a relation between reasonably light soils and the ability of runners to root freely and to establish a good stand of plants quickly.

Since the root system is shallow, the soil should be reasonably rich in humus in order to absorb and retain moisture. Occasionally soils are so rich that excessive growth is made at the expense of yield. Fall bearers do best on a soil that is naturally richer than is suitable for summer bearers.

Strawberries are not produced successfully on marshland, as it is highly subject to frost. Also, berries produced on muck are usually soft, and sometimes the fruit decays on the side in contact with the soil even before maturity.

Soil Reaction

The strawberry is not particularly sensitive to soil reactions, but it thrives best on a slightly acid soil, e.g., pH 5.5 to 6.5. It may grow well where acidity measures pH 5.0 to 7.0 if there is adequate organic matter present. When soil acidity is pH 4.5 to 5.3, lime may be needed. Apply it at least the year before planting strawberries. Otherwise broadcast it at least two months before planting and disk at intervals of a few weeks to mix the lime thoroughly with the soil.

Besides reducing acidity, lime ties up free Al, which is toxic to strawberry plants. In dolomite form it makes Ca and Mg available. It may also help the tilth of the soil. On new land that is usually acid, liming may improve the stand of plants and yield of berries. On overlimed soil the leaves may be yellowish because they are not obtaining Mn, Zn, or Fe. An excess may also dwarf the plants and berry size.

Water Drainage

Strawberries suffer on poorly drained soil. Waterlogging causes roots to be killed and new ones fail to develop fully. Even on land that is tiled or has an open subsoil, winter thaws may cause water to collect in low places, where it forms ice that may damage the plants. It is sometimes wise to plow furrows in autumn before applying mulch, to improve surface drainage and keep water from collecting around the plants in winter and spring. A poorly drained site encourages leaf and root diseases. Fruit rots are also more troublesome where the soil surface cannot dry quickly after rains.

In areas where the land is low and the drainage often poor, the plants may be set in rows raised 15.2 to 30.5 cm (6 to 12 in.) above the furrows that separate them. In furrow irrigation areas, strawberries are commonly grown on raised beds.

Standing water for a day or two is harmful, especially when the plants are growing actively.

ROTATIONS

Good strawberry crops usually result on newly cleared land, but most plantings must be made on sites that have been cropped for some time. Often the soil has lost much of its fertility, and its physical properties have been impaired.

Improving the fertility of the soil may not be enough. Soil structure may need to be improved. If so, incorporate organic matter into the soil; this gives better aeration, promotes the spread of roots both laterally and in depth, and permits better use of water. Soils with adequate organic matter lose less moisture than other soils.

Sod land is comparatively high in humus, but usually should be cropped for at least two years before planting strawberries. Untreated sod, particularly on sandy soils, is commonly infested with white grubs and other pests that cause a poor stand.

Do not grow strawberries continuously on the same soil. Some purposes of cropping systems are to grow legumes or green-manure crops in a rotation for the organic matter effects, and to precede berries with cultivated crops so as to reduce certain pests and to control weeds and grass. It is easier to eradicate certain perennial weeds before strawberries are planted.

Best rotation depends on previous soil treatment, adaptability of various crops to the soil and region, acreage, utilization of the crops in the rotation, ease of incorporating vegetative matter with the soil, limitations of growing season, and many other factors. In general, the length of time that other crops occupy the land in a rotation should at least equal that of strawberries.

Turning under one or more crops of soybeans before planting strawberries in northern areas helps prevent root rot.

In the South, one rotation plan is: after strawberries, drill in nematode-resistant soybeans or cowpeas. After this is turned under or harvested, sow winter oats. In spring, plow under or harvest the oats, and again sow soybeans or cowpeas. After this crop is plowed under or harvested, plant berries in autumn. Berries succeed well if planted after sweet potatoes, but in some sections may suffer from rhizoctonia root rot after potatoes, tomatoes, garden beans, or beets.

In the Pacific Northwest green-manure crops drilled in September make good growth in time to be turned under before berry planting in April. Abruzzi spring rye, fall-seeded, grows at lower temperatures than most kinds that are equally hardy.

Since verticillium wilt also attacks potato, tomato, eggplant, pepper and raspberry, and may occur where peaches or cherries grew previously, berries should not directly follow such crops. Root-knot nematodes that attack strawberries do not feed on oats, rye, wheat, corn, velvet beans, or hairy vetch, and these can be used to starve out these pests in rotations. Crops of beans, buckwheat, or pure stands of clover are distasteful to white grubs.

INTERCROPS

Strawberries are sometimes planted as intercrops in young orchards and vineyards. They furnish an income while the orchard or vineyard is becoming established. They bear the year after planting, give a cash return, and occupy the land for only a few years. But mice are sometimes harbored under the berry mulch and may attack the vines or trees; fire is a hazard when straw is placed in an orchard; orchard and vineyard operations are made more difficult; the berries may retard the growth of the trees and vines; fruit trees should not be cultivated as late as strawberries.

Many annual vegetables (direct-sown seeds do not commonly carry nematodes) and flowers (not gladiolus, which may carry verticillium wilt) may be used as companion crops with strawberries during the first summer. They are removed before the berry plants begin to spread over the ground.

PLANTING

To determine the number of plants required to set a hectare, multiply the distance between rows by the distance between plants within the row (in meters), and divide the product into 10,000, the number of square meters in a hectare. For an acre, divide the spacing product (in feet) into 43,560, the number of square feet per acre. For example, at 1½ × 4 ft spacing the number of plants needed to plant an acre is 7260; at 2 × 4 ft, it is 5445. A larger number of plants is required when double rows are planted, as on raised beds in Florida.

Preparation of the Soil

Begin preparation of the soil no later than a year before planting. It should achieve these objectives: destroy as many weeds as possible, especially perennials; incorporate organic material (such as manure, hay or straw, or green manures) into the soil and have the organic material sufficiently decomposed by planting time. Avoid plowing when the ground is too wet or too dry because it leaves the soil lumpy or cloddy. Such soil makes poor contact with the roots and dries out quickly at the surface. Unless serious erosion may result, fall plowing is preferred. Spring preparation then may require only leveling. Disk smooth to break up clods and to compact the soil before marking for planting.

Prior to planting, work the soil sufficiently to prepare a deep and reasonably loose "planting bed." However, it is not desirable to have the soil excessively loose (as could result from deep rototilling). This leads to breakdown of organic matter and it is difficult to do a good job of machine planting in such soils unless they are rolled, culti-packed, or allowed to settle for a few days before planting (Ricketson *et al.* 1976).

Soil fumigation, when used for control of nematodes, verticillium wilt, and some weeds, should be done in the fall prior to planting. This allows the fumigant to be effective and then dissipate out of the soil before spring planting.

Time of Planting

Actual date of planting varies with the locality. If possible, set the plants during cloudy weather. Keep the roots moist while the plants are being handled. Keep the main supply of plants in a shady spot, and the roots moist. Plants that are being dropped may be carried, for ex-ample, in a carpenter's apron lined with polyethylene.

North.—Plant early for these reasons: there is more moisture in the soil early in spring, and this greatly aids the establishment of the plants; the strawberry responds well to moderate to cool weather; and early spring planting promotes the formation of highly productive runners.

As a rule, early spring planting is one of the secrets of success in growing strawberries in the North, yet certain difficulties may be encountered. Some soils are made friable with difficulty if worked when too wet; and sometimes after the soil is made ready for early planting, adverse weather occurs or shipment is delayed and the soil must again be prepared, entailing extra expense. Normally the benefits of early planting greatly exceed the objections.

It is difficult in northern regions to obtain a good stand and high yield with plants set after the May rains. Plants set in dry, hot weather seldom do well unless irrigated. Usually the first fruiting year of a spring-set bed is a peak year. With summer planting of non-cold-stored stock even those plants that do become established may pro-duce low yields the next year since few highly productive runners form.

Freshly dug plants from a more southern latitude may be too far advanced in growth for successful planting in northern regions, espe-cially if hot weather follows soon after planting. Losses in planting can be largely avoided if completely dormant plants have been stored at about $-1.1°$ to $0°C$ ($30°$ to $32°F$) and 85 to 90% relative humidity. When the plants arrive, plant or store them immediately. Cold-stor-age conditions for apples are excellent for berry plants.

If the pack seems dry, make it moist but not so wet as to exclude air from the roots. Usually the plants need no water during storage if the humidity of the room is kept high.

It is not reasonable in northern regions to expect a full crop in the first summer after fall planting, because there is not enough time for the rooting of a normal number of highly productive runners in matted rows.

Fall-set plants, especially on light soils, start early in the non-bearing first summer, and this encourages rooting of highly productive runners. With fall-set plants, however, heaving on heavy soils may result in a poor stand the next spring. Roots of many surviving plants may be injured, and these may be unable to withstand later adverse conditions, including weeds, as well as thriftier plants. If fall-set plants are mulched to prevent heaving, there is extra expense for the material, its application, and its removal in spring to permit cultivation and the rooting of runners.

South.—In Georgia, plants set in September produce higher yields of marketable berries the following spring than those set later. This beneficial effect does not extend into the second season.

In most sections of North Carolina plants may be set during late fall, winter, and early spring. At higher elevations in the mountains, spring planting is best.

In some areas, e.g., North Carolina, large plants with well-developed crowns sometimes are set in November and December for a short crop in five months and may give yields of 3262 liters per hectare (1200 qt per acre) (the blossoms are not removed). Charged against the short crop are an extra mulching, scattered fruit for picking, and reduced yield for the main crop 12 months later.

In Maryland cold-stored June-set plants may yield as well as May or April-set plants. Success with June planting depends on the cultivar, district, quality of the cold-stored plants, and cultural practices. Irrigation is needed at planting time and occasionally thereafter, especially with late plantings.

In Florida during February or March set cold-stored plants obtained mainly from the North. During May to June set runners from the mother plants in other beds; these will in turn produce daughter plants. In August set the May to June runners for further increase. By September and October the plants set in August should have developed large runner plants. By transplanting in May and June, enough plants result to set 1.8 to 2 ha (4 to 5 acres) from an original stock of 100 plants. Plants raised in this way usually have larger crowns and bear better than those brought from the North about November 1 and set at once to fruit the following winter.

Midwest.—In southwestern Missouri, November-set plants produce a good row and a high yield since they start in early spring. It is necessary to mulch to prevent winter injury; only enough material is used to cover each plant; no advantage is gained by mulching the alleys between the rows because the mulch is lifted in spring. In central Missouri, November planting usually fails. Setting non-dormant plants during summer or early fall is not good anywhere in Missouri.

Planting dormant cold-stored plants later than April in central Arkansas and later than May in northwestern Arkansas reduces yield. Yields are closely associated with plant production. At both locations summer-set plants ripen most of the crop during the first three pickings. Only plants set in March, April and May produce well-filled matted rows. Poor plant production and low yields from summer-set plants seem to preclude commercial application of late planting in Arkansas (Moore and Bowden 1967).

With cold-stored plants in southern Illinois, planting after late June is not promising. In most years extra irrigation is necessary to establish later than normal plantings, and even then good rows of early rooted runners do not result.

Northwest.—In western Washington spring planting is usually best. If planting in autumn, set the plants early enough to become established before winter and thus be in place ready to grow in spring. Damage from soil erosion may follow fall setting. Also, especially after an open winter, weed control in spring is costly.

In irrigated parts of Idaho where the winters are not severe, plants can be set almost any time during the growing season except in hot weather. Planting in late August or early September is satisfactory in the warmer areas but only spring planting is suitable where the ground may freeze 10.2 cm (4 in.) or more.

California.—The main plantings can be grouped in two categories, both of which are soil-fumigated and covered with white polyethylene.

Winter plantings are made in October-November in the south coastal acreage. Some 50 to 75 million plants grown at high-elevation nurseries are stored annually for winter planting. They are dug during October and stored at 1.1°C (34°F) for 10 to 15 days. About 25% of California's acreage is winter-planted. Early fruit is the main reason for the winter planting, most of which is done in the southern area where the winters are mild.

Success with winter planting depends on how well the plants grow during the short days of December-January. The more active they are, the more flower buds are initiated and the greater the crop. Ambient temperatures control the growth rate, and soil temperatures may be increased by the use of clear polyethylene bed mulch. The chilling history of the plant also affects the growth rate and performance. If the plants fail to receive enough chilling, they lack vigor and will not grow fast enough for a good early crop, although they bloom profusely for a long time. If they receive too much chilling, they are very vigorous and produce runners instead of fruit. Heavy early production is obtained from plants dug in winter and stored at −1°C (30°F) until planted August 1. Short cold-stored periods are detrimental to early plantings since plants so treated tend to runner with subsequent reduction of first year production.

Summer plantings are made from 150 to 200 million plants grown at low-elevation nurseries. They are dug in late December to early February and stored at −2°C (28°F) in 1 to 2 mil (¹⁄₁₀₀₀ in.) polyethylene liners for planting from July through mid-September. This is the prevailing method because of the high yield and high fruit quality.

Since fruit quality of second-year plantings is relatively poor, about 2800 of the state's 3400 ha (7000 of 8400 acres) are replanted each year, and over 90% of the 2800 ha is mulched with white plastic.

Handling and Setting Plants

Good plants for spring setting in the North are thrifty and of the previous year's growth, with a well-developed root system of fibrous, light-colored roots, a single crown, disease-tested and free from pests. In a favorable planting season the plants may overcome mild root injury, but recovery may be slow.

Examine the plant packages as soon as they arrive, check them for condition, and if there is any damage or discrepancy in number of plants report it to the nursery and carrier immediately.

If planting is to be done the day of arrival of the plants, or the day after, store them in a cool place and keep them moist. If planting will be delayed for a longer time, place them in cold storage and keep them moist, or heel them in. Plants stored at 1.1° to 4.4°C (30° to 40°F) in polyethylene bags may grow better than those that have been heeled-in. The objective is to avoid freezing, over-heating, or drying out.

If plants are in polyethylene bags, there is little danger of their drying out. If the plants are not in plastic bags, keep the roots moist, but not wet. Do not leave plants in water.

While planting, avoid exposure of the roots to wind or sun. A good plan is to take the plants to the field in baskets lined with moist moss and covered with burlap or other material. The burlap also protects plants from wind. Drop only a few plants ahead of the planters, especially under drying conditions.

Plants set with the root system at right angles near the surface of the soil or folded in the hole may put out new roots slowly, and if the ensuing growing season is dry, they may die, sometimes long after they have made runners.

It may be unwise to leave soil on the roots after digging or at the time of planting, since certain pests may be carried in the soil. If washing is done, use a continuous stream rather than immersing the roots in a tub or pail of water. The usual procedure is to strip off the outer leaves, leaving 2 to 4 of the central ones at planting time. New leaves appear almost as soon as the new roots.

Root trimming facilitates machine planting. Trimming the roots ½ to ⅓ may promote copious production of laterals near the cut ends of the runner roots and six weeks after planting the bulk of roots may equal those of a "normal" plant. With ordinary planting little attention need be given to root trimming.

Marking the field in both directions speeds up planting and aids accurate spacing. A simple device for small areas consists of a handle long enough so that a person can pull the marker without bending, and a cross-piece that enables three rows to be marked at once. Movable pegs permit marking the desired spacing in the rows. In large plantings shallow furrows are usually made with a light plow or planting machine.

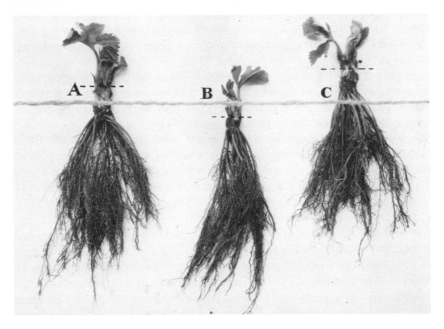

FIG. 2.3.   A—PROPER DEPTH OF PLANTING, B—TOO DEEP, C—TOO SHALLOW

Depth of Planting

Set the plants so that the midpoint of the crown is at the level of the soil surface. If they are set too deep, runnering is delayed and reduced, and the growing point of the crown may be damaged or rot; if set too shallow, the crown and tops of roots may dry out.

Methods of Planting

Success with different methods of planting may depend more on how the method is used than on the method itself.

Spade.—Two persons working together can set about 5000 plants in 10 hr. One makes a V-shaped opening fairly deeply into the soil; the other places and holds a plant in position while the spade is withdrawn and then used, about 7.6 cm (3 in.) from the plant, to push the soil against the roots on one side. Avoid excessive backward and forward movement of the spade and take care that no air space is left at the roots. The workers then firm the soil around the plant by foot. If the soil is so loose that it falls back into the opening before the plant can be placed, insert the spade at a slight angle from the vertical, lift it up, and place the plant under the spade before it is withdrawn.

Other Hand Methods.—Some other hand methods are the short-handled hoe, the trowel or dibble, and the punch and tongs used by sweet potato growers.

Furrow.—Some say that this method is quicker and cheaper than hand methods; others claim that it is slower, more expensive, and less reliable. The greater soil disturbance may lead to more drying out of the soil and less firmly set plants.

Machine.—Many large level fields are planted by machine. This method is quick ánd the plants can be watered as they are set. Three workers can plant 3 to 4 acres in 10 hr with some machines. One person drives and two others seated at the rear near the ground place the plants in a trench made by the machine. Plants should be uniform in size, "stripped," and with trimmed roots arranged in one direction in the containers. It is somewhat difficult to set all plants at the proper depth by machine. Someone should follow the machine to tramp the soil around the roots, to straighten misplaced plants and to fill gaps.

If the soil is packed by rain or mechanical means, transplanting may be easier and more successful. Some set single rows, or 2 rows on each side of 2 beds, or even 3 rows, one on each side of 3 beds. By proper arrangement of 1, 2, or 3-row setters, double-row beds can be set by making a round trip of the machine on the same bed or beds.

SYSTEMS OF TRAINING

Matted Rows

The matted-row system is used in most northern regions. Runners are allowed to set in all directions. Cultivation tends to straighten the runners into the rows and to limit the width of rows.

Spacing commonly is 107 to 122 cm (3½ to 4 ft) between rows and 45.7 to 60.9 cm (1½ to 2 ft) in the rows. Plants that are virus-tested often are set farther apart than infected plants. Rows closer than 91 cm (3 ft) seldom are suitable commercially. Instead of planting 46 to 61 cm (1½ to 2 ft) in the row, the spacing may be increased to 76 cm (2½ ft) on good soils with cultivars that are prolific plant makers, or it may be reduced, especially in small plantings, to 31 to 38 cm (12 to 15 in.) on rather poor soils with cultivars that are indifferent plant makers.

Usually a fruiting matted row 46 to 61 cm (1½ to 2 ft) wide is preferable to a wider or narrower one. With equal planting distance, the wider the row the greater the yield. But medium-width rows usually result in a better product and are easier to pick than those set farther apart and let become too wide. A point in favor of wide matted rows is that runners can space themselves better.

Two plantings with an apparently equal stand of plants in autumn may differ greatly in yields the next year if in one the stand is largely from early-rooted runners and in the other is largely late-rooted. Aim for a full stand of plants in matted rows by early fall in northern regions. Do not cut off early-formed runners, as these are the most productive ones. Late-spring planting usually results in low yield.

Dump rakes, side-delivery rakes, or spike-tooth harrows may be used to pull up many late-formed runners in matted rows. Then cut them off with rolling disks in front of the cultivator shovels and thus maintain the desired row width.

Hedgerows

Hedgerow training entails definite placing of runners from each plant, after which all later runners are removed. In single hedgerows set the plants 38 to 46 cm (15 to 18 in.) apart in rows to 61 to 107 cm (2 to 3½ ft) apart. Usually two runners are bedded in line with the parents. Another hedgerow system is to bed 4 to 8 runners from each plant at nearly equal distances apart, but kept from extending too far between the rows. In general, quality is improved but the cost is comparatively high.

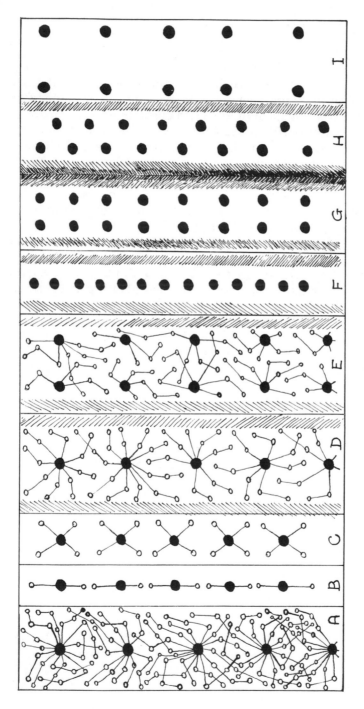

FIG. 2.4.   SYSTEMS OF TRAINING STRAWBERRIES

●—parent plant. O—runner plants. A—matted row; B—single hedgerow;
C—double hedgerow; D—spaced row (planted in center of raised bed); E—spaced row
(planted near edges of raised bed); F—single row hills; G—double (opposite) row hills;
H—double (alternate) row hills; I—stool hills.

Spaced Beds

Spaced beds are usually developed in the East by planting 61 to 91 cm (2 to 3 ft) apart in rows 107 to 122 cm (3½ to 4 ft) apart. Develop a bed 61 to 76 cm (2 to 2½ ft) wide early in the season with plants spaced 15 to 31 cm (6 to 12 in.) apart over the bed. When the tips of the first runners begin to enlarge, place them by hand in the rows between the mother plants, or to the side, and cover with soil. Place the next runners 15 to 31 cm (6 to 12 in.) out from the original row and on each side of it. Place additional runners until a wide row is formed, with the plants at least 15 cm (6 in.) apart. Thereafter, cut off all new runners.

Spaced plants may produce larger berries and a higher total yield than matted rows, but much hand labor is needed to space plants and to remove surplus runners. Responses from irrigation are often greater in spaced rows than in matted rows.

In Oregon, the rows are arranged 122 to 152 cm (4 to 5 ft) apart with the plants 61 to 91 cm (2 to 3 ft) or more apart in the row. Allow runners to fill in around the mother plants until spaced 18 to 25 cm (7 to 10 in.). Place soil on the strings. After spacing, remove all later runners. Aim for plant rows 51 to 76 cm (20 to 30 in.) wide. A medium-sized plant, which is the most productive in relation to its size, is developed by this method. Much labor is necessary for weeding and removing runners.

Hill Rows

Hill rows are used in areas where growth may continue most of the year, as in the Gulf Coast states. The beds are made 20 to 25 cm (8 to 10 in.) high and are let settle for at least 10 days before planting. The plants are set in late summer or in autumn for winter harvest. Usually the plants make no runners, but if they do appear, remove them. A large number of plants is required per hectare.

Single Hill Beds.—These are used in the Pacific Northwest, the Hammond, La. district, and the Chadbourn, N.C. district. Usually the plants are 30.5 cm (1 ft) apart in rows 91 cm (3 ft) apart.

Double Row Beds.—In Florida the berries are usually grown in beds 107 to 122 cm (3½ to 4 ft) apart with plants set in double rows 30.5 ×30.5 cm (12×12 in.) apart. Closer spacing may result in a higher yield. Average yields for 3 seasons were 2755 twelve-half-liter flats per ha (1115 twelve-pint flats per acre) at 22.9 cm (9 in.) spacing in double-row spacing (71,758 plants per ha, or 29,040 per acre) and 2357 flats per ha (954 per acre) at 30.5 cm (12 in.) spacing (53,793 plants per ha, or 21,780 per acre). A 25.4 cm (10 in.) spacing also gives better results than a 30.5 cm (12 in.) spacing (Albregts 1972; Locascio 1972).

In California, berries are planted 30.5 to 40.0 cm (12 to 16 in.) apart in double rows on raised beds spaced about 101.6 cm (40 in.) from center to center. In summer plantings double-row plants perform better than those in single-row beds because salt accumulation is a greater factor than the lower temperatures. The opposite is true of winter plantings because the lower temperature in the double rows is more important than salt buildup, since a shorter period of time is involved and less salt accumulates. Plants in low beds (10 cm, or 25.4 in.) high outperform those in high beds (20 cm, or 50.8 in.) in both winter and summer plantings. In both cases high beds are warmer than low beds and they accumulate more salt (Voth *et al.* 1967). Sometimes 3 or 4 rows are set on each bed.

Stool Hills.—For the stool or square hill system as used in British Columbia, all runners are removed before they root. This aids the parent plants to stool out in large multiple crowns. Spacing the plants 76 to 91 cm (2½ to 3½ ft) each way allows for cross-cultivation. Runners may need to be cut 5 to 10 times the first year, but less often in the second and later years. This system promotes superior quality and berry size in cultivars in climates adapted to them. Cultivars incapable of developing large, multiple crowns, as is the case with most cultivars, do not thrive in stool hills. For new plants, set mother plants in a separate planting to develop runners.

Solid Beds

Much higher yields can be obtained from solid-bed plantings than from matted rows. Yields as high as 29 metric tons per ha (13 tons per acre) have been obtained with multiple-pick harvesting, and as high as 8 metric tons (9 tons) with a once-over hand pick in tests in Ontario (Ricketson 1968, 1970, and 1973 correspondence).

Planting.—The mother plants are set as in matted rows, and are encouraged by good cultural practices to develop runners freely. In matted rows the space between rows commonly occupies 33 to 50% of the area of a planting. The proportion of a solid-bed planting sacrificed in wheel tracks in mechanical-aid harvesting depends on the width of machine used to carry pickers.

Spacing the Runners.—Good runner spacing is 15 to 23 cm (6 to 9 in.) apart in solid beds. This is done by hand several times between midsummer and early fall; some weeding may be done at the same time. Herbicides are available which give effective weed control without having to rely on cultivation. Irrigate lightly several times to pro-

Courtesy of E. T. Andersen, Hort. Res. Inst. Ont.,
Vineland Station, Ontario, Canada

FIG. 2.5.   SOLID BEDS

mote rooting of runners. Apply a winter mulch of wheat straw with
an ensilage blower; remove it completely the following spring.

First Fruiting Year.—In spring apply a suitable herbicide before
bloom and do some hand weeding. Irrigate to supplement rain in order
to supply 2.5 cm (1 in.) of water per week. Use a good spray program
with Captan or Benlate to control Botrytis rot.

A self-propelled, picker-positioner harvesting aid may carry 6 to 8
pickers; each picker lying on a padded-board, moving platform can
pick a strip 61 to 122 cm (2 to 4 ft) wide. The faster pickers are located beside slower ones, are assigned a wider strip to pick, and are
paid accordingly.

Once-over and Multi-picks.—The wide range of maturities in a
once-over harvest may be a problem to processors. Some of the berries may have been ripe seven days or more; these would be primary
berries and some secondaries. A hand-pick of these large, early berries
for fresh market is desirable. Multi-picks consist of pickings made at
3, 4, or 5 day intervals, as needed.

Renovation.—A solid bed in good condition may be renovated to
produce another year's crop. Aim to maintain or provide desirable
spacing of the plants, and to remove unrooted runners. This work is
done at the end of harvest, after fertilizing and mowing, by workers
riding on a moving platform.

Comment.—Probably no improvement in cultivars, use of growth substances, or change in cultural practices is likely, in the near future, to give such increases in yield as can be obtained from solid beds in areas where matted rows are common. Solid rows seem to have great potential for both fresh market and processing.

As long as growers can harvest berries in conventional ways they may not be interested in more machinery. But it is increasingly difficult to get pickers. Growers, particularly large operators, may need to resort to mechanical harvesting aids in order to attract pickers.

GROWING STRAWBERRIES IN A BARREL

As a novelty, strawberry plants may be set and fruited in a barrel. A good barrel for growing the berries is at least 3 to 3½ ft high and well-bulged. Remove the lid of the barrel. Bore 3 or 4 holes in the bottom. With a 5 cm (2 in.) auger, bore a series of holes in the sides, starting 15 cm (6 in.) from the bottom. Stagger the holes at 25 to 31 cm (10 to 12 in.) intervals in the sides, completely around the barrel. Start filling the barrel with fertile soil. Spread the roots inside the barrel so that they are angled slightly upward to allow for soil settling.

Keep the soil level with the rows of holes until the plants are set. Then add more soil and firm it. Make a sand cone extending upward through the center to facilitate proper moisture supply for the lower plants. Place 5 cm (2 in.) of gravel or broken crockery in the bottom to provide drainage for excess water. The core may be made from a 13 cm (5 in.) diameter tin can with both ends removed. The can is placed in the bottom of the barrel, filled with coarse sand, and gradually moved up and refilled with sand as soil is packed around it. Set a few plants in the top, but leave the center (sand cone) open for watering.

A handful of complete fertilizer may be added every 2 to 3 weeks if the plants appear to lack vigor. For winter, bring the barrel into a building or wrap with 15 cm (6 in.) of straw or other protective material to prevent excessive drying out and freezing.

Supply water at the top. As sun should reach all sides of the barrel, give the barrel a half turn from time to time; otherwise, set the plants only on the east, south and west sides of the barrel. If it is too hard to turn easily, set the barrel on coasters, an old wagon wheel, or on a clothesline turntable.

REMOVING FLOWER STEMS

To ensure strong, fruitful plants when the proper time comes, remove all flower clusters from newly-set plants. This helps the plants become established by preventing a severe drain on their vitality from untimely fruiting, aids in tolerating heat and drought, and increases early and total runner formation.

With cultivars that do not always make a desirable number of runners, the more often blossoms are removed the better it is for the plants. Usually make 2 or 3 trips over the planting. With cultivars having an excessive plant-forming habit, removing flower stems once may suffice.

Repeated removal is less costly if one waits until the bloom has progressed enough that the whole stalk can be picked off, not just individual flowers.

In the Pacific Northwest a few dried berries in the field due to lack of deblossoming may make weevil bait less attractive. The weevils may eat these berries instead of the bait.

Remove blossoms of fall bearers for 60 to 80 days after planting and from then on let them develop into fruit. It takes 3 to 5 weeks from blossom to ripe berry.

Single applications of gibberellic acid (GA), 50 ppm, to new and 1-year-old plantings of Geneva fall bearer in June, or double in June and July, may inhibit flowering, promote runner development, and increase the number of marketable runner plants the next year. The largest number of runners result from combining GA sprays with deflowering. GA may be useful to nurserymen who have been obtaining fewer than four runner plants per mother plant from fall bearers. Apply as a double spray 6 and 8 weeks after planting. Sprayed plants should be deflowered, but GA can reduce the number of inflorescences that must be removed (Dennis and Bennett 1969).

TILLAGE AND WEED CONTROL

Because of its low habit of growth, the strawberry cannot compete as successfully as other fruits with weeds that deprive the plants of moisture, sunshine and nutrients.

Rotation

Fewer weeds are likely to occur where strawberries are planted in a rotation.

Cultivation soon after planting and at frequent intervals controls weeds, conserves moisture, prevents the surface of the soil from becoming crusted, and facilitates rooting of runners. In the first year, cultivation should be increasingly shallow as the season progresses, and farther from the original plants each time, until the rows are of the desired width.

Pulling loose soil over runners helps anchor them and hastens rooting. In successive cultivations always work the same rows in the same direction to avoid disturbing plants already trailed into position by the cultivator. Moderate ridging in later years may help prevent water from standing around the plants, reduce winter injury to the crowns, and lessen loss from rotting of berries when rains occur during harvest. Avoid cutting close to the rows and then leaving an edge with roots exposed or poorly covered with soil.

Start cultivation early and continue until hard frost occurs. Since a mulch protects the late fall weeds as well as the strawberry plants, the planting should be relatively free of weeds before the mulch is applied.

A good mulch is an effective substitute for cultivation before harvest in fruiting years.

Growth of new leaves takes place at the top, so the crown grows out of the ground, though slowly. Because new roots are readily killed by dry air, hoe and cultivate moist soil toward the plants, not away from them, to give the roots a chance to form.

Hoeing and Hand Weeding

Some hand hoeing and weeding is usually necessary to keep weeds out of the row. At the first weeding uncover the buds of too deeply set plants. Such plants when neglected are unlikely to be thrifty, even though they live through the summer. Flower stems can also be removed at this time, but it is usually best to do this as a separate operation.

At later weedings train runners to vacant spaces, and remove those that extend far between the rows, or place them in better position. Several hand weedings may be needed the first year, or before picking the next year. It is important to have the planting weed-free during late summer when the fruit buds are forming.

It may be practical in some plantings to control weeds by special machines.

Herbicides

Certain chemicals are useful in weed control in berries, reducing the amount of hand labor and the number of cultivations.

New chemicals and research change the picture from time to time, and recommendations may quickly go out of date. It is important to read the product label carefully, to make certain that the herbicide has been cleared for use on strawberries, and to use the rate and time of application advised for the weeds to be controlled.

Overwintering weeds often grow through the mulch, and certain straw mulches may have grain seeds in them which germinate and become a problem. For a bulk-treated, herbicide-treated mulch, spread on the ground in a 15 cm (6 in.) layer the amount of mulch for a given field area. Spray it with the correct amount of the herbicide. Apply one-third at a time so that the mulch is sprayed and mixed three times for good distribution of the chemical. Spread the mulch soon after spraying. As an alternative, untreated mulch may be applied to the berry plants first and an herbicide applied on top of it.

Geese

Geese, particularly a heavier breed, will eat grassy weeds (e.g., young crabgrass and foxtail) in a first year planting until early fall without damage to the berry plants unless desperate for food. These birds are particularly effective in wet years, since they roam the planting when men and machine cannot.

Geese will not eat some weeds, e.g., many broadleaf ones. It may be possible to train them to eat certain weeds. Placing a few geese in a small enclosure and supplying them only with the kind of weeds prevailing in the planting is one way of determining whether they will eat them. Place the geese in the berry field if they become accustomed to eating these weeds. But, if weeds are allowed to "take over" the berry field, geese cannot clean it up. Do not use insecticides or some herbicides if geese are placed in the planting.

Usually 10 to 12 geese per ha (4 or 5 geese per acre) suffice or 15 to 20 (6 to 8) in wet season. Goslings are most efficient; they work best with a few old geese. Mature geese are less active in foraging and tend to compact the soil in spots where they congregate. Since geese prefer young tender growth, bring them in soon after planting, or when grass is appearing. In fruiting years, remove the geese from the berry field during the bloom and berry periods, and return them after picking is complete.

Supplement their diet, but not enough to satisfy their appetites or they won't eat weeds. About a handful of corn per goose per day is sufficient. Set a 190 liter (50 gal.) container, with a spigot to drip water continuously into a shallow basin, at one end of the row and scatter shelled corn or stale bread at the other end. The grown geese eat some of the corn, then waddle down the field toward the water, eating weeds as they go. Growing goslings may not eat whole corn and may require a standard growing ration during the first ten weeks. High-protein

Courtesy of W. W. Magill, University of Kentucky

FIG. 2.6.   GEESE CAN DESTROY MANY WEEDS WITHOUT
DESTROYING THE BERRY PLANTS

feeds are not suited to geese.

If the geese tend to fly out of the berry area, clip a few side-wing feathers, but do not clip the end feathers on the wings since these are essential for holding the wings on the back. Probably a better plan is to erect a portable fence, e.g., a 66 cm (26 in.) hay-wire fence when dogs and foxes are not a problem, or a 123 cm (4 ft) poultry fence against foxes and dogs. If shade trees do not occur near the planting, provide a shelter from hot sun; locate it about 6 m (20 ft) from the planting, or the geese will trample the plants around it.

Geese feed mostly on the weeds during early morning, late afternoon, evening, and moonlit nights. They seldom roam the berry field during the heat of the day.

When weeds are plentiful and the geese are confined overnight, give them a little feed before they are released in the morning. This is because geese do not have a crop for storing food as most birds do and when hungry may gorge themselves on grass and develop digestive troubles.

Using geese for weed control is not a new practice. Cotton growers have used them for many years.

IRRIGATION

Irrigation may be essential for consistent production. A conveniently reached source of water is an asset.

Supplemental Irrigation

Supplemental irrigation is the supplying of water in areas where the average monthly rainfall is usually sufficient for profitable farming. It is the watering of a planting during certain periods to furnish the water needed for good production.

Sprinkler systems used for supplemental irrigation consist essentially of pipes with sprinklers or nozzles for distributing the water, under pressure, over the area to be irrigated. The pressure may be provided by gravity from a water source at a higher elevation or by pumping. In sprinkler irrigation the water is distributed over the soil by mechanical means; in furrow irrigation it is distributed by the soil itself.

Purposes.—Timely irrigations may increase or save the crop, improve the size and appearance of the berries, and prolong the harvest. It is particularly in years when non-irrigated plantings suffer most that supplemental irrigation gives the best results. Usually the main purpose is to supply water near or during the picking season, but it is wise to irrigate in the first year, at planting time and later, to promote the development and rooting of runners. Irrigation aids in making fertilizer available to the roots.

Supplemental irrigation during fruit-bud formation may increase the yield. Berry size is not affected as much as by time of harvest. Largest size is produced by the primary berries. Irrigation increases the total number of berries, and a linear relation exists between number of berries and periods of harvest. Proper irrigation dies not affect the soluble solids content of the fruit or pH of the juice. Supplemental irrigation is both feasible and effective for production where rain is inadequate to maintain soil moisture at field capacity in the root zone.

Irrigation may aid in preventing frost damge to the blossoms. Compared with air, water contains considerable heat. If enough water is supplied it may release heat to keep the air temperature near the

FIG. 2.7.   ONE METHOD OF SUPPLEMENTAL IRRIGATION

ground above the freezing point. Turn on the sprinklers when the temperature drops to 0°C to 1.1°C (32° to 34°F) and keep it on until the temperature rises above 0°C (32°F) or until all the ice is melted. If water is turned on too late or is turned off while the ice is still on the plants, some blossoms probably will be injured.

Applying 2.5 mm (¹⁄₁₀ in.) per hour, or 2.27 liters (60 gal.) per minute, may protect the blossoms against −7°C (19°F). When the air temperature at plant level drops below freezing, water starts to freeze on the plants. The freezing water gives off heat, some of which goes into the leaves and blossoms to keep the plant at the freezing point of water, except when the air temperature is very low or during wind-borne freezes. Ice coats as thick as 6 to 13 mm (¼ to ½ in.) are not uncommon on the plants but often do not seriously damage them.

Excessive water during the fruit development period may result in softer fruit. Losses from fruit rot may be more serious with heavily irrigated berries unless thorough spraying for rot control is practiced. Normal root action and development may be hindered. Also, leaching of nutrients, especially N, may occur. Therefore, use irrigation with some care. Do not apply water at a rate faster than the soil can absorb it (Ricketson *et al.* 1976).

Soil Type.—Coarse-textured sandy and gravelly soils have a low water-holding capacity and absorb water rapidly, usually at any normal rate at which it might be applied with a sprinkler. Fine-textured silts and clays hold a large amount of water, but absorb it more slowly.

Since periods of several weeks without rain often occur, irrigation helps promote maximum yields.

Rainfall Distribution.—In Michigan, an annual precipitation of 50.8 cm (20 in.) is enough for good yields, if rain occurs when it is actually needed and if it falls slowly enough so that none runs off. That seldom happens. Sometimes almost the entire rainfall for a month may occur in one storm. Records for 20 years at East Lansing, Bloomingdale, Lake City, and Saginaw have shown drought periods (at least 2 weeks during which less than 6 mm (0.25 in.) of rain fell in 24 hr varying from 2 to 15 weeks; a dry period of 4 continuous weeks can be expected every 2 years. During that time strawberries could have used all the water available to their roots. A dry period occurring when a plant has its greatest need for water usually results in a serious decrease in both quantity and quality of the crop.

Strawberries may have poor flavor as a result of leaching of sugars from the fruit by excessive rain or prolonged irrigation. From green, immature fruits only 4 mg of carbohydrates, or 1.65% of the dry weight, can be leached; and from fully ripe fruits 84 mg, or 6.02%. During the first 7 hr of leaching, loss of carbohydrates is relatively small but steady (1 mg per hour). In the next 17 hr losses increase progressively to 7 mg per hour during the final 2 hr. After 24 hr of leaching, the fruits are insipid, lacking in sweetness, and of poor quality and aroma (Tukey *et al.* 1958).

Sprinkling differs from rain in several respects, and the effects on plants may be different, e.g., in relation to humidity and spread of disease. Since sprinkling is often done during warm, sunny days it has little effect on humidity except during application, whereas rain is generally associated with cloudy weather and prolonged high humidity.

Measuring Soil Moisture.—Soil moisture content may be measured in several technical ways. It may be estimated by the "feel" of the soil at depth of maximum rooting. When the soil will hold together n a firm ball when squeezed, start irrigating. A sticky ball when squeezed indicates enough moisture.

Check soil moisture before each irrigation to determine if the wilting point has been reached and if water should be added and after each irrigation to determine if the soil is supplied to the bottom of the root zone.

Streams, drainage ditches, ponds, lakes and wells are the chief sources of irrigation water. Certain laws, surface injunctions, or water rights limit or forbid such use of water. New irrigations up-stream, for example, may seriously reduce the water available to a down-stream irrigator.

Quality and Quantity.—Salt in brine wells may adversely affect the plants when applied to them. Generally, any drinkable water is suitable. If waters contain silt and organic matter, which may not be considered drinkable, screen out the foreign matter to prevent clogging of the nozzles. Sulfur water normally is not injurious to plants, but industrial wastes may be harmful.

The quantity of available water may limit the area that can be irrigated. It takes 27,154 U.S. gal. of water to supply 1 in. of water per acre. A well or stream from which 4285 liters (1132 gal.) per hour is pumped supplies enough water in 24 hr for 2.5 cm (1 in.) on 0.4 ha (1 acre). The quantity of water flowing in a stream or ditch at the driest time of year may determine how many hectares or acres can be irrigated from such a source. With a continuously flowing stream the flow should be at least 9.4 cm of water per week to each hectare (1½ in. per week per acre), with a system operating 20 hr a day for 6 days out of 7. When the water requirement exceeds the amount of such water available, dig a reservoir to impound the water, large enough to refill overnight, if only daytime irrigation is intended.

Amount and Frequency.—Most soils absorb water rapidly for several minutes, but in time the rate becomes nearly uniform. Set a few open-top cans along the lateral lines between sprinklers for measurement purposes. A knowledge of rainfall rates and of the ability of the soil to absorb rain aids in selecting suitable sprinkler rates.

Large drops resulting from low pressures tend to puddle and to seal the surface of the soil sooner than a fine spray. A cultivated soil left somewhat cloddy absorbs water more rapidly than a finely pulverized one. A compacted or crusted soil generally absorbs water slowly. Presence of organic matter increases the rate of absorption.

Apply sufficient water to penetrate 15 to 25 cm (6 to 8 in.) or slightly deeper. Crops on sandy soils require more frequent irrigation, in smaller amounts, than heavier soils.

A crop of 18,693 liters per ha (8000 qt per acre) removes from the soil nearly 5.4 metric tons (6 tons) of water in the berries. Also, many times this amount is lost by transpiration from the plants and by evaporation from the soil. This emphasizes the necessity of abundant moisture during the few weeks between bloom and harvest.

Water loss is greater during hot, sunny weather than during cool, cloudy periods. It is also greater in windy weather. Run sprinkler lines across the wind. With winds higher than 6.3 km (4 mi.) per hour it may be necessary to use twice as many sprinklers. The precipitation rate is the same if the liters (gallons) per minute discharged per sprinkler at 6.1 m (20 ft) spacing is half the amount at 12.2 m (40 ft) spacing.

Systems and Equipment.—The lightweight, aluminum alloy tubing of the rotary sprinkler type of overhead irrigation allows for easy portability. Sprinkler heads mounted on vertical risers above these portable lines distribute water through nozzles in a circular pattern. Sprinklers are spaced 12.1 or 18.3 m (40 or 60 ft) apart on a line, depending on the water pressure, and the portable lines are moved 12.1 to 18.3 m (40 to 60 ft) at each set; overlapping the spray pattern from adjacent sprinklers gives uniform coverage. The tubing comes in diameters of 5.1 to 20.3 cm (2 to 8 in.). The lengths, which are 6.1, 9.1 or 12.2 m (20, 30 or 40 ft) are easily connected through a quick coupler. Elbows, tees, valves, reducers, and other fittings are simply and quickly connected to the portable lines.

Furrow Irrigation

With plantings of raised beds, water can be supplied in furrows between the rows. The rows preferably should not exceed 91.4 m (300 ft) so that the water can run down the alleys without too much

FIG. 2.8.   FURROW OR FLOODING IRRIGATION

loss. During the planting and picking seasons, run water down every other alley, so that the workers can walk in the non-irrigated furrows, and at the next irrigation water the alleys previously omitted. Wherever possible cultivate the alleys about two days after each irrigation.

Apply water in the furrow between raised beds soon after planting. If the soil is not moist, failure to irrigate within a few hours after planting may result in a poor stand. Unless the field is level or slopes evenly, water collects in low spots, some plants are flooded, and others do not receive enough water. If lateral percolation is rapid and the entire bed is moistened quickly, width of the raised bed may be greater than where water soaks in slowly. When raised beds are too wide, it is more difficult to wet the soil in the middle of the bed.

In Washington state irrigation furrows are spaced close enough that the water wets all the soil to the depth of root penetration. Some growers irrigate at 2 to 3 week intervals in early spring, gradually lessening the intervening time, until during harvest each picking is followed by an irrigation in every furrow or alternate furrow.

In a year with little rain in early fall, irrigation in summer increases the next year's crop in Oregon. But even with three summer irrigations, best yields result with 34,580 to 79,040 well-spaced plants per ha (14,000 to 32,000 plants per acre), consisting entirely of spring-set mother plants, or of these plus early-rooted runners. The cost of keeping the plant population within the above limits is high in proportion to yield and returns, and it may be most profitable to irrigate only once in late summer.

Irrigation may be needed in Colorado every 4 to 6 days or even more often on light soils during the bearing season.

Hold irrigation in Idaho during the first year to the minimum for good vigor; restricted irrigation encourages deeper rooting. During fruiting, apply water every 4 to 6 days on light soils and every 7 to 10 days on heavier soils, or irrigate alternate rows after each picking.

In California, apply 3.7 to 4.9 m³ (3 to 4 acre-ft) of water in the Central Coast area, and 6.2 to 7.4 m³ (5 to 6 acre-ft) in southern California and the Great Central Valleys. Water is often applied in winter in southern California.

Salt Damage.—With furrow irrigation in some areas, the water reaches the surface of raised beds only by lateral and upward movement. Solar evaporation and plant transpiration remove the water, and the salts carried in by the water remain in the surface soil of the bed. In summer, little downward movement occurs through the top 15.2 cm (6 in.) of the bed to carry out the deposited salts. Because the young plants are shallow-rooted, frequent irrigations are necessary, and with each irrigation more salt is deposited. Maximum salt accumulation occurs in the surface 5 cm (2 in.) of the bed where the salt accumulation may be up to 25 times more than in the 5 to 15 cm (2 to 6 in.) depth. Damage from salt accumulation depends on the age and depth of the roots. In young plantings injury first shows as a lack of vigor. The most affected plants have a leaf-edge burn, and when the accumulation is high they die. The few roots which develop near the surface are short and thick with little fine root development.

In the second year, plants that have not been visibly affected in the first year and have attained normal size as well as deeper root development tolerate more salt and may show evidence of damage only by low vigor. As the season advances and salt accumulation increases, edge-burning appears. With increasing accumulation, scorching extends back into the plant until it dies.

When water containing more than 100 ppm of sodium chloride is used in furrow irrigation, sufficient salt may accumulate to cause a decrease in the first picking, although the plants seem normal. Aim to induce enough downward movement of water through the surface of the bed to leach out the salt left by the previous irrigation.

If the soil is sufficiently permeable to water, this can be done by changing from a furrow to an overhead system to reduce salt accumulation so that higher first pickings result. Sprinklers are less effective for this purpose during the second year because much salt accumulates while the first crop is being picked, when it is not practical to use sprinklers. Under most conditions the advantages of sprinkler irrigation in reducing salt accumulation in the root zone should not be offset by foliar absorption of toxic ions present in the irrigation water.

In Florida, a peaked bed offers protection from salt injury when two-row culture is used, as salt accumulates in an area of minimum root development (Locascio 1972).

Drip or Trickle Irrigation

Basically the trickle irrigation system consists of a series of pipes and tubes which apply water directly to the root zone. A timer programs daily water application rates, thereby maintaining a high water level in the root zones at all times. Conventional overhead and furrow methods apply large amounts of water at one time, only to leave plants under moisture stress between applications.

An advantage of the low-pressure trickle system is that a smaller pump can be used to distribute the water. The amount of water normally used is considerably less. Damage from salt accumulation is also minimized, since soil moisture levels are maintained at high levels and salts are moved away from the root zones by application of water. Foliar diseases may be reduced, since water is applied directly to the soil.

Tubing may need to be installed for new plantings, but a yield increase and a longer period of harvest are factors on the plus side.

In California the number of plants per acre can be increased 50% with equal plant performance by changing bed shape by at least that amount using the trickle system. A drawback is clogging of the small orifices. The use of filters is mandatory, and the smaller the orifice the more difficulties are encountered.

MULCHING AND WINTER PROTECTION

As winter protection, mulching checks heaving of plants and damage to the roots caused by freezing and thawing. It also prevents the plants from drying out or freezing excessively. In spring and early summer it helps to avoid injury from frost by delaying bloom, keeps down weeds (provided it is free from weed seeds), conserves moisture, replaces cultivation, reduces the number of dirty and rot-infected berries, makes picking more pleasant, may improve fruit color and increases yield. There may be some years when unmulched plants do not seem to suffer much injury and yield well. But it is possible that even higher yields and other benefits would have resulted if these fields had been mulched.

Objections are: cost of the material and its application; difficulty of obtaining suitable material in some cases; possiblity of weed seeds; in regions where the strawberry weevil or "clipper" is prevalent, a mulch may result in injury to the flower clusters; picking may be

FIG. 2.9.   AS A WINTER PROTECTION MULCH FOR STRAWBERRIES,
COVER BOTH THE ROWS AND THE SPACE BETWEEN THE ROWS

delayed somewhat. The advantages of mulching usually outweigh the objections.

Straw and Hay

Good mulch material is free from weed seeds, does not pack down and cause smothering, is not too coarse or so light that it blows away, has not been used previously as a mulch, and is not too expensive. Clean wheat straw or rye straw is usually the best material. Cornstalks are too coarse; chaffy straw, oat straw, and leaves pack down too much.

A straw mulch is more difficult to handle under furrow-irrigated conditions than on "dry land." Place the straw around the plants, leaving open spaces between the rows for irrigation.

Sometimes a cover crop of oats is sown in late summer or early fall between the rows, and is allowed to mat as it is killed by frost. But oats in dry periods may take moisture from the plants and in wet periods grow so rank as to shade the plants, crowd their roots, and thus cause smaller berries.

Where straw stacks are not plentiful, it may be wise to grow suitable crops for mulch material. Even low spots, which may be useless for berries, may produce a good growth of rye during winter and early spring and Sudan grass after that in some areas. A mixture of millet and Sudan grass may produce a large amount of dry mulch material. One hectare (2.47 acres) of lespedeza, cut before full bloom, may produce 3.36 metric tons (3.7 tons) of cured hay, or enough to lightly mulch 1 ha of berries.

In Kentucky, native broom sedge makes a good mulch. Cotton burrs, spread with a manure spreader, make a cheap mulch in Oklahoma. In Arkansas, rice straw generally carries less weed seed than other small grain straw.

Machinery is available for spreading straw in strawberries when they are grown on large scale.

When To Mulch.—The best time to mulch for winter in the North is determined by the temperature and previous exposure of the plants to frost rather than by the calendar. In general, mulch for winter only after the plants have been exposed to several frosts and growth has stopped, but before the plants have been exposed to temperatures lower than $-6.6°C$ (20°F). Apply it after a week or more of near-freezing temperatures and not soon after a period of warm weather that may reduce hardiness. The ideal period for mulching is rather short some years and varies from year to year.

The number of fall frosts may be a useful and simple index to determine when to mulch. Several light frosts previous to mulching may be necessary to avoid plant injury. Further delay may increase the hazard of a critically low temperature occurring before the plants are protected (Collins 1966).

Plant Injury from Cold.—The problem of winter injury is partly the effect of fluctuating temperatures on the carbohydrates in the plants. Respiration of the plants is more rapid after fluctuating temperatures than under constant temperatures, even though the latter may average higher. Accelerated respiration uses up the carbohydrate reserves, thus weakening the plants. A mulch, by maintaining more uniform temperatures, conserves the carbohydrate supply.

Most of the injury attributed to "ice smothering" is due to lethal temperatures, excess water when the plants emerge from dormancy, broken roots, or disease resulting from winter injury. The respiration rate of dormant plants is relatively low in winter, and an ice seal for ten weeks or longer may not cause serious injury in the North.

When temperatures of $-9°$ to $-11°C$ (10° to 12°F) or lower occur, with no snow on the ground, unmulched plants suffer. Fruit clusters may be injured, blossoming is reduced, and many plants do not bloom at all. These nonbloomers may grow strongly in spring and make many runners. Black root and root rot often occur, in part, from failure to mulch properly, since many feeding roots are destroyed or weakened by heaving and other causes. The effect may not be noticed until summer, when the grower may not have in mind that the trouble can be traced back to improper mulching the previous fall.

A light frost does not hurt the plants. A temperature of $-1.1°C$ (30° F) at plant level is likely to cause only slight injury, but $-3.3°C$ (26°F) is likely to cause severe injury. The length of time the low temperature persists has a great influence on the extent of injury. Protect plants from −9.4° to −6.7°C (15° to 20°F) and lower; at −6.7°C (20°F) the crown may turn brown internally. Waiting until the ground freezes before mulching is not safe, since injury may already have occurred. But subsequent resistance to cold depends on previous exposure to frosts at above −6.7°C (20°F). Too-early mulching, therefore, may be as harmful as too-late.

If mice are likely to cause damage the best plan may be to apply the mulch on top of an early snow in autumn, providing injuriously low temperatures have not occurred previously. When snow has covered the ground, mice usually have found winter quarters elsewhere than in the berry planting.

Depth of Mulch.—Apply dry, clean wheat straw several inches deep, both over and between the rows. A mulch 5.1 to 7.6 cm (2 to 3 in.) deep, when settled, requires about 6.7 metric tons of straw per ha (3 tons per acre). A clay soil subject to heaving needs a slightly heavier mulch than a lighter soil. A good mulch raked to between the rows aids in conserving moisture during growth and fruiting.

When baled straw or hay must be bought, the cost of the material is such that it may be necessary to reduce the amount applied. Too little mulch may shorten the picking period and result in small berries as well as in weakening of the roots. Where winters are milder than in the North, as in Tennessee, 3.36 to 4.5 metric tons of baled straw per ha (1½ to 2 tons per acre) is a good amount. The plants are partially visible through the mulch. Smothering may occur under too heavy a mulch in areas with mild winters.

Too heavy a covering is conducive to ice formation in the mulch; the ice layer tends to lower the temperature under the mulch and by doing so may defeat the purpose of the mulch as winter protection. To keep the mulch from blowing away in strong winds, long poles may be placed on top of it down the row.

Spreading straw by hand is slow work. It can be done fast and cheaply by an ensilage spreader. With a machine straw spreader having a capacity of 16 bales, two men can quickly cover an acre.

Weed Seeds.—Strawy manure may give good results, but it often contains weed seeds and may not keep the fruit as clean as wheat straw. If a field becomes weedy, yield is reduced and renovation for another crop is unlikely to be profitable.

Most new straw contains some grain seed that is likely to grow and become troublesome in spring. If the supply can be obtained a year before it is needed and is exposed to sun and rain, the grain seeds germinate and die. Shake new straw before it is used as a mulch. When using baled straw, thoroughly tear it apart and leave it in the rain and sun for several weeks before spreading; otherwise a weedy condition may result. Or, encourage weed-seed germination (especially wheat and cheat seeds) before applying the mulch by partly tearing open the bale of material, wetting it, and exposing it to the warmth of the sun. Bales of straw may be soaked for a week in a pond, then dried.

Removing the Mulch.—Remove the winter mulch in early spring after danger of severe frost is past but before there is much yellowing of the leaves. If the covering is thin, the plants grow up through it, though some shaking of the straw may be wise. But if the mulch is heavy, part it over the row with a fork, and push it into the alleys between the rows, tramp it down, and leave it there until after harvest. Remove the mulch from propagation rows earlier than from fruiting rows.

After the mulch is removed, cold weather may make it wise to cover the plants again for a short time. Where late ripening is desired, allow the mulch to remain on the plants somewhat later than usual. With this plan the leaves may become yellowish before the mulch is lifted. This is not usually desirable, but it delays the picking season and, in some cases, may offset the slight tendency to a temporary reduction in chlorophyll; of course, this should not be overdone. Windrow turning equipment and side-delivery rakes can be used for mulch removal.

When full winter protection is not provided, the chief objective is to apply straw mulch several weeks before bloom to protect the berries from dirt and so help them to be cleaner and brighter. Scatter the material over the beds, completely covering the plants, which may

FIG. 2.10.   STRAW BETWEEN THE ROWS OF PLANTS DURING THE FRUITING SEASON CONSERVES MOISTURE AND KEEPS THE BERRIES CLEAN

later be uncovered. If mulch is applied after the plants begin to bloom, do not cover the flowers and developing berries.

Mulching Fall Bearers.—Cultivate and hoe for the first two months after planting. When runners begin to form, cover the entire area around the plants and between the rows 2.5 cm (1 in.) deep with sawdust or chopped corncobs. Remove all flowers from the mother plants (during the planting year) until early July; ripe berries appear 3 to 4 weeks later. About 264 m³ of sawdust give a 2.54 cm layer over a hectare (140 cu yd give a 1 in. layer over an acre); maintain this depth.

Several systems of growing fall bearers mulched with sawdust have been tested in Ohio. When 7410 plants per ha (3000 plants per acre) are set 30.5 cm (1 ft) apart in triple rows, and 122 cm (4 ft) apart between centers, yields may average 40 to 60% higher in the first fall than when a single row of 27,170 plants per ha (11,000 plants per acre) is set out and a row of runner plants is established on each side, to make a total of 81,510 plants per ha (33,000 plants per acre), or than when fewer plants are set and more runners are trained in complete rows (Judkins 1950).

In Iowa, yields from a sawdust or chopped corncobs mulched 3-row system gave a higher net return than a 4-row system or matted rows not mulched for the late summer crop the first year. The original plants can be cropped three continuous years with comparatively high yields each year. Corncobs and sawdust differ little in effectiveness (Denisen *et al.* 1953).

Black Plastic Mulch

Several thousand acres of strawberries are grown in the annual hill system in Florida and Louisiana using black polyethylene mulch. Some advantages are: more vigorous plant growth, including periods when growth is often slow; higher yield; earlier ripening; reduced soil rot; hand weeding eliminated, except in the planting slits; more constant soil moisture; leaching of nutrients checked; washing down of beds avoided; cleaner fruit; less fruit cracking during wet periods; irrigation needs reduced.

Black plastic (1 or 1½ mil) comes in widths of 0.9, 1.2 and 1.8 m (3, 4 and 6 ft) or more, and 152 to 304 m (500 to 1000 ft) long in rolls. About half the growers form the beds and lay the plastic with a machine, then plant through the plastic by hand. Other growers apply the plastic and pull the plants through it. Some growers have constructed machines that lay the plastic and carry two men over the bed, where they can conveniently slit the plastic and pull the plants through (Locascio 1968).

Courtesy of S. J. Locasicio, University of Florida

FIG. 2.11.   STRAWBERRIES MULCHED WITH BLACK PLASTIC IN SOUTHERN FLORIDA

Apply the plastic to cover the top and sides of the raised beds. When transplanters are used, or difficulty is expected in plant survival, apply the plastic 1 to 4 weeks after transplanting.

Apply fertilizer after the beds are made up. Band it 35.6 to 38.1 cm (14 to 16 in.) deep in the center of the bed. Improper placement of the fertilizer may result in much damage. Both the fertilizer and a fumigant are applied before mulching with black plastic.

Biodegradable paper mulches with a polyethylene (PE) coating on both sides or with a single PE coating applied against the soil surface satisfactorily endures Florida's seven month growing season and gives fruit yields and fertilizer leaching results that compare well with black PE mulch, and it need not be removed from the field at season's end (Albregts and Howard 1972).

Clear Plastic Mulch

Clear polyethylene provides protection for strawberry plants by eliminating convection heat loss from the soil surface by reflection of soil heat back to the soil surface, and by maintaining a layer of insulating air over the plants. In contrast to straw mulch, clear polyethylene admits the sun's rays to the plant area, which adds heat to the enclosed system under the mulch and also provides energy for photosynthesis.

Mulching Winter Plantings.—Clear plastic mulch is applied in California within a few weeks after planting. Yields are increased 70% or more compared with no mulch. This is primarily a temperature effect. During the critical short-day period when flower-bud initiation takes place, soil temperatures are raised as much as 5°C (9°F) on clear polyethylene-mulched beds. Since the success of winter plantings depends on how much the plants grow in winter, the mulch must be used. When applied too late, the clear mulch actually reduces yield by stimulating runner production (Voth 1972).

Mulching Summer Plantings.—Over 90% of the summer plantings of about 2833 ha (7000 acres) in California is mulched. Pickers are reluctant to work in fields that are not mulched, especially when paid on an incentive basis.

The increase in production due to the plastic mulch is not as great as in winter plantings, but it does modify the production pattern favorably, increases fruit size and yield, and enhances earliness and fruit quality. The mulch is usually applied in January or February, depending on the area, plant size, planting date, and cold requirement of a given cultivar. If plants are under-developed or planted later than the recommended date, apply the mulch earlier, possibly even in November, as soon as runnering has ceased. But do not apply it early on properly timed plantings since yield and fruit size will be affected unfavorably (Voth 1972).

In California thousand of acres are fumigated annually with mixtures of methyl bromide-chloropicrin. Experiments on soil cropped 6 consecutive years with strawberries and fumigated 5 times with 2:1 mixture, 28 to 33 kg per ha (25 to 30 lb per acre), showed a yield increase of 25 to 30%, depending on the cultivar. This increase represents about 18 metric tons per ha (8 tons per acre) (Voth *et al.* 1971).

No Winter Mulch

Winter injury is a great limiting factor in strawberry production in southwestern British Columbia and northwestern Washington. The problem is accentuated by the susceptibility to cold and low fruit setting of the widely grown Northwest cultivar.

Mulching is not practiced in the region because of the high autumn and winter rainfall and the associated occurrence of crown diseases. Mulching is not advised in the Fraser Valley because the crop is washed before processing.

Two types of conditions may give rise to winter injury. The most severe yield losses occur from as low as $-23\,°C$ ($-10\,°F$) with little or no snow covering and frequent high winds. The second type of injury occurs after somewhat higher temperatures, which may range from $-9°$ to $-4\,°C$ ($15°$ to $25\,°F$) for varying lengths of time. The Northwest cultivar is particularly susceptible to injury from both conditions (Daubeny 1970).

Amount of crown injury increases with increasing rates of freezing, with the length of time the crowns remain frozen, and with repeated freezing and thawing. Rate of thawing increases the amount only when the rate is very rapid (Boyce and Smith 1967).

FERTILIZER

Basic Considerations

Conflicting experience on the role of fertilizers is to be expected since conditions vary with different regions, soils, years and many other factors.

In general, leaflets are best for indicating the status of N and Ca, the crown or leaflets best for P, the petiole for K, and the roots for Mg (Ballinger and Mason 1960).

Concentrations of Mn, Fe, B, and Cu show differences between leaflets and petioles. Leaf age has a profound influence on concentration of micro-elements which generally increase as leaf age advances.

Foliar analysis is a valuable tool in assessing the nutritional status of strawberry plants, but the interpretation of tissue analyses data requires an understanding of the many factors that influence chemical composition. While effects of cultural practices, climate, and soil are expected, tissue selected from sampling, leaf age, and physiological stage of growth also affect leaf composition.

Concentration of 13 major and minor elements in leaves and petioles of three strawberry cultivars were determined biweekly during the growing season. Concentration of most elements changed rapidly during flowering and fruiting. For most elements, leaf analysis was preferred since markedly greater concentration occurred in leaves than in petioles. Dates and tissue factors, and significant cultivar differences, must be considered in interpreting foliar analysis. Concentrations were relatively stable during the six weeks following harvest and this period seemed optimum for sampling (Jahn 1975).

Concentrations of macro- and minor-elements in the leaves of seven strawberry cultivars or selections (genotypes) were determined before flowering, at fruiting, and in the fall. Genotypic differences in nutrient concentration depend on sampling time, but genotype affected the levels of all 13 elements studied in leaves and the levels of Mg, S, Ca, Zn, Fe, Al, and Cu in petioles. There were effects of plant age on leaf concentration of some elements in 1- and 2-year representatives of 3 genotypes (John *et al.* 1976).

Practically all strawberry plantings benefit from application of fertilizer. In fact, a complete fertilizer is commonly applied to advantage when preparing the land for planting.

Fertilizer is not, as is often assumed, a cure-all. In the North, when the soil is reasonably fertile at the start, several factors, especially careful early planting in well-prepared soil, thrifty disease-tested plants, proper cultivars, adequate moisture, the quantity, quality, and time of applying the mulch, and weed and pest control may be as important as application of fertilizer. Later procedure may not be able to offset the lack of a good start for the plants.

It seems logical in a discussion of fertilizer to consider, as is done below, possible basic ways in which yield may be increased or a high yield made possible. The emphasis here is placed on systems in which much of the crop is produced on runners.

Suitable Cultivar.—Certain cultivars are inherently more productive than others in a given region. Fertilizer does not normally cause the yield of a low-yielding or a disease-susceptible cultivar to equal that of a high-yielding disease-tested one.

Fertilizer will not make a low-chilling cultivar succeed in the north, or a high-chilling cultivar succeed in the south.

Stand of Plants.—On a given area the number of fruit trees set at a certain spacing is not subject to increase, but with the strawberry in matted rows it is, because of the runners. A positive relation exists between number of runners rooted early and total number for the year. A primary aim is to encourage the plants to a good start after planting. Fertilizer does not necessarily make the yield from a given cultivar with a poor stand of plants, or a late-rooted stand, as high as that from the same cultivar with a good stand of early-rooted runners.

A wide row of plants does not in itself ensure a high yield. A larger number of comparatively narrow rows may more than compensate for wider rows spaced farther apart. In general, a good stand of plants is necessary for a high yield. Fertilizing does not guarantee a good stand of plants nor does it fully compensate for lack of a good stand.

Early Runners.—Two rows of plants that have received the same fertilizer treatment and appear equal in stand may vary greatly in their yield, if in one of these rows most runners rooted early and in the other they rooted late. Although more runners form late than early, yield may be about 14 times as great for a runner rooted in June than for one rooted in September or later.

TABLE 2.2

YIELD FROM RUNNERS ROOTED IN DIFFERENT MONTHS THE
PREVIOUS SEASON (PREMIER, OHIO)

Runners Rooted, Time	Number of Runners	Total Qt[3]	Yield per Plant, Qt
Parent Plant	375[1]	48.8	0.13
June	162	21.9	0.14
July	1989	79.0	0.06
August	3884	131.1	0.04
September-October 15[2]	1127	13.9	0.01
October 16-November	3375	23.2	0.009

Source: Shoemaker (1929).
[1] Original plants set out.
[2] Decrease in number of runners rooting due to drought.
[3] One quart (dry) is equal to 1.1 liters.

Since the yield from 1 plant rooted early may be equal to that from 14 plants rooted late, fertilizer would indeed have to cause a marked response to help a late runner to overcome its handicap. Weak runners, rooted late in the year, are "weeds" using the soil moisture and nutrients that are needed by the earlier-formed plants to develop and mature their buds and build up an adequate food reserve for fruit production.

Mother and oldest daughter plants have the largest carbohydrate reserves throughout the growing and are the most productive.

In matted or spaced rows, encourage the formation, rooting, and development of early runners. Several factors are highly influential in this respect, probably more so than fertilizer.

Fruit Buds.—Increased yield and higher earlier pickings may result from N applied near the start of fruit-bud formation. Although an increase in number of fruit buds is often an effect of fertilizer, other factors may be more important in the average planting, e.g., with the same number of plants in 2 given rows, if in 1 of these rows the runner rooted early and in the other they rooted late, there will be more fruit buds per plant in the first row.

A large plant does not necessarily result in a high yield. Certain cultivars make large plants but produce low yields. Also, too vigorous growth may be at the expense of yield. Thus too much as well as too little growth may reduce yield.

Yield is influenced by number of flower clusters and number of flowers that form fruits, i.e., by nutritive conditions at fruit-bud formation time.

Highest yield may result from N applied a month after planting and again in late summer. It stimulates fruit-bud formation and increases top and root growth. Applying N in early spring of the fruiting year to vigorous plants may cause a lower yield during the first half of the picking season but a slightly higher yield during later pickings. Spring application may promote darker-green leaves, slower picking, larger berries during the later part of the season, and more rot. Proper timing of fertilizer application is important.

Flower Clusters and Set of Fruit.—Fertilizer, particularly on soils low in N, may increase the number of flowers and set of fruit. But it is doubtful that an increase in set of bloom on a fair to poor stand compensates for a normal set on a good stand of plants. Total set may be increased 5% by an application of N before bloom.

Size of Fruit.—A good index to berry size is obtained by weighing lots of 20 berries from 2 replications for a total of 6 picking dates. The variability of berry size associated with harvest date is of such magnitude that generalized size comparisons are not as reliable as comparisons made at specific harvest dates (Janick and Eggert 1968).

When cultivars mature in different sequence it is difficult to compare them directly unless each cultivar is sampled at each picking. If this is done, it is possible to evaluate size directly throughout the season and calculate a yield-size relation. It is suggested to report the yield of berries averaging a minimum of 6.4 g (100 berries or fewer per qt) as well as total yield (Hill and Alban 1963).

Picking Period.—The effect from irrigation may be greater than that of fertilizer on extending the picking period, but there is a response from both practices.

Growth Status.—The response from fertilizer depends greatly on the condition or growth status. During a certain year the plants may respond to a given fertilizer in one way, but the next year a similar response may be made to abundant rainfall without any fertilizer.

Some Interactions.—Initial plant uptake of P fertilizer is enhanced when N fertilizer is applied directly in contact with phosphate. Proliferation of plant roots in the phosphate zone is increased by N and N/P interaction. Concentrating P fertilizer in bands reduces soil contact and decreases fixation of soluble phosphates by active aluminum and iron in the soil (Grunes 1959; Miller and Ohlrogge 1958).

Effect on Firmness.—Old-timers claimed that bone meal, largely because of its P, was the best fertilizer to produce firm berries. The fact that berries have long been shipped from the South to distant markets and that large amounts of P fertilizer are supplied may indicate a positive relation between P and firmness.

Claims that N fertilizer makes the fruit softer assume importance in cultural work and in marketing, particularly because higher yields are often possible from N applications and because strawberries are highly perishable. If increased N in the fruit promotes greater respiration intensity, application of P might reduce the intensity by lessening the N intake.

Water, especially heavy rain, may affect the firmness of berries more than fertilizer.

Total N in the berries increases with increased rates of applied N; titratable acidity in the fruit decreases with increased K rate; K level and titratable acidity in the fruit increase, whereas shear resistance of the fruit is not changed, although the compression resistance tends to be reduced with increased rates of K and of N. Various sources of K, i.e., K_2SO_4, KNO_3, and KCl, have little differential effect on quality of fresh fruit. The correlation is poor between various quality factors and fruit content of N, K, and Ca. Titratable acidity in the fruit and fruit content of K have the highest coefficient of correlation (Saxana 1968).

A relation may not necessarily exist between moisture content of a cultivar and suitability for shipping. For example, the firm-fleshed Blakemore ranks high in moisture content; Suwanee, a home-garden cultivar with soft berries, may be low in moisture content. A decrease in moisture content may occur between first and last pickings.

Organic Matter.—In a survey in southern Indiana of 63 plantings by M. McCown, yields ranged from 116 to 939 (24 qt) crates per ha (47 to 380 per acre). The 20 leading growers produced 623 to 939 crates per ha (252 to 380 per acre), averaging 739 crates per ha (299 per acre). In preparing the soil for planting, 4 of them each plowed under 45 metric tons of manure per ha (20 tons per acre); 2 plowed under cover crops; 2 plowed under heavy sod and grew corn 1 year before planting berries; 1 planted on new ground; and 1 plowed under manure before sowing wheat which was turned under the next year. Of the growers in the lowest-yielding group (116 to 168 crates per ha, or 47 to 68 crates per acre), 1 used 3.7 loads of manure per ha (1.5 loads per acre) in preparing the soil; 2 had plowed down 2 cover crops, but 2 intensive crops preceding the berries had benefited from them before the berries had their chance; and 1 plowed down orchard grass. Growers in the lowest-yielding group averaged 77% less crop than those in the highest group.

If 2 or more crops are to be picked from the planting, more organic matter in the soil is usually needed than for only 1 crop. The amount should not be excessive for the first crop and a fairly slow rate of decomposition or availability is desirable. Soils that contain more than 2½% organic matter usually supply sufficient N for a good berry crop, but the optimum percentage varies on different sites.

Chemical Composition

Analysis of eight cultivars gave the following averages: total sugars 10.0%; soluble solids 7.0%; insoluble solids 3.3%; titratable acidity 0.78%; total astringency 0.35%; tannin 0.20%; non-tannin 0.14% (Culpepper *et al.* 1935.)

Chemical composition is influenced by absorption of water and accumulation of sugar. These two processes are usually affected in their relative activity more by weather than by fertilizer. Cultivars may be grouped as: (1) low sugar, low acid, low astringency; (2) low sugar, low acid, high astringency; (3) medium sugar, high acid, medium astringency; and (4) high sugar, low acid, low astringency. The third group most nearly approaches the ideal chemical composition for processing.

The red color of strawberries is due to an anthocyanin pigment, pelergonin monoglucoside, which also occurs in carnations and some other flowers. Fresh fruit ranks fairly high in vitamin C; 50 to 90 mg per 100 g of fresh fruit.

Seven seedling populations of strawberry were analyzed for ascorbic acid content and color intensity. The amount and type of variation found showed both characters to be controlled by quantitative genes. It is postulated that two genetic systems control the inheritance of ascorbic acid and that the systems can interact with each other. Partial dominance was exhibited for high color intensity. Heritability estimates of 41% for ascorbic acid and 81% for color intensity were obtained. Flesh color and ascorbic acid content were not correlated characters (Lundergan and Moore 1975).

RENOVATING PLANTINGS

Strawberry plantings that are vigorous and reasonably free of weeds often are carried over for another year's crop. Cost of renovating is usually less than the cost of setting and caring for a new planting. The second crop ripens earlier than the first crop but the production period may be shorter.

Strawberry plants usually enter a stage of arrested activity toward the end of harvest. At this time very little new leaf or runner development occurs, many of the feeder roots die, and new root production is sparse.

Removal of Mulch

The tops of the plants may be mowed soon after harvest, e.g., with a rotary mower, high enough to avoid injury to the crowns. Mowing, provided the mowings are removed from the field, or burned, partially controls leaf-spot diseases.

Some claim that mowing, or otherwise removing the tops and old leaves, is a sanitary process for the beds, that growth is stimulated, and that further renewal is facilitated. Others claim that removing healthy foliage checks plant development.

Within certain limits at least, the smaller the leaf surface the greater is the transpiration per unit of leaf area. If part of the leaf area is removed the remaining leaves may transpire more water than they otherwise would. Also, stomata on plants in which the leaf area has been reduced may be open more of the time and function more effectively in photosynthesis than do stomata on many-leaved plants. After harvest, therefore, a relatively small amount of new foliage may be as efficient as a larger amount of old foliage.

Two-year-old plants have more leaves per plant at the end of the growing season and produce more flowers and fruits than new runners formed after renewal of the bed. The second crop on undisturbed plots often may be larger than on renewed plots.

Cutting off leaves or topping plants immediately after harvest is often done in the Pacific Northwest to control leaf spot, to reduce the leaf surface to lessen the loss of water during dry summers, and to control crown borers. Delayed topping after harvest decreases the yield the next year. Careless mowing may damage the crowns, and it may not cut off all the tops.

Burning Over the Planting

The old practice of burning over the planting soon after harvest has largely been abandoned, but some northern growers have persisted with this practice, or have returned to it. Do not burn until the mowed foliage and mulch are relatively dry, but the soil moist, and until there is enough breeze to sweep the blaze quickly across the field. To encourage quick passage of the fire, loosely scatter some dry straw across the field.

Novices often are unduly alarmed by the first appearance of a burned-over planting, but damage seldom is serious in matted rows if a good rain or irrigation follows soon after burning. Should the burning be done during a prolonged drought, the plants may be damaged unless irrigated. Some mulches are difficult to burn properly and some cultivars are more sensitive to heat than others.

Narrowing the Rows

In general, narrow the rows only to the width desired for picking, or a few inches more. Runner formation usually is not extensive after mowing.

Narrowing from One Side.—A plow may be used to narrow the rows from one side; a harrow or cultivator then levels the soil and tears out most buried plants. Many growers claim that the results are not commensurate with the cost.

A sharp grape hoe is useful for narrowing the rows after the mulch has been removed. About 30% of the same side of the row is sliced off 3.8 cm (1½ in.) deep to lay up the plants so that they may be gathered more readily than after plowing.

Narrowing Both Sides.—The rows are narrowed slightly from both sides and the plants left in the middle. Large rototillers (rotavators) will easily incorporate the straw, plants, and weeds between rows. Take care, by proper arrangement of the blades and/or by using shields, that the tiller does not throw a lot of soil on the plants in the row.

Some growers use a paraquat spray to kill weeds and strawberry runners in the alleys. Shields must be used to keep the spray off the plant row. With this method, the alleys are not cultivated and the straw mulch is left in place. This is a relatively fast and inexpensive renovation procedure and, by not working the alleys, there is little germination of new weed seeds. A second application of paraquat is usually required in the fall, for runner plant and weed control. Following irrigation the planting is handled like a first year planting (Ricketson *et al.* 1976).

Rows Not Narrowed

If renovation cannot be undertaken until it is too late to do more than make a narrow pathway between the rows, the plants may simply be thinned in the row or not thinned at all. Since the number of plants for fruiting the next year is reduced less than with "narrowing" systems, it may result in the highest yield.

In North Carolina, plants left to fruit for a second year may give higher yields than beds plowed to a narrow bar after the first crop. Two-year-old matted-row beds may yield 1½ times as much as beds that are renovated immediately after the first crop.

Some growers in southern Illinois first cover the old rows with soil by plowing or disking, then eradicate surplus plants by cross-harrowing and at the same time work fresh soil around the remaining plants.

Thinning Plants

Thinning reduces crowded conditions in the row, removes old plants, and affords opportunity for plants that are to fruit the next year to grow large and more productive. Thinning in renovation follows fruiting, and so the thinning is somewhat different than during the planting years.

When plants are crowded, early-thinned rows show advantages over unthinned or those in which thinning is delayed after renovation, provided the most productive types of plants are left and inferior ones removed. But under unfavorable conditions, better results may be obtained by leaving the rows with a later or reduced amount of thinning, or even without thinning.

Fertilizing and Cultivating

The kind and amount of fertilizer to apply when renovating plantings depend on the soil, the age, vigor, and stand of plants, the cultivar, the region, and other factors. A complete fertilizer is usually best.

HARVESTING

Strawberries are usually marketed in 1-qt, 1-pt, or ½-pt baskets (also called boxes, cups, hallocks, or tills). The U.S. Standard Container Act provides for three legal sizes of baskets (qt, pt, and ½ pt) based on dry measure, but not fixed standard dimensions, for interstate shipment. The U.S. quart is 20% smaller than the Canadian quart (a U.S. dry quart equals 1.1 liters).

Plastic containers have largely superseded wooden baskets in many regions. Paper pulp baskets have also assumed importance.

For many years the 24-qt basket crate was used. Use of 1-layer trays, especially the 8- or 12-qt capacity, have become popular for fresh markets and shipping. This container can be stacked 10 high at the farm or market.

Tests have shown little difference in time required to cool fruit in wood and paper baskets, compared with plastic baskets (Voth 1972).

Production Period

At Wooster, Ohio, a wheat straw mulch (11.2 metric tons per ha, or 5 tons per acre) in a first-crop planting was removed April 23; the plants began to bloom on May 11, were in full bloom on May 23, and the first picking was made on June 6. The winter was mild, severe spring frosts did not occur, and the "spring season" was somewhat later than usual. Corresponding dates for an adjacent second crop were April 19, May 9, May 21, and June 5.

In Louisiana the production period is 6 to 9 weeks. Counts of bloom in the field are useful for crop forecasting. Lowest interval for maturing of blooms for any cultivar and season could be 18 days compared with the highest of 41 days. For a three year period, average number of blooms matures in fewer than 24 days. A great increase in harvest occurs in the next 4 day period, particularly in the 24 to 26 day interval, or within 5 days, compared to the average of 16.6 days for all blooms (Wilson and Gimalva 1954).

Stage of Ripeness

Berries do not improve in quality after picking. Marketing insufficiently colored berries is not conducive to good quality. Berries picked immediately after reaching full color stand shipment for reasonably long journeys. Those that have stood in the field 24 hr or more after reaching good color may not ship well.

When berries that are greenish-white up to 10% pink are exposed to 29°C (85°F), full color may result in 48 hr. About 90% of full color may develop at 18°C (65°F) after 96 hr. At 13°C (55°F) good color may not develop. A low light intensity of 25 ft-candles slightly increases speed and degree of coloration at high temperature. Light has little effect at 13°C (55°F). Soluble solids content of berries ripened in the dark compares favorably with that of field-ripened fruits (Austin *et al.* 1960).

Berries picked 50% colored may be slightly smaller than those picked 75% colored. The flavor of half-colored fruit ripened at 21°C (70°F) is slightly lower in non-sweetened berries, but adding sugar to the ripened berries eliminates flavor differences. Quarter-ripened berries ripened at 21°C (70°F) are about equal in color to those picked with more color, but are slightly poorer in texture and flavor, and are smaller.

Berries picked when 75% red will develop full red color in 1 to 2 days at 21°C (70°F) and do not differ appreciably in flavor and size from fully ripened berries. Berries harvested when 50% red or less will also develop full red color but are poorer in flavor and texture and are smaller than berries 75% red. Growers who harvest berries that do not meet U.S. No. 1 grade for color sacrifice both quality and size.

It may be possible to pick at an earlier stage of development than is used commercially without having much effect on color, texture, or flavor if the berries are ripened and sweetened prior to use. In U.S. No. 1 Grade, strawberries must have not less than 75% of the surface showing pink or red. Therefore berries picked 50% colored may not meet U.S. No. 1 standards. Picking at an earlier stage should take into account the slight loss in size, the need to ripen the berries before use, and the risk of some decay while ripening. Subsequent handling, refrigeration, and transit conditions also have a bearing on the importance of the red color at harvest. When berries tend to be especially soft, e.g., during rainy seasons, growers would have a little more leeway in reducing losses if they could pick at an earlier stage (Smith and Heinze 1958).

Pickers and Picking

The number of pickers needed varies with their efficiency, the crop, and the method of harvesting. With a crop of 16,309 liters per ha (6000 qt per acre), about 20 pickers working daily should handle an acre. In warm weather, with higher yields, and at the peak period more are needed. Many growers employ enough pickers to complete picking before noon in order to avoid the heating of berries in full sun. Pickers work most efficiently during the cool part of the day. When the picking is fairly heavy at each picking it is easier to obtain good pickers.

As discussed elsewhere in the text, mechanical picker aids and machine harvesting have an important role in reducing the labor in harvesting.

For fresh market, leave the caps and about 12 mm (½ in.) of stem on the berry when picking. Pinch the stem close to the cap with thumb and forefinger. When hand-picking for processing, hold the stem and cap with the forefinger of one hand and pull off the berries with a slight twist of the other hand.

Most pickers are paid by piecework, though some may be paid by the hour or day. The punch-card system, like the book, check, or cash, has drawbacks as well as merits. Piecework pickers are inclined to pick where the berries are thickest, to leave the scattered fruit, and to fill the baskets without due regard to proper care. Pickers paid by the hour may not work as fast as they should. A common rate of paying is 20% of what the grower receives per unit of fruit. Sometimes 1¢ or so is retained to hold the pickers until harvest is over.

Those growers who depend largely on migrant labor during strawberry harvest should become familiar with any legal requirements.

Berries crush easily and then are not attractive as fresh-market fruit. Pick and discard overripe and unsound berries from the plants (such berries should not be left in the field even though worthless) to keep them from getting into later pickings and from spreading rot and mold. Hold only a few berries in the hand at a time. Berries decay quickly if overripe, or if they become soft or bruised in packing and handling. Berries picked on a rainy day may not keep well, but a little dew may not seriously reduce their keeping quality. Place berries in a cool place to delay deterioration.

Good supervision of pickers is important. Instruct them regarding the stage of ripeness or color, clean picking, sorting while picking, disposition of baskets, where to pick, and other details. Provide carriers or trays with handles that hold 4, 6, or 8 qt baskets, or 8 to 12 pt, for the pickers. Assign rows to pickers and thus check their work. Working between rows and picking half the row on either side may reduce damage to the plants and unpicked berries.

Shelter Shed

Keep picked berries out of the sun, wind, and dust. A shelter shed, even a structure with simply a roof and a wall on one side of the prevailing wind, often is an advantage. Locate it where pickers have a minimum walk when bringing in berries and so that it can be reached easily by truck. More than one shed may be needed in large plantings. A portable shed may be useful, or several shelters can be placed in different locations.

FIG. 2.12.   USEFUL SHELTER SHED

A ventilated picking lug developed in Michigan is adapted as a picking carrier for holding berries in bulk for processing and for fresh-market berries. It has a removable metal handle in an upright fashion which fits into grooves in the ends and a design which allows good ventilation.

Temperature

The length of time that berries keep after picking depends on the cultivar, degree of ripeness, care in handling, and temperature when they are picked and kept. For each rise of 8°C (15°F), the life of berries, other things being equal, is decreased 50%; i.e., if berries will keep for 8 days at 4°C (40°F), they will keep for only 1 day at 29°C (85°F). Berries picked in early morning while cool and placed at once in the shade, or precooled, keep longer and look better on the market than those picked at midday when they are warmer or left in the sun.

The temperature of the air and the berries at 6 a.m. may be much the same. By 9 a.m. there may be a decided difference. The difference is greatest about noon, though nearly as great from 12 to 4 p.m.

Picking is often continued into the heat of the day. If late-picked berries are to be kept overnight in a shelter shed, take special precautions with them. They are warmer than those picked earlier. If baskets filled with warm berries are placed in crates as they come from the field, only the top layer may cool sufficiently in a shed to prevent mold and other damage. It may be wise to let the berries stand uncovered in the cool shade of the shed or a tree until the temperature of the fruit becomes nearer the night temperature, or to use single-layer trays. Failure to precool is often the cause of shipped berries arriving on the market in unsalable condition.

Respiration

The life of strawberries after harvest is short owing to a relatively high rate of respiration. However, a high rate on a fresh-weight basis is often associated with firm berries of good shipping quality. Firm cultivars are high in total solids percent and their high respiratory rate is related to the large amount of respirable material per unit of fresh weight. The rate increases about 50% from the immature to the mature stage. Respiratory rate is 13 times as great at 26.7°C (80°F) as at 0°C (32°F) (Haller 1941).

Precooling

Strawberries arrive at markets in better condition if precooled at 4°C (40°F) within two hours and kept at this temperature. This is especially true during warm weather when fruit is picked during the heat of the day and fruit temperatures are 26.7°C (80°F) or higher. (See precooling and refrigerated shipping of strawberries from California.)

Storage

Short storage (2 to 3 days) at 12.6°C (55°F) results in little sweating after removal; temperatures below 12.8°C (55°F) may promote sweating. But berries stored for 7 days at −1.1°C (30°F) may show little ripening or breakdown and still be attractive after remaining at room temperature for 6 hr. Berries stored at 12.8°C (55°F) for 6 hr (often the storage time from picking to shipping) and then exposed to room temperature for 18 hr (includes the time in warehouse and retail store) may still make a good retail pack.

Probably the ideal holding temperature for fresh strawberries is 0.6° to 1.1°C (33° to 34°F). Berries keep better for 4 days at 4°C (40°F) than for 2 days at 21.1°C (70°F); weight loss and decay are less, and the berries are more attractive. Sprays of Ca salts may increase berry firmness (Eaves and Leefe 1962).

For maximum storage of fresh strawberries, keep the temperature below 4°C (40°F) to avoid rot. After 10 days, usually sooner, the fruit loses its fresh bright color, shrivels somewhat, and deteriorates in flavor. Good relative humidity is 85 to 90%.

Sodium dehydroacetate (Harven) has been used to stop mold in baskets of berries in storage for shipment at 0.6° to 2.8°C (33° to 37°F). Berries in pint baskets dipped in Harven (1 to 37 dilution in water) may keep for 8 days without molding and with only a low percentage of mold after 16 days. Besides mold control Harven may impart a glossy coating that persists during storage life and tends to delay breakdown slightly (Moore and Oberle 1961).

Berries sprayed with NaDHA for 60 sec and stored dry have a longer shelf-life. Decreased respiration of treated fruits is attributed to the fungicidal property of NaDHA or the inhibitory effect of the chemical on a respiratory enzyme of the fruit. A 0.5% solution may retard ripening (Watada 1971).

Exposing fresh strawberries to a low dosage of gamma rays generated by cobalt-60 can prolong shelf-life and reduce spoilage to about 5%. Similar results can be obtained with X-rays. It is estimated that savings from reduced spoilage losses in marketing could more than pay for radiation, or pasteurization, as this process is called. Unfortunately, the normal good flavor does not persist.

Grading and Packing

Grading in the field tends toward a minimum of handling but requires close supervision and a crop of good quality and condition. Grading at a field shelter or packing shed may consist of pouring berries

FIG. 2.13. PAN METHOD OF SORTING AND INSPECTING FIRM STRAWBERRIES

from one basket to another and removing culls.

In the pan method of sorting, empty each basket into a tin grading pan and remove defective berries as the fruit is gently poured back into the basket. Pull out the sides of the basket slightly and shake gently to allow the berries to settle; do not bounce the basket up and down. A useful grading pan is 25.4 to 27.9 cm (10 to 11 in.) long, 22.9 cm (9 in.) wide, and 4.4 cm (1¾ in.) deep. It can be made by a local tinsmith. For a smooth edge, bend back an extra ¼ in. around the longest sides.

Large growers may run the fruit over a belt, grade it, and then jumble-pack into 12-pint cardboard trays which can conveniently be stacked for precooling and marketing.

Standardized grades, properly and consistently used, promote honesty and fair dealing, and discourage careless and unscrupulous packing. They provide a common language with which to describe quality, maturity, size, condition, and other factors that determine the value of a given shipment. They serve as a convenient, fair, and understandable basis for inspection at shipping points and in receiving markets, for price quotations, for sales, for adjustment of claims, and for cooperative pooling.

In the major shipping areas inspectors sample the crates, cartons, or trays of berries delivered to assembly points and grade according to quality standards in terms of U.S. No. 1, U.S. No. 2, and Unclassified. Certificates describing the quality, condition, grade, pack, and any other important factors relating to the various lots of fruit for which inspection is requested are issued by licensed inspectors, and are generally accepted as a basis for buying and selling, and in settlement of allowances, claims, or rejections.

Properly filled baskets should be neither slack nor so full that berries will be crushed by covers or dividers. Baskets should be full enough to look attractive and to maintain a well-filled appearance for the consumer. Baskets in the lower layers should be well filled.

Weight loss is least in completely overwrapped baskets, intermediate with a film cap, and highest in open tops. A film cap reduces weight loss to 50% or less of that in open tops. Moistureproof films are most effective in reducing weight losses; non-moistureproof film is least effective. Weight loss is greatest in open-mesh plastic retail consumer baskets. Decay is slightly lower in film-overwrapped than in capped baskets and is lowest in open tops.

Berries in polyethylene-overwrapped baskets have more decay than with some other films. Little difference occurs in decay in various pint baskets. Berries wrapped with film, either as caps or overwraps, are better in appearance than those in open tops. A semi-moistureproof film cap reduces moisture loss and does not cause excessive condensation. With 1.0-mil ($\frac{1}{1000}$ in.) polyethylene crate liners stored at 4°C (40°F), a high build-up of CO_2 and nearly complete depletion of O_2 causes the berries to ferment. With thinner liners the atmosphere around the berries is not enough to affect the quality (Anderson and Hardenburg 1959).

A crate of strawberries is a closed package in that all its contents cannot be seen readily or inspected after such a package is prepared for market. A producer may find himself liable for fulfillment of the standardization law.

Baskets often are face-packed, which consists of placing berries in the top layer on their sides, all pointed one way, or placing each berry in the top layer with the stems down. Facing makes an attractive package and may be desirable provided the extra labor is warranted by the selling price.

Usually the fresh fruit trade prefers berries not less than 19 mm (¾ in.) in diameter. Do not pack baskets of generally small berries in crates that contain mostly larger berries. Do not mix cultivars in carrier containers, since this practice results in variable appearance and differences in carrying quality.

Besides the "U.S. Standards for Strawberries" that reach the consumer in fresh form, there are "U.S. Standards for Growers' Stock Strawberries for Manufacture" and "U.S. Standards for Washed and Sorted Strawberries for Freezing" for processing.

Pick-your-own Berries (PYO)

Shortage of labor and competition from distant areas forced many growers to adopt the pick-your-own method of harvesting. Customers drive to the planting and may supply their own containers when sales are made by weight. In some cases baskets may be obtained from the grower and used as the unit of sale. Many regard the opportunity to pick berries as an outing in the country.

Savings in costs of picking, packaging, and delivery to market may be passed on to the customer through the PYO method, and this method has greatly increased in recent years. It does not entirely replace a state's commercial crop, but it now accounts for an appreciable percentage of the total crop. Also, more strawberry plantings occur because of the PYO method.

In Wisconsin, in ten years PYO increased from 10% to 90% of the commercial crop from 809 ha (2000 acres). The plantings ranged upward from a few acres and were usually 2 to 4 ha (5 to 10 acres). In a 36 ha (90 acre) planting at Bristol on the last Saturday in June the grower checked out 1467 customers, and more than 1000 on July 4. He had as many as 12 supervisors in the field, 8 scales, and 2 cash registers at the check-out stand. Sales were by the pound (Gilbert 1968; McConnell 1973).

For the 10,873 liters per ha (4000 qt per acre) producer, profits from PYO sales at 27.5¢ per liter (25¢ per qt) may be $326 per ha ($132 per acre) greater than the wholesale markets at 38.5¢ per liter (35¢ per qt). With a higher yield, the advantage of PYO sales may be greater.

Average amounts picked by customers in Illinois were: less than 11 liters (10 qt), 21%; 11 to 33 liters (10 to 30 qt), 46.4%; 33 to 55 liters (30 to 50 qt), 19.5%; more than 55 liters (50 qt), 13.0%. Chief uses made of the berries were: freezing, 61.4%; fresh use, 28.3%; preserves, 9.6%; other, 7.0% (Courter and Zych 1971).

Location and Site

A location near large urban populations is best, but customers may travel 40 km (25 mi.) or more when they are assured of picking their supply of berries. Various methods of informing customers can be used to provide directions to the planting and to indicate when picking can be done. Allow adequate space for parking; uncontrolled parking may cause confusion.

Supervision

Before customers begin picking, the grower should inform them of the "ground rules"—prices, where and how to pick, and other significant matters. The rules should be posted.

One or more supervisors who can manage people and maintain row control are essential. Customers should not pick just anywhere in the field. The assigned area should be picked clean of ripe berries. Rotate the area to be picked, e.g., ½ may be picked each day to ensure ripe berries every day.

Many pickers are tempted to eat some berries as they pick, without paying extra. The loss may or may not offset the desirability of such pickers by making an issue of the matter.

Wider than normal spacing may be desirable to accommodate inexperienced pickers.

Prices

The prices charged should be made clear to the consumer at the outset; otherwise unnecessary bargaining may result later. Selling by weight eliminates the problem of over-filled or non-uniform containers; and customers can bring their own containers. A U.S. quart of strawberries weighs about 0.7 kg (1.5 lb); a gallon contains about 3.8 liters (3.5 qt). One price through the season is generally best. Changing prices may confuse customers from one picking to the next. Some growers charge more for the first picking (larger size, lower yield, and large crowd), and less for the last, clean-up pickings. PYO price should be lower than local retail prices.

Since prices are in cash, a definite place should be set up for an orderly checkout system which is fair and uncomplicated. The operator should have a plentiful supply of change on hand. Weighing should be done in full view of the customer and the scale must be accurate.

The use of a table and cash box has merit for even the smallest operation. For a large operation one or more cash registers may be essential. The records provided can be valuable for income tax purposes and for making business decisions.

Some basic rules for persons handling cash are: (1) Accept the money from the customer and lay it in full view of yourself and the customer. (2) Count out the change in your hand. (3) Recount the change into the customer's hand. (4) Wait until the customer is satisfied with the accuracy of the change and puts it away. (5) Then put the customer's money in the till (Vandenberg 1971).

In some cases the customer may offer to "pick on the halves," whereby half the quantity picked is kept as payment for picking the other half. The grower may be glad to have some picked berries on hand for sale.

Advertising, Insurance, and Other Considerations

Promotion is an important part of success with PYO, as are satisfied customers. Timely and carefully planned advertising is essential. All advertising methods may be used effectively—signs, newspapers, radio, TV, and direct mail. Long telephone conversations should be avoided.

Washrooms and good drinking water should be available, as should shade where picked berries can be placed. Some growers provide cold drinks for sale.

Many problems test the ingenuity of growers. There are as many good ideas and innovations as there are PYO operations.

PICKER POSITIONERS

The Moving Platform Method is adapted to the Solid-Bed method of culture, as discussed earlier. Excellent pickers have picked 16.5 to 27.5 more liters (15 to 25 more qt) per hr when working on a machine. In one comparison, an attendant supplied empty boxes and removed full ones when the pickers were working both on and off the machine. Normally, pickers spend considerable time taking containers to a packing shelter. When this lost picking time is considered, the increased picking rates obtained on a machine would be even higher than indicated.

Besides increased picking rates, which mean higher pay, working on a machine has several other advantages: fewer pickers are required, pickers can be kept in the shade continuously, there is no crushing of berries along the sides of the rows, and picking can even be done at night if lights are provided (Ricketson 1966).

For best results, rows should be uniform and pickers should have nearly equal picking ability. Machines should not be too large, probably large enough for 6 to 10 pickers. In solid-bed plantings, machines can be considerably larger, since selection of pickers with nearly equal ability is not critical. Faster pickers can be placed beside slower ones and allowed to pick a wider strip.

MACHINE-HARVESTING

The material which follows sets forth some of the early work in developing machine pickers.

Iowa Developments

The aim has been as follows: (a) concentrate ripening fruit with plantings established on beds with a minimum of ridging, the plants being closely arranged to support the fruit trusses. The necessary mulch for over-wintering is removed by a side-delivery rake in spring. (b) A fine corncob mulch is applied to retain moisture and prevent splash, and to keep the berries off the soil. The mulch is carefully leveled over the beds and wheel rows. (c) For a 76 cm (30 in.) picker head, make 71 cm (28 in.) beds on 92 cm (40 in.) centers for vehicles not wider than 132 cm (52 in.) across the rows. Beds are narrowed several weeks before harvest and wheel rows mowed and leveled. (d) Within the week prior to machine stripping, primary berries are hand-picked for the fresh market. (e) Just before machine harvest the upper leaves on the rows are mowed; the mower may be mounted on the picker itself (Quick and Denisen 1970).

Some further considerations are: (a) Of paramount importance to the success of any mechanical picking assembly is the need to stay below the fruit for maximum recovery. Any time fruit is left behind with certain machines, it is generally because the machine has been angled or raised so that the teeth ran above the fruit, with subsequent damage. (b) The beds need to be machine-prepared at all stages prior to harvest, with the harvest operation in mind. (c) The machine should have a built-in automatic height controller, so that the height of the picking teeth can be determined with precision. Most of the fruit damage occurs at the tips of the picking teeth; thus a soft or blunt tooth may reduce the damage.

Iowa State University (Denisen and co-workers) has obtained at least four patents on the various ideas or developments that have been generated from mechanical handling of strawberries. The latest innovation is the use of vinyl-coated rotating augers which harvest the ripe berries with a minimum of injury.

The basic design of an Iowa State self-propelled harvester (1962) consists of 16 scoops on a chain drive, cam and cam follower, chain and sprocket assembly, and supporting frame. The principle involved is a stripping action as the tines of the scoops are elevated through the foliage. The tines are curved slightly to facilitate entry into the bed and to prevent harvested berries from rolling off. The scoops are tripped above a collection box. Removal of the foliage with a rotary mower facilitates harvesting (Denisen and Buchele 1967).

Plastic or fiber-mesh netting placed over the beds before growth of leaves and inflorescence begins permits leaves and fruit to develop above the netting. The prototype machine developed for the system mows off leaves, raises the netting, cuts off the pedicels supported on the netting, and delivers the fruit to a conveyor and bulk box before rolling up the netting for storage. The harvester can readily be adapted to most conventional garden tractor designs. There is a sizable reduction in amount of injury to fruit compared with earlier designs (Stang and Denisen 1971).

An ideal netting should have the following properties: (a) firm fabric with sufficient flexibility to pass over 7.6 to 10.2 cm (3 to 4 in.) rollers; (b) heavy strands (40 mil [$^{40}/_{1000}$ in.] or greater) to reduce fruit bruising and cutting as the net is lifted; (c) mesh size of 19 to 24 mm (¾ to 1 in.) to permit emergence of leaves and inflorescences before full development occurs; (d) capability of withstanding weathering and machine stress (maintaining flexibility and strength) for at least three fruiting seasons (Stang and Denisen 1971).

High plant populations with subsequent competition could possibly further increase natural thinning by flower abortions and promote uniform or more concentrated ripening (Stang and Denisen 1967).

With machine harvest there may be a trend toward smaller berries (Denisen and Buchele 1967).

Arkansas Developments

The Sunrise cultivar has been outstanding in both concentration of ripening and total yield. Both total and acceptable yields are reduced by single harvests compared with multiple-harvester control. Highest yields of acceptable fruit from single harvests are obtained when the harvest is made during the second week of the ripening season, although the average size of acceptable fruit is larger when the harvest is made earlier (Moore and Brown 1970).

The machine performs three basic functions: fruit is (1) stripped from the plants, (2) separated from the leaves and other foreign material, and (3) conveyed to transporting containers. Since most of the mature fruit lies directly on the ground, a unique picking device lifts the fruit from the ground without disturbing the soil surface or damaging the berries (Morris 1972).

The basic components are a comb-brush stripping mechanism, a pneumatic system, and a conveying and collecting system. During the picking operation, high-velocity air lifts the fruit from ground level to a position above and in front of the comb-brush stripping mechanism in the picking chamber. Moving on a continuous belt, the comb-brush mechanism strips the fruit from the plants and conveys it to an air-lock valve; then the fruit is deposited in suitable containers.

Besides setting up the fruit for the combs, the high-velocity air flowing through the conveyor partially separates the fruit from leaves and other foreign matter. A cleaner (conventional blower) and a continuous sizer have been mounted as an integral part of the 1973 commercial model harvester.

Oregon

The "Stripper" is a full-row, self-propelled unit which travels at about 0.32 km per hour (0.2 mph). The picking finger bars are attached to two strands of roller chain and approach the plants from the side of the row to accommodate the low fruit setting characteristic of the Northwest cultivar, as well as the single-plant row system used in Oregon and Washington. Fruit is harvested on a conveyor belt. Leaves are removed by a pneumatic cleaning system.

The "Clipper" is a pull-type harvester utilizing the mowing method of harvesting and can operate at a higher ground speed than the Stripper, e.g., 0.8 km per hour (0.5 mph). It cuts off the plants above ground, removes leaves and other foreign matter with a pneumatic cleaning system, and places the fruit in containers for transport to the processor.

CAPPING (DECAPPING)

For processing, the calyx (cap) and stem usually are left in the field in handpicking. Large amounts of berries are capped at the processing plant, e.g., with a Morgan Capper or by other means. A necked berry is probably easier to decap than berries of other shapes. Since through pulping in processing the cap and stem material is eliminated from the pulp, machine-harvested berries should be suitable for manufacture of jams, jelly, and syrup.

Capping is defined as the removal of the fruit from the plant with the calyx remaining attached to the plant. Capping percentage, capping force, and pedicel breaking force are different genetic traits but they are significantly correlated with each other. The overall direction of dominance for the respective traits was for higher capping percentage, lower capping force, and lower pedicel breaking force. Because of the environmental influence on these traits, progeny tests such as diallele crosses provide a better evaluation of the genetic potential of a cultivar than its phenotypic performance (Brown and Moore 1975).

DISEASES

Leaf Diseases

The fungi which cause the common foliage diseases, except possibly mildew, infect only strawberry. Leaf diseases may greatly reduce yield. More than one leaf-spotting disease may occur on the same leaf.

Leaf spot spots are small and round, with a white or gray center and purplish margin. "Black seed" (1 to 10 black spots around a group of seeds) may occur on the fruit.

Leaf scorch spots are small, purplish, with no white centers. The spots may enlarge, coalesce, and cover the entire leaf. This disease, as with the preceding one, occurs on the underside of the leaf, thus making control by spraying or dusting difficult. It is often more damaging than leaf spot.

Leaf blight spots are first purple and later develop a dark-brown area surrounded by a purple ring. Often V-shaped infection occurs with the wide part at the leaf margin. During wet, warm weather leaf blight may cause a stem-end rot.

Powdery mildew shows as an upward curling of the leaf edges and a cobweb-like mold on the lower surface and on stem and fruit. Maturation of the fruit is interfered with.

Leaf variegation (June yellows, Blakemore yellows, spring yellows, yellows, chlorosis, gold disease, transient yellows, suspected mosaic, and non-infectious leaf variegation) may be due to some entity within the strawberry host cells. Generally the new leaves are faintly spotted or streaked with golden yellow to almost white in spring. These symptoms may disappear during warm weather and then reappear in the fall or the next spring. Each year it may become progressively worse until the plants become weak and stunted. There is no cure. Yield is reduced. Use non-variegated and virus-free plants (Zych 1964; Zych and Powell 1968).

Root Diseases

Red stele is caused by a fungus *(Phytophthora)*. It spreads by means of minute spores which are mobile when soil moisture is high, usually in lower or poorly drained sites. When infected roots are split lengthwise or peeled, their central core (stele) is reddish. This discoloration (which appears in no other strawberry disease) may show only near the dead tip, or it may extend the length of the root. Infected plants may have few new roots, and the roots may be gray. The leaves may appear off-color. The main periods of development are spring and fall. Infected plants commonly wilt and die rapidly in the first hot days of summer. Once the fungus is established in the soil it may remain viable for at least 12 years.

The fungus causing red stele has at least five races and these differ in their ability to infect different cultivars. A cultivar that is resistant in one area may be susceptible in another.

It is desirable that the genes for a high level of resistance to a composite of *P. fragaria* races, possessed by certain clones of *F. chiloensis*, be transferred to cultivars. It takes 2 to 3 generations beyond the F_1 of a *chiloensis* clone crossed with a cultivar to obtain selections with desirable combinations of characters. Large numbers of seedlings must be crossed; the standard technique for red stele resistance allows testing of many seedlings in any one year (Daubeny 1964, 1965).

Black root rot is a name for several troubles that produce similar symptoms, namely stunted plants; wilting and dying plants when the berries are half-grown; root system smaller than normal; main roots spotted with dark patches or zones; all or part, usually the tip, of main feeder roots dead; a cross-section of a dead root's being blackish; lack of vigor and few runners.

Some causes of black root are nematodes, soil fungi, winter injury, heaving, fertilizer burn, drought, and too much water, salt, or alkali in the soil. Set only healthy plants, obtained from a planting free from root rot; plant in a well-drained soil soon after digging; do not plant in the same soil more often than once in five years; sow a soybean green-manure crop on the site the year before planting strawberries; use cultural practices that promote vigorous plants.

Strawberries are accumulator plants and absorb silica from the soil continuously. The silica content of leaves, stems, sheaths, and crowns increases with age and is influenced by the soil in which the plants grow. There may be some relation between root rot and silica deposition in the plants. Silica deposited in such a way as to interfere with the transfer of food material from the leaves can weaken the root system (Lanning and Garabedian 1963).

Verticillium wilt, a soil-borne vascular disease caused by a fungus pathogen, is most active in cool weather. It invades the roots and interferes with movement of water to the leaves. Severely infected plants seldom produce a good crop. In new plantings symptoms appear about the same time as runners; in established plantings, they appear when the fruit begins to ripen.

Symptoms are: outer and older leaves wilt and dry at upturned margins and between the veins and become reddish to dark-brown; there are black spots on petioles; few new leaves develop and these tend to be stunted and may curl up along the midvein; central younger leaves are small, and have a dull, dark cast; new roots from the crown are short, with blackish tips; plants look dry and may suddenly collapse. The plants are often stunted and flattened, as if suffering from lack of water. Culturing in the laboratory is necessary for positive identification.

Many crop-growing soils contain one or more races of *Verticillium*.

The fungus infects several hundred host plants. Do not plant strawberries in soil where tomato, eggplant, pepper, melons, okra, potato, mint, brambles, stone fruits, chrysanthemums, or other susceptible crops have been grown the past several years. Once the fungus becomes established in an area it may remain alive in the soil for 25 years. Fumigation is effective control. Certain cultivars are more resistant than others.

Fruit Diseases

Gray mold (Botrytis) often starts as a blossom infection; preventing this may double the normal yield. Wind may disseminate thousands of spores over the planting. Diseased tissue is covered with a light-gray fluffy mold composed of fungus growth containing the spores. Temperatures of 21° to 27°C (70° to 80°F) and rains encourage infection. Pickers handling infected berries may spread infection to healthy berries. Within two days after good berries are picked, they may become rotted.

Leather rot (Phytophthora) causes berries on or near the soil to turn brown and appear water-soaked. Berries at all stages of maturity may become hard and leathery.

Rhizopus rot is primarily a post-harvest disease. Juice from infected berries leaks out of the bottom of the container. In packaged fruit this rot may be confused with gray mold rot, since the entire surface of the package soon becomes covered with a white, fluffy mycelium mat. Sanitation, careful handling, and precooling to 10°C (50°F) or lower are helpful control methods.

Important reductions in postharvest rots have resulted from (a) field use of plastic film to prevent fruit contact with soil; (b) eliminating fruits with visibly rotted leaves at harvest; (c) wound avoidance during harvesting and handling; (d) prompt transport to the cooler; (e) rapid cooling by forced-air and low-temperature transit; (f) elevated CO_2 in the atmosphere during transit; and (g) expedited marketing made possible by high-speed trucks.

Virus Diseases

Several virus diseases cause damage to strawberry plants. They may produce either mottling, mild yellow-edge, crinkle, vein chlorosis, leaf curling, or dwarfing.

The two general types of viruses that affect strawberries are (a) killer and (b) latent. The former, e.g., aster yellows, produces severe symptoms and kills individual mother plants and attached runners. The latent viruses are often responsible for progressive weakening of a planting stock. A latent virus by itself may produce no obvious symptoms in a strawberry plant. But combination of two or more viruses may produce yellow leaves, crinkled foliage, or severe stunting of plants (McGrew 1964).

A single virus may limit the number of runners that form and result in a low yield and small dull berries. Two or more viruses, or virus strains, may be present in a plant and be carried directly to daughter plants, or the viruses may be transmitted together by aphids.

As it is impossible to cure an established virus infection, destroy all infected plants as soon as they are seen. Spraying to control aphids that spread virus may be helpful. The spread of viruses in the Deep South by aphids is so limited that the use of insecticides to control aphids is probably not warranted.

DISEASE-TESTED PLANTS

A disease-tested program with strawberries is designed to control viruses, red stele, Verticillium wilt, nematodes, cyclamen mite, and several other pests. The plants also must meet minimum size standards and be true-to-name.

The terms "virus-free," "disease-free," etc., are misleading because there can be no guarantee that plants propagated on a commercial scale in the field will be 100% free of viruses or other diseases (Ricketson 1976).

Several stages are involved in the production of Registered and Certified Stocks. It takes several years to develop stocks of a given cultivar sufficient for the nursery trade.

Indexing for freedom from the pests mentioned above is done by trained personnel using special techniques. The indexed plants are grown under strict isolation for a year in a screenhouse, where only indexed plants are located. Different cultivars are separated in the screenhouse by a mechanical barrier at least 30.5 cm (12 in.) high. The screenhouse keeps out aphids, and soil fumigation controls nematodes and other harmful organisms. The fumigant is allowed to disappear before placing plants. Routine inspections and insect control applications are made.

Registered or Foundation Stock is then grown for a year by two or more nurseries. Requirements are soil fumigation, 610 m (2000 ft) isolation from other strawberries and regular insecticide applications to control aphids and cyclamen mite. The nursery may now sell these plants and identify them with a special tag.

The entire field must meet the requirements, including spraying, and no portion of a field shall be accepted for inspection. Normally, each year the plants are officially inspected in spring, summer, fall, and at digging time.

In a Certification Program Registered Stock may be grown for a year by Certified Stock growers and must be isolated by at least 305 m (1000 ft) from non-certified and wild strawberries.

Aphids injure plants in three ways: (a) by sucking sap from the plant, (b) by injecting toxic material into a plant, thereby causing stunting or deformation of tissues, or (c) by acting as carriers of virus diseases.

Cool, wet springs usually result in high aphid populations. Ladybird beetles, which normally keep aphids at low levels, are not as active during cool, wet weather. Hot, dry summer weather favors rapid development of two-spotted spider mite populations.

The Lesser and Thomas species insert their slender beaks into leaf tissues and are involved in spread of virus diseases. If recently tested plants are set out it is not necessary to spray or dust the first year. If, however, non-disease-tested plants are used, it may be possible to reduce virus infection by spraying or dusting plants less than one year old.

INSECTS

Chewing Insects Which Eat Holes or Portions of Leaves

Strawberry leaf roller, a small, reddish or brownish moth, deposits small eggs on leaves. The larvae cause the leaflet to fold at the midrib and feed within this shelter. Only the epidermis is eaten but continuous feeding causes the entire leaf to turn brown and die. The insect is susceptible to attack by certain parasites and this usually keeps the populations at non-economic levels.

Strawberry sawfly larvae (green with black eye spots on each side of the head) eat portions of leaves, mostly at night. When abundant they may completely destroy foliage in a few days. The adults are black-bodied, four-winged flies, with a row of whitish spots on each side of the abdomen.

Strawberry flea beetle adults (small, brownish black) may riddle the leaves with "shot holes."

Mites Which Injure Leaves by Sucking Sap

Cyclamen mite, scarcely visible to the naked eye, pale in color, feeds on young unfolded leaves in the crown; failure of stems to elongate causes a leaf rosette; berries may be distorted. It is mainly a greenhouse pest but may cause serious losses in strawberries. Once established it is difficult to control.

Spider mite (two-spotted mite), pale in color and usually with two darker spots on the back, sucks the sap from the underside of the leaves, causing a rusty brown color. Plants are stunted and yield reduced. Hot weather favors rapid population increase.

Insects and Other Pests Attacking Buds and Fruits

Strawberry weevil or "clipper" is a dark, reddish brown, snout beetle. The head is prolonged into a slender, curved snout about as long as the body. It girdles flower stems, causing buds and newly formed fruits to dry up.

Cutworms and armyworms (several species) which are large, stout caterpillars, striped, mottled, or gray, eat large holes in berries. They feed at night and hide during the day. They cut off young plants at ground level and may eat leaves and berries of established plants.

Tarnished plant bug adult is a small coppery brown bug with piercing and sucking mouth parts. It feeds on individual achenes (seeds) and destroys their contents. "Catfacing" may result. *Stink bug* also punctures the berries, causing uneven ripening or "catfacing."

Ground beetles are long, hard-shelled, black or brown, and active at night. They eat the skin of injured berries, largely for the seeds.

Insects Attacking Stems and Crowns

Strawberry crown borer beetle lays eggs on the crown near the base of a leaf stem about the time of bloom. These soon hatch and burrow downward toward the center of the crown. The white, legless, grublike stage lasts 4 to 8 weeks, and by midsummer most of the inside of the crown may be eaten out.

Strawberry crown girdler feeds on the crown (see Root Weevil).

Insects Attacking Roots

White grubs, larvae of May beetles or June bugs, are dirty white with brown heads, usually coiled and with distinct legs. They feed in the ground, especially grassy areas and sandy soils. They eat off roots and kill plants, usually between planting time and runner formation. They have a three year cycle. Since most damage is caused by two-year-old grubs, the injury is more severe every third year. Chickens or hogs may destroy many grubs on land soon after it is broken up.

Strawberry root aphid, bluish green, inserts a slender beak to suck sap from the roots. Infected plants lack vigor, have pale foliage, and berries dry up or fail to develop properly. Ants carry them to strawberry roots and from plant to plant.

Strawberry root weevil, a small legless grub, feeds on small rootlets. As the larvae become larger they feed on larger roots and crowns.

Wireworms are small, shiny brown larvae that feed on roots.

Grape colaspis beetles are yellowish brown, with brown legs and yellow brown antennae. The larvae sometimes attack roots and the adults feed on foliage of strawberries during the day.

Other Pests of Strawberries

Spittlebugs cause white, frothy, irregular masses on leaves, flowers, and stems. The young insects suck juices from the plants. The plants are stunted and the berries do not reach full size. The spittle masses are annoying to pickers.

Slugs or snails are elongated slimy mollusks with or without a shell. They eat out holes in the foliage and berries, leaving slimy trails. They may be troublesome during wet seasons and are night feeders.

Nematodes are microscopic, wormlike creatures. They usually are more destructive in sandy soil than in clay or soil with a high organic matter content. Some are more widespread than others, and different ones are more serious in some regions than in others. In many regions, plantings are not so heavily infested that soil fumigation is warranted. But in some areas soil fumigation is required for successful strawberry growing. (See Disease-tested Plants.)

Lesion nematodes (Pratylenchus) attack the roots and initially cause small spots that are amber to dark-brown. In older infections, root decay is extensive and much like that caused by root-rot disease. Leafstalk lengths are shortened, leaves may become slightly yellow, and emerging leaves on seriously infested plants appear bluish. Nematodes may increase Verticillium wilt.

Strawberry bud nematode (Aphelenchoides) causes the bud disease called spring crimp or red plant. A related bud nematode causes summer crimp or summer dwarf. These nematodes live among developing leaves and feed on the leaf surface.

Sting nematode (Belonolaimus) is more destructive to strawberries than any other nematode in some areas, but occurs mainly in the light, sandy soils of the lower coastal plains. It is comparatively large, lives in the soil, and feeds on the roots.

Root-knot nematode (Meloidogyne) penetrates and feeds in small roots and causes knotlike enlargements. Severe infestation has the same effect as removing most of the roots; plants are weakened, more subject to drought injury, have few runners, and less fruit. Nematodes that enter the roots to feed can stay alive when the plants are dug, stored, and shipped.

All soil-inhabiting nematodes can be checked by fumigating the soil with nematocides. Nematodes in roots, leaves, and buds can be killed by hot-water dip of dormant plants at 52.8°C (127°F) for 2 to 3 min.

Control is obtained when fumigation treatments are used before planting. In general, successful fumigation consists of careful application of the correct amount of nematocide at the proper soil depth. Follow the directions on the container.

REFERENCES

ALBREGTS, E.E. 1972. Influence of plant density on strawberry fruit production. Proc. Fla. State Hort. Soc. 84, 156-59.

ALBREGTS, E.E., and HOWARD, D.M. 1972. Comparison of polyethylene-coated biodegradable paper mulch on strawberry. HortScience 7, 568-69.

ANDERSON, J.F. 1964. Mineral content of strawberry leaves as influenced by rate and placement of fertilizer and lime. Proc. Am. Soc. Hort. Sci. 84, 332-37.

ANDERSON, R.E., and HARDENBURG, R.E. 1959. Effect of various consumer baskets and film wraps on quality of strawberries. Proc. Am. Soc. Hort. Sci. 74, 394-400.

ANTLE, G.G. 1972. Why are we having trouble marketing strawberries? What can be done about it? Rpt. Dept. Hort., Mich. State Univ., 12-16.

AUSTIN, M.E. et al. 1960. Color changes in harvested strawberry fruits. Proc. Am. Soc. Hort. Sci. 75, 382-86.

BAILEY, J.S., and ROSSI, A.W. 1965. Response of Catskill strawberry plant to digging date and storage period. Proc. Am. Soc. Hort. Sci. 84, 310-18.

BAKER, C.E. 1951. Cooperative fruit and vegetable shipping-point auctions. U.S. Dept. Agr. Bull. 64.

BALLINGER, W.E., and MASON, D.D. 1960. Selection of tissue for use in strawberry nutritional studies. Proc. Am. Soc. Hort. Sci. 76, 359-65.

BARRITT, B.H. 1974. Single harvest yields of strawberries in relation to cultivar and time of harvest. J. Am. Soc. Hort. Sci. 99, 6-8.

BOOSTER, D.E. 1962. Mechanical harvesting of strawberries. Ore. Hort. Soc. Proc. 54, 135-41.

BOYCE, B.R., and SMITH, C.R. 1967. Low-temperature crown injury of dormant Catskill strawberries. Proc. Am. Soc. Hort. Sci. 91, 261-69.

BRIGHTWELL, W.T. 1964. Yield of Dixieland strawberry in Georgia as influenced by date of setting plants. Am. Soc. Hort. Sci. 84, 338-40.

BRINGHURST, R.S. 1955. Strawberry growing in California. Market Grow. J. 20-21.

BRINGHURST, R.S. 1956. California strawberries aren't everbearers, but they act like they are. Am. Fruit Grower, April.

BRINGHURST, R.S.   1960.   Relationship of root starch and chilling history to performance of California strawberries.   Proc. Am. Soc. Hort. Sci. *75*, 373-81.

BROOKS, J.F. *et al.*   1971.   Commercial strawberry production.   N. Carolina Ext. Circ. *422*.

BROWN, G.R., and MOORE, J.N.   1975.   Inheritance of fruit detachment in strawberry.   J. Am. Soc. Hort. Sci. *100*, 569-572.

COLLINS, W.B.   1966.   Effect of winter mulches on strawberry plants.   Proc. Am. Soc. Hort. Sci. *89*, 331-35.

COLLINS, W.B., and SMITH, C.R.   1970.   Soil moisture effects on rooting and early development of strawberry runners.   J. Am. Soc. Hort. Sci. *95*, 417-19.

COREY, J.   1962.   Tar heel berry growers have bright red future.   Am. Fruit Grower, March.

COURTER, J.W.   1969.   Guidelines for "pick-your-own".   Processed material, Univ. of Illinois, Urbana.

COURTER, J.W., and ZYCH, C.C.   1963.   Response of dormant strawberries to late summer planting in southern Illinois.   Trans. Ill. State Hort. Soc. for 1963, 1-3.

COURTER, J.W., and ZYCH, C.C.   1971.   Survey of pick-your-own strawberry customers.   Ill. Growing Rpt. *24*, 1-4.

CULPEPPER, C.W. *et al.*   1935.   Physiological study of development and ripening in the strawberry.   J. Agr. Res. *50*, 645-96.

DAUBENY, H.A.   1961.   Powdery mildew resistance in strawberry progenies.   Can. J. Plant Sci. *41*, 239-45.

DAUBENY, H.A.   1964.   Effect of parentage in breeding for red stele resistance of strawberry in British Columbia.   Proc. Am. Soc. Hort. Sci. *84*, 289-94.

DAUBENY, H.A.   1965.   Relative resistance of various *Fragaria chiloensis* clones to *Phytophthora fragariae*.   Can. J. Plant Sci. *45*, 365-68.

DAUBENY, H.A.   1968.   Cream strawberry.   Can. J. Plant Sci. *48*, 629.

DAUBENY, H.A.   1970.   Winter hardiness in strawberries for the Pacific Northwest.   HortScience *5*, 152-53.

DAUBENY, H.A.   1971.   Totem strawberry.   Can. J. Plant Sci. *51*, 176-77.

DENISEN, E.L. *et al.*   1953.   Influence of summer mulching and runner removal on everbearing strawberries.   Proc. Am. Soc. Hort. Sci. *62*, 235-45.

DENISEN, E.L., and BUCHELE, W.F.   1967.   Mechanical harvesting of strawberries.   Proc. Am. Soc. Hort. Sci. *91*, 267-75.

DENNIS, F.G., and BENNETT, H.O.   1969.   Effect of gibberellic acid and deflowering on runner and inflorescence development in an everbearing strawberry.   J. Am. Soc. Hort. Sci. *94*, 558-60.

DENNIS, F.G. *et al.*   1970.   Effect of photoperiod and other factors on flowering and runner development of three strawberry cultivars.   J. Am. Soc. Hort. Sci. *95*, 750-54.

EATON, G.W., and CHEN, L.J.   1969A.   Effect of captan on strawberry pollen germination.   J. Am. Soc. Hort. Sci. *94*, 558-60.

EATON, G.W., and CHEN, L.J.   1969B.   Strawberry achene set and berry development as affected by captan sprays.   J. Am. Soc. Hort. Sci. *94*, 565-68.

EAVES, C.A., and LEEFE, J.S.   1962.   Note on the influence of calcium on the firmness of strawberries.   Can. J. Plant Sci. *42*, 746-47.

EGBERT, R.L.   1940.   Retarding the ripening of strawberries.   Mich. Quart. Bull. *23*, 20-26.

ENLIG, C.N. 1961. Salt tolerance of strawberries under irrigation. Proc. Am. Soc. Hort. Sci. 77, 376-79.

FORSHEY, C.G. 1969. Potassium nutrition of deciduous fruits. HortScience 4, 39-41.

GILBERT, F.A. 1968. Small Fruit Workers Conf. Rpt., Beltsville, Md.

GOOD, J.M. 1972. Nematodes. U.S. Dept. Agr. Farm Bull. 2246.

GRUNES, D.L. 1959. Effect of nitrogen on availability of soil and fertilizer phosphorus to plants. Advan. Agron. 11, 369.

HALLER, M.H. 1941. Respiration of strawberry and raspberry fruits. U.S. Dept. Agr. Circ. 613.

HANSEN, C.M. 1972. Strawberry mechanization. Am. Fruit Grower, June, 17.

HEILMANN, P.E. 1968. Heavy application of nitrogen early in spring fails to aid strawberry yields in the field. Better Fruit, March, 16-18.

HILL, R.G., and ALBAN, E.K. 1963. Strawberry stands and yields as related to weed control methods. Proc. Am. Soc. Hort. Sci. 82, 892-98.

HOOVER, M.W. 1955. A rapid objective method for evaluating color in strawberries. Proc. Am. Soc. Hort. Sci. 65, 195-98.

HOOVER, M.W., and DENNISON, R.A. 1955. Treatments influencing the quality of Florida strawberries. Proc. Am. Soc. Hort. Sci. 65, 188-94.

HOWELL, G.S. et al. 1972. Horticultural Rpt., Mich. State Univ., East Lansing.

JAHN, O.L., and CROSBY, E.A. 1958. Growth of strawberry plants as affected by several nitrogen carriers. Proc. Am. Soc. Hort. Sci. 71, 207-15.

JAHN, O.L., and DANA, M.N. 1966A. Fruiting and growth of the strawberry plant. Proc. Am. Soc. Hort. Sci. 88, 352-59.

JAHN, O.L., and DANA, M.N. 1966B. Dormancy and growth of the strawberry. Proc. Am. Soc. Hort. Sci. 89, 322-30.

JAHN, O.L., and DANA, M.N. 1970. Growth relationships in the strawberry plant. J. Am. Soc. Hort. Sci. 95, 745-49.

JANICK, J. 1960. Evaluation of strawberries. Indiana Res. Bull. 695.

JANICK, J., and EGGERT, D.A. 1968. Factors affecting fruit size in strawberry. Proc. Am. Soc. Hort. Sci. 98, 311-16.

JANICK, J., and MARSHALL, G.E. 1966. Yield-size relationship of strawberry varieties. Fruit Varieties and Hort. Digest 15, No. 2, 29-32.

JOHN, M.K. et al. 1975. Influence of sampling time on element composition of strawberry leaves and petioles. J. Am. Soc. Hort. Sci. 100, 513-17.

JOHN, M.K. et al. 1976. Genotypic influence on elemental composition of strawberry tissues. J. Am. Soc. Hort. Sci. 101, 438-41.

JOHNSON, F.D., and WALKER, R.B. 1963. Nutrient deficiencies and foliar composition of strawberries. Proc. Am. Soc. Hort. Sci. 83, 431-39.

JUDKINS, W.R. 1950. Everbearing strawberries. Ohio Farm Res. 35, 6-7.

KIRSCH, R.K. 1959. Importance of interaction effects in fertilizer and lime studies with strawberries. Proc. Am. Soc. Hort. Sci. 73, 181-88.

KWONG, S.S. 1967. Leaf age and leaf function influence of concentration of microelements in strawberry leaves. Proc. Am. Soc. Hort. Sci. 91, 157-60.

KWONG, S.S., and BOYNTON, D. 1959. Time of sampling, leaf age, and leaf function as factors influencing concentrations of nutrient elements in strawberry leaves. Proc. Am. Soc. Hort. Sci. 73, 168-73.

LANNING, F.C., and GARABEDIAN, T. 1963. Distribution of calcium, iron, and silica in tissues of strawberry plants. Proc. Am. Soc. Hort. Sci. *82*, 187-91.

LATIMER, L.F. 1943. Responses of strawberries to boron. Proc. Am. Soc. Hort. Sci. *42*, 441-42.

LOCASCIO, S.J. 1965. Strawberry revival in Florida. Am. Fruit Grower, May.

LOCASCIO, S.J. 1968. Black plastic ups Florida strawberry yields. Am. Fruit Grower, June.

LOCASCIO, S.J. 1972. Strawberry yield and soil nutrient levels as influenced by plant population, fertilizer rate and bed shape. Proc. Fla. State Hort. Soc. *84*, 160-62.

LUNDERGAN, C.A., and MOORE, J.N. 1975. Inheritance of ascorbic acid content and color intensity in fruits of strawberry. J. Am. Soc. Hort. Sci. *100*, 630-32.

McCONNELL, G.E. 1973. Pick your own. Am. Fruit Grower, June.

McCOWN, M. 1933. Humus and cultivation govern berry yields. Hoosier Hort. *15*, 43-46.

McGREW, J.R. 1964. Strawberry diseases. U.S. Dept. Agr. Bull. *2246.*

MILLER, M.H., and OHLROGGE, A.J. 1958. Principles of nutrient uptake from fertilizer beds. Agron. J. *50*, 95-97.

MOORE, J.N., and BOWDEN, H.L. 1967. Response of strawberry varieties to date of planting. Proc. Am. Soc. Hort. Sci. *91*, 231-35.

MOORE, J.N., and BROWN, E. 1970. Yield and maturity of strawberries in relation to time of once-over harvest. J. Am. Soc. Hort. Sci. *95*, 519-22.

MOORE, R.C., and OBERLE, G.D. 1961. Strawberry mold stopper. Am. Fruit Grower, April.

MORRIS, J.L. 1972. Strawberry mechanization. Am. Fruit Grower, June.

MORRISON, W.W. 1968. Preparing strawberries for market. U.S. Dept. Agr. Farm Bull. *1960.*

MORROW, E.B. *et al.* 1959. Genetic variances in strawberries. Proc. Am. Soc. Hort. Sci. *72*, 170-84.

NITSCH, J.B. 1950. Growth and morphogenesis of the strawberry as related to auxin. Am. J. Botany *41*, 152-59.

NITSCH, J.B. 1955. Free auxins and free tryptophan in the strawberry plant. Plant Physiol. *30*, 33-39.

NORTON, R.A., and WITTWER, S.H. 1963. Foliar and root absorption and distribution of phosphorus and calcium in the strawberry. Proc. Am. Soc. Hort. Sci. *82*, 277-86.

NYE, W.P., and ANDERSON, L. 1974. Insect pollinators frequenting strawberry blossoms. J. Am. Soc. Hort. Sci. *99*, 41-44.

OFFENBACHER, A.G. *et al.* 1971. Leaf variegation in strawberries. Ill. Dept. Plant Pathology Circ. *706.*

OURECKY, D.K. 1976. Frost tolerance in strawberry cultivars. HortScience *11*, 413-14.

PIRINGER, A.A., and SCOTT, D.H. 1964. Interrelation of photoperiod and flower cluster and runner production of strawberries. Proc. Am. Soc. Hort. Sci. *84*, 195-200.

QUICK, O.H., and DENISEN, E.L.   1970.   A strawberry harvest mechanization system.   HortScience 5, 150-51.

RICKETSON, C.L.   1966.   A mechanical harvest aid for strawberries.   Hort. Res. Inst. Ont. Rpt., 6-9.

RICKETSON, C.L.   1968.   Solid-bed plantings.   Hort. Res. Inst. Ont. Rpt. for 1967.

RICKETSON, C.L.   1969.   Ontario strawberry plant certification.   Hort. Res. Inst. Ont. Rpt. for 1968.

RICKETSON, C.L.   1970.   Plant spacing in solid-bed strawberry plantings. Hort. Res. Inst. Ont. Rpt. for 1969.

RICKETSON, C.L.   1976.   The strawberry in Ontario.   Ministry of Agr. and Food, Ontario.

RINGS, R.W., and NEISWANDER, R.B.   1966.   Insect and mite pests of strawberry.   Ohio Res. Develop. Center Res. Bull. 987.

ROM, L.C., and DANA, M.N.   1960.   Strawberry root growth studies on fine sandy soil.   Proc. Am. Soc. Hort. Sci. 75, 362-67.

SAXANA, G.K.   1968.   Fruit quality of fresh strawberries as influenced by nitrogen and potassium nutrition.   Proc. Am. Soc. Hort. Sci. 92, 354-62.

SCOTT, D.E.   1971.   Strawberries: changing production and patterns.   Am. Fruit Grower, Feb.

SCOTT, D.E., and DARROW, G.M.   1972.   Growing strawberries in the Southeastern and Gulf Coast States.   U.S. Dept. Agr. Farm Bull. 2246.

SHERMAN, W.B., and JANICK, J.   1967.   Greenhouse evaluation of fruit size and maturity in strawberry.   Proc. Am. Soc. Hort. Sci. 89, 303-15.

SHOEMAKER, J.S.   1929.   The strawberry.   Ohio Agr. Expt. Sta. Bull. 444.

SHOEMAKER, J.S., and GREVE, E.W.   1930.   Relation of nitrogen fertilizer to the firmness and composition of strawberries.   Ohio Agr. Expt. Sta. Bull. 466.

SIMONS, R.K.   1958.   Response of Howard Premier and Vermilion varieties of strawberries to supplemental irrigation.   Proc. Am. Soc. Hort. Sci. 71, 216-23.

SISTRUNK, W.A.   1963.   Field conditions and processing practices relating to frozen strawberry quality.   Proc. Am. Soc. Hort. Sci. 83, 440-46.

SMITH, W.L., and HEINZE, P.H.   1958.   Effect of color development at harvest on quality of post-ripened strawberries.   Proc. Am. Soc. Hort. Sci. 72, 207-11.

SOMNER, N.F. et al.   1973.   Reduction of postharvest losses of strawberry fruits from gray mold.   J. Am. Soc. Hort. Sci. 98, 285-88.

STANG, E.J., and DENISEN, E.L.   1970.   Inflorescence and fruit development in concentrated and nonconcentrated ripening strawberries.   J. Am. Soc. Hort. Sci. 95, 7-11.

STANG, E.J., and DENISEN, E.L.   1971.   A proposed system for once-over machine harvesting of strawberries for fresh use.   HortScience 6, 414-15.

TUKEY, H.B. et al.   1958.   Loss of nutrients by foliar leaching as determined by radioisotopes.   Proc. Am. Soc. Hort. Sci. 71, 496-506.

VANDENBERG, J.   1971.   Pick-your-own harvesting.   Ont. Dept. Agr. Factsheet, March.

VOTH, V.   1955.   Stored strawberry plants.   Calif. Agr. 9, 9-16.

VOTH, V.   1961.   Pruning and polyethylene mulching of summer-planted strawberries in southern California.   Proc. Am. Soc. Hort. Sci. 78, 275-80.

VOTH, V.   1972.   Plastic in California strawberries.   HortScience 7, 378.

VOTH, V., and BRINGHURST, R.S.   1958.   Fruiting and vegetative response of Lassen strawberries in southern California.   Proc. Am. Soc. Hort. Sci. 72, 186-87.

VOTH, V., and BRINGHURST, R.S.   1970.   Influence of nursery harvest date, cold storage, and planting date of winter-planted California strawberries.   J. Am. Soc. Hort. Sci. 95, 496-500.

VOTH, V. et al.   1961.   Response of strawberries to nitrogen in southern California.   Proc. Am. Soc. Hort. Sci. 78, 270-74.

VOTH, V. et al.   1967.   Effect of bed system, bed height, and clear polyethylene mulch on yield, salt accumulation, and soil temperatures in California strawberries.   Proc. Am. Soc. Hort. Sci. 91, 242-56.

VOTH, V. et al.   1971.   Effects of successive soil fumigation with methyl bromide on strawberry replanting.   Calif. Agr. 25, No. 3, 14-15.

WADE, E.E.   1965.   Strawberries: the strange malady.   Am. Fruit Grower, May.

WATADA, A.E.   1971.   Postharvest physiology of strawberry fruits treated with sodium dehydroacetate.   J. Am. Soc. Hort. Sci. 96, 177-79.

WILSON, W.F., and GIMALVA, N.J.   1954.   Number of days from bloom to harvest of Louisiana strawberries.   Proc. Am. Soc. Hort. Sci. 63, 201-02.

WORTHINGTON, J.T., and SCOTT, D.H.   1970.   Successful response of cold-stored strawberry plants dug in the fall.   J. Am. Soc. Hort. Sci. 95, 262-66.

ZYCH, C.C.   1964.   Leaf variegation in strawberry seedlings.   Trans. Ill. State Hort. Soc. 98, 117-21.

ZYCH, C.C., and POWELL, D.   1968.   Commercial production of strawberries.   Ill. Circ. 983.

Chapter 3

Bramble Fruits

The fruit of raspberries, blackberries, and related types *(Rubus)* is an aggregate fruit. It consists of a collection of drupelets, which are partly fleshy and partly hard (the seed). In a raspberry the core remains on the bush when the "berry" is picked; in a blackberry the core comes with the picked fruit and becomes part of the edible fruit.

The canes of *Rubus* are biennial. The term *primocane* was proposed by L. H. Bailey for the first year growth, and *floricane* for the second year.

The bramble fruit discussion is classified into (1) red raspberry, (2) black raspberry, (3) purple raspberry, (4) erect and semi-erect blackberry, (5) western trailing types, including the evergreen blackberry, loganberry, and boysenberry, and (6) southern trailing blackberry or dewberry.

PART 1

RED RASPBERRIES

In most red raspberry cultivars which become leaders in this continent and which originated here, the native *Rubus strigosus* predominates. However, indications of the European red raspberry *R. idaeus* appear in most newer cultivars.

Probably 75% or more of the raspberries in the United States and nearly 100% in Canada are reds. The red raspberry succeeds farther north than any of the bramble fruits, but its chilling requirement is too high for production in the South, except possibly at high elevations.

There is an undersupply of raspberries in the East. Some reasons for this are disease, labor (particularly for picking), grape expansion, dislike for the thorny condition, and desire to try other crops. Substantial progress has been made in the knowledge of diseases and in a certification or indexing program for planting stock.

REGIONS AND DISTRICTS

East and Midwest

Rather than large, concentrated plantings many comparatively small ones are scattered throughout the East and Midwest, including Michigan, New York, Pennsylvania, Ohio, Minnesota, Wisconsin, Iowa, Illinois, Indiana, and New England.

West

Red raspberries are produced in Colorado in a way that has three distinctive features: they are grown under irrigation; the canes are for the most part laid down and covered with soil for winter protection; and they are grown at elevations of 1220 to 2134 m (4000 to 7000 ft).

Most of the red raspberry acreage in Washington state (an extensive one) occurs in the Puget Sound area in the coastal region or western part of the state, centering largely in the Puyallup and White River Valleys around Puyallup and Sumner, both in Pierce County. Snohomish, Whatcom, Thurston, and King Counties have large plantings. A smaller area occurs in Clark County in southwestern Washington, across the Columbia River from the northern part of the area in western Oregon. Processing is the main outlet.

Canada

Production for all of Canada is about 13.2 million liters (12 million qt) per year with about 75% of it in British Columbia and 20% in Ontario. Most of the remainder is in Quebec Province (1.1 million liters, or 1 million qt), largely near Montreal, in Nova Scotia (82,500 liters, or 75,000 qt), and in New Brunswick (55,000 liters, or 50,000 qt).

Ontario's production on 364 ha (900 acres) is scattered over much of the province. The British Columbian acreage is mostly in the Fraser River Valley. The red raspberry is grown with protection as far north as the Peace River District in Alberta.

RED RASPBERRY CULTIVARS

There is an old horticultural expression that "varieties (cultivars) are characterized by their faults." It is recommended that prospective red raspberry growers consult their Extension Service on the merits and weaknesses of different cultivars for a given area.

If a large quantity of red raspberry seed is planted an occasional seedling may have yellow or amber berries, as the result of genetic segregation. The berries are comparatively mild but of little or no commercial value. They may be thought to be something new, but not so.

POLLINATION, DRUPELET SET, AND CRUMBLINESS

Most red raspberry cultivars are self-fruitful. Cultivars which show regularity of drupelet set have a high level of self-fertility and this is often a factor in their success. However, self-fertility is not always complete, i.e., all the drupelets may not be well developed. Percentage of drupelet set is of concern in production.

One indication of the trouble is crumbly berries. Crumbliness (reduction in drupelet set) can cause serious losses in yield. Some causes of crumbliness are virus-disease infection (tomato ringspot, mosaic, tomato black ring), and variations in male and female sterility. Also, weather may be involved. Certain cultivars may be more tolerant than others. Good growing conditions may help to counteract the effects of virus infection and minimize or mask the symptoms.

Partial male sterility may limit self-fertility and result in crumbliness in certain virus-infected clones of some cultivars (Freeman *et al.* 1969).

Reductions in yield from self-pollination seem most likely to involve self-incompatibility or reduced pollen fertility. Reductions from open pollination may involve reduced numbers of functional embryo sacs (Daubeny 1971; Virdi *et al.* 1972A).

It seems unlikely that reduced set from open-pollination would be caused entirely by lack of fertile pollen or by self- or open-pollination, since the availability of pollen from many clones would mask any sterility or incompatibility reactions. It seems more likely that open-pollination reductions are caused by lack of full female fertility of functional embryo sacs (Daubeny 1971; Virdi *et al.* 1972B).

Another example of incomplete self-fertility is a crumbly-fruit condition of a clone of the Sumner cultivar due to retarded embryo sac development and more non-fertile pollen than normal. This may occur when there is no evidence of aphid-transmitted red raspberry mosaic in plants of crumbly Sumner, and when results of indexing for mechanically transmitted viruses are negative (Daubeny 1969).

Virus affects on embryo-sac development probably are not severe enough to account for failure of fruit-set or yield reduction (Eaton and Turner 1971).

FRUIT-BUD FORMATION

Fruit-bud formation takes place in late summer or fall of the year preceding the crop year. Cultural practices can influence the time of flower initiation and the rate of development. Those factors that advance primordial development are usually associated with slowing or stopping of primocane growth (Crandall and Chamberlain 1972).

FRUIT GROWTH STAGES

There are three definite fruit growth stages: (a) a period of rapid growth beginning at full bloom; (b) reduced growth rates, during which the endocarp hardens; (c) rapid growth continuing to maturity. Most of the growth of the developing fruits is accounted for by the carpellary tissue. Berries grow more in basal than in polar diameter and during development they increase proportionally more in weight than in volume. There is similarity between the development of the aggregate fruit and that of various drupe fruits. Evidence supports the use of the term drupelet for the individual developing ovaries (Hill 1958).

PROPAGATION

Sowing seed is used in breeding new cultivars, not for the reproduction of named cultivars. Extract the seed from the berries in water in a blender. Store it for several months at 4° to 7°C (40° to 45°F) under moist conditions before sowing it. Time the after-ripening period with suitable conditions for planting.

Red raspberries are usually propagated by suckers that grow from the roots. These suckers appear in spring, continue to do so into summer, and are the forerunners of nursery plants.

Red raspberry plants may be obtained by digging entire nursery rows or by digging near mature plants. Plants with well-developed T-roots are desirable. Usually plants are dug by hand, but large nurseries use a machine when the rows are dug clean. Young plants should actually be dug; if pulled, only a straight stub with few roots poorly equipped for growth may be left.

An example of increase in number of plants that can be dug in a red raspberry nursery is shown in Table 3.1. In established fields 10 times as many new plants per hectare from reds than from blackcaps is not uncommon.

Spring suckers sometimes thrive when set in early summer of the year in which they appear. But they are not ordinarily used, chiefly because of their perishability.

TABLE 3.1

STOCK INCREASE IN A RED RASPBERRY NURSERY
PLANTING CHIEF CULTIVAR

Year	Plants Set	Dug in Fall	Sold
First	14	157	0
Second	157	1,765	75
Third	1,690	13,230	5,980
Fourth	7,250	—	

Source: W.G. Brierley, University of Minnesota, 1939.

Red raspberry is rather difficult to root from cuttings. However, most cultivars can be rooted nearly 100% from young leafy shoots as they emerge 15.2 to 20.3 cm (6 to 8 in.) from the soil. If cuttings are taken repeatedly from a vigorous stock plant and placed under mist, many plants can be obtained from a single clone.

LIFE OF PLANTING AND YIELD

Red raspberries should fruit for at least 6 years; some plantings have produced for 20 years. Each succeeding profitable crop reduces production costs and emphasizes the importance of healthy plants for setting, isolation from disease sources, suitable soil, adequate drainage, and proper culture.

Yield per hectare varies with many factors, such as age of planting, cultivar, cultural practices, weather, prevalence of diseases and insects, and thoroughness of picking. Red raspberries take three years to develop enough strong canes in the row for a high yield.

LOCATION AND SITE

Soil

Information given previously for grapes and strawberries applies, for the most part, to the bramble fruits.

Raspberry roots are sensitive to poor soil aeration. Low O_2 supply in the soil may limit the production of growth-promoting substances responsible for bud development and rapid subsequent cane growth. This may occur coincidentally with limitation in water supply due to restricted root systems.

Improved root growth at temperatures below 15.6°C (60°F) may mean that high temperature is an important factor that limits the growth of raspberries in the warmer parts of the temperate zone. Also, northern cultivars do not succeed in the Deep South because they do not receive adequate winter chilling at 7.2°C (45°F) or lower.

The ideal soil probably is a deep sandy loam, well supplied with humus and retentive of moisture, but well drained. Since fruiting occurs at a time when soil moisture is low, select a soil that retains moisture. Where crown gall is a factor the heavier soil types may aid the plants in tolerating the disease. Soil reaction, other than extremes, is not greatly significant, but a slightly acid soil is usually best. For propagation, a light soil has an advantage.

A compact impervious subsoil that retards downward movement of water checks root development. Determine the character of the subsoil before choosing the site, either by boring with a soil auger or by digging holes at intervals over the field. Subsoil should be loose enough for good drainage and good root growth, but should prevent excessive loss of water. In general, brown or reddish subsoils are more open and drain better than yellow or gray soils. Very sandy and gravelly subsoils may allow too much drainage.

Water Drainage

Since the root system of most bramble fruits is mostly in the upper 91 cm (3 ft), the water table should not be less than 91 cm (3 ft) below the surface of the ground for more than a few days at a time. Plants whose roots penetrate comparatively deep and are not partly killed by poor drainage or a high water level can best absorb moisture from the lower depths in dry periods. Adverse effects due to reduction of the feeder roots appear in dry summer periods when the plants are growing and maturing their fruit.

Where the water table is low throughout the year or approaches the surface for only a few days in spring, roots penetrate deeply and branch profusely, shoot growth is vigorous, and yields are moderate to heavy. Where the water table is high throughout the year or for a long period in spring, the root system is shallow, cane growth is poor, yields are low, and plants are short-lived. Reduction in root system may promote winter injury.

Excessive water late in the growth period may delay maturity of the wood, and the following spring canes may show various degrees of weakness or death from winter cold. Also, the natural rise of the water table in winter and spring may suffocate roots and weaken the crowns. Growth on the fruiting canes cannot be supported by the depleted root and crown systems, and turns yellow, wilts, and dies prior to harvest. New canes may also show drooping, yellowish leaves, and even purplish striping. Often, however, especially toward fall after new roots have developed, the growth of new canes may be normal; but such growth is ineffective, because drowning of the roots occurs again in winter and early spring and the canes collapse while fruiting.

Wind

Protection from wind has some advantages, such as steady bushes in picking. Also, since snow drifts less and remains longer, less evaporation occurs from the soil and canes, and consequently there is less winter injury. In some cases, strong winds may dry out the soil rapidly and take much moisture from the canes. Where air drainage is poor, fungus diseases may become more serious.

A structural weak point in the raspberry plant is the attachment of the canes to the crown. Whipping of canes by wind or striking them in tillage often partially disrupts this union. The breakage may be underground and go unnoticed. Injured canes may wilt completely and die in a few days, or they may live for several days or even weeks. When new shoots are injured, the tips may die back, a broad blue stripe may creep up the stem from the base, the leaves may gradually turn yellow and drop, and weak, new growth from the secondary buds on the cane may give the plant a peculiar bunchy appearance. Such symptoms may be mistaken for disease, winter injury, or injury by root-feeding insects.

If a wind-damaged cane is held near the tip and moved back and forth, the looseness at the crown will be evident, and a gentle pull usually breaks it away completely. The basal end shows callus and brown, dry wood, and pith over most of its surface where the partial break occurred some days previously. Callus formation does not repair the injury. To avoid this damage, select sites that have some protection from strong winds. Otherwise, arrange a trellis to support the canes.

Previous Crops

It is often wise to plow under a green-manure crop before planting bramble fruits. Land on which corn or other frequently cultivated crops have grown a year or more previous to planting bramble fruits is usually suitable. If a sod site is selected, plow it down in early fall and thoroughly work it before planting in spring. Fields infested with grasses are difficult to keep clean.

Isolation from Disease Sources

Red raspberries should be separated by 100 m (20 rods) or more from sources of infection.

Planting Raspberries in Orchards

Bramble fruits occasionally are interplanted in a young orchard as a source of income before the orchard bears. The disadvantages usually exceed the merits.

Do not set bramble fruits within 3 to 4.6 m (10 to 15 ft) of newly set trees. Plant only between every other tree row, to allow for passage of machinery. When apple trees are spaced 12.2 m (40 ft) apart, up to 3 rows 2.4 m (8 ft) apart of bramble fruits can be set between them. With peaches or other trees only 6.1 to 7.3 m (20 to 24 ft) apart, do not set more than 1 row of brambles between the 2 rows. Bramble fruits can be set between the trees in the row. They may be damaged by the spray material used on fruit trees.

Bramble fruits grow taller than strawberries or most vegetables or flowers and the habit of growth and spiny canes make them more difficult to handle in an orchard. Bramble fruits, well-spaced, can be cultivated in one direction throughout their life, but cross cultivation of the orchard is precluded. Bramble fruits draw heavily on the soil for moisture and nutrients and return little in plant residues. More fertilizer is needed when they are grown in an orchard.

Verticillium wilt may spread from brambles to orchard trees, and vice versa, with disastrous results.

HARDINESS AND WINTER INJURY

The red raspberry thrives farther north than most fruits, but is sometimes damaged by cold in important production areas.

Severe Cold

There are inherent differences between cultivars in their tolerance of severe cold. In Alberta, Canada, for example, the Chief cultivar, with only windbreak protection, produced a good crop following a winter in which the temperature dropped to −45.6°C (−50°F) at Edmonton; the Taylor cultivar was killed to the ground line.

Vigorous, robust canes are desirable, providing the main growth is made early in the year. If, however, first year canes continue to grow late, they may be succulent and tender when a fall freeze occurs. Damage from cold is usually most pronounced on the upper part of the canes, but even the basal part may be injured. A common type of immaturity extends only a few inches down from the tips and so is of little importance, since the tips are removed in spring pruning.

Almost any source of injury, whether pests, wind, or mechanical, may cause severe enough defoliation or damage to the photosynthetic tissue to result in reduced resistance to freeze injury.

Premature defoliation by wind and mites often occurs in western Washington. The pith in the basal portion of the buds is most susceptible to freeze damage, followed in order by the pith of the cane, the vascular tissues in the base of the buds, and the floral primordia. Defoliation and mite injury increases the susceptibility of the bud tissues to freeze injury and reduces starch and sugar reserves. Severe mite defoliation reduces the number of buds the following year (Doughty *et al.* 1972).

Rest Period

In autumn in northern areas the canes become dormant (without leaves). The buds enter a rest period, and while in it the plants are most resistant to damage from cold. Resistance decreases after the rest period breaks.

Alternating Cold and Warm Weather

Injury may result in well-matured canes from alternating spells of cold and warm weather in late fall or early winter. If the warm weather lasts for several days the buds may begin early stages of development; they may swell and show green tips and die when the weather turns cold again. When the buds are killed, the cane dries up in spring. The cane itself may be injured and some buds survive. These buds develop, but the canes dry up during hot summer weather because they cannot carry enough water.

Much cane injury may occur when temperatures vary from cold to warm and to cold again at almost any time from November to April. Factors involved are: (1) The rest period is broken. (2) A few days of temperature above freezing can cause loss of cold resistance. (3) If the temperature rises above 7.2°C (45°F) for a few days, with little or no frost at night, buds can begin early stages of growth and be neither resting nor hardy. (4) Subsequent cold, particularly sudden cold, may cause severe injury to canes that have lost their resistance to cold or to those that actually have begun the early stages of bud activity.

Hardening

A raspberry cane must be hardened to withstand low temperatures. Rest begins during relatively warm fall days, and deep rest can be reached before hardening begins. Hardiness, or resistance to cold, is developed by exposure to cold. It proceeds gradually when hard frosts occur frequently. Exposure for several nights to around $-6.7°C$ $(20°F)$ or lower is necessary to harden the cane fully, but the rest is not broken until after the canes are exposed to a certain accumulation of cold.

Dehardening and Rehardening

The rest period may end in early winter and is brought about by the effect of the accumulated hours of cold below about $7.2°C$ $(45°F)$. Cold-resistant cultivars, like Chief and Latham, enter a deeper rest and come out more slowly than more tender ones.

Frequently canes not only dry out in winter or early spring following injury from fluctuating temperatures, but also after injury from such causes as borers, tree crickets, or even severe crown gall infestation.

Composition

The percentages of soluble solids, total N, pectic compounds, ether extract, and moisture have little relation to hardiness of winter hardy and tender red raspberries. High retention of water under pressure is associated with the capacity to withstand low temperatures. The percentage of total moisture which can be expressed by pressure varies, and may reach a very low minimum for either type of cane in midwinter. Injury tends to be greater in winters with wide fluctuations of temperature than steady cold. Peroxidases and acid and alkaline phosphates are active; catalase is inactive (Bennett and Weeks 1960).

Latham canes deharden in early winter in Minnesota and may reharden to some extent if the buds do not become active. But fully dehardened canes cannot reharden enough to escape injury at below $-18°C$ $(0°F)$. If bud development occurs, injury may follow subsequent exposure to below $-6.7°C$ $(20°F)$.

Sudden Cold

Sudden cold occurring relatively early, perhaps in mid-November, may cause much injury. Effects of sudden cold during winter depend largely on the occurrence and duration of mild spells immediately preceding cold weather.

Cane injury may occur when temperature suddenly falls below −18°C (0°F). But Latham and Chief can endure severe cold if well-hardened. Light frosts and one night at −6.7°C (20°F) do not harden well-matured canes enough to prevent killing by sudden exposure to −18°C (0°F). This temperature may kill cane tissue while buds are uninjured. After exposure for 4 nights to −6.7°C (20°F) and then to −18°C (0°F) there may be slight injury to cane tissues and no injury to buds. Such injury, which is due to early, sudden cold before the canes are fully hardened, may promote subsequent drying of canes at harvest time.

Drying Air

In regions with severe winters, particularly where the air is relatively dry, unprotected canes may dry out beyond recovery at temperatures above freezing. The intake of the roots may be so slow in cold soil that replacement of water losses from the roots is inadequate to hold the moisture above 50% of the fall (mature) content. Again, when the soil freezes deeply and drying winds are frequent in winter or early spring before the soil thaws, the roots cannot replace the water evaporated from the buds and canes.

Sometimes the canes cannot recover even when conditions are favorable later or in spring. Such injury often occurs in western Minnesota, where rainfall is low and drying winds common. It is not wise there to mulch the field when the ground is frozen, since the soil under the mulch may remain frozen late enough for drying to occur before the roots become active.

Root Injury

No root injury may occur at soil temperatures above −19°C (−2°F). The killing point is between −21° and −22.8°C (−6° and −9°F). Therefore, under usual winter conditions severe root injury is not likely to occur.

Hardiness Complex

Several specific factors in the hardiness complex must be recognized. If "hardiness" means a high degree of cold resistance, this factor has long been present in such cultivars as Latham and Chief. Objectives in breeding for hardiness in northern raspberries should include, besides a high degree of cold resistance and ability to harden rapidly, factors such as: retention of cold resistance once attained; longer rest or deeper dormancy in order to avoid out-of-balance bud activity; and ability to reharden if initial cold resistance is lost.

WINTER PROTECTION

Colorado

To protect against severe winter cold, cover the canes completely with soil about November 1. Winds tend to blow straw, cornstalks, and other materials away, and these materials may harbor mice that damage the roots. Remove the old canes before the covering is done, but do not prune the new canes until they are uncovered in spring.

First bend down the canes as flat as possible without breaking, and weight them down at the right side of the row so that the ends are not plowed into when uncovering. Then plow furrows 15 cm (6 in.) deep on both sides of the row to throw soil on the canes. This does not completely cover them; finish the covering with shovels. Cover the canes 10 to 15 cm (4 to 6 in.) deep at their highest point, but not while frozen, brittle and difficult to bend to the ground without breaking. In old plantings where the hills may be root-bound, remove a shovelful of soil from the front of the hills before the canes are bent down.

Uncover the canes in spring before the buds swell much; they may withstand −15°C (4.8°F) without injury. If canes are left covered until the leaves appear, the leaves may be killed by frost after uncovering. But if canes are lifted before growth starts, the leaves come out gradually and become hardened.

Partially uncover the canes by plowing away from both sides of the row. Then thrust a 4- or 6-tine fork under the soil. Rake soil from between the canes and leave the row level; otherwise, a ridge forms in a few years and makes irrigation difficult.

Minnesota

Several red raspberry plantings of 50 to 200 plants were tip-covered late in October by W.G. Brierley in 1943. In spring the canes were lifted before the buds started. In early June the tip-protected canes showed no injury at all and were alive to the tip buds. In other cases there was slight injury to the tips, but the injured portion ordinarily would have been removed in spring pruning. Some buds in the arched-up portion of the canes were killed, but the same injury was more extensive in unprotected parts of the field. In tip-covered plots the average injury did not exceed 5%; in unprotected plots it was 40%. It seemed likely that cane injury would reduce the crop 10 to 50% in the unprotected areas, but protected plants would bear nearly a full crop.

Covering can be done over a period of several weeks, with the canes in full foliage. In fact, leaves help to hold the canes down. The work can be done later, in October, but the risk of soil freezing is greater. Winter covering with soil may protect the canes against warm weather, which causes loss of cold resistance.

PLANTING

Red raspberry suckers that have completed a growing season are usually best. Good-quality planting stock is a key to success. The disadvantages of poor stock, particularly disease-infected stock, can often never be overcome.

Time of Planting

In general, early spring planting before growth starts is usual in most regions. In some areas, red raspberry plantings are often started with "green plants." These young plants or suckers are transplanted 4 to 6 weeks after growth begins in spring. This practice is satisfactory in favorable seasons, but if drought or hot weather occurs soon after transplanting, the young plants may suffer severely.

On light soil, fall planting may be better than spring, particularly when adverse weather or other factors prevent early spring planting. Fall planting helps avoid the rush of spring work. Plants bought in autumn are freshly dug; those bought in spring may have been stored over the winter under none too favorable conditions, especially when one nurseryman buys the plants from another. Ordinarily, late is better than early fall planting. With too early planting, drought and relatively warm days may reduce the stand. Plants set too late may not become sufficiently established to resist heaving out.

Pruning at Planting Time

Uusually 30.5 to 45.7 cm (12 to 18 in.) of a vigorous red raspberry cane are left in planting, and of less vigorous ones 15.2 to 30.5 cm (6 to 12 in.). A poor stand of reds often results when the plants are pruned to ground level at planting, especially with plants set in late spring when pruning causes loss of food reserves.

Distance of Planting

Spacing 0.61 to 1.2 m (2 to 4 ft) in the row with 2.1 to 2.7 m (7 to 9 ft) between rows usually is suitable for reds in hedgerows. The fact that the red raspberry is a prolific plant maker, fills the row quickly, and is comparatively long-lived affects the spacing. In Washington state, reds are often spaced 0.61 to 0.76 X 1.8 to 2.1 m (2 to 2.5 X 6 to 7 ft), but spacing varies with soil fertility, moisture, training system, and harvesting method.

Setting the Plants

Set the plants at the same depth or slightly deeper than they grew previously. If set too shallow, or if the soil is not firmed well around them, many of the plants may dry out; take care not to injure young shoots. Poor root development, heaving out, weak plants, injury from drought, and blowing over of the canes may also occur. If set too deep, the growing points may not push through the soil, especially if it is heavy.

FIG. 3.1.   RED RASPBERRY PLANTING OFF TO A GOOD START

One plan is to mark the row locations with a few stakes which are used as a guide for plowing furrows 12.7 to 15.2 cm (5 to 6 in.) deep to receive the plants. Set the plants against the side of the furrow and partially cover the roots with soil; complete the planting operation by covering with more soil. It is not necessary to cross-mark for hedgerows, but this should be done for the hill system.

TILLAGE

Shallow working of the middles is usual early-season practice. When roots are cut, even though the ends heal, the injured area may become infected with crown gall.

If cultivation is done after each picking to loosen the soil packed down by the pickers, many berries may be knocked off and those in the bushes may become dirty.

Cultivate soon after harvest, but then cease tillage to permit good maturing of the canes. The land needs preparation if a cover crop is to be grown. Tillage usually extends later into the year when the objective is both plants and fruit, instead of fruit only.

If reds are highly mounded in autumn and left that way over winter, the buds that form new canes may be produced so high above ground that the new plants are weakened the next year.

HERBICIDES

A number of different herbicides, applied according to manufacturer's directions, are useful in raspberry plantings.

MULCHING

Merits of a straw mulch are: higher yield in many cases; moisture conservation; prevention of erosion; elimination of cultivation; more vigorous cane growth; reduced heaving of fall-set plants in heavy soils; cooler soils in summer; more uniform soil moisture (Kelsall 1946).

Objections are: cost of the mulch and its application; danger of fire and mice; possible delayed maturity of canes in autumn; interference with producing plants for sale; possible blockage of furrow systems of irrigation by the mulch material.

IRRIGATION

Earlier discussion of irrigation of strawberries applies also, for the most part, to bramble fruits. For a high yield it is important that in the year preceding the harvest a large number of robust canes be produced, and that they make their chief growth early rather than late in the season. Hence a good supply of soil moisture is important during the period preceding late summer. For greatest efficiency, cultivate after irrigation. Some noteworthy points follow.

Ontario.—The maximum or peak moisture use rate is about 5 m (0.2 in.) per day. This peak is useful when the moisture-storage capacity of the soil is known. Raspberries obtain most of their moisture from the top 61 cm (2 ft) of soil. Well-drained sandy soils may hold only 5.1 cm (2 in.) and loams up to 10.2 cm (4 in.) of available water. Start irrigating when 50% of the available moisture in the soil has been used. With peak-use rates this generally is 5 to 10 days, depending on the soil type.

It is generally advisable to use enough water to bring the available moisture in the top 61 cm (2 ft) back to 100%. But as irrigation equipment may be only 75% efficient, about 3.8 cm (1.5 in.) of water would need to be discharged from the sprinklers to supply 2.54 cm (1 in.) of available soil moisture. Do not apply water faster than it can be absorbed by the soil.

Ohio.—For maximum size of red raspberries, there must be ample moisture during the "final swell" of the individual berries. For maximum benefits from any special soil-management practice designed to conserve moisture or from a supplemental irrigation, initiate these practices 2 weeks before the first picking or 3 weeks after first bloom. Also, since the bloom and harvest seasons extend over a 3 to 4 week period, continue these practices throughout the harvest season.

Reds require 2.54 to 3.8 cm (1 to 1.5 in.) of water per week, either from rain or irrigation. The use of fairly tall risers with the sprinkler heads above the plants gives more uniform coverage than low risers.

More fertilizer and less pruning may be necessary in heading back of canes when irrigation is practiced. Anthracnose, spur blight, and mildew may be more prevalent unless adequate control is provided.

Colorado.—Soon after planting, make shallow furrows a few inches from one side of each row and run a small stream of water through them until the soil is thoroughly wet around the roots; from then on, irrigate at least every two weeks. During harvest, irrigate twice a week, except on very light soils. On irrigation days turn on the water as soon as picking is over for the day, so that the surface soil can dry before the next picking. When pickers must work in a muddy field, the soil becomes packed and hard, and many berries dirty. After mid-August, irrigate only often enough to avoid checks from lack of water. This, combined with fewer cultivations, hinders rapid growth and causes the plants to mature their wood for winter. In autumn, just before covering for winter protection, irrigate to make the soil easier to handle when covering the plants. Even if covering is not necessary, give this irrigation to keep the soil from drying out during the winter.

Run the water long enough to wet the soil at least 30.5 cm (1 ft) deep. The more thorough the irrigation the less frequent the need for it. Some growers irrigate frequently, yet their plants suffer because they do not apply enough water.

FERTILIZER

Base the fertilizer program on soil and leaf analyses determined by local sources.

The soil should be well supplied with organic matter, which is easier to provide before planting than later. The best cover depends on the soil and locality.

The quantities of waste vegetative material (mainly spent fruiting canes and surplus new canes) removed from a 5- to 6-year-old planting in Scotland may be about 57% per year. The amounts of dry matter and of the nutrients N, P, K, Ca, and Mg removed in the waste may be greater than the amounts either in the fruit harvested or (possibly for K) in the leaves returned to the soil (Wood and Anderson 1962).

The number, diameter, and height of canes are related to yield. Thicker and taller canes provide a higher yield per given area. Since there is a relation between vigor and yield, adopt fertilizer and other practices that promote vigorous canes early in the season.

Application of N fertilizer early each spring is advised, but avoid excessive amounts. Apply it near the plants between the rows. If applied directly on the crowns it may cause injury. N fertilizer may make the fruit softer, but not as much as heavy rains. Color, texture, and flavor of the fruit and growth of the plants may be better when P, K, and trace elements occur with N in the fertilizer in proper balance.

TRAINING

Red raspberries send up shoots from leader buds at the base of the canes, usually at least 2 such buds forming on each cane. Thus, if 2 canes grow the first year after planting and each produces 2 buds, 4 canes would appear the second year, 8 the third year, and 16 by the fourth year. But since some buds do not start and many make weak canes, when plants are in bearing, about the same number of strong canes may be produced the first year after the planting comes into full bearing as during later years.

Besides the shoots from leader buds, reds send up suckers from underground stems. If some system of training were not used, the field would soon become a dense thicket of canes, each competing with others for food, moisture, and light, and picking would be difficult.

Hedgerow System

Commonly in the East red raspberry suckers are allowed to develop between the plants in the row to form a hedgerow. The wide hedgerow, often 0.9 to 1.2 m (3 to 4 ft) in width, though yielding well, has several drawbacks. Fruiting shoots in the center of the row are crowded and many die prematurely; berries are overlooked by the pickers and are either lost or picked later when overripe; weak canes are produced

FIG. 3.2.   EXCELLENT HEDGEROWS OF RED RASPBERRY

that bend over and allow the berries to become dirty; and certain fungus diseases may be more severe on the shaded canes in the middle of a wide row.

A high-quality crop may be obtained by restricting the row width by cultivation and pruning to a width of 30.5 to 61 cm (1 to 2 ft) (narrow hedgerow). Because of the larger number of canes per hectare, higher yields are possible than with the hill system and, because of the narrower rows, the faults of the wide row are avoided.

It is usually better to support tall red raspberry canes in hedgerows by wire than to prune back too severely.

In Ontario a 1-sided and a 2-sided trellis were compared with tall-growing cultivars. New suckers tended to grow well in both systems and did not interfere with the fruiting canes or harvesting (Ricketson 1970).

In both systems the wires along the sides of the row are 76.2 cm (30 in.) apart. In the 1-sided trellis the fruiting canes are confined to a 38.1 cm (15 in.) row and are bent to one side of the row in the spring. A wire on the swinging arms holds these canes against the side wire. The 2 wires are held together with clips every 3 to 4.6 m (10 to 15 ft). In this system most of the new suckers tend to grow on the side of the row opposite the fruiting canes. The next year the wire on the swinging arm is moved to the opposite side of the row and the fruiting canes are held against the wire on this side. Thus, in one year the fruiting canes are bent to one side of the row and in the next are bent to the other.

In the 2-sided trellis half of the fruiting canes are bent to one side of the row and half to the other. They are held to the side wires by 2 other wires on swinging arms. This system gives a V-shaped row and most of the new suckers tend to grow in the center. The 2-sided trellis is very productive, since rows can be quite wide (61 to 76.2 cm, or 24 to 30 in.) and practically all strong-fruiting canes can be left when irrigation is practiced. With both systems, take care in bending canes so the wires do not break off buds.

Staked Hills

Reds sometimes are grown in hills. Set the plants 1.8 x 1.8 m (6 x 6 ft) apart, sometimes 2 in each hill. Stakes are usually set at the start of the second year; tie 5 to 8 canes to each stake, depending on the vigor of the plant and soil fertility. Make 2 to 3 ties, pulling the canes close to the stakes, so that the fruiting shoots tend to grow outward and are not entangled with the canes, thus making picking easier. Cut back the canes in spring and tie to about the height of the 1.5 to 1.7 m (5 to 5.5 ft) stake. If canes are left longer, in windy weather much injury may be done to the succulent shoots.

FIG. 3.3.   STAKED HILLS OF RED RASPBERRY

Teepee-hill System

Select 5 to 8 canes far enough apart to make the base of a hill 35.6 cm (15 in.) wide; draw them together at the top and tie tightly. Make 2 ties, the first at the top and the second 20.3 cm (8 in.) lower. Teepee-hill plants sometimes twist and fall over. To avoid this, make the hill with a wide base, shorten the canes to 1.2 m (4 ft), and tie tightly. Yield is somewhat lower than with staked hills. Keeping the hills free from grass and weeds is a little more difficult, but the cost of stakes is eliminated.

Hill-row System

Set the plants 91.4 cm (3 ft) apart in the row. This system is useful in areas where canes are laid down in one direction and buried over the winter.

Trellising Reds in the Pacific Northwest

Set stakes 2 to 2.1 m (6.5 to 7 ft) by 7.6 to 9.1 m (25 to 30 ft) apart and 45.7 to 60.9 cm (1.5 to 2 ft) into the ground; end posts should be even farther apart. Usually there is 1 top wire and 1 or 2 pairs of lower wires. The top or support wire supports the canes that are tied to it. The other wires, called guard wires, protect the canes from passing machinery. The wires are usually fastened directly to the posts; nail hooks permit easy moving of the wires.

In another plan, nail cross-arms to the posts and fasten the wires to them; making and keeping these up is an extra expense. More common practice is to use spreaders and cross-arms 5.1 × 5.1 × 40 cm (2 × 2 × 16 in.).

Spread Trellis.—This system is the most used in British Columbia. A 5 × 10 cm (2 × 4 in.) cross-arm is securely fastened 1.37 m (4.5 ft) above the ground to cedar posts placed 9.1 m (30 ft) apart at 395 posts per ha (160 posts per acre). A 61 cm (2 ft) long cross-arm is centered and stapled to each end of the first cross-arm. Two 10-gauge wires are stretched along the top of the long cross-arm and stapled to the cross-arms at each end of it. Half the canes from each crown are tied to one wire and the other half to the other wire.

Another method requires a second set of 14-gauge wires to be placed near the main wires so that the canes are held between the 10- and 24-gauge wires. These two wires are then held by means of metal clips.

The spread trellis encourages the new canes to grow in the center of the row where they are supported and out of the way of the pickers. There are about 2410 linear meters of row per ha (3200 ft per acre). This system requires 404 kg of 10-gauge wire per ha (360 lb per acre) and 159 kg of 14-gauge wire per ha (142 lb per acre) (Carne 1965).

Three-wire Trellis.—Staple a support wire to the top of each post 1.37 m (4.25 ft) high. Keep the wire tight so that when the canes are tied to it, it holds them in place. Erect one pair of guard wires 76 cm (2.5 ft) above ground. Do not staple them to the posts, since they are moved from time to time to place the new canes inside the wires. As new canes grow, they become too tall for the wire at 76 cm (2.5 ft). By putting in two sets of nail-hooks, one at 76 cm (2.5 ft) and the other 25.4 cm (10 in.) higher, the wire can be moved up as the canes grow.

Four-wire Trellis.—Erect two sets of guard wires. Canes may or may not be tied to the top wires. In any event, both the top and bottom wires protect the new canes. Staple the top set 1.2 m (4 ft) above ground, and hook the lower set 0.61 m (2 ft) above the ground.

Five-wire Trellis.—Erect two sets of guard wires, the lower 61 cm (2 ft) above the ground and the other 46 cm (1.25 ft) higher. There is no need to raise these wires as the new canes grow. The extra wires also give more protection than one set.

The number of canes left in the spring depends on the vigor of crown. Leave only 6 to 8 canes for a full crop. The first shoots to grow in the spring produce the best canes. Cut out excess shoots that grow during the season. Remove them before picking starts (Carne 1965).

PRUNING RED RASPBERRIES

Pruning at planting time is discussed under Planting. Avoid summer topping of reds because most tests have shown appreciable damage, e.g., promotion of branches that are susceptible to winter injury.

Heading Back Dormant Canes and Branches

Dormant pruning is best done in late winter or very early spring before growth starts. Swollen buds are easily broken off in pruning. With too early pruning, the canes may be too brittle and break easily and, when cut back to proper lengths, subsequent winterkilling or drying out of the end portions may unduly reduce the amount of fruiting wood left.

Pruning is concerned mostly with unbranched canes. With some cultivars, however, some shortening of branches is required.

Some 45 years ago R. V. Lott showed in Colorado that the highest-yielding buds of a cane are in the third, fourth, and fifth sections, measuring upward from 91.4 to 182.8 cm (3 to 6 ft). Therefore, bud distribution may be added to the factors that determine yield, along with weight per berry, number of berries per fruit shoot, and percentage of bearing buds. A consistent increase of only one bud in either the third or fourth section would give, in productive buds, an increase of 20 g per cane, or 815 liters per ha (300 qt per acre), in a linear hedgerow with 8.2 canes per meter (2.5 canes per ft) and rows 2.4 m (8 ft) apart. When canes are headed to 91.4 cm (3 ft), 2 of the 3 heavy-producing sections (fourth and fifth) are removed. To benefit from such heading, the 3 remaining feet must make a yield increase greater than the fourth, fifth and sixth feet. Such fruiting response may not occur. Growers who prefer short to tall canes may need to plant a larger acreage to obtain the same yield.

In the 1920s S. Johnston and R.E. Loree, in Michigan, showed that about 62% of the buds on a Cuthbert cane may produce shoots that mature their fruit; 10% remain dormant; 12% grow into vegetative, unfruitful shoots; 10% winterkill, chiefly at the tips of the canes; a few buds develop into shoots that are mechanically injured; and a few produce shoots that dry up.

Naturally branched canes are more vigorous and more productive than unbranched ones. Buds 1 to 5 on the branches give rise to some vegetative or barren shoots; buds 10 to 15 produce the best-yielding laterals. Beyond bud 15, yield and size of fruit decrease rapidly.

In the 1930s W.G. Brierley found, in Minnesota, that Latham yields in proportion to cane length, but yield is affected by the following factors. Fruit shoots grow longer as pruning severity increases. Canes cut short increase in height proportionally more than longer canes, because of longer fruit shoots. Canes cut to 1.5 m (5 ft) bloom and produce ripe berries a few days earlier than severely pruned ones. Taller canes yield slightly more early fruit than 1.5 m (5 ft) canes. Low pruning does not greatly lengthen the harvest. Drought and unusually hot weather reduce berry size and yield. Rain, even light showers, increases berry size and yield for 1 or 2 pickings. Berry size becomes larger from successively shorter pruning, in part due to the effect of pruning and in part because berry size decreases toward the tips of the canes. Severe pruning, by affecting the vigor of remaining laterals, increases berry size, but not enough to offset loss in yield. Winter injury, drought, and high temperatures may reduce yield of long canes to that of those cut to 91.4 cm (3 ft). Probably the performance of the cane as a whole depends more on moisture supply than on pruning treatment.

In Washington state, plants pruned to 9 canes per plant may yield 1120 kg more per ha (0.5 tons more per acre) than those pruned to 6 canes. Leaving 15 canes per plant does not increase yield over those thinned to 12.

Thinning Canes.—In general, thinning of strong canes reduces the yield without increasing berry size. Thin out the small, slender canes in the hedgerow. Fruiting canes that average 15 to 20 cm (6 to 8 in.) apart are usually well spaced in the row. Keep hedgerows fairly narrow. In hill systems leave 5 to 10 vigorous canes per hill.

Removing Canes After Fruiting.—Bramble-fruit canes are biennial. They complete their growth the first year, bear fruit the second year, and then die. The underground stem is perennial and sends up a new set of canes each year.

After the canes have fruited in summer remove them, either soon after harvest or in early spring. On the one hand, canes that have fruited are of little further value in the field; their early removal permits next year's canes to grow without obstruction; the field looks neater; some pests may be checked; the canes are less tough and easier to remove at this time; there is little or no loss of food supply in the roots; the plant may use in the first year canes the water and nutrients that would otherwise have been taken up by the second year canes. Disease is detected more readily; and rush of other work often is less pressing than in the spring.

On the other hand, second year canes may protect and support the first year canes against breakage by storms and heavy weight of drifted snow; second year canes do not greatly obstruct the growth of first year canes; the first year canes may mature a little earlier than otherwise. Removing the second year canes soon after harvest is usually best.

About 40 years ago, studies by W.G. Brierley, University of Minnesota, disclosed the following information. In moisture-deficient soils, removal of second year canes soon after harvest may save for the plants the water that would be transpired by these canes from them until the end of the season. When rain and soil moisture delay maturity of first year canes, leaving second year canes in place until the end of the season reduces the excess of water and tends to hasten maturity of the first year canes. Transpiration is more rapid in second year canes until the last picking.

Transpiration rate of first and second year canes differs little until late in the season; but second year canes usually have more foliage, so the total volume of water is greater, at least in late summer.

Cambium in the canes begins to decline in meristematic activity in the first year and is feeble the second year. Apical meristem ceases to function at the end of the first year; no winter buds are formed in the second year; and cambium in the second year forms little new xylem and phloem. Canes of both ages increase in diameter in the central and tip regions in the second year; but 90% of the second year canes show no increase at the base. Cambial activity, as shown by new xylem, occurs in most growing canes in the second year; but it is feeble and related to vigor of fruiting shoots rather than to cane vigor in the first year. New xylem does not appear in second year canes until fruiting shoots have several leaves.

Cambium activity progresses slowly and is mostly on the side of the cane where the shoot is growing. Easy breaking of fruiting shoots is ascribed to this limited development of new xylem. But where fruiting shoots are numerous, a general activity of cambium occurs, with the formation of a complete, narrow ring of new xylem. Degeneration of phloem at the base and tip of canes occurs at about the same time; the former is associated with senility of the cambium and the latter with inadequate water supply.

While the fruiting laterals are growing rapidly, food stored in canes and roots is transported upward and used for growth. When fruiting laterals have about ended their growth and a large leaf area is forming photosynthate in excess of the needs of the fruiting canes, the surplus is transported downward.

After harvest the foliage on second year canes is still active photosynthetically, but the photosynthate is not transported out of the old cane system. Phloem of second year canes may break down at the base soon after harvest and thus prevent downward movement of carbohydrates. But under good nutritive conditions, the phloem may not break down immediately after harvest.

"I have repeatedly observed in Colorado that the base of the cane was the last to dry up. In Latham it was common for 4 to 6 in. at the base of the cane to be green when fall pruning was done about November 1. The rest of the cane was dead and dry long before that time." (R. V. Lott correspondence, 1934.)

Short-handled pruners are commonly used to cut the old canes just above ground level. Ordinarily hand pruners require more stooping or kneeling.

Usually head back dormant canes as lightly as is compatible with suitable training and support, freedom from damage in cultivation, ease of harvesting, and avoidance of small berries near the end of the canes. Some growers do not remove the tip portions because, even though the berries there may be rather small, they may bring a good price because of their earliness. Probably it is better to say that a certain proportion of the cane should be cut at a definite height irrespective of amount of growth. In general, 15 to 25% is often the right amount to remove.

HERITAGE FALL-BEARING RED RASPBERRY

For many years fall-bearing red raspberries were recommended only for home gardens. However, with the release of the highly productive Heritage cultivar the situation has changed. Heritage originated from a cross between (Milton × Cuthbert) × Durham and was released

Courtesy of D. K. Ourecky, New York State Agr.
Expt. Station, Geneva, New York

FIG. 3.4.   VIGOROUS HERITAGE BUSHES

by the Geneva, N.Y. Experiment Station in 1969 (Ourecky and Slate 1969).

The term "fall-bearing" denotes fruiting on the current season's growth. Fall bearers in late summer produce flowers and fruits on the upper part of the new canes. The fruiting surface may extend down one-third the length of the canes.

Heritage is far superior to any of the present fall-bearing red raspberry cultivars. It is very vigorous, suckers prolifically, and produces very erect primocanes which are exceedingly sturdy and do not require support. The fall-crop berries are medium-sized, very firm with coherent drupelets and remain in good condition on the plant even when overripe. Heritage will bear a light summer crop, but if only a fall crop is desired mow the canes to ground level after a hard frost, thus sacrificing the summer crop for a slightly earlier fall crop.

A new approach to raspberry culture may be possible with the fall-bearing habit. Since fruit is borne on the current season's growth, there is no need for hand-topping and after frost all canes may be mowed or brush-hogged to ground level, thus eliminating hand removal of the old canes.

HARVESTING AND MARKETING

Hand-picking

Pickers and Picking.—Number of pickers needed for a given planting or for a district as a whole would be decreased, or the acreage available pickers could handle would be increased, if full-day picking could always be practiced. But conditions are not always such that full-day picking is possible or wise. It is often important that picking be done in early morning; otherwise, the berries may heat. Picking in the afternoon of hot days adversely affects the appearance of the ber-

Courtesy of D. K. Ourecky, New York State Agr.
Expt. Station, Geneva, New York

FIG. 3.5.   HERITAGE BERRIES

ries and total yield because the berries become dryer and smaller, and pickers do not work most effectively in hot weather.

The length of time between pickings usually does not influence the mold count of freshly picked berries. Overripe berries, which are the most likely to mold, fall off the bushes if not picked, and therefore may not contribute to the mold count. (See Mold, Chap. 3; also see "Pick-Your-Own" discussion, Chap. 2.)

Careful handling for market is necessary. Pick the berries directly into the basket in which they are sold and do not handle again for grading or sorting, though some filling of baskets or culling may be needed. Trays or other containers that hold a given number of units (qt, pt, or ½ pt) are used.

It takes longer to hand-pick red raspberries than it does the other small fruits. The picking period of reds is usually fairly long. In picking, waist carriers are more convenient than picking stands, but the berries are shaken up more. As soon as the baskets are filled, transfer them to larger-unit containers. Raspberries are ready to pick when they separate readily from the receptacle or core.

The H-ion concentration and the titratable acid of the developing berries increases uniformly until ripening processes start, as indicated by pigmentation of the berries, and then decreases as ripening progresses. These changes help to account for the increase in palatability from pigmentation to maturity.

Storage.—Raspberries may be stored in the fresh condition for a few days at $0°C$ ($32°F$) and 85 to 90% RH. Marketable quality of harvested berries may be maintained for several days longer than usual by fumigation, where acceptable, with SO_2 for 15 to 20 min and then storing at $10°$ to $21°C$ ($50°$ to $70°F$).

The berries have a high degree of perishability. For example, the limit of storage life is 2 to 3 days at $0°C$. Increasing the CO_2 concentration up to 30% with the aid of dry ice retards the rate of softening and fungal growth. Use of machine harvesters increases the need for greater berry strength.

Preharvest sprays of $CaCl_2$ or water-soluble wax may increase berry size (by weight) and decrease the rate of softening during storage for 48 hr at $21°C$ ($70°F$). With 4 cultivars and 3 dates of harvest, preharvest sprays of wax may increase firmness but have no effect on total acidity, acid loss, water loss, or fungal decay. There is, however, a positive reaction between cultivars and harvest dates in relation to firmness, acidity, and rot development (Eaves *et al.* 1972).

Shipping and Processing.—For shipping, pick over the planting every day; for processing, every second or third day, unless the weather is hot. Reds are divided into "shippers" (berries that are large, firm, and in prime condition) and "canners" (berries that are too soft to ship fresh but are still in good condition for a lower price). The soft texture makes the berries subject to spoilage in transit. Precooling soon after picking and refrigerated shipping are helpful.

Machine-harvesting

Machine harvesters have been used for some time in the Pacific Northwest in harvesting bramble fruits for processing.

One type is pushed like a wheelbarrow under the canes. Two forces oppose each other: (a) gravity and the eccentric action of the catching board, and (b) a gentle flow of air evenly distributed across the board. Berries are shaken from the canes by hand onto the sloping catching board and roll gently and slightly downward into boxes. The gentle flow of air from blowers removes leaves and trash.

Another type of machine goes over the rows. Sets of flexible rubber fingers vibrate back and forth through the plants to shake the berries onto a catching platform. The berries are then eased into a cup-type elevator that lifts them to a platform, a blast of air from a compressor unit, operated by the same motor that does the elevating, cleans them.

Still another type involves suction (see Blueberries).

The softness of fruit, vigorous new cane growth, and long ripening period make it comparatively difficult to harvest reds mechanically.

The following two pruning and training systems protect the new cane growth, give high yields, and are well adapted to machine-harvesting. (1) The fruiting canes are woven on a 2-wire trellis. New canes grow up through the middle and the fruiting surface starts about 51 cm (20 in.) from the ground, so the fruit is in good position for machine-harvest. Fruit is removed from the plants by shaking the wire over which the canes are woven, either by hand or mechanically. (2) In a 1-sided trellis, all canes are trained between 2 closely spaced wires and are topped at a height of 1.8 to 2 m (6 to 6.5 ft). The wires are tied together between each hill to keep the canes in place and new canes develop on the opposite side of the row. All fruit on a row can be harvested with 1 trip down the row; 2 trips are required with the spread trellis. With high topping, most of the lower fruit buds remain dormant, thus raising the fruiting surface off the ground. This method also spreads the fruiting area out more than with the weaving system and allows free air movement around the berries, thus reducing the amount of fruit rot.

A self-propelled catching frame with air cleaner is combined with hand shaking to harvest the berries. The catching frame has a 40.6

cm (16 in.) wide conveyor belt 4.27 m (14 ft) long in the bottom of the apron; the row side of the apron is 50.8 cm (20 in.) from the ground. The whole machine is 4.9 m (16 ft) long and 1.4 m (4.5 ft) wide. Harvested berries are conveyed to the rear where they fall across an air stream into the flat (Crandall *et al.* 1966).

Another machine harvester is tractor-towed, hydraulically operated, and requires a driver plus 1 to 4 sorters, depending on the yield. Best results are usually obtained when the picker is towed at about 0.8 km per hr (0.5 mph). The picking drum speed is adjustable, but optimum speed is about 600 rpm. A blower removes debris, and berries are conveyed to a belt for sorting. The machine measures 5 m long, 3 m high, 3.7 m wide (16.5, 10, 12 ft, respectively), with platform down, on a 2.7 m (9 ft) wheel base. Minimum height is 2.1 m (6 ft 10 in.) under arches. The harvester has a manually adjustable machine height, so ground clearance may be changed to suit this type of berry or the field to be harvested. An optional leveler attachment is available to keep it level on uneven terrain.

Using a "shake and catch" method of machine-harvesting with canes attached to a trellis, up to 70% of hand-picked yield was collected from a clonal raspberry planting at Ottawa, Canada. Characters related to berry quality and to the machine, such as shape of receptacle, ease of picking, and fruit removal force, were related to characters indicating susceptibility to winter damage. Thus, selection for winter hardiness is an important first step in further improving this material. Leaf retention in the fall was not a reliable indicator in winter hardiness. Efficiency was slightly reduced with a method using untrellised plants and less dependence on winter hardiness (Fejar and Spangelo 1973).

PART 2

BLACK RASPBERRIES

The black raspberry (*Rubus occidentalis*) is adapted to moderate winter climates. It is not as hardy to cold as the red raspberry. It is not adapted to the South, where it does not receive adequate chilling. Production of blackcaps has greatly declined in the last 20 years. There is presently a scarcity of this fine fruit.

The main problem, and it is a serious one, in successful black raspberry production is disease control. Set only disease-tested plants and isolate the planting a good distance away from other brambles. Consult your Extension Service as to cultivars and sources of plants.

FIG. 3.6.   DUG A BIT LATE TO SHOW NEW CANE DEVELOPING

POLLINATION

Most blackcaps are self-fruitful. However, increased yield and perfection of fruit often results when bees are placed near the planting during bloom for pollination.

PROPAGATION

Occasionally, long canes of black raspberries bend to the ground, become covered with soil (largely by rain splashing), and take root. But for good multiplication and good plants, layer the tips properly by hand at the right time.

Disease Effect

Obtain plants from disease-tested sources for setting. Virus diseases may increase rapidly from year to year. Growers who set diseased plants commonly harvest a first or partial crop, 1 or 2 good crops, and then find that the planting runs down badly. But if healthy plants are set, effectively isolated, and inspected at regular intervals, the disease problem can be reduced. Rogue out any plants as soon as they show symptoms of virus diseases and verticillium wilt.

In a test by S. Johnston in Michigan half of a 572 plant field (Section A) was set with plants that seemed to be disease-free. The other half (Section B) was set with plants bought from the trade and appearing as vigorous as the other lot. In the first summer, 20% of the plants in Section B showed mosaic or wilt and were removed. Only 1 mosaic-infested plant appeared in Section A. That was the first fruiting year, and Section A yielded 26 cases and Section B 5 cases. In June of the second year so many plants in Section B showed virus diseases and wilt that the entire section was removed to prevent infection of nearby plantings. Section A continued to yield well (36 cases the second year and 50 cases the third year). Section A would have done better if it had not become infected from Section B.

Branching of Laterals

Each lateral may produce more than one tip plant, since the laterals may branch just before rooting. Thus more plants are obtained, but they are smaller and lack the well-developed root systems of unbranched tips. As many as 10 secondary laterals may develop; 60 have been counted in an exceptional case. Secondary laterals that are 20 cm (8 in.) long usually form good root systems. But often the secondaries are short when layered, and the increase in number of new plants is offset by poor, or only fair, root development.

Development of secondary laterals is due chiefly to bruising of the

FIG. 3.7.   DAMAGE TO THE TIP OF THE PARENT CANE RESULTED IN THIS DEVELOPMENT OF SMALL NEW PLANTS

FIG. 3.8.   TIP LAYERED TOO EARLY

tips of primary laterals as a result of whipping by wind. To determine whether or not a late-summer cover crop would reduce whipping injury to the tips, soybeans, oats, golden millet, and buckwheat were tested in successive years in Ohio; but less than 50 plants rooted of their own accord each year in an 850 plant field.

Summer Topping

Tip portions of unchecked first year canes are often so spindly that sturdy new plants are not obtained. As plantings become older, the canes often become higher and many laterals fail to reach the ground. Proper summer topping prevents this condition.

Time for Layering

The best time to layer is when the tip portion of the laterals lengthen in rat-tail fashion, with small curled leaves. Begin layering when some laterals have reached this condition and most of them are nearing it. Tips put down too early usually push out of the ground. They can again be layered, but the part of the shoot initially underground makes a poor plant at the first point of contact. Late tipping may promote several small plants from secondary laterals instead of one well-rooted plant per main lateral and also results in loss from heaving out. Layering usually begins in late August or early September, depending on the region. Since all tips are unlikely to be ready at one time, go over the field several times.

Use of a narrow spade or heavy trowel results in better plants than plowing a furrow.

For propagation a fairly light, well-drained soil is desirable; but a soil that is too light, loose, and dry falls back into the hole easily and makes successful tip-layering difficult.

An Ohio survey by the author showed, in 50,000 plants, a loss of more than 50% of rooted tips on heavy, rather wet soil in contrast to 15% on sandy or gravelly loam. Losses were especially severe with tips that did not become well rooted because of late layering and heaving. On heavy soils it is often impossible to dig plants in spring until growth is so far advanced that much injury results to the plants; also, digging is slow and costly.

Age of Field

Black raspberries are seldom grown in nursery rows simply to obtain new plants by tip layering. Nurseries commonly buy plants, often under contract, from growers who sell berries. One-year-old fields often show less disease than older fields. But thorough inspections of fields started from disease-tested plants can make tips from mature plants as suitable as those from young plants.

Number of New Plants

With good care 5 to 10 new black raspberry plants can be obtained from each vigorous parent plant after a year's growth. About 24,700 plants per ha (10,000 plants per acre) is a fair estimate for mature fields. More can be obtained if the plants are kept low and the stand is good.

Method

Insert the tips 7.6 to 10.2 cm (3 to 4 in.) deep. With shallow tipping much loss may result from whipping out, heaving out, and poor root development. Deep placement of tips, especially in heavy soils, may result in breakage of the tender growing points in digging. Use a vertical rather than a horizontal method of tip layering.

Rate of Tipping

The number of tips layered in a 4.9 ha (12 acre) field in 10 hr, with a narrow spade or heavy trowel on clay loam in Ohio, averaged about 2500 per man. Under good conditions one man, exerting himself for an hour, placed 900 tips in the soil.

Removal of Second Year Canes

Remove the canes soon after fruiting. This permits thorough inspection for diseases, avoids tramping on the tip plants when removing the brush, and facilitates layering.

Digging

The tips, under favorable conditions, become well rooted by the end of the growing season. Leaving them attached to the parent plant over the winter is better than severing them in the fall, unless for fall planting.

A 4-prong potato hook or a 5-prong potato fork is good for digging. Tying in bundles of 25, with one tie near the crown, is better than throwing the plants into baskets where they may break and be difficult to separate.

In separating layer plants from the parent canes, leave 15 to 20 cm (6 to 8 in.) of cane on the tip plants. Shorten these "handles" later to 10 to 15 cm (4 to 6 in.), or so that the end of the tied bunch is uniform. Late digging interferes with work involved in fruit production and increases anthracnose infection. It is one of the few ways in which propagation of new plants may reduce the crop.

To dig, bundle, and pack 1000 plants is a good average per man per day. Charge some expense to the field against growing the plants; fruit production receives the major charge. The cost of producing both those plants that are sold and unsold should be considered. Advertising adds to propagation costs.

Leaf Stem and Leaf Bud Methods

Black raspberries can be propagated by leafy stem cuttings. Cut tender new growth into 3-bud pieces 15 to 18 cm (6 to 7 in.) long. Place the cuttings upright in a perlite mixture under mist. In about three weeks, set the plants in a nursery to harden for field planting. However, tip layering is the chief method.

PLANTING

A healthy field of black raspberries should produce 6 to 8 or more crops; the average is lower largely because of disease. Each succeeding profitable crop reduces costs and emphasizes the importance of healthy plants for setting, isolation from disease sources, suitable soil, adequate drainage, and proper culture.

When to Plant

Early spring planting of dormant stock is usually best. Stage of growth of tip plants is important in relation to time of spring planting. The growing points that give rise to new canes are easily injured. Plants growing in a region with a comparatively early spring or on light soil are more advanced at a given date than those in a region with a somewhat later season or on heavy soil; keep this in mind when ordering plants. With plants set after having been heeled-in or stored for some time or shipped late, a comparatively large number of spindly canes may result instead of a limited number of strong new canes. It is risky to set plants after the leaves appear.

"Handles".—The "handle" left on the plants at digging time aids in planting and in locating the plants, but it may be a source of anthracnose infection. At planting, cut it off, leaving none of it above ground. If removal of the handle is delayed until after growth is well started, infection of the young canes may have occurred. In brief, if the plants are thrifty and are planted early, cut off the handles immediately after setting; but if they are weak or are set in late spring, it may be best to leave the handles on and control anthracnose by spraying. Remove any growths from the handle that produces berries, or the plant will be weakened; also, if the growth is only of this kind, the plant is likely to die.

FIG. 3.9.   POOR DRAINAGE IN A LOW SPOT

FIG. 3.10. THE "HANDLE" FROM THE PARENT CANE UNLESS REMOVED MAY IN-TRODUCE ANTHRACNOSE TO THE NEW PLANTING

Depth of Planting.—Usually the entire crown is covered with 7.6 to 12.7 cm (3 to 5 in.) of soil when planting. In West Virginia, plants covered with 12.7 cm (5 in.) of soil had a higher survival rate, the new canes appeared above ground more rapidly, and total growth was greater on a heavy soil. The plants covered with 12.7 cm (5 in.) had a distinct advantage in survival rate and total growth where the handles were left attached until the new plants appeared (Childs 1963).

Good spacing for blackcaps is 1 to 1.2 m (3.5 to 4 ft) × 2.1 to 2.7 m (7 to 9 ft). Relatively close spacing reduces wind damage, but this may also be avoided by low summer topping, production of canes of thick diameter, supports, or certain other procedures.

Tillage, Herbicides, and Mulching

Clean cultivation from early spring until after harvest is commonly practiced. When the soil is heavy and the drainage none too good, the rows may be ridged.

Weeds and grasses often become established in the planting, thus harboring pests and sapping moisture from the berry plants. The use of herbicides may result in increased yields, longer life of a planting, and less labor and cultivation.

The responses from mulching black raspberries are much the same as described earlier for red raspberries.

FRUIT-BUD FORMATION

The black raspberry differentiates its flower buds somewhat earlier in the year than red and purple raspberries and erect blackberries.

FERTILIZER

Although fertilizer is helpful and even essential, it does not completely offset a poor stand of plants, poor drainage, pest damage, or many other factors. Wise use of fertilizer, including trace elements, is a part of good cultural practice. Response from fertilizer is not fully evident the year of application because the canes are produced one year and the fruit the succeeding year.

Use fertilizer practices based on soil and leaf analysis. Place some emphasis on treatments that promote vigorous growth of canes early in the season.

N-fertilized plants have dark green leaves. Yields of individual shoots and also the average size of their berries are related to amount of foliage.

The more robust the canes and the more of them per hill, up to a point, the higher the yield. Canes 12 mm (0.46 in.) in diameter may yield 186.5 g (6.58 oz) of berries; and 16.5 mm (0.65 in.) canes 340 to 1332 g (12 to 47 oz). With 7 canes per hill left for fruiting, averaging 12 mm (0.46 in.) thick, yield per hectare may be 8700 liters (3200 qt per acre). With 4 canes per hill, averaging 11 mm (0.43 in.) thick, it may be 3044 liters (1120 qt).

Annual application of sulfate of ammonia may cause the soil to be somewhat more acid. In a planting in Ohio, where 258 kg per hectare (230 lb per acre) of sulfate of ammonia were applied annually for five years, the soil acidity dropped from pH 5.3 to 4.8, which is too acid, for example, for best growth of some cover crops without liming. However, the plants produced high yields in the fifth year.

N fertilizer may make the fruit softer, but not necessarily as soft as a period of heavy rain. Many growers could beneficially apply more N than has been their custom. In many cases, however, successful black raspberry growing, apart from freedom from disease, may depend more on the physical than the chemical condition of the soil.

It may not be necessary to apply P every year. If cover crops are grown, however, the need may be greater.

Leaf samples of black raspberry may show K deficiency when the %K (dry weight) is 0.8 or less (Forshey 1969). Leaves taken from first year canes in New York in August contained 0.5 to 0.7% K (dry weight). Many, but not all, plants showed a basal leaf scorch which was not obvious in July on first year canes, although some of the scorch was evident in early June. Application of K sulfate reduced the amount of basal leaf scorch; check plots continued to show much scorch during the same period. Application of K in August increased the leaf content of K from 0.65 to 1.15% by August in the next year and resulted in 20% increase in yield, more canes, and 100% increase in weight of dormant prunings (Tomkins and Boynton 1959).

TRAINING AND PRUNING

Black raspberries are maintained in the original crowns in the row. Although trellises and supports have certain merits, wiring or staking is seldom necessary with properly summer-topped plants.

Pruning at planting time is discussed under Planting. Thinning in the row is considered in the general treatment.

Summer Topping

Proper summer topping of the terminals of the new canes of blackcaps, when the plants are 46 to 61 cm (18 to 24 in.) high, checks the terminal cane, promotes strong branching, results in a steady, low, stocky plant that is not top-heavy, and facilitates picking the next year. Low, stocky plants also are best for tip layering.

Go over the field several times in order to top the first year canes at the desired height. It is not necessary, and may be somewhat harmful, to remove only the extreme tip, because the top lateral may then extend as an upright terminal with a narrow crotch that is unduly subject to breakage. It is better to pinch or cut the main cane 7.5 to 10 cm (3 to 4 in.) or so from the tip. This causes a wider-angled, stronger union.

Topping is more difficult in established plantings (because fruiting canes are present) than in young ones. It is hard to keep up with the work without encountering some tall canes. When most of the canes have been left unchecked until late in the year, the best plan may be to support them by wires to avoid wind damage.

For a uniform topping height for first year canes, wait until all become slightly higher than 46 to 61 cm (18 to 24 in.) and then cut all of them back at one time. This also prevents the problem that arises af-

FIG. 3.11. SUMMER TOPPING IS ONE OF
THE SECRETS OF SUCCESS IN GROW-
ING BLACK RASPBERRIES WITHOUT
SUPPORT

TABLE 3.2

RELATION OF NUMBER OF CANES PER PLANT TO TOTAL YIELD,
BLACK RASPBERRY

No. Canes per Plant	No. of Plants	Avg. Two Year Yield in Oz[1]
2	12	16.8
3	16	22.4
4	25	26.1
5	33	27.5
6	20	34.5
7	20	33.4
8	4	42.0
9	5	46.3
10	4	40.3

Source: Johnston and Loree, 1927.
[1] One ounce equals 28.3 grams.

ter the field has been gone over several times, when the earlier-topped
canes have branched and their tips are difficult to distinguish from
those on unchecked canes. But when canes become higher than 91 cm
(3 ft), topping may promote growth from weak buds. It seems better to
top tall canes severely than to leave them tall without support.

Removal of Old Canes

After the first year, removal of the old canes soon after harvest is best, for reasons given previously for red raspberries. In fields used for both fruit and propagation, removing the old canes soon after harvest prevents tramping on the tip layers.

Dormant Pruning

Pruning of blackcaps has to do mostly with branches, because the main terminals are, or should be, eliminated by summer topping. Most terminals encountered in dormant pruning are weak. Cut them off just above a strong branch. Pruning decreases the number of berries and tends to increase their size. In fact, at times, increase in berry size offsets the decrease in numbers and results in little difference in marketable yield, particularly in dry seasons and on poor soils.

Shorten the branches to 10 to 18 cm (4 to 7 in.) the first year and to 20 to 30.5 cm (8 to 12 in.) in mature fields for a good correlation between berry size and yield. The more vigorous and healthy the cane, the more fruiting wood it can usually support to advantage. This must be considered when increased growth results from fertilizer. Too much fruiting wood may reduce the number of canes developing for future years

FIG. 3.12.   THE OLD CANES (THOSE THAT HAD FRUITED) WERE REMOVED
SOON AFTER HARVEST

unless soil fertility is high. Remove weak, slender canes, but avoid excessive thinning of strong canes.

Two ways to maximum yield are to increase the amount of fruiting wood per hectare by leaving longer branches when pruning, and to produce and retain more canes per hectare. In a vigorous planting in Ohio, branches left 15 to 30.5 cm (6 to 12 in.) long, retaining up to 10 canes per hill for the third, fourth, and fifth crops, did not result in a decrease in the succeeding number of canes, in their diameter, or in yield of the sixth crop.

Some soils are not fertile enough to maintain 9 to 10 canes per hill. But in many fields it would be profitable to build up fertility and regulate pruning so that more than 4 or 5 canes per hill could be maintained annually. It would often be wise to increase the number of strong canes per hill and to shorten the branches more than is the custom.

Heavy yields may not occur with less than 7410 fruiting canes per hectare (3000 per acre). Maximum yield may only be possible with 12,350 to 19,760 canes per hectare (5000 to 8000 per acre). Individual canes in thickly stocked fields may be less productive than in those thinly stocked, but yield per hectare is greater with the larger number of canes.

FIG. 3.13.   PRUNING BLACK RASPBERRIES—BEFORE AND AFTER

HARVESTING AND MARKETING

Baskets are usually filled quickest with blackberries, followed in order by black, purple, and red raspberries. The remarks on harvesting given previously for red raspberries apply also in general to black raspberries.

PART 3

PURPLE RASPBERRIES

The purple raspberry (*Rubus neglectus*) is a hybrid of black and red raspberries. The black raspberry is usually the seed parent and the red raspberry the pollen parent. The plants are larger than the parents, an example of hybrid vigor.

Plantings of purples are scattered in small plantings throughout the East. The purple raspberry is well liked by the processors and, when they can obtain them in sufficient quantity, they may pay a premium for them. Some persons consider ice cream made with purples to be the best of all.

In an Illinois study, red × black and purple × black combinations were completely incompatible. Red × purple, purple × purple, and purple self-fruited produced fruit usually of normal appearance, but with some incompatibility. All other combinations were fully compatible. Pollen tubes in the incompatible combinations did not progress beyond the upper third of the style and exhibited a thickening of the wall at the tip. Normal pollen tube growth and fertilization occurred in the compatible combinations (Zych 1955).

Most named purple cultivars are self-fruitful. Sometimes, however, crumbliness of the drupelets occurs.

CULTIVARS

As with other small fruits, your instructor or Extension Service can indicate the most suitable cultivars to plant in your area.

PROPAGATION

Most purple raspberries are propagated, like the black raspberry, by tip layering. However, some can be propagated from suckers, like the red. The purple raspberry matures its crop later, tip layering is later, and a lower percent of tips take root than with the black raspberry. But the purple, owing to greater vigor, may produce as many plants, or more, than the black.

PLANTING

A healthy field of purple raspberries should produce 6 to 8 or more crops. The average is not more than 3 or 4 crops, largely because of disease. Hectare averages of fairly good fields of purples are 4620 to 6250 liters (1700 to 2300 qt per acre).

Time of planting and spacing are much the same as given earlier for black raspberries, viz., early spring at 1.1 to 1.2 × 2.1 to 2.7 m (3.5 to 4 × 7 to 9 ft).

PRUNING

Summer-top purple raspberry a little higher than black raspberry. The proper amount to head back purple raspberry bushes depends on their vigor. Usually shorten the branches to 15 to 25 cm (6 to 10 in.) the first year and 25 to 36 cm (10 to 14 in.) in succeeding years. Strong, healthy canes can support more fruiting wood than weak canes.

PART 4

ERECT AND SEMI-ERECT BLACKBERRIES

The genus *Rubus*, and especially its subgenus *Eubatus*, are composed of a highly heterogeneous series of species and species hybrids. Polyploidy in somatic cells ranges from diploids or 14 (2X) to dodecaploid or 84. Certain crosses which normally are not successful may be achieved by colchicine treatment, which affects the chromosome status. For example, 14 (2X) × 28 (4X) crossing results in triploids (21 or 3X chromosomes), which are sterile in varying degree; but the cross can be made more effectively by doubling the 14 chromosomes to 28 by colchicine treatment and then crossing this "induced" type with the "natural" 28 type (Britton and Hull 1957; Shoemaker and Sturrock 1959).

Some examples of (2n) blackberry chromosome numbers are:

14 chromosomes: McDonald, Burbank Thornless, Oklawaha
28 chromosomes: Eldorado, Nanticoke, Brazos
42 chromosomes: Cory Thornless, Chehalem, Olallie
49 chromosomes: Boysen, Young, Lucretia

FIG. 3.14.   COMPANION CROPPING MAY PROVIDE AN INCOME IN EARLY
YEARS, BUT FOR REASONS GIVEN IN THE TEXT THERE ARE DISADVANTAGES
FOR BOTH FRUITS

53 chromosomes: Carolina
56 chromosomes: Austin Thornless
63 chromosomes: Cascade, Pacific

The erect or semi-erect type of blackberry is the main type grown in northern regions. It is distinguished from trailers by its squarish stems and can be grown without support, especially when summer-topped.

Blackberry production is "big business" in certain areas in Texas. In the Lindale-Tyler area alone the commercial planting exceeds 2430 ha (6000 acres); 10% of the fruit goes to fresh markets and 90% is processed. Besides the commercial plantings in Smith, Wood, and Henderson Counties there are numerous small plantings in other parts of Texas.

Other leading erect-type blackberry production areas are in Arkansas, Oklahoma, Missouri, Michigan, New York, and several other eastern states.

CULTIVARS

As with other small fruits, your instructor or Extension Service can indicate the most suitable cultivars to plant in your area.

SEED SIZE AND INHERITANCE

Nine seedling populations involving small, intermediate, and large-seeded clones of tetraploid blackberries (*Eubatus*) were evaluated for seed size inheritance. All seedling progenies exhibited a wide range of seed sizes with high frequencies of transgressive segregations, especially for small sizes. The data support a model for quantitative inheritance with partial dominance for the small seed size. Calculations of heritability showed an average maximum estimate of 97%, supporting previous observations of the lack of environmental effects on the expression of seed size in blackberries (Moore *et al.* 1975).

POLLINATION

Erect blackberries are potentially self-fruitful. Failure to set well is often due to a virus-induced sterility. (See Sterile Plant, under Diseases.)

PROPAGATION

Most erect blackberries can be propagated from suckers, but the rate of increase is much greater from root cuttings. Good root cuttings are made 10 to 18 cm (4 to 7 in.) long, and slightly less than 1.3 cm (0.5 in.) in diameter. Root pieces over 1.3 cm (0.5 in.) thick may be too old for best results; those 3 mm (0.125 in.) or less thick may not produce strong, vigorous plants.

For a nursery row, place the cuttings 7.6 to 15 cm (3 to 6 in.) apart horizontally in a furrow, or scatter them on the surface of a nursery bed, and cover with 5 cm (2 in.) of soil. Many cuttings can be made from a blackberry plant with a strong root system. After a year in a nursery the young plants should have developed sufficiently to be dug and set in a permanent planting.

Plants can be obtained by plowing a deep furrow away from an established plant row, gathering the exposed roots and placing them in damp burlap or strong plastic bags to avoid drying. Cut the roots to the desired length.

When all the old plants are removed from a part of the field, new plants grow from pieces of roots left in the soil. Plants from a healthy planting may be set out; they may be followed by a second stand of plants.

YIELD

Yields of healthy, established erect blackberries in northern regions may be 4620 to 6250 liters per ha (1700 to 2300 qt per acre). No fruit is borne the first year. It may take three years from planting to obtain a high yield.

Commercial growers in the Lindale section in Texas obtain 1233 to 2130 kg per ha (1100 to 1900 lb per acre) of berries during the second year. Yield increases rapidly during years 3 to 7 and levels off from years 8 to 10. If plant loss has been high during the early life of the planting, yields may start to decline around the seventh year. Favorable yields from plantings with good stands and vigorous growth range from 3923 to 7286 kg per ha (3500 to 6500 lb per acre) (Morris 1970).

PLANTING

Planting in early spring usually gives the best results. In Texas plantings can be made from November on.

A common spacing in the East is 1.2 to 1.5 × 1.8 to 2.7 m (4 to 5 × 6 to 9 ft). In Texas and Arkansas 3.7 m (12 ft) between rows is the minimum commercially, and many growers prefer 4.3 to 4.9 m (14 to 16 ft) for machine-harvesting.

Root cuttings can be spaced 30 to 91 cm (1 to 3 ft) apart in the row and the plants allowed to grow in hedge fashion. Many growers prefer to place two root pieces in the same spot to assure a more perfect stand.

Set rooted cuttings at the depth they formerly stood in the nursery or slightly deeper. Open the furrow for them immediately before planting to avoid loss of soil moisture. In light sandy soil, root cuttings are dropped flat in the furrow and soil is firmed around each cutting by foot.

TRAINING AND PRUNING

Retain slightly fewer vigorous first year canes per foot of row with the erect blackberry than with the black raspberry. A longer branch should remain after pruning the former.

Summer Topping

Topping the terminals of erect blackberries usually prevents the need for support and promotes fruitful branches. Topping is done when the new canes are 76 to 91 cm (2.5 to 3 ft) or slightly higher. The optimum height varies with different cultivars and their vigor, and with the kind of machine used for harvesting large plantings.

FIG. 3.15. WHEN THE CANES ARE TOPPED 45.7 to 76.2 cm (18 to 30 in.) HIGH, THE TOP LATERAL MAY DEVELOP IN A WEAK WAY IF 7.6 to 10.2 cm (3 to 4 in.) OF THE CANE ARE NOT REMOVED

Shortening the Branches

This is done during the dormant season. It is sometimes wise to delay this pruning until fruitful and unfruitful clusters can be distinguished, since different cultivars vary in fruiting habits. When it is seen that the fruit will be borne relatively far out on the branches, prune comparatively lightly. Shortening such branches too much may reduce yield. In general shorten the branches about 50%.

Clipping the top and sides of the row sometimes is done in large plantings by means of a cutter machine.

Removal of Old Canes

Remove all old canes at ground level after they have fruited. Also remove weak and spindly canes. The removal and burning of the old canes immediately after harvest may help control some insects and diseases. For areas where the growing season is long and double blossom occurs, see Diseases That Primarily Affect Flowers and Fruit (Chap. 3).

CULTIVATION

In the young planting, cultivate shallowly so as not to disturb the root system, and frequently to prevent grass and seedlings from becoming established. Hoeing is one of the tedious and expensive operations. A newly emerged sprout is tender and easily broken. Rarely does a strong, acceptable plant come from a root cutting that has lost its first sprout.

COVER CROPS

Growing and turning under a cover or green-manure crop before planting is a good practice, especially when the soil is deficient in organic matter and is susceptible to wind and water erosion.

Two major disadvantages may be encountered where cover crops are used after the berries are planted. Deep-plowing to incorporate the cover crop in the soil cuts the blackberry roots, which in turn develop many suckers that are difficult to eradicate. Aphids, thrips, plant bugs, and other insects feed on cover crops, especially legumes. Some of these insects attack the berry plants and the fruit after the cover crop has been plowed under.

When a cover crop is grown in a berry planting, a rotary-type mower or shredder can be used to cut it down before plowing under. This eliminates deep-plowing (Morris 1970).

HANDLING HARVESTED BERRIES

Immediately after harvest place the berries in a cool place. If the berries are to be processed, deliver them to the plant as soon as possible. The quality of non-refrigerated berries deteriorates rapidly when they are held at 26°C (75°F) for over 24 hr. If the berries cannot be processed immediately, store at 0°C (32°F) and 85 to 90% RH. Since blackberries can be held for only 4 or 5 days under these conditions, it is not general practice to store blackberries that are to be processed (Morris 1972).

MACHINE-HARVESTING

Under optimum conditions in Arkansas, plants grown from good root cuttings are ready for machine-harvesting two years after planting and reach peak production in the fourth and fifth years.

Pruning is one of the chief cultural practices in producing blackberries for machine-harvesting. Top the new canes of semi-erect cultivars like Brazos at a height of 76 to 82 cm (36 to 40 in.) This can be done with a mowing machine modified to do the job. Side-mounted cutters will prune the sides of the hedgerow to the desired width.

A self-propelled over-the-row machine developed in Arkansas shakes the fruit from the plant, taking advantage of the natural abscission of the blackberries. When the fruit reaches maturity, it falls from the plant at the slightest agitation. Unripe berries are left on the bush for later harvest (Morris 1972).

Operation is by electric power from a gas motor-driven generator unit. The beater mechanism consists of four arms on each side, adjustable for length and frequency of stroke, essentially in the range of 100 strokes per minute. It is vital to provide complete shaking, because the berries left on the bush may develop mold and infect berries of the next harvest. The berries fall on fold-away spray-mounted catcher frames located along the outer edge of the catcher system to minimize fruit loss. Belts on each side of the row convey the berries to field containers, where the trash and leaves are blown away. Two lug tenders are positioned on the rear of the machine.

The machine has a harvesting capacity of 0.4 to 0.6 ha (1 to 1.5 acres) of blackberries per hr. Set up a harvesting schedule for 4 ha (10 acres) per day on a 4-day schedule. Maintain this rigid schedule once the berries start to mature to prevent the problem of a build-up of overripe, moldy berries that can create a severe mold problem during transit.

FIRMNESS

The large Humble cultivar berry is rather soft. Preharvest sprays of 0.2 and 0.4% $CaCl_2$ and 6 g per gal. Botran 75W applied 1, 2, and 3 times delayed postharvest softening of Humble for 4 days. A single spray of 25% water-soluble wax 1 day before harvest also delayed softening. Storage at reduced atmospheric pressure (185 mm) delayed softening for 8 days, possibly as a result of ethylene removal. Softening caused by 1 ppm ethylene was partially overcome by addition of 10% CO_2 and 10% benlate (Lipe 1976).

PART 5

WESTERN TRAILING TYPES

The western trailing types do not succeed well in the East. Large quantities of these fruits are produced in the Pacific Northwest and California, as well as in British Columbia.

The main western trailing forms are the Thornless Evergreen blackberry, Marion blackberry, Boysenberry, Youngberry, and Loganberry. Some others are Aurora, Brainerd, Himalaya, and the hybrids such as Cascade, Pacific, and Olallie.

Trailing blackberries and related types develop deep roots, can obtain moisture from a considerable depth, and are more tolerant of drought than raspberries and erect blackberries. Also, some of them, e.g., Evergreen, endure more winter soil water than most other berries.

The western trailers produce higher yields than erect blackberries, but the latter are hardier. The fruit, for the most part, bruises easily. Its main use is for wine and freezing. Frozen berries are used for pie fillers, jams, and jellies.

THORNLESSNESS

Thornless trailing types may be chimeras: i.e., the outer tissue of the cane is thornless but the center tissue of both canes and roots has the characteristics of thorniness. Perpetuation of such thornless forms must be from stem cuttings or by tip-layering; shoots from the roots always bear thorns. Therefore, in growing them avoid cutting the roots, because shoots that arise from these cut or damaged roots will be thorny and should be discarded.

Some plants, including the roots, are genetically thornless. The thornless characteristic is recessive. When a genetically thornless plant is crossed with a thorny cultivar, all the resulting seedlings are thorny, and further populations must be grown or backcrossed to recover the thornlessness.

Several thornless trailing cultivars have been grown for many years, e.g., Thornless Evergreen blackberry, Thornless Boysenberry, Thornless Loganberry, and Thornless Youngberry. These have largely replaced their thorny ancestors.

WESTERN TRAINING AND PRUNING SYSTEMS

New canes arise in the spring of each year. Choose a training system and erect it, usually in the planting year. Train the canes in late winter or early spring to permit tillage during the growing season. Bend the canes carefully to avoid breaking or forming sharp angles that may break later. Many branch canes form when a cane is broken; these usually are slender and increase the number to be handled in training. The outer end of the cane usually can be cut off without greatly reducing the yield. The size of the berries may be increased when half or more of the cane is cut off, but the number of berries produced may be reduced.

Vertical Training Systems

One-wire.—String a heavy wire tightly 152 to 168 cm (5 to 5.5 ft) high on posts 4.9 to 6.1 m (16 to 20 ft) apart. Take up and twist the canes along the wire in either one or both directions from the plant. Since many canes are wrapped together around one wire it must be strong or it may break. All the berries are at one height for harvesting.

Two-wire.—Set posts 4.9 to 7.3 m (16 to 24 ft) apart along the row. Large posts may be set farther apart and smaller posts or stakes set every 3.1 to 3.7 m (10 to 12 ft). Stretch two wires between the posts, the upper wire at 137 to 168 cm (4.5 to 5.5 ft) and the lower wire at 76 to 107 cm (2.5 to 3.5 ft).

Weave or Wreath System.—Take 2 or 3 canes together and pass them from upper to lower wire and back again to form circles or wreaths. All the space between wires is utilized. More time is needed in training than with some other systems.

Loop System.—Divide the canes of each plant into 2 parts. Take each part separately to the top wire. Make 1 or 2 twists around the wire and

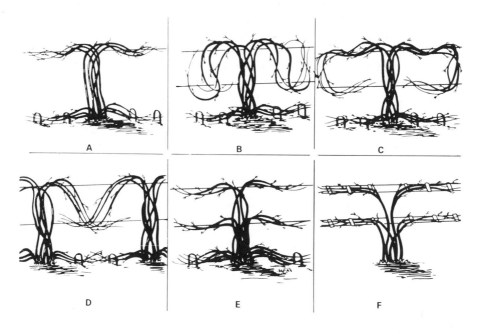

FIG. 3.16.   TRAINING WESTERN TRAILING BRAMBLE FRUITS

A — single wire (fruiting canes above, growing canes below); B — weave or wreath system; C — loop system; D — half loop or interlocking system; E — four-arm system; F — four-wire horizontal trellis (fruiting canes above, growing canes below).

then bring the canes down to the lower wire and turn inward with 1 or 2 twists. Similarly loop the other half of the canes on the other side of the plant to form a double loop. The canes can be trained quickly.

Half-loop or Interlocking System.—Do not turn the canes inward. Instead, bring them down to the lower wire and interlock with the canes of the next plant.

Rope System.—Divide the canes into four bundles and extend them in both directions along both wires. Take the longer canes to the top wires. Canes may be cut off and tied at the point of intersection with those of the next plant or interlocked with them.

Fan System.—Distribute individual canes on the wires in fan form. Tie them to the wires, or interlock and twist along the upper wire. Much tying is needed.

Horizontal Training Systems

Two-wire.—Support two wires on cross-arms (30.5 to 61 cm, or 1 to 2 ft) nailed to posts. Lay other cross-arms of wood or wire on the wires and place the canes on them.

Four-wire.—Here a top pair of horizontal wires is 2 ft above a lower pair. If the fruiting canes are placed on the upper wire, train new growth on the lower wires. After removing the old canes, take up the new canes to the upper wires, or leave them to fruit on the lower wires. In this case the new canes are trained up to the upper wires where they remain until after they have fruited.

THORNLESS EVERGREEN BLACKBERRY

The Evergreen was introduced into Oregon early in the history of the state.

The rope, loop, and fan training systems are used, as well as some of the other systems discussed. Many growers prefer to run the bundies of canes in one direction on the wires.

A new system which appears promising in British Columbia is to pinch back all new canes when 46 to 61 cm (18 to 24 in.) long. Although the canes are shorter the number is increased. This system may give higher yields (Littler 1965).

After harvest cut down and burn the old canes and keep the new canes trained along the row. When placing these canes on the wires the following spring some thorny canes may be noticed; cut these off at ground level.

In late winter or early spring shorten the canes to 3 m (10 ft), lift them to the wire and wrap or tie them in place.

A planting grown under suitable conditions may produce for up to 15 years. Average yields are about 11.2 metric tons per ha (5 tons per acre). Pick every 4 or 5 days when the berries are completely black but still firm. If a spell of hot weather occurs during this period, complete the picking by noon.

MARION BLACKBERRY

Marion ripens 3 to 5 days later and is smaller than Boysen. It is a *Rubus* hybrid with parentage going back to the native western selections and the Himalaya. Very good flavor.

When Marion is spaced 76.2, 132.4, and 304.8 cm (2.5, 5, and 10 ft) apart and trained in late summer, increased yield occurs at the higher plant densities. The increase is attributed to stimulation of axillary buds and their subsequent lateral growths on which fruit buds develop (Sheets *et al.* 1972).

BOYSEN (BOYSENBERRY)

Boysen is usually more vigorous than Young and ripens slightly later. The berry is large (3.1 cm or 1.75 in. long) with a purplish-black cast, excellent flavor and large seeds. Like Young the plants are prickly. It has a distinctive aroma (which Young lacks) and is covered with a dusty bloom (Young is shiny). There is also a more distinct core in Boysen than in Young. It is not quite as sweet as Young. California 1935. It is extensively planted in California because of its high yield and high fresh and frozen quality, and for its quality for pies.

The first crop is picked in southern California May 20 to June 25; in the San Joaquin Valley May 23 to June 25; in the Sebastopol June 2 to July 10; in the Central Valley June 20 to August 10. A second crop is produced in southern California and in the Central Coast area, thereby extending the picking season through August. Propagate the thornless form by tip layering, not from root cuttings.

YOUNG (YOUNGBERRY)

Young is earlier than Boysen. It is popular in local markets in Texas because of its large fruit and excellent flavor. The plants are vigorous and easy to pick. It yields better in east Texas than in central and south Texas. It is susceptible to anthracnose. Sunscald may cause some injury when the canes are tied to stakes. It produces 2 to 3 trailing new canes each year from the base of the main cane. It has more prickles than most cultivars and those on the canes are unusually long. These prickles are not considered a deterrent in harvesting, since the fruit is produced on racemes 12.7 to 15.2 cm (5 to 6 in.) long growing perpendicular to the cane. The fruit is large and purplish-black. The few large seeds are scarcely noticeable. It makes an attractive pack.

LOGAN (LOGANBERRY)

The berry is reddish purple, long, and acid. There is no naming of its cultivars, other than that the thornless type is preferred.

Production of Logan is largely restricted to the Central Coast region of California, the Willamette Valley of Oregon, the lower Columbia River area in Washington, the southern tip of Vancouver Island, and sheltered locations in the Fraser Valley in British Columbia.

The three main outlets for loganberries, each of which requires a specific maturity are: *Fresh market* berries must be bright and in prime condition. Pick every day to maintain this condition. *Canning* or *freezing* berries must be firm, reddish purple, and in good condition. Pick every second day. *Wine* berries must be thoroughly ripe, i.e., dark purple but not shriveling. At this stage the berries contain a high percentage of juice and have reached maximum weight. Pick by appearance (Littler 1964).

In the second year after planting, a hectare of loganberries in an area suitable for this fruit may produce 6.7 to 11.2 metric tons (3 to 5 tons per acre) of berries. This yield can be maintained until the planting is about 12 years old.

The rope, loop, or fan systems of training can be used to advantage.

During the growing season train the canes flat along the ground and keep them in place with stakes 61 cm (24 in.) long. Drive these stakes into the ground deeply enough to make them firm.

When canes have fruited they are removed and burned. Head back new canes to the desired length when they are put up on the wires in spring. A plant should produce 10 to 14 healthy canes each year, but if more than this are produced remove the weaker ones. If laterals occur remove them entirely or cut them back to 5 or 6 buds.

HYBRID WESTERN BLACKBERRIES

The trailing type that is native west of the Cascade Mountains from northern California to British Columbia probably has the finest flavor of any blackberry, but yields are not high. Cascade, Chehalem, and Olallie were developed by Waldo *et al.* in Oregon.

PART 6

SOUTHEASTERN TRAILING BLACKBERRIES OR DEWBERRIES

Fruiting clusters of this southern trailing type of blackberry are smaller and more open than in the erect and western trailing types. They have a low chilling requirement and will not succeed in the North. The berries are large and soft. Interplanting with an effective pollinator is required in most cases. Because the trailing canes have little wood fiber, they must be supported. Support may consist of bundles of canes tied in "hills" to a stake. Another method is to extend and tie the canes on horizontal wires.

In the Deep South a good practice is to cut back to ground level both old and new canes after harvest. A supply of new canes has adequate time to develop in the long growing season.

BRAMBLE FRUIT DISEASES

Certified or disease-tested plants are the best for planting in the cultivars available. Set them a safe distance from other bramble fruits to prevent spread of viruses, and of verticillium wilt in particular, into the certified plants. Aphids can spread viruses 0.8 km (0.5 mi.) or more. In a certified program plants initially free of viruses are propagated by qualified growers under strict regulations designed to prevent virus infection and to control crown gall, verticillium wilt, nematodes, and other important pests.

Diseases That Affect Entire Plants and Cause Stunting

Virus Diseases.—The exact nature of viruses is not well understood. They are transmitted from plant to plant, chiefly by aphids. Infected bushes never recover. All stock propagated vegetatively from infected plants also is infected. When a planting becomes more than 3% infected with virus diseases the plants seriously decline in vigor and yield. Plant only virus-tested plants.

Leaf curl leaves are darker green than normal, small, and tightly curled inward and downward. Infected plants may assume an upright habit of growth and be conspicuous alongside normal plants. The fruit is small. Purple raspberries seem immune to leaf curl. At least two blackcap cultivars, Plum Farmer and New Logan, seldom seem to be infected.

Mosaic (combination of black raspberry necrosis and Rubus yellownet virus) symptoms are a mottling of the leaves and splotches of shades of yellow and green that vary in size and contour. Yield suffers, flavor is lost, the fruit crumbles easily, and the planting is short-lived.

An aphid is the vector of the components of red raspberry mosaic. Until recently the red raspberry aphids in Europe and North America were thought to be biological races of the same species *Amphorophora rubi*. However, the North American species is rightfully *A. agathonica* (Converse *et al.* 1971).

Because immunity appears to be determined primarily by a single dominant gene, selections that are homozygous for the characteristic should be obtained with relative ease and, when used in breeding, ensure immune progeny. It should be possible, therefore, for all red raspberry breeding programs in North America to produce aphid-immune cultivars that will ensure control of red raspberry mosaic (Daubeny 1972).

Green mosaic (green mottle mosaic, red raspberry mosaic, mild mosaic, raspberry necrosis) is found in red, purple, and black raspberries. It is most serious in its effects on blackcaps, but is more widely distributed on reds. Infected blackcap canes are retarded in leaf development on their fruiting canes in spring. In yellow mosaic of black raspberries, the foliage becomes yellowish, with different mottling, seldom with the dark green "blisters" of green mosaic.

The large aphid *Amphorophora* spreads both green and yellow mosaics. A single aphid can acquire at least one of the component viruses of black raspberry necrosis after ½ hr of feeding and transmit within a 2 min transfer feeding. Rubus yellow-net virus has a similar vector relationship (Stace-Smith 1956).

The aphid that spreads mosaic seems to be reluctant to feed on some cultivars, e.g., Washington, in the Pacific Northwest.

Streak symptoms do not appear on blackcaps until the temperature becomes fairly high. Affected plants are stunted. The leaflets are slightly or distinctly rolled, and a coarse splotching or obscure mottling may occur; those at the tips of canes are twisted or distorted. Purplish stripes may appear on the canes.

Control of virus diseases is hopeless in heavily infected plantings, but in nursery or new plantings it requires roguing out and destroying all diseased plants, including all nearby diseased wild or cultivated plants. In roguing, diseased plants may be dug, carried from the field and burned, or burned in place. They should not be dug and allowed to wilt, because the aphids present may crawl off and find their way to other plants. For new plantings, obtain disease-tested stock, isolate it from disease sources, and rogue out infected or suspected plants as soon as noticed. Do not confuse frost damage with virus-diseased plants.

Orange rust, a systemic fungus disease, is the chief disease in erect blackberries. Before the leaves are full-grown, many orange-colored blisters occur on the lower side of the leaves and give an orange cast to the plant. Recovery that seems to take place relatively late in the season is temporary, for all diseased plants will have rust the next year. Destroy all rusted plants (including the root system) in the field as well as nearby wild plants before the spores are shed.

Diseases That Primarily Affect Canes

Anthracnose (light-colored sunken, cracked spots surrounded by a red ring, chiefly on the canes) of black raspberries can largely be checked by removal of the "handles" at planting time and/or by spraying with 3.8 liters (1 gal.) of Elgetol or Krenite in 378.5 liters (100 gal.) of water when the buds show 6 mm (0.25 in.) of green in early spring, and again just before bloom. When cane infections on red raspberries are numerous, the fungus grows throughout the bark, thus producing gray bark in the fall. Severe infection may contribute to winterkilling.

Cane blight shows as smoky-colored, cankered areas with dying or dead wood and bark. Weakening of the plant by freezing is a common forerunner of cane blight. Good culture, including removal of the second year canes soon after harvest, helps avoid the trouble. To control Gloeosporium blight (wilting of the tips and canes turning blue), spray as for anthracnose.

Spur blight shows on new canes as brownish discolorations in the bark just below the leaf attachment. These spots extend along the cane but may be confined to small areas with green bark between. On second year canes infected the previous year, small yellow leaves result on weak laterals that wither and dry early in the season. Provide for free circulation of air, as by thinning of canes, good spacing of rows, or other procedures that prevent dense growth. Good drainage and weed control are important. Spur blight seems to occur less frequently on seedlings with hairy, spine-free, non-pigmented canes, and also on seedlings whose canes have a moderately dense wax covering.

Verticillium wilt in blackcaps is indicated by yellowing and dropping of the leaves. Stunting results from a shortening of the internodes. Tips of the first year canes wilt first. The woody cylinder of the roots is brownish. Root infection may not involve all of the root system, and so symptoms may develop on one side of a first year cane or on 1 or 2 of several in a group. Canes infected the previous year often die or show poorly developed buds in the fruiting year; second year canes may open their buds, but the expanding leaves and laterals are stunted, yellowish, and withered. If fruit forms in infected canes, it is small and insipid. A thin stand of plants in reds may result because suckering is reduced. Soil fumigation at planting time may be helpful.

Diseases That Primarily Affect Leaves

Mildew may seriously affect red raspberries, particularly if air circulation is poor. Leaf spot, if it becomes a problem, can be checked with a fungicide, as can mildew and rust. Yellow rust appears late in the season. Infected leaves are covered with orange-colored masses of fungus spores. Spores may also be produced in the fruit. Spruce trees are an alternate host.

Diseases That Primarily Affect Flowers and Fruit

Rosette (double blossom) attacks blackberries in the Deep South. Early in spring the fungus-diseased buds are more swollen than normal buds and often are reddish. Small buds may form laterally to the main buds. Sepals and petals are increased in size and number; the petals are more or less crinkled and pink. Fruit either does not mature or is small and worthless. The fungus promotes bushy growths called witches' broom. Where the growing season is long, cut back both old canes and new shoots of susceptible cultivars to ground level after harvest and then spray the new growth 3 times at 10-day intervals with a fungicide.

Sterile-plant virus causes an effect often referred to as nubbins, three-seeded, he-berry, and buckshot. Flower parts become dry. Poorly developed fruit occurs in the same cluster with normal fruit. As the growth spreads, set of normal fruit lessens. Plants eventually show decreased vigor and many new, thinner canes per crown. There are fewer laterals than in healthy plants. No effective control is known, nor is the method of transmission (Morris 1970).

Fruit rot caused by a Botrytis fungus organism results in losses of fruit by rotting and reduction of quality by discoloration of the drupelets. The disease enters mainly through the blossoms and develops slowly until moisture content of the fruit increases, when it develops rapidly.

Mold growth may be so heavy that the berries mat together. Flavor is impaired, and moldy fruit should be discarded if mold is visible. Often mold cannot be seen with the naked eye. Rain falling 1 or 2 days before picking is the chief factor determining the amount of mold in freshly picked berries, so pick as rapidly as possible after rain and process the berries with a minimum of delay.

The Howard mold count of pulped fruit is based on the percentage of microscopic fields (100X) showing mold filaments. Canned berries shipped in interstate commerce may be seized if the mold count is much higher than 40% positive microscopic fields.

Diseases That Affect Roots

Root rot has been discussed under Strawberries. Nematode activity may intensify root rot losses.

Crown gall (bacterial) shows as warty galls on the roots or base of crowns. The disease may enter through wounds caused mechanically or by insects. Avoid planting on infected sites. The disease may be spread through a planting in soil cultivation.

Mushroom root-rot can be detected by removing soil from around the crown and peeling back the bark. Fan-shaped, felt-like, white mold growth can be seen beneath the bark and wood. Within the bark of decayed parts, dark brown or black strands occur. Mushrooms of the disease may be seen at the base of affected plants. Avoid sites where oak trees grew previously.

BRAMBLE FRUIT INSECTS

Insects That Attack Fruit and Foliage

Byturus fruitworm causes wormy berries. Canners may refuse fruit when infected berries are detected, because of pure food laws. The larvae (light-brown areas on each segment) feed chiefly on the berry's core; some remain in picked fruit and may cause crumbly berries. Adult yellowish-brown beetles feed on fruit buds and unfolded leaves, on stamens and pistils, and around the base of stamens on open flowers.

Sawfly injury appears as brown blisters or tunnels with a flattened, active larva less than 8 mm (⅓ in.) long feeding within; 2 broods may occur.

Red spider mites feed on the underside of the leaves. The combined rasping and sucking mechanically disturbs the leaf tissues and results in sap losses. At first the foliage seems to be covered with minute yellow spots; later it is grayish; and still later the entire leaf may turn brown and die. Hot, dry weather favors the pest. Drenching rains or overhead irrigation help overcome infestation.

Two-spotted mite is usually pale yellow to green, sometimes reddish-brown, with two large indefinite black spots on the back and body. It may cause a whitish flecking on the upper surface of the leaves. The leaves may dry up and drop. Damage is usually during a dry period.

Blackberry mite, of microscopic size, feeds between the drupelets and core of the berry causing, in the West, the "redberry disease of blackberries." Affected berries are brighter red than unripened fruit, become hard, and remain on the bushes. "Red berry" may vary from a single drupelet in a black berry to many red drupelets.

Aphid injury is indirect, by spreading virus diseases.

Insects That Affect Stems and Roots

Cane maggot adults lay a single egg on leaves at the tip of a young shoot. The egg hatches within a week, and the resulting maggot bores down about 15 cm (6 in.) inside the shoot and then turns upward and girdles it, leaving a bluish ring. The shoot drops over at the point of girdling, shrivels, and dries up. The maggot remains in the shoot until the next spring, when it becomes an adult fly.

Red-necked cane borer causes swellings 2.5 to 5 cm (1 to 2 in.) long on the basal portion of the canes. The damage may result in failure to fruit and in much breakage.

Crown borer adult is a clear-winged moth that superficially resembles a yellow jacket. Eggs are deposited on the leaves in late summer or early fall. Upon hatching, the larvae crawl down to the base of the cane where they winter in small cuts in the cane, usually just below the soil surface. Next spring the larvae bore into the crown, causing swelling there. The larvae again winter in their tunnels. When the new canes attain full growth, they are broken off by wind at a point about 5 cm (2 in.) below ground. The life cycle requires two years.

Snowy tree cricket deposits its curved, light-orange eggs in closely spaced, single rows about 5 cm (2 in.) long in the canes in late summer or early fall. The egg punctures may weaken the cane so that it breaks.

Nematodes (microscopic worms) feed on the roots. They tend to be spotty in their distribution.

REFERENCES

BARRITT, B.H., and TORRE, L.C. 1975. Fruit anthocyanin pigments of red raspberry cultivars.   J. Am. Soc. Hort. Sci. *100*, 98-100.

BELL, R.C. 1951. Mechanical raspberry harvesting. Am. Fruit Grower, May.

BENNETT, E., and WEEKS, W.D. 1960. A partial chemical analysis of two varieties of raspberry which differ in winter hardiness. Proc. Am. Soc. Hort. Sci. 76, 366-69.

BOOSTER, D.E. 1962. Mechanical harvesting of berries. Am. Fruit Grower, May.

BOYNTON, D., and WILDE, M. 1959. Development of black raspberry fruit. Proc. Am. Soc. Hort. Sci. 73, 158-63.

BRITTON, D.M., and HULL, J.W. 1957. Chromosome number of Rubus. Md. Contrib. 2776.

CARNE, L.C. 1965. Red raspberry growing with particular reference to the Fraser Valley. Brit. Columbia Dept. Agr. Lft., 1-7.

CHILDS, W.H. 1963. Growth response of Cumberland black raspberries to variations in planting behavior in a heavy soil. Proc. Am. Soc. Hort. Sci. 83, 428-30.

CONVERSE, R.H., and BAILEY, J.S. 1961. Resistance of some Rubus varieties to colonization by Amphorophora rubi. Proc. Am. Soc. Hort. Sci. 78, 251-55.

CONVERSE, R.H. et al. 1971. Search for biological races in Amphorophora rubi agathonica, Hottes. Can. J. Plant Sci. 51, 81-85.

CRANDALL, P.C., and CHAMBERLAIN, J.D. 1972. Effects of water stress, cane size, and growth regulators of floral primordia development on red raspberries. J. Am. Soc. Hort. Sci. 97, 418-19.

CRANDALL, P.C. et al. 1966. Mechanically harvesting red raspberries and removal of insects from the harvested product. Proc. Am. Soc. Hort. Sci. 78, 251-55.

CRANDALL, P.C. et al. 1974. Influence of cane number and diameter, irrigation, and carbohydrate reserves on the fruit number in red raspberries. J. Am. Soc. Hort. Sci. 99, 524-26.

DAUBENY, H.A. 1966. Inheritance of immunity in red raspberry to the North American strain of the aphid Amphorophora. Proc. Am. Soc. Hort. Sci. 88, 346-51.

DAUBENY, H.A. 1969. Some variations in self-fertility in the red raspberry. Can. J. Plant Sci. 49, 511-12.

DAUBENY, H.A. 1971. Self-fertility in red raspberry cultivars and selections. J. Am. Soc. Hort. Sci. 96, 588-91.

DAUBENY, H.A., and STACE-SMITH, R. 1963. Note on immunity to the North American strain of red raspberry mosaic vector, the aphid Amphorophora. Can. J. Plant Sci. 43, 413-14.

DAUBENY, H.A. et al. 1970. Effects of virus infection on drupelet set of four red raspberry cultivars. J. Am. Soc. Hort. Sci. 95, 730-31.

DENISEN, E.L. 1968. Amethyst raspberry. Iowa Farm Sci. 23, 8, 11-12.

DENISEN, E.L. 1976. Liberty raspberry. Hort Sci. 11, No. 4, 433.

DOUGHTY, C.C. et al. 1972. Cold injury to red raspberries and the effect of premature defoliation and mite damage. J. Am. Soc. Hort. Sci. 97, 670-73.

EATON, G.W., and TURNER, N. 1971. Embryo sac development in relation to virus infection of four raspberry cultivars. J. Am. Soc. Hort. Sci. 96, 159-61.

EAVES, C.A. et al. 1972. Influence of preharvest sprays of calcium salts and wax on fruit quality of red raspberry. J. Am. Soc. Hort. Sci. 97, 706-707.

FEJAR, S.O., and SPANGELO, L.P. 1973. Red raspberry yield components and their relation to mechanical harvesting. J. Am. Soc. Hort. Sci. *98*, No. 5, 432-36.

FORSHEY, C.G. 1969. Potassium nutrition of deciduous fruits. HortScience *4*, 39-41.

FREEMAN, J.A. et al. 1969. Increased pollen abortion caused by viruses in four red raspberry cultivars. Can. J. Plant Sci. *49*, 373-74.

GRIGSBY, B.H. 1938. Physiological investigations on red raspberry plants inoculated with red raspberry mosaic. Mich. Agr. Expt. Bull. *169*.

HALTVICK, E.T., and STRUCKMEYER, B.E. 1955. Blossom bud differentiation in red raspberry. Proc. Am. Soc. Hort. Sci. *86*, 234-37.

HILL, R.G. 1958. Fruit development of red raspberry. Ohio Agr. Expt. Sta. Res. Bull. *803*.

HILL, R.G., and BANTA, E.S. 1971. Bramble fruit culture, Ohio State Univ. Bull. *411*.

JENNINGS, D.L. 1962. Some evidence on the influence of the morphology of raspberçs ianes upon their ability to be attacked by certain fungi. Hort. Res. (Scotland) *1*, 100-11.

JENNINGS, D.L. 1967. Observations on some instances of partial sterility in red raspberry cultivars. Hort. Res. (Scotland) *7*, 116-22.

JOHNSTON, S., and LOREE, R.E. 1927. Pruning the red raspberry. Mich. Bull. *162*.

KEEP, E. 1961. Autumn fruiting in raspberries. J. Hort. Sci. *36*, 174-75.

KEEP, E. 1968. Incompatibility in Rubus with special reference to *R. idaeus*. Can. J. Genet. Cytol. *10*, 253-62.

KELSALL, A. 1946. Mulches on small fruits. Nova Scotia Fruit Growers' Assoc. *83*, 69-71.

KNIGHT, R.L. 1958A. Genetics of resistance to *Amphorophora rubi* in raspberry. II. A_2-A_7 from the American variety Chief. Genet. Res. Cambridge, L. *319*.

KNIGHT, R.L. 1958B. Resistance in red raspberry to *Amphorophora rubi*. Intern. Cong. Vol. *II*.

KNIGHT, R.L. 1960. Genetics of suckering and tip rooting in raspberry. Ann. Rpt. E. Malling Sta. for 1959.

KNIGHT, R.L., and KEEP, E. 1956. Fruit Breeding and Genetics to 1955, Rubus and Ribes. Commonwealth Agr. Bur. Farnham Royal, England.

KNIGHT, R.L. et al. 1959. Genetics of resistance to *Amphorophora rubi* in raspberry. I. Gene A, from Baumforth. J. Genetics *56*, 261-80.

KOLBE, M.H., and BROOKS, J. 1962. Small fruit culture. N. Carolina Ext. Circ. *333*.

LIPE, J.P. 1976. Effect of preharvest CaCl, wax, Botran, and Benlate sprays and ethylene manipulation on blackberry storage. HortScience *11*, 224.

LITTLER, A.E. 1964. Loganberry culture in British Columbia. Brit. Columbia Dept. Agr. Hort. Circ. *100*.

LITTLER, A.E. 1965. Blackberry culture in British Columbia. Brit. Columbia Dept. Agr. Hort. Circ. *65-10*.

MOORE, J.N. et al. 1975. Inheritance of seed size in blackberry. J. Am. Soc. Hort. Sci. *100*, 377-79.

MORRIS, H.F. 1970. Growing blackberries. Texas Agr. Ext. Serv. Publ. *B-990.*

MORRIS, J.R. 1972. It takes more than a machine to mechanize. Am. Fruit Grower, July.

OURECKY, D.K., and SLATE, G.L. 1969. Heritage, a fall bearing red raspberry. Res. Circ. *19,* New York Agr. Expt. Sta., Geneva.

RICKETSON, C.L. 1970. Raspberries and blackberries. Ontario Dept. Agr. Publ. *473.*

SHEETS, W.A. *et al.* 1972. Effect of plant density, training, and pruning on blackberry yield. J. Am. Soc. Hort. Sci. *97,* 262-64.

SHERMAN, W.B., and SHARPE, R.H. 1971. Breeding Rubus for warm climates. HortScience *6,* 147-49.

SHOEMAKER, J.S., and DAVIS, R.M. 1966. Blackberry production in Florida. Fla. Agr. Expt. Sta. Circ. *294.*

SHOEMAKER, J.S., and STURROCK, T.T. 1959. Chromosome relations in blackberries. Fla. State Hort. Soc. *72,* 327-30.

SHOEMAKER, J.S., and WESTGATE, P.J. 1964. Oklahawa blackberry. Fla. Agr. Expt. Sta. Circ. *S-159.*

SHOEMAKER, J.S. *et al.* 1958. Flordagrand blackberry. Fla. Agr. Expt. Sta. Circ. *S-112.*

SNYDER, J.C. 1936. Flower bud formation in Latham raspberry. Proc. Am. Soc. Hort. Sci. *33,* 41-44.

STACE-SMITH, R. 1955. Black raspberry necrosis. Can. J. Bot. *33,* 314-22.

STACE-SMITH, R. 1956. Separation of components of raspberry mosaic. Can. J. Bot. *34,* 435-42.

TOMPKINS, J.P., and BOYNTON, D. 1959. A response to potassium by the black raspberry. Proc. Am. Soc. Hort. Sci. *73,* 164-67.

VIRDI, B.V. *et al.* 1972A. Meiotic irregularities associated with a partially male-sterile red raspberry selection. HortScience *7,* 263.

VIRDI, B.V. *et al.* 1972B. Embryo sac development in a partially male-sterile red raspberry selection. HortScience *7,* 263-64.

WOOD, C.A., and ANDERSON, M.M. 1962. Quantities and composition of crop materials removed from an established raspberry planting. Hort. Res. (Scotland) *1,* 85-94.

WU, L., and OVERCASH, J.P. 1971. Anatomical structure of red raspberry hybrid cuttings rooted under mist. J. Am. Soc. Hort. Sci. *96,* 437-40.

WYLIE, W.D. 1970. Raspberry crown borer. Ark. Farm Res. (Oct-Dec).

ZYCH, C.C. 1965. Incompatibility in crosses of red, black, and purple raspberries. Proc. Am. Soc. Hort. Sci. *86,* 307-12.

ZYCH, C.C. 1967. Thornless erect blackberries. Ill. Res., Winter.

ZYCH, C.C. 1972. Leaf-bud method of propagating brambles. Ill. Fruit Growing Leaflet, *11.*

Chapter 4

Currants and Gooseberries

Botanically the fruit of both the currant and gooseberry, like the grape, is a true berry. Horticulturally these two fruits are not major crops, but they are widely grown in northern regions. Long before vitamins were well known, housewives preserved black currants for making a hot drink for use against colds.

The commercial market is practically limited to fruit-product manufacturers. For home gardens or local markets, the ease of culture, small amount of space required, long life of the plants, and the many culinary uses to which these fruits are adapted commend them to consideration. (See White pine blister rust under Diseases.)

CULTIVARS

Red Currant Cultivars (Mostly *Ribes sativum*)

Cascade.—A week later than Red Lake and the berries are larger but the clusters are shorter. Minnesota origin.

Cherry.—The Cherry offered in the trade is usually some other cultivar.

Fay.—Once a leader, blooms comparatively early, making it subject to frost damage. Its weak bush allows the canes to sprawl and be broken.

Filler.—More productive than Fay, which it resembles in fruit.

Red Lake.—Fruit large, in large clusters with long stems, good quality, lighter color than most cultivars, midseason to late. Vigorous, hardy and productive. Minnesota.

Stephens No. 9.—Fruit large, good quality. Clusters medium to large with fairly long stems. Moderate vigor, rather sprawly. Ontario.

Wilder.—Once a leader but now excelled in several respects by some other cultivars. Indiana.

White Currant Cultivars (Mostly *Ribes sativum*)

White Grape.—Probably the leader.

Some other cultivars are White Dutch, White Transparent and White Imperial.

Black Currant Cultivars (Mostly *Ribes nigrum*)

Black currants owe their characteristic odor to the glands on the leaves and new growth.

Boskoop Giant.—Fruit large, good quality, early. Production variable (see Pollination). England.

Climax.—Heavy yielder. Berries medium to large. Ontario.

Consort, Coronet, and Crusader.—These seem resistant to rust (see Pollination).

Kerry.—Highly productive. Clusters large, fruit large, ripens evenly, early midseason, susceptible to mildew. Ontario.

Magnus.—Early. Berries large, firm, even-ripening. Good for machine-harvesting.

Naples.—Strong grower, large berries. England.

Saunders.—Early midseason. Even-ripening. Good for machine-harvesting. Ontario.

Seabrook.—Midseason. Fairly even-ripening. Good for machine-harvesting.

Topsy.—Early, very productive, clusters medium size. Berries large. Good for machine-harvesting.

Gooseberry Cultivars (Mostly *Ribes grossularia* or *R. rusticum*)

Captivator.—Fruit dull red. Plants almost spineless, except for a short distance at base of canes. Upright. Good for machine-harvesting.

Chautauqua (Columbus, Portage, Triumph).—Fruit pale green, European type, larger than that of American kinds but more subject to mildew.

Clark.—Fruit large, red when ripe. Generally free from mildew. Outstanding in Ontario except in the colder parts. Late. Natural hybrid of

European and American cultivars. Careful pruning required for machine-harvesting, since growth normally is dense and with many branches close to the ground. Can be propagated by layering. Ontario.

Fredonia.—Plants vigorous and open. High yielder. Fruit large, good quality, late, dark red when ripe. New York.

Oregon Champion.—Fruit green, medium size, late. Grown in Pacific Coast States. Oregon.

Pixwell.—Few thorns. Canes rather slender and somewhat drooping on old plants. Very hardy. Berries oval, medium size. Fruit hangs away from the stems, making it easy to pick, hence its name. North Dakota.

Welcome.—Dull red with pink flesh, medium size. No spines on the fruit; few on the plant. Minnesota.

POLLINATION

Most currants and gooseberries are self-fruitful, hence there is usually no need to provide for cross-pollination. However, there are some pollination exceptions in black currants.

Crusader pollen tends to stick together in clumps so that bees do not readily pick it up. The flowers of Coronet do not open widely at the top so that bees often reach in from the side without contacting the anthers.

The flower structure of some black currants (e.g., Boskoop Giant) may prevent self-pollination. In most cultivars the first few flowers at the base of a cluster usually hold their stigmas level with the anthers, or slightly above or below, and this situation prevails to the tip of the cluster. But in Boskoop Giant many flowers toward the tip of the cluster may hold their stigmas out beyond the anthers. This difference in stigma position in relation to the anthers affects the fruit set. If the weather during bloom favors insect activity, a good set of fruit may be expected; but if conditions are unfavorable for pollination, only a few easily self-pollinated flowers at the base of the cluster may set fruit.

PROPAGATION

Hardwood Cuttings

Currants usually are propagated by hardwood cuttings, which are made from dormant, well-matured, new wood of canes of medium size. They are usually made about 20.3 cm (8 in.) long; in the Pacific Northwest 25.4 to 30.5 cm (10 to 12 in.). When gooseberries are propagated by cuttings, the procedure is like that for currants. But set them 15.2 cm (6 in.) apart in nursery rows 91.4 cm (3 ft) apart. Leave only 1 or 2 buds above ground to prevent drying out and to encourage rooting.

Layering

Simple Layering.—If only a few plants are needed, bend down several branches, partly cover them with soil, and hold in place by pegs. This can be done in the fall or spring and by the next fall the layers should have enough roots to be set in a nursey row. Slow-rooting cultivars may need another year before they are moved.

Mound Layering.—For quantity production of gooseberry cultivars that are difficult to propagate from cuttings, first cut back the main branches severely in the dormant season to encourage numerous vigorous shoots. In midsummer, mound earth halfway up the shoots. If root development is good by fall, cut the rooted shoots off the parent plant and set in nursery rows to grow for 1 to 2 years; otherwise, leave the shoots attached to the parent plant for another year.

LOCATION OF PLANTING AND YIELD

Good currant or gooseberry plantings should give at least 10 to 12 crops; some may produce until 20 or more years old. Keep the plants thrifty by liberal fertilizing, proper pruning and pest control. The bushes produce longer in the north than toward the southern limits.

Good yields per hectare, with plants 1.2 × 2.4 m (4 × 8 ft), are about 8700 to 13,000 liters (3200 to 4800 qt per acre) for red currants and a little less for black currants, and 10,900 to 17,400 liters (4000 to 6400 qt per acre) for gooseberries. Yields of these fruits under favorable conditions may be as high as 11.2 metric tons per ha (5 tons per acre); yields per large bush often are 5.5 to 11 liters (5 to 10 qt).

LOCATION AND SITE

A rich well-drained clay loam is good. In dry soils gooseberries may suffer from premature defoliation, thus exposing the fruit to sunscald. In selecting a site much the same considerations apply as for the other fruits previously discussed. Gooseberries and currants bloom earlier than the other small fruits, but their hardiness is indicated by their northern distribution.

Reduction in exposure to sunlight by providing some shade, which also results in cooler air, helps control mildew and avoids sunscalding of gooseberries. Shade should not be so low and dense as to increase mildew by preventing good air circulation or come from taller plants that are so near these fruits as to compete with them for moisture and nutrients.

PLANTING

Vigorous, well-rooted, one-year-old plants are best for planting; two-year-old plants usually cost more. Also, two-year plants may be the cull stock left after the best one-year stock has been sold. But weak one-year plants may be less satisfactory than good two-year-olds. A vigorous, well-rooted one-year plant is usually more easily set, suffers less in transplanting, and makes more progress toward producing a crop in the permanent planting than it would during the same time in a nursery row.

Time of Planting.—Since currant and gooseberry bushes start growth early in the spring, fall planting merits attention, especially if the plants would otherwise be set in late spring. They lose their leaves early in autumn. Setting the plants soon after they become dormant gives the roots ample time to become established before winter. Gooseberries may not be ready for fall planting until several weeks later than currants. If the ground is dry in autumn it may be wise to delay planting until early spring; late spring planting may adversely affect the year's growth.

Spacing.—Common spacing for red currants and gooseberries is 1.2 to 1.5 × 2.1 to 2.7 m (4 to 5 × 7 to 9 ft). Black currant plants grow larger than the red and are set about a foot farther apart in the rows. A wide space between rows facilitates cultivation and spraying. In dry years a closely spaced planting may suffer most.

Commercial growers use large sprayers that require adequate space to pass, e.g., in a long narrow planting so that all rows can be reached from the outside or an occasional wide space every 5 to 6 rows.

The spacing often suggested is 2.4 to 3 m (8 to 10 ft) between rows and, in the rows, red currants and gooseberries 1.5 m (5 ft), and black currants 1.8 to 2.1 m (6 to 7 ft). This comparatively wide spacing results in a greater feeding area and water supply per bush and in more vigorous growth and higher yield per bush. Excessive spacing reduces yield per hectare.

Setting the Plants.—Set the plants slightly deeper than they grew previously. Heading back the top at planting time may or may not be necessary according to conditions.

TILLAGE

Currants and gooseberries need considerable moisture and a cool soil. Practice frequent shallow cultivation to control weeds during the life of the planting. Herbicides should be considered.

In a newly set planting on heavy soil, plowing toward the plants as soon as they are set in autumn provides extra soil cover immediately around the young plants and helps to prevent heaving due to thawing and freezing. With older plantings in autumn, it may be wise to plow a drainage furrow between the rows. The tractor disk makes for rapid tillage but may seriously reduce the shallow root system.

MULCHING

A mulch maintained from year to year, as a substitute for cultivation, keeps the soil moist and cool, and smothers weeds. Mice or fire may damage mulched plants. Supplement straw mulch with N fertilizer. In an outstanding gooseberry planting in Ontario the grower applied alfalfa screenings around the bushes to a maintained depth of 12.7 to 15.2 cm (5 to 6 in.) with a resultant increase in size of bush, size of fruit, and yield.

FERTILIZER

Currants and gooseberries are heavy feeders. It is helpful to turn under manure and cover crops, especially before planting.

In Ohio, both manure and N fertilizer increased the yield of Wilder red currant. Mulching with straw without addition of N resulted in yellowish foliage. When N was added to the straw, the foliage became dark green, and both yield and growth were increased. P, K, and lime were less beneficial than N on this soil (Shoemaker 1935).

With leaf samples taken in September, K deficiency may occur at less than 1%. Comparable value for leaf blade samples taken in June may be 0.9%. The optimum value for both reds and blacks may be over 1.0% (Forshey 1969).

PRUNING

Red and white currants fruit at the base of 1-year-old wood and more so on spurs on 2- and 3-year-wood. Older wood produces inferior fruit. The object of pruning is to remove wood older than three years and to replace it with a suitable number of younger growths. It is largely a thinning and renewal process. The average well-pruned dormant bush when 3 years old may consist of about 3 shoots each of 3-, 2-, and 1-year-old wood. With older bushes a few more canes of the various ages are usually left.

Black currants bear the most and best of their fruit on wood of the previous year's growth. Therefore, leave a plentiful supply of young wood while pruning.

Pruning of currants, done in the dormant season, consists mostly in thinning out the canes. Head back too high or straggly branches. In red currants the young vigorous shoots that are to replace the older ones may be shortened to prevent the bush from becoming straggly, and to promote even development of fruit spurs along their whole length instead of mostly at the ends. Avoid this shortening of the branches in black currants. In all types remove weak growth and branches close to the ground. Also remove and burn any dying canes promptly throughout the season to kill the borers inside them.

The fruiting habit of the gooseberry is much like that of the red currant; hence the method of pruning is much the same. After a few years of bearing the wood begins to fail and produces inferior fruit in smaller total quantities. Thus there should always be vigorous growths coming on to replace older wood as it is removed.

HARVESTING AND MARKETING

Hand-picking

A large percentage of the crop is sold on a PYO (Pick-Your-Own) basis. Picking may last a month or more, but for processing, the crop may be harvested in one picking by machine.

Pick red currants by separating the stem of the cluster from the bushes with the fingers. Picking for jelly making may be done while the fruit is slightly immature.

Gooseberries are usually stripped from the bushes by hand or with a special scoop. Thorny bushes make picking disagreeable. Sometimes pickers wear heavy canvas aprons which are spread under the bush as the picker circles it in raking berries from the branches with glove-covered hands. The berries are poured from these aprons into field boxes and cleaned later. For the general market, pick gooseberries more carefully than by a method in which some of the fruit is cut by the thorns and spoils quickly. Some cultivars are less thorny than others.

Probably green-colored gooseberries are the most popular, but some markets prefer the pink or red types. The latter are often considered by customers as green-colored fruit that is overripe and therefore less desirable.

Machine-harvesting

An electrical self-propelled sucking device features a vacuum hose as the machine moves along the row. A 5.1 cm (2 in.) hose has a cutting head at each end to cut off stems, and the vacuum sucks currants through the hose into a chamber. After the fruit arrives in the chamber, the leaves left after clipping are blown out through the exhaust system. The fruit then drops down a chute into one of two crates attached to the back, under the machine. As the crate is filled a crank handle moves vacuum to the second crate; while this crate is being filled, the first crate is removed from the machine and placed on trucks (Dyment 1972).

In machine-harvesting of currants and gooseberries care should be taken that the foliage is not damaged excessively; 50% destruction one year may mean a serious loss the next year.

Some success has been obtained with the European type in harvesting by application of Ethephon (Ethrel) as an abscission agent so that fruit can be shaken and gathered from the canvas by hand. The European type may be trained to a bushlike form with short legs. The American type is grown as a distinct bush.

DISEASES

Anthracnose causes small brown spots on the leaves, young canes, fruit stems, and fruit, as well as early defoliation.

Leaf spot adversely affects leaves, which turn yellow and drop; bushes may be defoliated early in the season. The spots are at first brown, but later become pale or gray and, under a hand lens, little black spots (fruiting bodies of the fungus) may be seen in them. To control these, use a mildew spray with a suitable fungicide just before the blossoms open, just before the fruit sets, and soon after harvest.

European currant rust shows on the lower side of leaves as little clusters of orange-colored spots. Later they are replaced by elongated, threadlike, reddish-brown structures. If these are numerous they give the lower surface of the leaves a feltlike appearance; hence the name "felt rust of currants." Treat with sulphur.

White pine blister rust spends part of its life cycle on currants and gooseberries. Because of this, growing these fruits, particularly black currants, is banned in some areas.

INSECTS

Imported currant worm adult is a sawfly. It often strips red currants and gooseberries of almost all their foliage, but it seldom attacks black currants. The mature worm is 1.9 cm (¾ in.) long, bluish-green, and with a black head and many black spots over the body. There may be 2 or 3 broods each year.

Currant borer works inside the canes, especially in the larger canes. Affected canes may become sickly and in the next year some may die. The borer is the white larva of a clear-winged wasplike moth. The moths appear in early summer and lay eggs in the axils of the leaves or in little openings on canes. Young larvae, on hatching, bore into the pith where they feed until full-grown and remain over the winter. If an infested cane is cut through, the darkened pith shows the work of the borers. (See Pruning.)

Rose stem girdler injury on the canes is mostly due to the larvae tunneling in the canes, frequently girdling them and killing the stem above the point of attack.

Currant aphid-infested leaves curl downward. The parts of the upper surface between the veins are usually elevated in large, irregular blisters that are often reddish. Leaves may be weakened so much that they die. Treat with an aphicide while the buds are dormant or bursting.

Red spider mites feed on the underside of the leaves, causing them to become brownish or yellow. Such leaves dry up and die in dry weather, when the plants need them most. Mites spin a fine web on the underside of the leaves and lay their tiny, pearl-like eggs there. They winter in the soil around the base of the plant and attack the plants in spring soon after the buds burst. Supply water. Spray with a suitable miticide.

Scales of several kinds suck juices from the tender wood of the bushes and may weaken or even kill the plants. The covering of San Jose scale is circular and ashy brown; that of Oyster Shell scale is brownish, resembling a tiny oyster shell. Treat with a suitable scalecide when the buds are dormant or bursting.

Currant fruit fly causes wormy currants and gooseberries. The flies begin to emerge during bloom, but egg-laying does not start until bloom is nearly over. The female fly inserts eggs into the young fruit by means of her ovipositor. The eggs hatch in about a week and the maggots consume the surrounding tissue. Infested berries develop discolored areas around the spot where the egg was inserted, and ripen unevenly and prematurely. Many drop from the bushes before the main crop is ripe, but others remain and are picked with the normal berries. The maggots leave the fruits soon after they fall and enter the soil to a depth of 2.5 to 5.1 cm (1 to 2 in.), where they pupate and pass the winter. For control, contact a local entomologist.

REFERENCES

DYMENT, R. 1972. Currant harvester. Am. Fruit Grower, Western Edition (Sept. 13).

FORSHEY, C.G. 1969. Potassium nutrition of deciduous fruits. HortScience 4, 39-41.

KNIGHT, R.L., and KEEP, E. 1958. III. Grundlagen und methoden der zuchtung und zuchterfolge, subgenus Coreosmam. Handbuch der Phlanzenzuchtung 2, No. 6, 450-60.

SHOEMAKER, J.S. 1935. Fertilizer and mulch on red currants. Ohio Bimonthly Bull. 20, 82-83.

Chapter 5

Blueberries

Botanically the blueberry, like the currant, gooseberry and grape, is a true berry. Horticulturally the blueberry is a substantial and fast growing fruit-crop industry.

Blueberries (*Vaccinium*) have small, soft seeds; true huckleberries (*Gaylusacia*) have ten large, hard seeds. So-called "huckleberries" usually are fruit of one or more wild blueberry species.

PART 1

NORTHERN LOWBUSH BLUEBERRIES

Northern lowbush blueberries consist of several species, chiefly as follows:

V. myrtilloides, velvet leaf blueberry. The leaves and stems are hairy. The leaf margins are non-toothed. The colonies are dense and of moderate size. The fruit is bright metallic blue. It ripens later than the next species.

V. angustifolium, low sweet blueberry. Gradually replaces the above species in northern regions subjected to rotational burning. Leaves shiny, smooth and with toothed margins, the points of which have minute glands. Colonies are dense and often large. The bright blue fruit is excellent in flavor.

V. lamarckii probably developed from a doubling of the chromosomes of *V. angustifolium*. Its colonies are smaller, the plants taller, and the fruit larger than *angustifolium*. Fruit is bright blue and of excellent flavor.

V. vacillans, low dryland blueberry, covers the same range as *an-*

gustifolium, with which it crosses freely and which, in some places, it seems to be replacing. Fruit is black of fair flavor.

The genetic sources of the richly diverse morphological specialization exhibited by modern North American diploid species are likely the result of gene mutation and recombination within spatial groups. Occurrence of many broadly adapted polyploid species (discussed later in this chapter) has seemingly further reinforced the isolation of the diploids in nature (Hall and Galletta 1971).

FRUITING AND GROWTH HABITS

The flowers and fruits are borne on the previous year's growth. Determinate growth may result from formation of an apical primordium, or it may result twice a year from death or inactivation of the growing tip.

Vegetative branch elongation ceases in early summer owing to death of both the apical meristem and distal portion of the axis. Coincident with this is the development of a flowering branch primordium in the axis of the penultimate leaf. In midsummer the apical meristem of the flowering branch becomes inactive. It is either laterally displaced or it elongates as a minute unbranched columnar structure. Coincident with this inactivation, the proximal flower primordia develop florets in which all flower parts may be recognized, but the distal flower primordia (those adjacent to the inactivated apical meristem) are retarded in development. Retarded distal flower primordia, but not the proximal flower primordia, develop in acropetal succession (Bell 1950).

FIG. 5.1.   LOWBUSH BLUEBERRIES ARE UPLAND SPECIES

LOWBUSH BLUEBERRY INDUSTRY

Lowbush blueberry occupies an intermediate place in the succession of plants between field and forest. The plants are essentially wild. No named cultivars exist and little or no attempt is made at propagation, planting or other common horticultural practices. However, the commercial crop has some intensive culture features.

Lowland blueberries are upland species, usually 10.2 to 12.7 cm (4 to 15 in.) high, that stool late colonies by means of underground shoots (rhizomes). Even though only a part of the total wild crop is harvested, annual volume of that harvested in North America is about $10,000,-000; more than half of the crop is canned or frozen.

Maine.—The chief blueberry areas are in a strip along the northeast, in Washington, Hancock, Knox and Lincoln counties, which produce 900,000 kg (2 million lb) for fresh fruit and 1.36 million kg (3 million lb) for processing annually. About 8900 ha (22,000 acres) are periodically burned, dusted and otherwise cared for. It is the leading lowbush commercial area in the world. Most of the blueberry land is owned by growers and managed as a special fruit crop.

New Hampshire.—*V. myrtilloides* predominates in the northern third of the state, mostly on hilly land, where a late crop is harvested.

Michigan.—A rather distinct line divides the lowbush and highbush areas. It extends southwest from Bay City to about 33.8 km (20 mi.) north of Grand Rapids. As the line nears Lake Michigan it turns northwest to some extent, because of the moderating influence of the lake on the climate. South of this line highbush blueberries thrive; north of it, including the Upper Peninsula, only lowbush species occur.

The lowbush type matures its fruit and forms fruit buds for the next year's crop in a shorter growing season than the highbush. Lowbush plants occur abundantly where the average growing season is only 60 to 70 days. But to avoid frosts during bloom or soon after, and to have enough time to harvest the crop before early September frosts, requires a growing season of at least 120 days.

Other United States Areas.—In Massachusetts the chief wild blueberry acreage is in Worcester County. In New York the wild type occurs mostly in eastern Rensselaer County. Lowbush blueberries also are harvested in northern Wisconsin and northern Minnesota. In West Virginia they occur chiefly on the fairly level, rocky land on the crest of the Allegheny Mountains as a part of Monongahela National Forest, 914 to 1219 m (3000 to 4000 ft) above sea level and covering 647 to 777 sq km (250 to 300 sq mi.).

Canada

Large quantities of wild blueberries are picked in eastern Canada. Besides domestic consumption, some 7.3 million kg (16 million lb) a year may be shipped to the United States from the 5 eastern provinces.

In Nova Scotia an important area of wild blueberries occurs in the western counties, e.g., Cumberland. With the rotation of burning, two-thirds of the acreage bears each year; much of the crop is processed. In Prince Edward Island both climate and soil are suitable for an expanding industry. In New Brunswick blueberries occur on large areas that have been burned over at various times, chiefly in Charlotte and Gloucester counties. Yields are 0.68 to 2.27 million kg (1.5 to 5 million lb) a year, with an average of 1008 kg per ha (900 lb per acre).

In Quebec about 3.2 million kg (7 million lb) are picked annually. The Lake St. John and Chicoutimi area leads. Other important areas are Bay St. Paul and Saguenay, Abitibi, Three Rivers, Bay St. Laurent, Gaspesie and Joliette. In northwestern Quebec, adjacent to Ontario, two important areas are Rouyn-Noranda and Ville Marie-Temiskaming. Several large processing plants are operating.

In northern Ontario large areas of wild blueberries are picked, centering at Chapleau, Sudbury, Algoma, Kirkland Lake and Muskoka.

PROPAGATION

Lowbush blueberries are not planted like other small fruits. Initially the plants probably start naturally in fields from seeds left in the droppings of foxes, raccoons and birds. Development of a plant from seed is slow. As the plant grows larger it sends out rhizomes (underground stems) and increases in area until it spreads to other patches or clones.

There is a record of a clone 805 m (½ mi.) wide. Probably at least 100 years passed before it reached this size from the original plant. Thus, when a blueberry field is established, it may last a long time (Eaton 1957).

Many different methods of propagation have been tried, but none has worked well in the field.

Under field conditions rhizome development is greatly restricted or completely suspended in transplanted rooted cuttings, thus accounting for poor establishment of new plants with this method.

How the Plant Develops

New shoots of mature plants develop from dormant buds in the rhizomes. The tips of growing shoots die in the summer and the buds develop into either vegetative or flowering types. Whether a particular bud will be vegetative or flowering is determined the year the shoot arises. By fall most flower buds can be distinguished from vegetative buds, as they are larger.

The ratio of flower to vegetative buds is greater on new shoots than on older twigs. The flower buds formed on new shoots also are hardier and contain more flowers per bud (Hall and Aalders 1967).

Development of Fields

Development of a lowbush blueberry field is done by selecting a site which has potential for production of this crop and encouraging blueberry plants already on it to spread faster.

First cut and remove any trees on the area. Haul the brush to a barren area, such as a rock pile, for burning. Do not burn such brush in the field as the intense heat may destroy underlying blueberry plants. Mow hardwood saplings before burning.

On smooth land a rotary mower aids in clearing or mowing prior to burning. It is more rugged than the conventional cutter-bar mower and eliminates the need for hand-cutting heavy brush before mowing. It may also reduce the loss due to breakdown which often occurs with cutter-bar mowers. The machine shreds the trash into small pieces, thus leaving a clean field for harvesting the next year.

Abandoned farmland has the greatest potential in eastern Canada for blueberry production since the land has previously been leveled and cleared of rocks. It is then easier to burn, dust and handle. In Maine blueberry lands consist of fairly level, elevated plateau areas or barrens, or of moderately sloping to steep, rocky hillsides. Most of the production is on acid soil (pH 4.5 to 5.7), sandy or gravelly loam, and rather shallow low-humus soils. In New Hampshire some of the crop is borne on steep hills.

Rhizomes

Rhizomes originate at the base of aerial stems. Secondary and later rhizomes originate from buds at nodes on older rhizomes.

The potential of lateral buds on the rhizomes to develop into shoots declines steadily from spring to early July in Maine; then the buds become inactive. In late June a sharp increase in bud activity occurs and remains high for the rest of the year (Kender 1968).

BURNING AS A PRUNING AND WEED CONTROL PRACTICE

After certain forests have been cut or burned over, lowbush blueberries come in naturally. If burning in later years is prevented, sooner or later the area becomes brush and woodland again. Thus, areas that yield large quantities of berries for a few years may produce none later, as a result of crowding and shading of the bushes.

Burning of fields, forests and woods is not legal in some areas, particularly where lowbush blueberries are not grown commercially. Prospective growers in new areas wishing to develop or improve blueberry fields with the aid of burning should first obtain information on the legal status of burning.

In commercial lowbush areas burning is an approved pruning and weed-control practice. To reduce the fire hazard neighbors may exchange work in burning; several men equipped with brooms, shovels, fire pumps, and other firefighting equipment are necessary. A back swath is burned before starting a large fire.

Since the plant's above-ground portion forms only a small part of the total, the blueberry is less damaged by burning than is most competing vegetation. Its extensive root system allows the plant to compete with other plants on land of low fertility.

Shoot Emergence

After burning, new shoots emerge for about four weeks; highest emergence rate is 5 to 7 days after the first shoots appear. The later the emergence the smaller the average number of flower buds and flowers per shoot. The number of flowers may be five per bud on all emergence dates. First shoots to emerge are taller and have the most fruit-cluster buds per stem. Tall stems usually have more flower buds per cluster than short stems.

When to Burn

Early spring, when the snow has left the fields but remains in the woods and before green grass appears, especially in fields near timber or slash land, is a good time to burn. An early burn may provide a longer growing season for developing new growth and fruit buds for the next crop. The ground should be wet or frozen in order to protect the topsoil and the blueberry crowns and roots.

In Nova Scotia the number of sprouts, the total number of flower buds, the number of flower buds per sprout, and the proportion of sprouts with flower buds are greatest when burning is done in early spring. No new sprouts emerge during the burn year on plants burned after July 1. Sprouts which appear on these plants the next spring are similar to those following spring burning (Eaton and White 1960).

Since the first stems to emerge are potentially the most fruitful, early-spring burning would seem to be better than later burning. But more often than not in New England, average stem length from a mid-May burn may be slightly greater than from mid-April burns, owing to accelerated growth following a late burn. Stem length is determined by both growth rate and length of growing season. In general, late burning shortens the growing season, but not in direct relation to deferment of burning. For example, 33 days' difference in date of burn (April 9 versus May 12) may make 16 days' difference in date of shoot emergence, but only 5 days' difference in length of season during which shoots grow.

The year after burning, growth is an unbranched shoot. Lateral shoots are seldom produced unless the meristem is damaged by insects, frost, or other agency. Even though rhizomes occur below ground their growth habit tends to be long and unbranched (Hall *et al.* 1969).

If short, uninjured stubs remain after a "light burn," a minimum interval occurs between burning and shoot emergence; but the interval is somewhat lengthened by a burn severe enough to destroy all the old stem above ground. In such a case new shoots arise at or slightly below the soil surface from the ends of a rhizome, which serves as a "crown." The interval between burning and shoot emergence becomes maximum if intense burn destroys the crown area so that new shoots arise farther back on the rhizome (Trevett 1955).

Frequency of Burning

One plan is to divide the area into three parts, burning one-third each year. Burning once in 3 years results in 2 crops in 3 years. With a three-year burn the second crop usually is smaller than the first. New growth from burned plants comes from buds on the rhizomes and averages less than two new stems from each old stem. The burn-to-harvest period is about 15 months. The first crop obtained the year after burning is larger than succeeding crops where *angustifolium* dominates; when *myrtilloides* dominates, the second crop may be larger than the first.

Burn Materials

Straw or Hay.—Distribute it in small piles after the blueberry leaves have turned red or fallen. Winter snows crush the mulch around the old stems, thus aiding a thorough clean-up. Partly burned stubs may interfere with rake harvesting. Mowing the weeds and bushes in the fall may promote a better burn and make it easier to spread the material. Where the fields are located on steep hills it is not practical to transport hay or straw, nor is it necessary on new areas because of grass and dry vegetation already there.

Oil.—Set the burner so that it burns 373 to 467 liters of oil per ha (40 to 50 gal. per acre), just enough to kill the twigs. First burn a 15 m (50 ft) lane around the outer edge of the field. The fire is spread quickly with a 5 cm (2 in.) pipe with a wick in one end and a screw cap on the other end. Oil torches and machine-mounted flame throwers are also used. Oil must be burning when used; otherwise, it may kill the plants. Repetitive burning with a flame thrower may have detrimental long-term effects on the rhizomes of lowbush blueberry clones.

Propane Gas.—Propane is suitable for small fields or acreages, but is slower than oil burning.

Materials Compared.—Five pruning methods were tested in Maine: standard oil burning (applied with a hand flame thrower; fuel oil); mowing with a Gravely mower; mowing plus herbicidal oil (Provedent No. 3); herbicidal oil applied with a knapsack oil pressure sprayer; fortified herbicidal oil (302 liters or 80 gal. of a chemical weed killer) (Kender *et al.* 1964).

Yield and plant stand were poorest in plots pruned with herbicidal oil. Pruning which entirely destroyed the above-ground plants (burning or mowing plus oil) caused new, vigorous stems to emerge from buds on the rhizomes. Treatments which allowed portions of stems to remain intact above the soil surface (mowing) caused many new, unproductive stems to emerge from the basal buds of these above-ground portions. With the use of oil alone, dead plants remained in place in the field and resulted in low yields and poor fruit quality the following year.

SOIL

Organic Matter

In New Hampshire high-producing soils have a 2.54 cm (1 in.) duff layer made up largely of roots, dead and decaying twigs, and leaves; in low-producing soils the duff layer is missing or very thin. With burning once in 3 years an area that has been in production for 60 years may have been burned 20 times. This probably accounts for the low organic content, because the duff is flammable, and burning is accompanied by normal decomposition. Much of the "blueberry barrens" is land that has been carelessly and deeply burned and cropped for many years, resulting in a depletion of the organic litter and a poor stand of plants.

Commercial acreages in Maine are mostly on well-drained sandy loam or loamy sand. These soils are covered with a mat of organic litter that may be 2.54 to 10.2 cm (1 to 4 in.) deep, depending on the number of deep, hard burns. Light burns made when the soil is either frozen or wet do not greatly reduce the depth of the organic matter.

A fairly thick surface of organic matter serves as a matrix to help rhizomes resist high temperatures during burning and to hold water in a dry season. It is also important to organisms associated with the blueberry plants both as a source of nutrients and as a medium in which to grow.

Soil Tests

Most lowbush blueberry soils are not fertile soils. Of 215 samples taken in Washington County, Maine, 97% were low or very low in available P, 75% were very low in available K, and 80% were low or very low in available Ca. No relation was found between mineral content of the soil and yield (Dow *et al.* 1955).

FERTILIZER

During the burn year aim for a strong, tall stem early in the season to ensure abundant fruit-bud formation for the first crop. In the year after burning, aim to produce many branches without decreasing the first crop yield. These branches are essential for a large second crop in a three-year cycle. Although fertilizer may improve yields, too much growth in the year of burn may result in slender stems with few buds. Fertilize at rates that will not upset the balance between vegetative growth and yield or cause a luxuriant growth of weeds that crowd out the blueberry plants. Even on fairly weed-free fields, compromise between the amount of fertilizer that the blueberries actually need and the amount that causes least weed growth.

On land relatively free of grass in Maine, when only one application is made between burns, if most of the blueberry stems have been less than 10.2 cm (4 in.) long, apply, for example, 179 kg per ha (160 lb per acre) ammonium sulfate. If the stems have been more than 15.2 cm (6 in.) try 189.6 kg per ha (180 lb per acre) of ammonium sulfate.

In a three-year period between burns, fertilizer applied 7 to 10 days before bloom in either the year before, or the year of, the burn usually increases the yield of only the first crop. Fertilizer applied in the spring of the first crop year results in a higher yield for the two crops. If the land is burned every other year, instead of every three years, fertilize in the spring of the year of the burn.

May and June applications in New Hampshire of 7-7-7 fertilizer at rates of 224.1, 560.2 and 1120 kg per ha (200, 500 and 1000 lb per acre), respectively, increased the yield of weak plants. The result was due to more fruit-bud clusters, more fruit buds per cluster, and greater resistance of the bloom to spring frost. The productive period of plants with 2-year-old tops was lengthened at least 3 to 5 years.

FROST DAMAGE AND POLLINATION

Killing of blossoms and young fruits by late spring frost may cause great loss. Often, however, frost is blamed for a poor crop when the fault is due mostly to inactivity of bees and other pollinators. If the pistils are black when examined several hours after low temperatures occur, the damage is probably due to frost. If, however, the flower parts are green and healthy, poor fruit set probably has some other cause, such as poor pollination.

Most clones of lowbush blueberry are self-sterile and require cross-pollination. Under natural conditions in Nova Scotia pollination is accomplished by bumble bees (Bombus) and solitary bees (Andrena, Delictor, and closely related species). Unlike most insects which visit the blossoms for nectar, bumble bees collect pollen for food. Since the flowers of lowbush blueberries are an inconspicuous, pale white color and are often hidden by foliage, pollinating bees may find nectar by olfactory stimuli. As determined by isothermal gas liquid chromatography analysis on nectar volatiles, *V. angustifolium* evolves acetaldehyde and ethyl alcohol, but not in quantity high enough to be smelled (Hall 1971).

Good pollination may increase production by increasing the number and size of berries that set and develop. In Maine, averages per berry may be: small berries 6.4 mm (¼ in. or less) in diameter, less than 8 seeds; medium-sized berries 6 to 13 mm (¼ to ⅜ in.) 10 to 15 seeds; large berries 11 to 13 mm (⁷⁄₁₆ to ½ in.) 16 to 18 seeds. In order to develop, each blueberry seed must result from pollination by an individual pollen grain. Therefore, for most seeds and largest berries pollination must be thorough (Trevett 1959).

When the blueberries start to bloom, place hives on areas where experience has shown a scarcity of native bees. Place 2 to 3 strong colonies per hectare. Remove the bees after bloom, before any spraying or dusting is done.

High yields in certain years may be attributed to a greater concentration of bees working on blueberries because of a scarcity of nearby floral competition (West 1969).

HARVESTING AND MARKETING

Harvest for an attractive pack when 90% of the berries are blue. Try to delay harvesting as long as possible, but do not delay too long in a season of cold weather, as berries touched with frost are of little market value.

In Maine, harvesting for fresh-fruit market begins about June 20 and for canneries about August 10. Harvesting usually lasts about a month or until ended by killing frosts, but in a hot, dry season it may last only 2 to 3 weeks.

FIG. 5.2.   THE RAKE IS USED FOR COMMERCIAL HARVESTING OF THE
LOWBUSH BLUEBERRY

RAKING

The rake (shaped like a dustpan) which is used for harvesting is made of metal, is 25.4 to 30.5 cm (10 to 12 in.) wide, and contains 42 to 48 comblike teeth. A raker averages 5 to 10 bu or more a day. Where the site permits, large fields may be divided by cord into lanes 1.8 to 2.4 m (6 to 8 ft) wide to help control the crew for a complete harvest. Assign a picker to each lane to pick only an allotted strip.

Where possible, have the pickers with their backs to the sun in order to see the fruit better. Do not rake until the dew is off the berries because of the difficulty in winnowing wet berries.

Raking is done by a backward rolling of the implement as it is pulled through the plants. With another type, pickers run the rake through the plants in a forward and upward motion. The berries catch on the teeth and roll back to the heel of the rake. After several scoops of the rake, the berries are dumped into a shallow container, the rake being held close to the container so that leaves and grass collected with the berries go into the box with them and act as a cushion to prevent crushing.

A machine harvester can speed up work in large areas.

Cleaning

The gasoline-operated cleaner has a paddle fan that blows the loose leaves, grass and other material from the berries as they fall from the feeder belt onto an inclined belt. The large round berries roll down the belt faster than it moves upward. Smaller berries, soft berries, those with stems, and the clusters, which do not roll so easily, are carried with the belt and are thus separated from the marketable fruit. A commonly used cleaner handles about 1410 liters (50 bu) of dry berries a day.

Consumer Packaging

Thin transparent plastic covers usually are placed on filled baskets

FIG. 5.3.   CLEANING AND PACKAGING WILD LOWBUSH BLUEBERRIES FOR MARKET

and held tightly in place with an elastic band. If a box is loosely packed, the berries roll around and rub off the bloom, especially from those on top of the basket, thus causing them to be dark and unattractive for market.

Customers prefer a light-blue berry. The gray bloom of the berry depends on the amount of waxy covering, and it is this covering that keeps the berries dry and causes them to hold up longer. If this protective waxy covering is lacking, or if it has been rubbed off so that the dark skin of the berries is exposed, the fruit may quickly pick up moisture, become soft, and soon deteriorate.

PART 2

HIGHBUSH BLUEBERRIES

V. corymbosum is the northern highbush type and *V. australe* the southeastern. Terminal growth is added to the canes each year. Individual bushes may persist for many years and become thick and tall. Eventually the old canes die and are replaced by young ones coming up from the crown. Old canes are relatively unproductive and yield small berries. Highbush plants do not spread by rhizomes as do the lowbush.

For those who cannot study the basic materials in the field, a good way to gain an understanding of *corymbosum* is to read descriptions of *akransanum, simulatum, marianum, lamarckii,* and *brittonia.* Then mix them together, much as if one were producing all possible hybrid combinations in a long-term breeding program, and in succeeding generations, over at least 1000 years, to back-cross, and re-cross further in all possible combinations, and then select all those plants over 1 m (3.3 ft) high whose leaves are over 13 cm (5.1 in.) wide and 26 cm (10.2 in.) long. The result would be *V. corymbosum,* which is not an imaginary population but a very real one and as complex as the results of the hypothetical experiment would have been (Camp 1945).

Highbush blueberry plants are exacting in climatic and soil requirements. Selection of an unfavorable site is costly, not easily rectified, and is likely to result in failure. Highbush blueberry is about as hardy as peach in its northern range and is subject to prolonged dormancy (insufficient cold to break the rest period) in its southern range.

INDUSTRY

Total annual value of the crop is more than $18 million.

TABLE 5.1

PHYLETIC PATTERN AND ORIGIN OF THE POLYPLOID SPECIES OF BLUEBERRIES[1]

Diploids	Tetraploids	Hexaploids
myrtilloides		
vacillans	alto-montanum	constablaei
pallidum	simulatum	
?	brittonii	NORTHERN HYBRID COMPLEX = corymbosum
angustifolium	lamarckii	
caesariense	australe	
	marianum	
atrococcum	arkansanum	
	fuscatum	A SERIES OF SOUTHERN HYBRID COMPLEXES
darrowi		ashei
	myrsinites	
tenellum	virgatum	amoenum
elliottii		
?	hirustum	

Source: Camp (1945).

[1]Straight, horizontal lines indicate the autoploids; allopolyploids are shown as being derived from two or more sources; the two chief tetraploid complexes are indicated by boxes.

New Jersey (4856 ha or 12,000 acres)

Production has exceeded 1 million 12 pint flats. Burlington County, the original center of the industry, and Atlantic County are the leading areas. Camden and Ocean counties also produce substantial crops. Leading shipping centers are New Lisbon, Brown's Mills, Pemberton, Hammonton, and Tom's River. About 90% of the crop is marketed fresh.

Michigan (4050 ha or 10,000 acres)

Blueberries are the major berry crop in Michigan. Production in favorable years is about 18,144,000 kg (40 million lb) with a value of over $8 million to growers. Successful production is mostly limited to a 32 to 48.2 km (20 to 30 mi.) area along southwestern Michigan from the Indiana border northward to Muskegon. The crop is later than in New Jersey.

The highbush succeeds in the northwestern part of the lower peninsula if the plantings are made near Lake Michigan. Plantings near Ludington and on the Old Mission Peninsula near Traverse City are fairly successful, but plantings a few miles inland are not. Soils in southeastern Michigan are usually not suitable for blueberries, but successful plantings occur on some selected sites.

Reasons for rather general failure of the highbush blueberry in northern Michigan are: too short a growing season (number of days between killing frosts) to develop and mature wood and fruit buds; killing of wood protruding above snow level by late fall and winter temperatures (much of the supposed greater hardiness of the lowbush blueberry is actually due to protection by snow cover); and breakage of the plants from heavy accumulation of snow (the rigid, brittle wood of the highbush plants breaks more easily than that of the lowbush).

For best results, highbush blueberry needs a growing season of 160 to 165 days. Average length of growing season in the Traverse City, Old Mission Peninsula, is 154 days, in the Houghton area 145 days, at Lake City 123 days, and in the interior parts of the upper peninsula 60 to 100 days.

Flower-bud hardiness of seven commercial highbush cultivars was determined from fall to spring for two consecutive years in Michigan. Hardiness was expressed as T_{50}, estimated by Spearman-Karber equations. The T_{50} values for cultivars showed good agreement with spring field survival. Distal buds were less hardy than proximal buds of the same twig. Average Exotherm methods were more variable than the T_{50} method, based on ovary browning, for determining flower-bud hardiness (Bittenberger and Howell 1976).

North Carolina (1619 ha or more than 4000 acres)

Some of the plantings are 16 ha (40 acres) in extent. Most of the acreage is in Pender, Bladen, Duplin and surrounding southeastern counties. Some commercial plantings occur in the western North Carolina mountains. Early season (three weeks ahead of other commercial areas) and ideal soil type have made this crop profitable. Yield averages about 400 12-pint flats per acre.

In the coastal area water is a problem—too much in spring unless adequate drainage is provided prior to planting, and too little at harvest time unless irrigation is available. Growers who have irrigation use this facility for frost control. New plantings in the mountains show promise. Upland soils are planted on the contour with sod between the rows and sawdust around the plants.

Other Areas.—About 324 ha (800 acres) of highbush blueberries occur in Washington state, and some in Oregon, Massachusetts, New

York and Indiana. Most highbush cultivars do not succeed south of northern Georgia, but plantings of hybrids are showing promise in Florida.

Highbush cultivars are recommended for northern Arkansas, and rabbiteye cultivars for southern and eastern areas. Surface organic mulches greatly stimulate plant growth and production on the upland soils (Moore 1976).

In Canada 650 ha (1600 or more acres) of highbush blueberries occur in British Columbia, chiefly in the Richmond and Pitt Meadows areas in the lower Fraser Valley Delta region. There are some plantings in Nova Scotia.

CULTIVARS

Because of stem canker in the major producing area of the Coastal Plain of North Carolina, high tolerance or resistance to this disease is essential there. The most suitable cultivars for North Carolina differ from those in comparatively canker-free northern regions.

Early

Angola.—Canker-resistant. Berry large, somewhat soft. Very sensitive to soil and water variations. North Carolina 1951.

Morrow.—Canker-resistant. Bush medium size, semi-erect and broad, slow-growing after fruiting age. Fruit clusters usually borne upright, at the periphery of the bush. Cuttings root readily. Better fruit size than Angola. North Carolina 1964.

Weymouth.—Bush medium upright. Fruit dark, medium large, fair quality. New Jersey 1936.

Wolcott.—Bush semi-upright. Fruit large, well-shaped, round, medium blue, small scar. North Carolina 1950.

Earliblue.—Bush upright, comparatively hardy. Fruit large, light blue, firm, good scar, resistant to cracking; cluster loose. Pollination sometimes is a problem. New Jersey 1952.

Northland.—Bush spreading, 122 cm (4 ft) high at maturity. Hardier than many others. Fruit medium size, round, medium blue, moderately firm, good flavor. Michigan 1968.

Patriot.—Bush upright, relatively open, highbush (even though one of its grandparents was lowbush). Very hardy. Berry large, firm, scar very small, color good. New Hampshire 1976.

Midseason

Collins.—Matures between Earliblue and Bluecrop. Medium-hardy. Fruit large, light blue, firm, sweet. New Jersey 1959.

Bluecrop.—Upright, medium-hardy, but the fruit may stand more cold than some others. Fruit large, light blue, somewhat tart, excellent shipper and keeper. Satisfactory for machine-harvesting. Makes up 35% of the Michigan acreage. New Jersey 1952.

Bluehaven.—Upright, to 152 cm (5 ft), comparatively hardy. Michigan 1968.

Blueray.—Upright spreading, medium-hardy. Fruit very large, firm, sweet. New Jersey 1959.

Berkeley.—Bush medium upright, medium-hardy. Fruit very large, lightest blue, firm, medium quality, resistant to cracking. New Jersey 1949.

Croatan.—Canker-resistant. Erect. Fruit medium size, medium firm, ripens quickly in warm weather. Performs best on light soils. North Carolina 1954.

Herbert.—Dwarfish bush. Fruit large, fine flavor, rather dark. New Jersey 1952.

Coville.—Bush only medium-hardy. Fruit large, light blue, tart until fully ripe. Inconsistent. New Jersey 1949.

Late

Murphy.—Canker-resistant. Bush medium-low, spreading. Leaves large. Cluster long, loose, open, excellent type. Fruit large, medium size, scar large but shallow, fairly good quality. North Carolina.

Jersey.—Bush spreading, vigorous. Fruit large. Cluster long and loose. Some tolerance of canker. Makes up 50% of the Michigan acreage. New Jersey 1928.

Scammell.—Bush erect, moderately canker-resistant. Fruit small, dark, firm, good dessert quality. North Carolina 1931.

Rubel.—Bush upright, willowy. Fruit cluster loose. Fruit small to medium, firm, ships well, medium dessert quality, among the best for processing and machine-harvesting; an early selection from the wild. Comprises 15% of the Michigan crop. New Jersey 1911.

Elliott.—Bush vigorous. Fruit borne in loose clusters, firm, light-blue, medium size, good mild flavor. Resistant to both phases of mummy disease. Michigan 1973.

FIG. 5.4.   JERSEY HIGHBUSH BLUEBERRY

Fruit Shakeability

An estimation of the fruit shakeability for machine-harvesting of several cultivars in North Carolina is as follows (ideal 100): Murphy 98; Morrow 95; Wolcott 93; Croaton 92; Earliblue 92; Jersey 81; Bluecrop 76 (Brooks 1970).

POLLINATION

Most cultivars are self-fruitful and fruit well in large blocks. This simplifies cultural operations, especially harvesting. However, improvement in fruit set and size generally results from effective cross-pollination.

Bees

To increase the population of pollinators, when the blueberries start to bloom place beehives on areas where experience has shown a scarcity of native bees. Place one strong colony per hectare on small areas; on large areas one hive may serve more land. Remove the bees soon after bloom, before any spraying or dusting is done.

Early pollination favors increased yield, primarily in the first two harvests, and increases fruit size in the last two harvests. Growers using honeybees for pollination should contract to ensure field placement of hives not later than 25% of full bloom (Hull et al. 1971; Howell et al. 1972).

The honeybee colony which will collect pollen of blueberry to the substantial exclusion of other species seemingly has not been found (Eaton and Stewart 1969).

Pollination Conditions

Highbush blueberry flowers remain receptive to pollination for eight days after anthesis, but percentage set, average berry weight, and number of seeds per berry decrease when pollination occurs more than four days from anthesis. Berries from self-pollinated flowers have smaller and fewer seeds than cross-pollinated ones.

Temperatures of 16.1° to 27.2°C (61° to 81°F) hasten pollen-tube growth in the style and improve fruit set. Berry weight is largest at the higher temperatures. Cross-pollinated fruits usually ripen more rapidly than self-pollinated ones and ripen much more rapidly at higher than at lower temperatures (Knight and Scott 1964).

Coville Cultivar

Coville has been inconsistent in bearing in solid blocks. Planting several cultivars nearby that ripen in succession rather than only one extends the harvest and distributes the risk. Coville is largely self-incompatible. Therefore, without cross-pollination it may fail to set good crops, particularly of large, early berries. Bumblebees will work Coville flowers as readily as other cultivars, but domestic bees may work other blueberry cultivars in preference to it.

Microspore development is abnormal in 75% of Coville's locules. Irregular metaphase plates occur at meiosis 1 and premature cytokinesis at meiosis 2. An unidentified substance is associated with microspore breakdown. Both normal and abnormal development occurs in the same locule during meiosis; only abnormal pollen occurs when the globular bodies are also present. Each microspore of a tetrad is binucleate shortly after anthesis. The generative nucleus divides mitotically in the pollen tube 6 to 7 hr after pollination. Coville does not dehisce readily from the anther sacs and does not germinate *in vitro*. When fertilization occurs, development of the endosperm and embryo is normal (Stushnoff and Hough 1968).

Jersey Cultivar

Without adequate pollination Jersey produces small, seedless, late berries in Michigan. Its flowers are less attractive to bees and have less pollen per flower than some other cultivars. More bees are needed if it is to attain pollination results equal to those of some other cultivars.

Degeneration of Embryo Sac

Progressive degeneration of the embryo sac occurs after anthesis in Rancocas; 33% of the embryo sacs may degenerate 3 days after anthesis (Eaton and Jamont 1967).

Distance Between Stigma and Anther Tip

High fruit set is associated with a short distance between stigma and anther tip. The ideal flower from the standpoint of maximum fruit set appears to be one with a short corolla that widens at the middle to more than 8 mm (0.31 in.) and then narrows perceptibly at the base (Eck and Mainland 1973).

Gibberellin (GA)

Both KGA (potassium gibberellate) and NAA (auxin), 500 ppm, may induce fruit set on Coville without benefit of pollination. Commercially a set of about 80% is required for a good crop; 6 of the treatments resulted in sets of over 80%. The treatments were applied with a small dropper to the style base in March. At high concentrations, NAA and KGA combinations promoted earlier ripening and higher soluble solids levels than occur in pollinated fruit (Mainland and Eck 1968).

Under field conditions GA does not reduce the number of flower buds formed in Coville. It results in smaller berries that require a long maturation period. There is a strong positive correlation between seed number and berry size in a cultivar. Some factor required for large berry size seems to be lacking in parthenocarpic fruit (Mainland and Eck 1969; Eaton and Stewart 1969).

GA (250 and 500 ppm) applied at 75% full bloom to Jersey bushes caged with and without bees and to open pollinated bushes increased fruit yield per bush, reduced seed weight per fruit, and increased the rate of berry enlargement compared with fruit not pollinated. No effect occurred on soluble solids and titratable acidity. GA appeared to duplicate the effect of pollination and fertilization (Hoods and Kenworthy 1971).

Exogenously applied GA remains in the blueberry fruit a relatively short time (Mainland and Eck 1971).

PROPAGATION

Hardwood Cuttings

Blueberries are more difficult to propagate from hardwood cuttings than are grapes. Hardwood grape cuttings may be stored in a cool place until callused, and then planted directly in nursery rows for footing. Blueberry cuttings are more easily rooted in propagation beds from softwood cuttings under mist (see Part 3, Rabbiteye Blueberries).

Ground Beds.—Fill the bed to a 15.2 cm (6 in.) depth with a mixture of 1 part coarse sand, 1 part well-rotted sawdust, and some perlite. Very fine sand tends to pack, causing poor aeration and retaining excessive moisture. The medium should have a pH of 4.5 to 5.0. In some cases, bottom heat 21.1°C (70°F) is beneficial but is usually not necessary. Frames may be covered with clear plastic reinforced with fine wire mesh.

Making the Cuttings.—Make hardwood cuttings 7.6 to 12.7 cm (3 to 5 in.) long from well-hardened, thrifty, disease-free, pencil size dormant shoots of the previous season's growth. Wood for cuttings may be taken after the leaves have dropped during late fall or early winter before heavy frosts occur, or delayed until late winter but before growth starts.

The cuttings should have only leaf buds. Avoid slender growth, those damaged by cold, and those with brown pith (see Canker).

Often the upper portion of the whips is of late growth, is not stout or firm like the lower sections, will not root readily, and should be discarded. Take as many cuttings as possible from the basal and intermediate portions of the shoots where the factors that influence rooting seem to be most favorable.

Rooting the Cuttings.—Place the cuttings 2.54 to 5.2 cm (1 to 2 in.) apart in rows 5.1 to 7.6 cm (2 to 3 in.) apart, or slightly more, under partial shade. Leaving 1 or 2 buds exposed is good. Do not insert the cuttings too deeply. Firm the soil around the cuttings and water thoroughly to eliminate air pockets.

First top growth occurs while the cuttings are callousing. When roots start developing, top growth stops temporarily. As top growth begins again, the roots should be well established. At this stage increase the light and reduce the humidity level.

Cuttings of some cultivars (e.g., Bluecrop) rooted in full sun are superior to those rooted in partial shade.

The propagation medium is very low in nutrients. When the second flush of new growth appears and the plants are well-rooted, apply a dilute solution of a fertilizer weekly, or Hygro at half the strength advised for house plants. Rinse all foliage immediately after application. Wet the plants in the evening to runoff condition.

Nursery Rows.—Established rooted cuttings are transferred to nursery rows in a well-drained good blueberry site, and spaced about 30.5 cm (1 ft) apart in rows 61 cm (2 ft) apart. After a year in the nursery they are called 2-year-old plants. These usually are the best for field planting. Remove by hand all blossoms from plants in the nursery; even one berry on a small plant may check shoot growth.

Softwood Cuttings

Cuttings taken in early summer from new growth root readily under mist. Make them with 2 to 4 leaves, and set at once in a rooting bed under intermittent mist, which maintains the foliage.

Mist nozzles that deliver 7.57 liters (2 gal.) of water at 13.4 kg (30 lb) pressure provide near 100% humidity; 6 sec of mist every 2 min is satisfactory. Good underdrainage is essential. Reduce misting when the cuttings have rooted, and water only when the surface soil becomes dry, to allow the cuttings to harden.

Plants may be left in the bed for protection over the winter. Then they are grown for at least a year in the nursery before planting in their permanent location.

Mound Layering

Many cultivars root freely on the branches when mounded with sawdust or granulated peat. Plants thus obtained are irregular in shape when first transplanted but rapidly become normal.

Grafting

Grafting scions of highbush cultivars onto rabbiteye rootstocks is a possible means of taking advantage of the superior soil adaptability and vigor of the latter species. Spring grafting and midsummer T-budding are the best methods. Remove suckers from the rootstock annually (Galletta and Fish 1971).

ESTABLISHING A PLANTING

Site

Plants related to blueberries (e.g., huckleberries, azaleas, or laurel) growing on a site are good indicators of success, as is a mixture of pine, red maple, and white cedar, or peat 10.2 to 20.3 cm (4 to 8 in.) thick. Pure sites of white cedar may be difficult to drain. Pine and oak forest, unless irrigated, may be too dry for blueberries. Sites covered with thin pine growth and sheep laurel can be used, but even with irrigation such land shows its scarcity of peat a few years after planting.

Newly cleared land often is best. It usually contains more organic matter than older land. Thoroughly work the soil for at least two years preceding planting to subdue weeds and grasses. Drainage outlets should remove the runoff of heavy rain in 12 hr. Young plants may start well on poorly drained land and die later. In fact, if the water table is high, set the plants on wide raised beds.

Soil and Soil Acidity

Heavy clays are seldom suitable for blueberry production and very light sands may be deficient in organic matter.

Good blueberry soil in the East is an open, porous, sand-peat mixture with a water table at least 35.6 cm (14 in.) but not more than 76 cm (30 in.) below the surface. High acidity of such soil was long believed to be the main feature making it suitable for blueberries, but other factors are also important. In such soil, nature has produced an ideal combination of aeration, moisture supply and fertility for the highbush blueberry. The fine, fibrous roots cannot readily penetrate a compact, heavy soil.

A soil that dries out, even for short periods, may not be suitable without irrigation. Plants set on thin land with a meager water supply may do well for several years, but after the bushes attain full growth shortages of both moisture and soil humus may cause trouble, first in the poorest parts.

In New Jersey after installing the chief drainage ditches and removing the heaviest brush, plow deep enough to go through the peat and bring some of the sand to the surface. If the land is kept fallow for a year before planting, many injurious grubs leave the site, certain weeds are checked, and the coarse roots and sticks start to decay. "Thin" spots where the land is a few inches higher than the rest of the field and the peat deposit is shallow are improved by spreading peat 7.6 cm (3 in.) thick before a plowing or by placing it in the deep furrows alongside the plant rows. If set without the peat, the plants may grow poorly.

Shallow soils may result in plant injury by flooding, poor drainage, drought and low temperature.

Most commercial highbush plantings are on naturally acid soils that test in the range of pH 4.5 to 5.2. A low pH value may cause loss of elements due to chemical action.

Organic Matter

Growth and yield are often roughly in direct ratio to the amount of organic matter in the soil.

Most commercial plantings in eastern North Carolina are on sandy soils characterized by 2% or more organic matter, underlain with a white sand layer above an organic matter hardpan (Brooks 1970).

Water Table

Sparse leaf growth, smaller leaves with severe yellowing, and premature leaf abscission occur under high water table conditions. A too-high water table caused by an impervious clay subsoil is undesirable; the water table should be kept 35.6 to 81.3 cm (14 to 32 in.) below the surface by ditches, etc. Dormant plants may tolerate standing water, but during growth an excess may be fatal, especially in hot weather. Good surface drainage is important since the roots need adequate aeration.

Soil Moisture

Highbush blueberries often grow wild along the edges of ponds and even in swamps. Actually, however, those in swampy sites are situated on hummocks so that they are above the water level and the roots are not completely and continuously submerged.

Blueberry bushes are shallow-rooted and will not tolerate either extreme of drought or prolonged periods of excessive water in the root zone. They require a well-drained soil.

COLD INJURY

Frost injury in commercial areas is usually limited to killing of the flowers, but partially developed berries also may be injured. In Michigan blueberry flowers in full bloom may not be injured at −5°C (23°F) but −6°C (21°F) may reduce the yield of Rubel 12% and some other cultivars 50%. In a swamp half the wild crop may be destroyed at −7.2°C (19°F). Where blueberries are growing on an old cranberry bog, frost damage may be decreased by partial flooding on cold nights.

PLANTING

Good 2-year-old nursery plants commonly are 30.5 to 45.7 cm (12 to 18 in.) high. A plant older than three years may lose most of its root system when moved, perhaps enough to set it back one year or more. Planting 3-year-old rather than 2-year-old stock may result in a crop 1 year earlier, but the net return may not exceed the extra cost of the larger plants. A grower can reduce his initial costs by planting 2-year-old stock. He can reduce them still more by obtaining rooted cuttings and growing them in a nursery for 1 to 2 years before field planting.

Because of the fibrous root system, set the plants in a well-prepared soil. Plant slightly deeper (5.1 cm, or 2 in.) than in the nursery.

Spacing the Plants

The plants should usually be set 1.2 × 2.4 m (4 × 8 ft) apart, 3360 plants per ha (1360 plants per acre), or 1.5 × 3.0 m (5 × 10 ft) apart and 2149 plants per ha (870 plants per acre), according to adaptability of the equipment to be used. Provide roadways at intervals in large plantings.

When to Plant

Early spring planting before growth starts is safest, but fall planting (November) may be successful in areas where the climate is moderated by a large body of water and winter snow is heavy. Some early fall planting is done in New Jersey. In western Oregon planting is done in fall, winter or early spring. Planting in late spring, especially if followed by warm, dry weather, may weaken the plants so that they make little growth the first year.

TILLAGE

Clean cultivation is commonly practiced and is essential the first few years. Cultivate no deeper than 5.1 to 7.6 cm (2 to 3 in.) and only often enough to check weeds. An automatic rotary hoe is useful for working close to the plants along the row and saves much hand labor.

Herbicides (e.g., Diuron, Simazine) at 2.24 to 4.5 kg per ha (2 to 4 lb per acre) before the buds open usually provide season-long weed control. The higher rate is for heavier-textured (loam) soil or for areas with intensive infestations. Annual applications of herbicides for 2 to 3 successive years may result in a nearly weed-free blueberry row (Hull et al. 1971).

For particularly troublesome perennial weeds, application of 4.5 kg of the herbicides per ha (4 lb per acre) may help reduce, but not eliminate, the problem. These herbicides may be ineffective on organic soils at the aforementioned rates.

In bearing plantings in Michigan, sow an annual cover crop after harvest. In young nonbearing plantings sow the cover crop earlier. Use, for example, a mixture of 2 parts oats and 1 part buckwheat at 131 liters per ha (1.5 bu per acre).

The spacing on raised beds made before planting is usually 2.7 m (9 ft) between rows. If soil washes down the slope of the ridge, open the central depression between the rows from time to time and re-make the slopes.

GROWTH FLUSHES

Early ripening highbush cultivars usually produced more vegetative growth flushes than later ripening ones. Multiple buds were found most frequently on thick wood regardless of cultivar. Most distal buds on any flush were flower buds, while proximal buds were usually vegetative (Gough 1976).

GROWTH AND DEVELOPMENT OF FRUIT

Blueberry fruit shows a cyclic growth in size: (1) a period of rapid growth of the pericarp for about 29 days after fertilization; (2) a retarded pericarp growth of 5 to 56 days, with rapid development of the embryo; and (3) a second period of rapid pericarp growth that continues to maturity, but varies from 16 days in a lowbush type to 26 days in Jersey highbush.

FIG. 5.5   HIGHBUSH BLUEBERRY CLUSTER

Fruit maturity is related to the condition of stages (2) and (3). Fully mature fruits may remain on the bush 10 days without loss in size even under slight drought. Berries that receive most sun tend to be the largest. No definite order of fruit maturity occurs in the cluster and maturity has no correlation with fruit size or location within the cluster. The median cluster portion of Jersey yields most fruit for the first picking; the second picking is usually divided among terminal, medial and basal portions. Late-bloom clusters (three weeks later than average berries) mature most evenly within the cluster and often require only one picking. Variation in moisture conditions influences fruit size but not the durations of stages (2) and (3) (Young 1952; Shutak *et al.* 1957).

The type of wood on which the berries grow does not affect the time from blue coloration to abscission. Elapsed time from blossom drop to fruit maturity is too variable for predicting time of harvest. Berries in shade ripen a little later than those in sun.

Berries on the thickest, most vigorous wood are latest in ripening in autumn and opening in spring. Both leaves and berries are largest on the most vigorous wood. In general, more than 65% of the time required to reach maturity is for the first third of the total berry volume, and only 9 to 10% for the last third. A berry may increase 25% in volume after it has turned blue. Temperature is more important than light in influencing ripening, but light can be more important in effecting flower-bud formation (Shutak *et al.* 1957).

Application of Alar mid to late summer retards shoot elongation, but the number of buds per unit length of new growth may be increased. Blossom opening and ripening of berries may be delayed, but fruit size may not be affected (Hapitan *et al.* 1969).

SEED SIZE AND FRUIT SIZE

Fruit size and seed number decrease with progressively later harvests in all cultivars. Seed size differs among the cultivars, but it is not related to fruit size. The percentage of total seeds that develop varies among cultivars and is related to fruit size (Moore *et al.* 1972).

According to the above authors, fruit size in the blueberry is partially determined by the number of seeds and the percentage of seed development. Other factors, such as the amount of growth hormone produced per seed, possibly exert some influence.

Several genetically controlled factors influence fruit size development. Fruit size in the highbush blueberry is quantitatively inherited (Draper and Scott 1969).

FERTILIZER

Since fertilizer recommendations vary with locality, site, soil and other conditions, consult a local authority. Soil and tissue analyses are useful guides to fertilizer needs in a given planting.

"Complete" fertilizer recommendations often have a 1.0-0.43-0.83

ratio. In some cases one or more minor elements are added to the NPK mixture.

On newly set plants in Michigan apply fertilizer thinly by hand around each plant four weeks after planting, keeping 30.5 to 45.7 cm (12 to 18 in.) from the crown. After the first year fertilize just before the buds break. On both newly set and 1-year-old plants apply 72.8 kg per ha (65 lb per acre) of 16-8-8 plus 4 Mg on mineral soils and 8-17-16 plus 4 Mg on organic soils around the plants. During the next year apply 152, 228.5, 304.7 and 380.9 kg per ha (136, 204, 272 and 340 lb per acre), respectively. On 6-year and older plants on mineral soils apply 457.1 kg per ha (408 lb per acre), 72.8 kg (65 lb) of actual N, and on organic muck apply about half as much (Bell and Johnston 1962).

The blueberry grows and fruits at a lower fertilizer level than most other fruits. Heavy fertilization may retard, but not stop, the natural increase in yield due to increase in age and size of the bushes.

Some Leaf Analyses

Four types of leaf samples were taken in British Columbia in June and August from 11 early, midseason and late cultivars. The first three were, respectively, the first, second and third leaves of current season shoots subtending first clusters and the fourth was a composite collection of these leaves.

Each cultivar had less Ca in June than in August, and most cultivars had lower Mg in June than in August. Most cultivars had similar N and Fe content in both months, but had higher P and K in June than in August. In June, K was lower in samples of young leaves than in composite samples. In August, young leaves were higher in Mg. In June, composite samples were higher in P than the second and third leaves. Cultivars, as well as sampling positions and time, are important in evolving diagnostic criteria in analysis (Eaton and Meehan 1971).

Healthy blueberry plants usually show lower levels of K, Ca, Mg and P than most other fruits. Midsummer levels of 2.2% N, 0.97% K, 6.4% Ca and 4.5% Mg seem adequate. Corresponding average ratios in the fruit are approximately 7.2, 1.0 and 6.5 for N, P, and K, respectively (Ballinger and Kushman 1970; Bishop et al. 1971).

Seasonal changes in content of N, P, K, Ca, and Mg in leaves of Rubel were followed during two years. Except for K, the seasonal curves of the elements were similar to those in late apples and Elberta peach. Leaf K showed a late-season increase which did not occur in late apples and Elberta peach (Bailey et al. 1962).

Manure

For many years it was believed that manure would kill cultivated blueberries. But bushes have thrived where as much as 44.8 metric tons per ha (20 tons per acre) of horse manure have been applied. There seems to be little difference among manures if they provide the same amount of N per hectare.

Nitrogen (N)

Ammonium N seems superior to nitrate for blueberries and may be essential; nitrates actually may be harmful. One reason for failure of blueberries on marginal soils may be a lack of ammonium N. Soil conditions there are usually favorable for nitrifying organisms, resulting in a high concentration of nitrates. Ammonium N is short-lived under such conditions. But in the acid soils that are naturally favorable for blueberries, denitrifying organisms predominate, and nitrates may be quickly converted to the ammonium form.

Ammonium N may be associated with Fe nutrition. This is not an effect of the availability of Fe in the solution or absorption by the roots but is an internal function, since plants receiving nitrate N and showing Fe deficiency contain as much or more Fe as normal leaves. Soil pH may not necessarily directly control Fe absorption because plants growing in soils high in pH often contain as much Fe in their leaves as those growing in a lower pH (Cain 1954).

N is often the only element required and may be supplied as urea if the soil pH is below 5.0. Above pH 5.0 use ammonium sulfate.

However, Wolcott plants under a constant-flow gravity system in the greenhouse were able to utilize either nitrate N or ammonium N and maintain a healthy growth for two growing seasons (Hammett and Ballinger 1972A).

Phosphorus (P) and Potash (K)

Interveinal chlorosis, less foliage and lighter berries may appear when the foliar level of P is below 0.40%.

N and P increase the rate of growth of Wolcott young plants in North Carolina. A direct relation may exist between the rate of N, P, or K and the foliar content (Cummings et al. 1971).

As stated earlier, the source of K fertilizer should be sulfate of potash.

Harmful effects due to KCl on highbush blueberries have been reported. However, in North Carolina the leaf Cl content must exceed 0.50% of the total foliar area dry matter before any foliar symptoms of injury appear (Ballinger 1962).

Magnesium (Mg)

In Mg deficiency the leaves turn yellow and red between the veins. Discoloration starts at the leaf tip and spreads along the margins toward the base. Application of 28.0 to 33.6 kg per ha (25 to 30 lb per acre) of magnesium sulfate or 22.4 kg per ha (200 lb per acre) of dolomitic limestone (contains Mg) may eliminate the deficiency symptoms. Lime applied before or after establishment of a planting may raise the soil pH and depress yield.

Iron (Fe)

Fe deficiency, particularly on upland soil in Ohio, is due to the inability of the blueberry to take up available Fe. In all observed cases of this type of chlorosis, weed and cover crops within the rows showed no Fe deficiency symptoms (Hill 1956).

Fe deficiency may be temporarily corrected by a foliar spray of 1% ferrous sulfate or the incorporation of Fe sulfate into the soil. In a soil that is not sufficiently acid, applications are soon converted to unavailable forms and yellowing occurs on new growth.

One soil application of chelated Fe compounds at 45 g ($\frac{1}{10}$ lb) per plant may correct visual symptoms of Fe chlorosis for at least two years. Treated plants may show increases in Fe content of the leaves and improved growth and fruiting. Chelated Fe compounds may also be effective as foliar sprays in 2 applications of 0.96 kg per 400 liters (2 lb per 100 gal.) of water. In severe chlorosis a combination treatment may be warranted. For immediate correction a foliar application can be made; for a more permanent correction, a soil application is required. Avoid using an excess.

A high P content appears to have the effect of lowering the Fe percentage in a nutrient solution and thereby produces Fe chlorosis.

MULCHING

Mulching is not the usual practice in most blueberry plantings. In fringe areas, home gardens, and even larger plantings on non-organic soil it may merit attention.

IRRIGATION

About 2.54 cm (1 in.) of rain or irrigation each week is needed in a mature planting during the growing season. Owing to the long ripening season of the blueberry, during drought it may be necessary to make 2 or 3 applications of 2.54 to 5.1 cm (1 to 2 in.) of water 10 days apart in the picking season and as needed during the heat of the summer.

Overhead sprinkler irrigation can give frost and freeze protection in early spring. Apply 2.5 to 4.6 mm (0.1 to 0.15 in.) per hour when the temperature around the plant drops to 0.5° to 1.1°C (33° to 34°F). Continue to sprinkle for the duration of the low temperature or until all ice melts off the plants. This may save the blossoms and/or young fruit even if the temperature outside the protected area drops to −3.9°C (25°F) (Sneed *et al.* 1970).

Ripe fruit may split in plantings under a steady wetting by an overhead system. Sprinkler applications may be made prior to ripening or directly after a picking in the early morning so the plants will dry rapidly.

Optimum soil moisture is possible with supplemental irrigation and proper drainage. There are several types and systems of irrigation. Interested growers should consult local authorities for the kind and layout best adapted to their planting.

PRUNING

Pruning helps regulate both the current year's crop and the fruiting potential the following year.

No pruning results in thin, weak growth and small late-ripening fruit. Total yield may be higher than on pruned plants, but the size and quality of the fruit are comparatively small and poor. Most cultivars tend to overbear.

Young Plants

In pruning young plants survival may be ensured by a balance between root and top in planting, a good early start, good establishment of the plants and development of desirable wood.

Either before or soon after planting, rub off by hand some or all of the large, compound fruit buds that may be present on the shoots. Cut back, on the average, about one-fourth of the top soon after planting. Remove small bushy growth near the base of the plant to obtain a more upright bush and to keep the fruit off the ground. Little if any further pruning may be needed until the third year after planting.

Older Plants

By the fourth year the plants are reaching maturity and should be conditioned for full production. Practices now are aimed at size and quality of the crop. Open up dense centers by cutting out thin wood, removing low spreading branches, and reducing the number of fruiting areas to promote good berries.

The two main classes of growth habit of the bushes are upright and spreading. Erect cultivars require most center-thinning. Spreading cultivars require little center-thinning but need low-branch removal.

Fruiting Habit

The fruit is borne on wood of the previous year's growth. Largest and best quality fruit is borne on vigorous wood. Try to have the fruit buds well distributed on the bush by wise selection of canes and lateral shoots. Since the tendency is toward over-bearing, unless some buds are pruned off or thinned later, the berries are relatively small and too little vigorous wood may result for the next year's crop. Over-bearing results in small, poor-quality fruit and may shorten the life of the bush because of greater drought injury during periods of low rainfall.

When to Prune

Usually pruning is done in the dormant season. It should be completed before the plants start to grow in the spring. Annual pruning helps to initiate new, vigorous growth on which the next crop is borne.

Amount of Pruning

Regulate the amount of pruning according to the comparative value of total yield, size of berries, and season of maturity.

Heavy pruning may reduce the crop, increase berry size, and shift the ripening period forward. The fruit ripens in a shorter time and earlier than on lightly pruned bushes.

In Michigan late berries bring higher prices than larger, early berries. This is because of the competition with wild blueberries, the bulk of which ripen earlier than the cultivated blueberries, and from other fruits of the same season, such as strawberries, raspberries and cherries. Therefore, a light pruning that promotes later berries, even though somewhat smaller, seems best.

General

Prune enough, along with a good fertilizer program, to strengthen the plant so that enough new growth is produced for a subsequent crop. Often, weak bushes require more severe pruning than vigorous ones. Heavy pruning causes thicker and more leafy shoots than light pruning. Thick and late-developing shoots tend to set fewer buds than early and weak shoots.

Systematically thin out the shorter, weaker shoots, leaving enough of the thick shoots to bear the crop and provide new growth on the selected canes. Tip back long fruiting shoots to leave 4 to 6 buds for adequate fruit size.

There should be enough leaves around fruiting clusters to provide adequate food materials (mostly sugars) for the developing fruit, but not enough to over-shade the fruit or to reduce spray coverage.

Certain cultivars (e.g., Rubel) need much thinning out of small branches, and so are expensive to prune. To increase berry size, cut back the fruiting shoots of some cultivars to 3 to 5 buds per shoot, depending on the number of fruit buds per shoot. Do little of such pruning with Earliblue, Ivanhoe, Bluecrop and Coville (Hull *et al.* 1971).

Facts to Remember When Pruning

(1) Blueberries produce fruit on the previous season's growth. (2) Fruit buds are formed during the summer. (3) Vigorous growth produces high-quality fruit. (4) Most cultivars tend to overbear, thus causing small fruit. (5) Erect cultivars need center-thinning. (6) Spreading cultivars require little center-thinning, but require low-branch removal. (7) Heavy pruning increases fruit size, hastens ripening, and reduces yield very little. (8) No pruning results in thin, weak growth, and small late-ripening fruit. Yield may be higher than from pruned plants, but the size and quality of the fruit will be poor and over-bearing may result.

THINNING DEVELOPING BERRIES

Rubbing off excess blossoms with the fingers may promote larger, more uniform berries and avoid over-bearing. Removing clusters of flowers is more rapid and as effective as thinning berries in the clusters. Freezing temperatures may be a determining factor in deciding whether or not to thin the blossoms or clusters.

HARVESTING

Plants 6 years and older may produce 2.24 to 11.2 metric tons per ha (1 to 5 tons per acre). Higher yields may be obtained under ideal conditions, but excessive crops may be associated with over-bearing.

Hand-picking

Maturing highbush berries change from green to red and then to blue. Once the epidermis of the berries becomes completely blue, it is hard to tell by sight if the berries are ripe enough for harvesting. Position on the panicle does not indicate the degree of maturity.

When to Pick.—The berries become mature-ripe 60 to 80 days after bloom, depending on the cultivar and temperature. The fruit is borne in clusters of 5 to 10 berries. Individual berries in a cluster ripen in succession for several weeks.

As blueberries ripen, total sugars and soluble solids content of the fruit increases, and titratable acidity (as citric acid) decreases. Other indications of the loss of fruit acidity during ripening are increases in berry pH and in sugar-acid or soluble solids-acid ratios. Low total sugars or soluble solids ratios are associated with good keeping quality and high ratios with poor keeping quality (Galletta *et al.* 1971).

Courtesy of Elizabeth C. White

FIG. 5.6.   HARVESTING SCENE IN A HIGHBUSH BLUEBERRY FIELD

Highbush blueberries are harvested in mid to late May and continue through June in North Carolina in the coastal area, ahead of any other region. Peak harvest occurs around June 1 when the Wolcott cultivar reaches maximum harvest, and in the Canner Elk area of Avery County in late September or early October. North Carolina blueberries may be found on the market both early and late in the season (see also Rabbit-eye type).

Harvesting begins about June 15 in New Jersey.

In southwestern Michigan harvest of early cultivars starts in early July; late cultivars extend to mid-September and later in some years. Peak harvest of the Jersey cultivar is in early August. About 25% of the Michigan blueberry crop is hand-picked.

How to Hand-pick.—Cup the hand under a cluster and roll off the desirable berries between thumb and forefinger, without squeezing, as they are pulled gently from the cluster. Fast pickers use both hands. Fill the baskets rounding full.

Pick carefully so as not to damage the "bloom" or light blue color of the fruit. Handle the fruit as little as possible when picking and packing.

A good picker can pick up to 75 half-liters (75 pints) in 8 hr if the crop is heavy and the bushes are optimum size. Generally, 25 to 37 pickers per ha (10 to 15 pickers per acre) are needed during the peak of the season in mature plantings.

Picking directly into shallow baskets allows more of the "bloom" to remain than picking into small pails fastened around the picker's waist. Each picker may have a carrier, e.g., one which holds 8 half-liter (pint) boxes. In most large plantings the main harvesting is done with harvesting aids or machines.

Number of Pickings.—Pick only ripe berries. Many underripe berries result if picking is done too frequently, and many overripe ones if picking is not done often enough.

When machines are used the crop is harvested in a once-over manner. Often several hand-pickings are made for fresh-fruit market before the machine harvest. Some hand-picking may also be done after the machine harvest.

In North Carolina commercial harvesting varies from about twice a week to once or twice a season, after most fruits have ripened (equivalent to 12 to 14 days of ripening). Harvesting patterns often are based on factors other than those influencing fruit quality. Fruit harvested by different growers with different picking schedules is often graded the same because grade is based mainly on average size of fruit. Some crops are harvested in a manner designed to obtain and preserve the highest possible quality (Kushman and Ballinger 1963).

Berry Firmness.—On 15 occasions either Wolcott, Jersey, Morrow or Murphy cultivars were harvested by commercial hand-pickers and over-the-row machine harvesters in 1970 and 1971. Compared with commercially hand-picked fruit, machine-harvested fruit was 30% softer in compression tests. When held for 7 days at 21°C (70°F) the fruit developed 11 to 41% more decay. Machine-harvested fruit sorted on a commercial cleaner was softened still more and developed 5 to 10% more decay than fruit machine-harvested but not sorted. Fifty times as many canes were damaged by machine as by hand-picking (Mainland *et al.* 1975).

Delayed Harvesting.—A berry ripened after harvest never achieves the sweetness of a ripe berry at harvest. The sugar content of berries ripening after harvest is proportional to the stage of ripeness at harvest. The difference may be as great as 30%.

The berry continues to increase in size after turning blue. Commercially, it is often too expensive and unwise to harvest berries before they achieve their full size. Whenever possible a six-day delay in harvest after berries have turned blue should be employed; this may mean a volume increase of as much as 20%.

When berries are sold by weight, delayed harvesting may also mean increased profits. Berries harvested while still unripe lose moisture more rapidly than those fully ripened. Berries in the green-pink stage may lose 6%; those in the fully ripe stage only 4% when kept at room temperature (Gough and Shutak 1973).

Some Quality Considerations.—Blueberries ripened on the bush may average 3.6% higher in soluble solids than those ripened off the bush. Soluble solids content commonly is 10 to 17%. Underripe berries lack good blueberry flavor.

Wolcott berries harvested at 3, 6, 9, and 12-day intervals at Currie, N.C. exhibit little difference in yield, dry weight and soluble solids, but lengthening the harvest interval increases size of fruit, sugars and pH, and decreases total titratable acidity and keeping quality. Keeping quality is correlated with soluble solids to acid ratio (Kushman and Ballinger 1963).

The primary changes during ripening relate to citric acid. Minor changes in malic and quinic acids are detectable, but no significant changes occur in amounts or kinds of amino acids (Kushman and Ballinger 1968A).

Changes in titratable acidity are greater than for other constituents durung ripening and may serve as a harvesting index. Most of the sugar is present prior to red color development in the fruit. Titratable acid content decreases continuously as ripening progresses.

Mechanical Aid and Machine-harvesting

Hand-held Vibrating Units.—This type of mechanical aid is used to harvest about 25% of the Michigan crop. The picking fingers are mounted on a vibrating head. They shake the berries from the canes and the fruit is collected on a portable canvas frame placed under the bush. The vibrating units also remove some leaves, twigs and immature fruit. Prior to packaging or processing, special equipment removes trash, leaves and small immature fruits. Removal of larger, immature berries and undesirable fruit is done by hand as the fruit moves over a sorting table (Hull *et al.* 1971).

Hand-held vibrators can harvest up to 362.9 kg (800 lb) per day compared with 45 to 68 kg (100 to 150 lb) by hand-picking. Electric and compressed-air vibrators are manually controlled. The batteries may require charging or changing, perhaps every other night.

Self-propelled Over-the-row Harvesters.—With this type of harvester the berries are shaken from the bush, deflected by collecting pans beneath the bush and moved onto conveyors. The fruit is then conveyed to the rear of the machine and collected in field lugs for transportation from the field. The machine harvests about 0.3 ha (0.75 acre) per hr. About 65% of the Michigan crop is harvested by this method.

Another harvester has four-wheel drive, power steering, hydraulic controls throughout and travels easily over soft-bottom land on special tires. The assembly includes a bush-divider shaker assembly, catch pans, conveyor and pneumatic separators. Each wheel can be adjusted vertically up to 45.6 cm (18 in.) to adapt to different bush heights. Speeds range from 3.2 km per hr(2 mph) up to 9.7 km per hr (6 mph).

The machine measures 5.49 m (18 ft) long, 3.25 m (10 ft 8 in.) wide, with a minimum height of 3.53 m (11 ft 7 in.) and a maximum of 3.96 m (13 ft). It has a 40 cm (16 in.) turning radius and requires only 5.49 m (18 ft) of space at the end of a row to turn without reversing. Standard equipment includes lights for night operation, signal horn and two lug-type trailers. Extra trailers, flasher lights and driver canopy are optional.

In another machine aluminum fingers vibrate the branches throughout the entire bush, shaking the ripe fruit onto catch trays and into stainless-steel bucket conveyors. As the machine travels past the base of the bush, catch disks turn and slowly open and close, giving maximum catching ability.

Established sod or other ground cover between the rows may keep machine harvesters or other heavy equipment from bogging down. Mowing the cover occasionally, irrigating, and applying herbicides in the row appear encouraging. The mummy berry disease, which can be more serious in noncultivated fields and where sod culture is practiced, requires extra care for control.

Chemical Fruit Looseners

The harvest period for individual blueberry cultivars ranges from 3 to 6 weeks. This prolonged harvest period for any given cultivar presents a problem to machine-harvesting of these cultivars. Many growers have experienced difficulty in adapting the large and expensive commercial blueberry harvesters to more than one harvest per cultivar. The machines inevitably leave sufficient ripe fruit to pose a quality problem in subsequent harvests.

2-Chloroethylphosphonic acid (Ethephon, Ethrel) applied as a spray to highbush blueberry two weeks before first harvest results in an increase in percentage of the total yield of ripe fruit harvested in the first two pickings. This increase may occur at a concentration of Ethephon as low as 240 ppm in Weymouth cultivar, but for Blueray a higher ppm is needed to produce the same effect. Ethephon seems to accelerate the production of anthocyanins, but not other maturity indices (Eck 1970).

Ethephon reduced fruit removal force as much as 50% depending on concentration and time of application. This allowed reduced machine-harvesting vibration frequency which reduces damage to berries during harvest and thus increases shelf-life. Machine harvest was further facilitated by Ethephon-induced color development and hastening of abscission, which reduced the number of harvests required (Howell *et al.* 1976).

HANDLING HARVESTED FRUIT

Moisture content of the berries averages about 86%. Placing the fruit in a cool place soon after harvest helps to reduce moisture and weight loss.

Cooling the harvested fruit retains quality and prolongs shelf-life. Cool quickly to 4.4°C (40°F) or lower, but not below 0°C (32°F). If cooled promptly and kept cool, blueberries packed ready for retail sale may hold up well at 0°C (32°F) for 2 weeks, at 4.4°C (40°F) for 1 week, and at 21.1°C (70°F) for 2 days.

A capping machine helps speed the packaging process. Filled baskets are put on a sliding platform and slid into the capping area four pints at a time. Film is brought across the top of the baskets and each pint basket is capped as the anvil is brought down. When the capped baskets get over to the other side of the unit they are removed and put into flats to complete the process.

Automated packaging using existing packaging equipment and folded waxed master cartons may be feasible for fresh-market berries. The 36-pint master requires only 56% as much space as 12-pint flats in conventional packaging.

There are a number of different covers for pint baskets, such as: (1) a glued-on lid; (2) film put on by heat-shrink; (3) flat-packed formed cartons; (4) cellophane and rubber band or contact cement; (5) plastic tops snapped on.

Cleaning

Machine-harvested berries require more cleaning than hand-picked berries.

It is important to provide sufficient cleaning equipment to handle mechanically harvested berries, because the large machines harvest fruit as rapidly as 2 to 3 cleaning units can handle it. A cleaning-packing line, including a destemmer and sizer where needed, as well as automatic in-line packaging equipment, is used in modern handling of the crop.

Sorting and Packaging Berries Electronically

The acid composition of blueberry fruit appears to afford a mechanism of resistance to decay-producing organisms. There is a relation between acidity and soluble solids as berries develop. This indicates a potential means of sorting blueberries electronically according to their anthocyanin content. Studies with a light transmittance difference meter indicate that sorting according to anthocyanin content nondestructively is feasible (Birth and Norris 1965; Ballinger et al. 1968, 1970; Ballinger and Kushman 1970; Dekazos and Birth 1970).

Regardless of season, location, harvest date or size, Wolcott fruits sorted with transmission light according to their anthocyanin (ACY) content were reasonably well separated for quality as expressed by pH, titratable acid (AC), soluble solids (SS) and the SS/AC ratio. Quality of fruits of the same ACY class differed according to cultivar (Wolcott, Berkeley, and Jersey). AC content of the fruit decreased slightly during the season regardless of the ACY class or cultivar. This consistent reduction in AC as the season progressed was accompanied by increases in the SS/AC ratios and development of decay. Location of harvest (farm to farm) influenced SS somewhat. A long harvest interval produced a small but consistent effect on all quality parameters (Kushman and Ballinger 1975).

Anthocyanin expression depends on one or two genes and its content may be inherited. For cultivars whose fruits are not normally blue, the commercial use of blue color as the major criterion of marketability (ripeness) may not be valid since color development is not necessarily related to berry ripeness and quality (Ballinger et al. 1972).

Individual fruit pH, total acidity (AC as %), and SS/AC ratios correlated significantly with anthocyanin content in Wolcott, Jersey, and

Tifblue, as measured by light transmission Δ(OD 740 to 800 nm).

The development of machine harvesters has produced a need for new methods, as discussed previously, of grading the fruits when they arrive at the grading station, when they may be green, ripe, or bruised.

RENOVATING OLD PLANTINGS

Many blueberry plantings are more than 21 years old. Production begins to decline in old plantings, largely because of the shading effect. Severe hand-pruning may or may not bring the overgrown planting back to an economic production level. The ever-increasing limitation on labor available to prune blueberries makes it important to explore ways to restore production.

One scheme is to root out the old plants and plant new cultivars. Another is to cut back the plants severely. With the tractors owned by most growers the clearance is not adequate to cut down the plants. Both cutting and shredding modifications of equipment have been tried, as well as circular saws, flaming, and use of chemicals in relation to width of row.

These questions are yet to be answered: What is the effect of flame or chemicals on longevity of a planting? How often must a given operation (cutting back, narrowing of row, or regrowth control) be performed? What is the optimum width of a recut plant for maximum yield and harvester efficiency? What chemicals can be used and what rate would give most effective control of regrowth? What combination of treatments will give the least reduction in income during the rejuvenation process? (Hansen *et al.* 1972).

In early spring, while the bushes were still dormant, a 26-year-old field of Jersey plants that were in a state of low production (less than 3361 kg per ha or 1.5 tons per acre) was sawed off at ground level with a circular saw to produce 20, 25, and 30 cm (8, 10 and 12 in.) row widths and an unnarrowed control approximately 40 cm (16 in.) in diameter. The method returned poorly productive bushes to superior production in two years. After four years the yield was still greater. Paraquat was used to maintain a narrow crown width (Howell *et al.* 1975).

PROTECTIVE DEVICES

Birds often take many berries and rabbits often damage the stems. Protective enclosures of 1-in. mesh poultry wire may be useful in home gardens. No single protective device seems to have been successful against birds. Some combination or rotations of explosive devices or flashing strips have limited value, as has a shotgun.

PART 3

RABBITEYE BLUEBERRIES

The rabbiteye blueberry (*Vaccinium ashei*) was so named because when the fruit begins to ripen the pink color resembles a rabbit's eye. It is hexaploid and native to the Southeast and South, especially along many of the large streams in northwestern Florida, southwestern Georgia and southeastern Alabama. Native plants are generally vigorous and may grow 3 m (10 ft) or more tall and send up few to many stems. In general its range is much the same as that of the muscadine grape.

Highly successful commercial plantings occur in at least North Carolina, Georgia and Florida. Both highbush and rabbiteye cultivars succeed in North Carolina, but the highbush does not succeed in Florida.

Some attributes of the rabbiteye are great vigor and adaptability to a wide range of growing conditions in the area where it succeeds, as well as to heat, drought and canker tolerance.

Insufficient and natural chilling affected vegetative bud break less than floral break. Plants flowered normally only after receiving 500 or more hours of constant or intermittent artificial chilling. A high temperature alternated with low temperature slowed but did not

Courtesy of J. F. Brooks, North Carolina Agr. Ext. Service

FIG. 5.7.   RABBITEYE BLUEBERRY

nullify the low temperature effect. A close association exists between artificial constant chilling and natural chill-unit data on floral or vegetative bud break. Chill-unit models have potential use in predicting completion of the rest period in rabbiteye blueberries (Spiers 1976).

Rabbiteye berries are generally darker-colored, larger-seeded, smaller-fruited and less finely flavored than the northern lowbush or highbush types. But the flavor is quite acceptable for a wide range of purposes and the berries of newer cultivars are lighter blue in color.

Where both highbush and rabbiteye are grown, the latter is later in the beginning and ending of harvest. In North Carolina, for example, highbush berries generally begin ripening in late May and harvest is concluded by late June. Rabbiteye harvest, on the other hand, begins in late June and continues into late August.

CULTIVARS

Woodard.—Early; two weeks before Tifblue. Bush medium size; produces many suckers. Berries comparatively large, light blue, slightly more acid than Tifblue. Does not crack in rainy weather following a dry period. Good shipping quality. Georgia 1960.

Tifblue.—Leading rabbiteye cultivar. Bush very vigorous. Late midseason. Fruit large, round, heavy waxy bloom, light blue, sweet, very firm. Often appears to be ripe several days before full flavor. Scar small and dry. Seeds medium small and soft.

Homebell.—Bush upright; produces enough new stems to renew the plant. The top is spread by heavy crops, thus facilitating harvest. Fruit medium-large, medium-dark blue, medium-firm. Does not attain a blue color until almost mature, thus it is easy to pick only ripe berries.

Bluebelle.—Plants upright, produce large light berries with a small scar and good flavor. Good for PYO because the berry sizes well throughout the season. Georgia 1976.

Climax.—It allows 50% of the crop to be harvested at once and so is excellent for machine-harvesting. Cross-pollination is needed. Georgia 1976.

Bluegem.—Plant size intermediate between Woodard and Tifblue; moderately spreading; makes a limited number of suckers. Woodard overlaps it in bloom. Fruit remains on the bush for a long time in firm condition. Picking scar small and dry, thus inhibiting decay and increasing shelf-life. Both fruit and young leaves have a heavy glaucescence or wax that results in a light-blue appearance. Florida 1970.

Floridablue and Sharpblue.—These extend the area for growing high quality blueberries 161 km (100 mi.) farther south, and begin the ripening season more than a month earlier. Neither is recommended for shipping because of the wet scar, but they are suitable for PYO and local markets. Florida 1975.

Delite.—Fruit medium-large, round, small dry scar. Although the berries have a fairly heavy bloom the red undercolor may show through when ripe. Ripe and immature berries separate from the bush easily so machine-harvesting should be delayed until most berries are ripe. This seems to be the first cultivar with berries that are not tart before reaching maturity. Georgia 1969.

Brightblue.—Bush moderately vigorous and spreading. A waxy bloom gives the berries a light-blue color. Berries large, especially early in the season. Berry firmness, heavy bloom, and small, dry scar combine to make this an excellent shipper. Georgia 1969.

Southland.—Berries firm, with a waxy bloom giving a light-blue color; scar small and dry. Skin may be somewhat tough late in the season. Georgia 1969.

Menditoo.—Late midseason. Bush medium-vigor, spreading. Fruit dark-blue, large, round, medium-firm, sweet. Long ripening period. North Carolina.

FRUITING NURSERY PLAN IN EVALUATING SEEDLINGS

About 80% of blueberry seedlings fruited the second year after seed harvest when grown rapidly at densities of 16 plants per m^2 in Florida. This permits roguing of plants on the basis of fruit characters in the second year from seed harvest (24 months) and evaluation of remaining plants the following year. The fruiting nursery system, based on intensive care of seedlings at ultra-high densities to achieve rapid growth, improves breeding efficiency (Sherman *et al.* 1973).

PROPAGATION

Digging suckers or sprouts from parent bushes will produce a small number of plants quickly. Cut them back severely when planting. For quantity increase the main method is softwood cuttings. If hardwood cuttings are used, proceed as outlined for highbush blueberry.

Softwood Cuttings Under Mist

Placing softwood cuttings under mist in a prepared medium is the chief method of propagating rabbiteye cultivars in quantity. Avoid using cuttings that have fruit buds.

Making the Cuttings.—Take the cuttings soon after the first flush of spring growth. Most shoots are then at the same stage of growth and large numbers of cuttings may be made at one time. Cuttings should not be so tender that they wilt soon after being stuck in the propagation bed.

Cuttings 7.6 to 10.2 cm (3 to 4 in.) long commonly root within 6 to 8 weeks in a suitable medium under mist.

In a test in Georgia treatments consisted of removing all leaves except the three terminal ones (designated as "stripped"), compared with leaving all the leaves on the cutting ("not stripped"). Also, half the lots were cut with a sharp knife below a bud before putting in the bed ("cut"), in contrast to those "not cut." The highest total percentage of rooting was in cuttings that were stripped and cut; but there was little difference in percentage of cuttings with excellent roots between lots having leaves stripped and recut and lots not stripped but cut. A large leaf area is desirable for formation of large root system, but the number of cuttings that produce roots may be lowered slightly by a large leaf area (Brightwell 1971).

Rooting Medium.—This often is a mixture of 60% peat and 40% perlite by volume. Some prefer to raise the peat percentage and lower the perlite percentage. Perlite makes the mixture light so that cuttings may be easily removed from the medium.

On a small scale the rooting may be done in flats or trays in a greenhouse. Commercially the rooting usually is done in a coldframe. A good coldframe for the purpose is 30.5 cm (12 in.) high on one side and 45.7 cm (18 in.) on the other.

Place 5 cm (2 in.) of coarse cinders in the coldframe or series of coldframes for good drainage. On top of the cinders add 2 parts peat, 1 part coarse sand and 1 part old sawdust.

Native peat often is variable and may contain so many weed seeds that imported peat (Canadian or German) may be preferable.

Cover the bed with sash, e.g., saran cloth (63% shade), to maintain a high relative humidity, and keep it heavily shaded to lower daytime temperatures and to protect cuttings from direct sun rays. Instead of the coldframe, a structure which can be shaded with saran cloth may be erected and the bed made inside it.

Growing Newly Rooted Cuttings.—Well-rooted cuttings may be grown in full sun or in partial shade. The use of liberal amounts of peat often may increase growth.

Cuttings may be left in the rooting beds until they are ready to be set in a nursery or they may be potted. Good results have been obtained by allowing cuttings to remain in the cutting beds, potting and plunging in the cutting beds, or potting and placing pots in a cool greenhouse.

Good root development may occur if cuttings are potted in late summer or fall and placed in protected coldframes or in a greenhouse during the winter. In Georgia rooted cuttings potted in November in 7.6 cm (3 in.) peat pots produced over 2½ times as much top growth as plants in composition dirt bands, and almost 5 times as much as those in clay pots by December 23, when grown under identical greenhouse conditions. More buds were breaking on plants in peat pots than on those in dirt bands or clay pots (Brightwell 1971).

Rooted cuttings may be grown in full sun or in partial shade such as that provided by various shade materials or the natural shade of pine trees. The soil must be well prepared and weeds eliminated prior to setting the plants.

Various potting mixtures may be used. Good growth has resulted from use of imported peat moss, imported peat moss and perlite, and a 3:2:1 mixture of sandy soil, peat moss and sawdust.

To eliminate noxious plants and to reduce nematodes and soil fungi, soil may be fumigated with methyl bromide. This treatment increases plant growth and spacing may be as close as 30.5 × 45.7 cm (12 × 18 in.).

Grow the rooted cuttings in a nursery or coldframe for a year, often under partial shade, before field-planting.

To study the influence of soil fumigation on growth of rooted cuttings, a uniform area in a Georgia nursery was selected for six 15 × 4.6 m (50 × 15 ft) sections. Alternate sections were treated with methyl bromide 2.44 kg per 100 m² (4.5 lb per 100 sq yd). The plastic cover was left on the treated area for 48 hr. Treatment was two weeks before planting to allow excess gas to escape. Plants were spaced 30.5 × 45.7 cm (12 × 18 in.).

At the end of the first growing season the average plant height in the treated areas was 38.1 cm (15 in.) compared with 15 cm (5.9 in.) for the untreated. Average total growth in the treated areas was 65.7 cm (25.9 in.) compared with 35.1 cm (14.3 in.) for the untreated. The differences may be attributed in part to high populations of *Pythium* species and stubby-root nematodes in soil from the untreated areas, compared with low populations from the treated areas (Brightwell 1971).

PRODUCING THE CROP

Soil

Most commercial plantings in the Southeast are grown in the sandy soils of the Coastal Plains area in Georgia, in North Carolina and in north central Florida. They can be grown on clay soils of the Georgia Piedmont if sufficient mulch (e.g., sawdust) is used. A pH of 4.5 to 5.5

is desirable. Arrange the rows to ensure adequate drainage.

Planting

Rabbiteye plants usually are set while dormant in late fall or winter in North Carolina. Planting may extend from late fall through March in Florida. Spacing commonly is 1.8 m (6 ft) apart in rows 3.66 m (12 ft) apart.

Fertilizer

The plants are sensitive to readily soluble fertilizers and may be injured or killed by excessive amounts. Moderate to low amounts of cottonseed meal, azalea-camellia fertilizer, or ammonium sulfate applied after new growth begins may increase growth. The latter material is especially effective in correcting a yellowing of the leaves due to high pH or N deficiency.

It is essential that young plants receive adequate moisture during the growing season. In the second season spread 28 to 57 g (1 to 2 oz) of a high organic fertilizer around each plant. As the plants grow larger the type and amount of fertilizer must be determined by soil analysis and growth. Do not apply nitrate of soda. In field tests all plants that received 57 g (2 oz) of nitrate of soda were dead after 2 years (Brightwell 1971).

Firmness and Decay

Spraying Woodard bushes with 2.3 kg per ha (2 lb per acre) Defolian at 24-day intervals in 5 applications tended to increase firmness, and when applied 21 days before harvest decreased the number of decayed fruits (Austin 1976).

Pruning

Pruning of young plants consists mostly of removing low branches and some thinning of crowding branches in the center of the plant.

With older plants, eliminate surplus stems to keep the bushes from becoming too dense or tall. Thin branches to facilitate harvesting. In general prune rather lightly, since the rabbiteye can support heavy crops.

Pollination and Yield

Plant two or more cultivars which overlap in bloom to assure adequate pollination of each other. Two examples, in alternate rows, are Tifblue and Woodard; Woodard and Bluegem.

Yields of 3-year-old plants may average 3.3 liters (3 qt) per plant. Yields increase until the plants are about 12 to 15 years old and may be 16.5 liters (15 qt) or more per plant.

Courtesy of J. F. Brooks, North Carolina Agr. Ext. Service

FIG. 5.8.   BEFORE AND AFTER PRUNING LARGE RABBITEYE BUSH

Picking

Picking in north central Florida begins in May and extends into late June. In North Carolina it begins in late June and continues into August.

With most cultivars begin pickling 1 to 2 weeks after the first blue color development, or when the red has disappeared from around the stem. Only a few berries in a cluster may ripen at one time. Some cultivars ripen their fruit within a 3 to 5 day period; others may ripen over a considerably longer period. A desirable feature is long retention on the bush in firm condition for PYO or for picking for market sales. Delay machine-harvesting until most berries are ripe.

Courtesy of J. F. Brooks, North Carolina Agr. Ext. Service

FIG. 5.9.   THESE PLANTS WERE NOT VIGOROUS AT TIME OF PRUNING, BUT WERE IN GOOD SHAPE A YEAR LATER

BLUEBERRY DISEASES

Stem canker is caused by a fungus in infected bark. It weakens or kills the stem above cankered and girdled areas. It is seldom serious in northern regions but may be so severe in eastern North Carolina that only resistant cultivars are successful. In general, cultivars grown in the North are not successful in the major area of North Carolina for this reason.

Stunt is transmitted by a sharp-nosed leafhopper, shows as shortened internodes, clustered young shoots, and small, curled, often cupped leaves, with marginal chlorosis, and a usually green midrib. The tiny leaflets are chlorotic. Premature red coloring occurs. Vigor, flavor, size, and yield are reduced. Rogue out infected plants. Take cuttings only at least ¼ mi. from the nearest diseased plant.

Mosaic, a virus disease, causes individual shoots to be light green or mottled with yellow. Later, mottled leaves occur throughout the plant with some yellowing near the base of the shoots.

Shoestring, a virus dease, shows as red streaks and vein bending in the spring. The leaves become distorted or have narrow strap-leaf deformities.

Red ringspot, a virus disease, causes red rings on the upper surface of the leaves.

Stem blight or "dieback," like its relative stem canker, is serious only in North Carolina. Both highbush and rabbiteye cultivars are susceptible to it. Infection occurs primarily through wounds. Remove all dead or dying branches as soon as possible.

Necrotic ringspot is soil-borne and is transmitted by nematodes. The leaves become puckered and distorted. The spots may drop out.

Mummy berry shows as a dieback of shoots and a hard rot of fruit. Give frequent tillage in early spring, before the spores are discharged, to disturb the over-wintered mummies, thus stopping further apothecial development.

Leaf rust has an alternate stage on hemlock (*Tsuga*) in areas where this tree occurs. In southern regions it may overwinter on the blueberry. Discolored spots appear on the lower side of the leaf. Defoliation usually occurs late in the season but may occur early and result in berries shrivelling and dropping.

Witches'-broom infects the stems and results in clusters of slender shoots. It has fir (*Abies*) as an alternate host and does not spread from plant to plant of blueberry. Remove infected blueberry plants.

Blossom and twig blight often cause damage on sites where water stands for some time during the growing period, and in years of foggy weather during and just before bloom.

Anthracnose-infected fruits show orange-colored spore masses.

Powdery mildew may cause extensive defoliation. Resistance to mildew has been important in selection of new cultivars by breeders.

Alternaria and *botrytis* are fruit-rotting fungi. Various fruit acidity and soluble solids may account for 80% of the decay variability in different clones. Differences in ripening season, temperatures, fruit/leaf ratios and moisture all affect the soluble solids/acidity ratio. Seasonal fluctuations in rot organism and populations, differences in fruit pedicel scar area and moisture content, and fruit firmness may contribute to the other 20% of the decay variability (Galletta *et al.* 1971).

BLUEBERRY INSECTS

Scales (several kinds) feed on twigs and may greatly reduce vigor.

Blossom weevil beetles bore into swelling buds and blossoms from the side and consume the contents. Most buds so injured do not open, and the few that do form a small rosette of malformed leaves. Egg-laying begins when the flowers show white. A female punctures the corolla and lays a single egg among the anthers. The grub hatches in 1 to 2 days and eats the stamens, pistil, and part of the ovary, leaving a mere shell. The crop may be reduced over 50%.

Plum curculio adult is a rough-looking grayish to dark-brown snout beetle with a hump on the middle of each wing cover. The chewing mouth parts are on the end of a long snout which projects from the head somewhat like an elephant's trunk.

Cranberry fruitworm larvae web clusters of berries together, feeding within and leaving filth in the fruit.

Cherry fruitworm red larvae feed in the developing berries.

Sharpnose leafhopper is a vector of the virus stunt disease.

Blueberry maggot-infested berries, even a few of them, may cause an entire shipment to be condemned. The adult resembles a housefly in shape but is slightly smaller, with black bands across the wings and white lines on the abdomen. The egg is laid beneath the skin of the fruit. A few days later the maggot hatches and may feed in the fruit for about two weeks.

REFERENCES

AUSTIN, M.E. 1976A. Comparison of hand and machine harvest of rabbit-eye blueberries. HortScience *11*, No. 3, 244.

AUSTIN, M.E. 1976B. Effect of difolatan on shelf life of rabbiteye blueberries. HortScience *11*, No. 3, 224.

BAILEY, J.S. *et al.* 1962. Seasonal changes in nutrients in leaves of Rubel blueberry. Proc. Am. Soc. Hort. Sci. *80*, 327-30.

BALLINGER, W.E. 1962. Sulfate and chloride ion effects on Wolcott blueberry growth and composition. Proc. Am. Soc. Hort. Sci. *80*, 331-39.

BALLINGER, W.E., and KUSHMAN, L.J. 1970. Relationship of stage of ripeness to composition and keeping quality of highbush blueberries. J. Am. Soc. Hort. Sci. *95*, 239-42.

BALLINGER, W.E. *et al.* 1968. Progress in maturity measurements of blueberries using light-transmittance technique. HortScience *3*, 99.

BALLINGER, W.E. *et al.* 1970. Anthocyanins in ripe fruit of highbush blueberry. J. Am. Soc. Hort. Sci. *95*, 283-85.

BALLINGER, W.E. *et al.* 1972. Anthocyanins of ripe fruit of a pink fruited hybrid of highbush blueberries. J. Am. Soc. Hort. Sci. *97*, No. 3, 381-84.

BALLINGER, W.E. *et al.* 1975. Factors affecting the firmness of highbush blueberries. J. Am. Soc. Hort. Sci. *98*, No. 6, 583-87.

BALLINGTON, J.R. *et al.* 1968. Effects of soil amendments on growth of rabbiteye blueberry. S. Carolina Res. Ser. *117*.

BELL, H.P. 1950. Determinate growth in blueberry. Can. J. Res. *28*, 637-49.

BELL, H.P. 1953. Growth cycle of blueberry. Can. J. Botany *31*, 1-6.

BELL, H.P., and BURCHELL, J. 1955. Flower development in lowbush blueberry. Can. J. Botany *33*, 251-58.

BELL, M.K., and JOHNSTON, S. 1962. Hints on blueberry growing. Mich. Agr. Ext. Folder *119*.

BIRTH, C.S., and NORRIS, R.K. 1965. The difference meter for measuring interior quality of foods and pigments in biological tissue. U.S. Dept. Agr. Tech. Bull. *1341*.

BISHOP, H.F. *et al.* 1971. Effect of source and rate of N and Mg on nutrient levels in highbush leaves and fruit. HortScience *6*, 37-38.

BITTENBERGER, B.C., and HOWELL, G.S. 1976. Cold hardiness of flowerbuds from selected highbush blueberry cultivars. J. Am. Soc. Hort. Sci. *101*, No. 2, 135.

BOLDER, C.A. 1951. Growing blueberries. Ore. Agr. Expt. Bull. *498*.

BRIGHTWELL, W.T. 1971. Rabbiteye blueberries. Ga. Agr. Expt. Res. Bull. *100*.

BRIGHTWELL, W.T., and WOODARD, O.J. 1960. Blueberry breeding in Georgia. Fruit Varieties and Hort. Digest *15*, No. 2, 39.

BROOKS, J.F. 1970. Blueberries: production guide for North Carolina. N. Carolina Agr. Ext. Circ. *474*.

CAIN, J. 1952. Cultivated blueberries must be cultivated. N.Y. Farm. Res. (Jan.)

CAIN, J. 1954. Comparison of chlorotic and green blueberry leaf tissue with respect to free amino acid and basic cation contents. Proc. Am. Soc. Hort. Sci. *65*, 49-53.

CAMP, W.H. 1945. North American blueberries. Brittonia *5*, No. 3.

COLLINS, W.B. *et al.* 1966. Growth substances in the flower bud and developing fruit of *V. angustifolium*. Proc. Am. Soc. Hort. Sci. *89*, 243-47.

CONSTANTE, J.F., and BOYCE, B.R. 1968. Low temperature injury of highbush shoots at various times of the year. Proc. Am. Soc. Hort. Sci. *93*, 267.

CRAIG, D.L. 1967. Highbush blueberry culture in eastern Canada. Canada Dept. Agr. Publ. *1279*.

CUMMINGS, G. *et al.* 1971. Fertilizer and lime rates influence highbush blueberry growth and foliar element content during establishment. J. Am. Soc. Hort. Sci. *96*, 184-86.

DEKAZOS, E.D., and BIRTH, G.S. 1970. A maturity index for blueberries using light transmittance. J. Am. Soc. Hort. Sci. *95*, 610-14.

DOW, G.F. *et al.* 1955. Producing blueberries. Me. Agr. Expt. Sta. Bull. *479*.

DRAPER, A.D., and SCOTT, D.H. 1969. Fruit size inheritance in highbush blueberry. J. Am. Soc. Hort. Sci. *94*, 417-18.

DRAPER, A.D. *et al.* 1972. Two tetraploid sources of resistance for breeding blueberries resistant to Phytophthora Cinnamomii. HortScience 7, 266-67.

EATON, E.L. 1957. Spread of blueberry seed through manure and by migrating robins. Proc. Am. Soc. Hort. Sci. *69*, 293-95.

EATON, E.L., and WHITE, R.G. 1960. Relation between burning and development of sprouts and flower buds in lowbush blueberry. Proc. Am. Soc. Hort. Sci. *76*, 293-95.

EATON, G.W., and JAMONT, A.M. 1967. Megagametegenesis in *V. corymbosum*. Can. J. Botany 44, 712-14.

EATON, G.W., and MEEHAN, C.N. 1971. Effect of leaf position and sampling date on leaf nutrient composition of eleven highbush cultivars. J. Am. Soc. Hort. Sci. *96*, 378-80.

EATON, G.W., and STEWART, M.G. 1969. Highbush blueberry pollen collection by honeybees. HortScience *4*, 95.

ECK, P. 1970. Indluence of Ethrel upon highbush blueberry fruit ripening. HortScience *4*, 95.

ECK, P., and MAINLAND, C.M. 1973. Highbush blueberry fruit set in relation to flower morphology. HortScience *6*, 484-95.

EDWARDS, T.W. *et al.* 1972. Seed development in certain Florida tetraploid and hexaploid blueberries. HortScience *7*, 127-28.

FORSHEY, C.G. 1969. Potassium nutrition of deciduous fruits. HortScience *4*, 39-41.

GALLETTA, G.J., and FISH, A.S. 1971. Interspecific blueberry grafting, a way to extend Vaccinium culture to different soils. J. Am. Soc. Hort. Sci. *96*, 294-98.

GALLETTA, G.J. *et al.* 1971. Relationships between fruit acidity and soluble solids levels of highbush blueberry clones and fruit keeping quality. J. Am. Soc. Hort. Sci. *96*, 758-62.

GOUGH, R.E. 1976. Observations on vegetative and reproductive growth in blueberry. HortScience *11*, No. 3, 260.

GOUGH, R., and SHUTAK, V.G. 1973. Key to quality blueberries. Am. Fruit Grower (June).

HALL, I.V. 1971. Volatiles of lowbush blueberry nectar. HortScience *6*, 493-94.

HALL, I.V., and AALDERS, L.E. 1967. Lowbush blueberry production and management. Can. Dept. Agr. Publ. *1278*.

HALL, I.V. *et al.* 1969. Apical dominance in lowbush blueberry altered by indolebutyric acid. HortScience *4*, 27-28.

HALL, S.H., and GALLETTA, G.J. 1971. Comparative chromosome morphology of diploid Vaccinium species. J. Am. Soc. Hort. Sci. *96*, 289-92.

HAMMETT, L.K., and BALLINGER, W.E. 1972A. A nutrient solution-sand culture system for studying the influence of N form on highbush blueberries. HortScience 7, 498-500.

HAMMETT, L.K., and BALLINGER, W.E. 1972B. Biochemical components of highbush blueberry fruit as influenced by nitrogen nutrition. J. Am. Soc. Hort. Sci. *97*, 742-45.

HANSEN, C.M. *et al.* 1972. Rejuvenation of old blueberry plants. Mich. State Univ. Duplicate.

HAPITAN, J.C. et al. 1969. Vegetative reproductive responses of highbush blueberry to succinic acid, 2,2-dimethylhydrazide (Alar). J. Am. Soc. Hort. Sci. 94, 26-32.

HEPLER, P.R., and DRAPER, A.D. 1976. Patriot blueberry. HortScience 11, No. 3, 272.

HERATH, H.M., and EATON, G.W. 1968. Effects of water table, pH, and nitrogen on growth and nutrient-element content of highbush blueberry plants. Proc. Am. Soc. Hort. Sci. 92, 273-74.

HILL, R.G. 1956. Iron chelates help correct chlorosis in blueberries. Ohio Farm and Home Res. 41, 23, 31.

HOOKS, R.F., and KENWORTHY, A.L. 1971. Influence of gibberelin A_3 $(GA)_3$ on fruit of highbush blueberry. HortScience 6, 139-40.

HOWELL, G.S. et al. 1972. Influence of timing of hive introduction on production of highbush blueberries. HortScience 7, 129-31.

HOWELL, G.S. et al. 1975. Rejuvenating highbush blueberries. J. Am. Soc. Hort. Sci. 100, No. 5, 455-47.

HOWELL, G.S. et al. 1976. Ethephon as a mechanical harvesting aid for highbush blueberries. J. Am. Soc. Hort. Sci. 101, No. 2, 115.

HULL, J. et al. 1971. Stake your claim on blueberries. Am. Fruit Grower (May).

KENDER, W.J. 1965. Factors affecting the propagation of lowbush blueberries. Proc. Am. Soc. Hort. Sci. 86, 301-306.

KENDER, W.J. 1966. Rhizome development in lowbush blueberry as influenced by temperature and photoperiod. Proc. Am. Soc. Hort. Sci. 90, 144-48.

KENDER, W.J. 1968. Rest period in rhizome buds of lowbush blueberry. Proc. Am. Soc. Hort. Sci. 93, 254-59.

KENDER, W.J., and ANASTASIA, F. 1964. Nutrient deficiency symptoms of lowbush blueberry. Proc. Am. Soc. Hort. Sci. 85, 275-80.

KENDER, W.J., and EGGERT, F.P. 1966. Several soil management practices influencing the growth and rhizome development of lowbush blueberry. Can. J. Plant Sci. 46, 141-49.

KENDER, W.J. et al. 1964. Growth and yield of lowbush blueberries as influenced by various pruning methods. Proc. Am. Soc. Hort Sci. 84, 269-73.

KNIGHT, R.J., and SCOTT, D.H. 1964. Effect of temperature on self-pollination and fruiting of four highbush varieties. Proc. Am. Soc. Hort. Sci. 84, 302-306.

KOCHER, F. 1972. Endogenous nitrogen status on rhizome bud activity in lowbush blueberry. HortScience 7, 128-29.

KUSHMAN, L.J., and BALLINGER, W.E. 1963. Influence of season and harvest interval on quality of Wolcott blueberries grown in eastern North Carolina. Proc. Am. Soc. Hort. Sci. 83, 395-405.

KUSHMAN, L.J., and BALLINGER, W.E. 1968A. Acid and sugar changes during ripening in Wolcott blueberries. Proc. Am. Soc. Hort. Sci. 92, 290-95.

KUSHMAN, L.J., and BALLINGER, W.E. 1968B. Commercial forced-air cooling of blueberries in North Carolina. Proc. Am. Soc. Hort. Sci. 92, 284-89.

KUSHMAN, L.J., and BALLINGER, W.E. 1975. Relation of quality indices of individual blueberries in photoelectric measurement of anthocyanin content. J. Am. Soc. Hort. Sci. 100, No. 5, 561-64.

MAINLAND, C.M., and ECK, P. 1968. Induced parthenocarpic fruit development in highbush blueberry. Proc. Am. Soc. Hort. Sci. 92, 284-89.

MAINLAND, C.M., and ECK, P. 1969. Fruit and vegetative response of the highland blueberry to gibberellic acid under greenhouse conditions. J. Am. Soc. Hort. Sci. *94*, 19-20.

MAINLAND, C.M., and ECK, P. 1971. Endogenous auxin- and gibberellin-like activity in highbush blueberry flowers and fruit. J. Am. Soc. Hort. Sci. *96*, 141-45.

MAINLAND, C.M. *et al.* 1975. Effect of mechanical harvesting on yield and quality of fruit and bush damage of highbush blueberry. J. Am. Soc. Hort. Sci. *100*, No. 2, 129-34.

MAKUS, D.J., and BALLINGER, W.E. 1973. Characterization of anthocyanins during ripening of fruit of *V. corymbosum*, cv Wolcott. J. Am. Soc. Hort. Sci. *98*, 99-101.

MOORE, J.N. 1976. Blueberry production and research in Arkansas. HortScience *11*, No. 3, 224.

MOORE, J.N. *et al.* 1972. Effect of seed number, size, and development of fruit size of cultivated blueberries. HortScience 7, 268-69.

MOORE, J.N. *et al.* 1975. Inheritance of seed size in blackberry. J. Am. Soc. Hort. Sci. *100*, No. 4, 377-79.

OBERLE, C.D. *et al.* 1960. An unusual winter effect on highbush blueberry. Fruit Varieties and Hort. Digest *15*, 13-14.

O'ROURKE, F.L. 1942. Influence of blossom buds on rooting of hardwood cuttings of blueberry. Proc. Am. Soc. Hort. Sci. *40*, 332-34.

SHARPE, R.H., and DARROW, G.M. 1959. Breeding blueberries for the Florida climate. Fla. State Hort. Soc. *72*, 306-11.

SHARPE, R.H., and SHERMAN, W.B. 1971. Breeding blueberries for low-chilling requirement. HortScience 6, 145-47.

SHARPE, R.H., and SHOEMAKER, J.S. 1958. Development of temperate-climate fruits for Florida. Fla. State Hort. Soc. *71*, 194-200.

SHERMAN, W.B. *et al.* 1973. The fruiting nursery: ultrahigh density for evaluation of blueberry and peach seedlings. HortScience 8, 170-72.

SHUTAK, V.G. 1956. Sawdust mulch for blueberries. R.I. Agr. Expt. Sta. Bull. *339*.

SHUTAK, V.G. *et al.* 1956. Ripening of cultivated blueberry fruits. Proc. Am. Soc. Hort. Sci. *68*, 178-83.

SHUTAK, V.G. *et al.* 1957. Growth studies of cultivated blueberry. R.I. Agr. Expt. Sta. Bull. *339*.

SMITH, D.W., and HILTON, R.J. 1971. Comparative effects of pruning by burning or clipping on lowbush blueberries in north-eastern Ontario. J. Appl. Ecol. *8*, 781-89.

SNEED, V.G. *et al.* 1970. Irrigation of blueberries. N. Carolina Agr. Ext. Circ. *474*.

SPIERS, J.M. 1976. Chilling regimes affect bud break. J. Am. Soc. Hort. Sci. *101*, No. 1, 84-86.

STUSHNOFF, C., and HOUGH, L.F. 1968. Sporogenesis and gametophyte development in Bluecrop blueberries. J. Am. Soc. Hort. Sci. *93*, 242-47.

THORPE, G.R. 1971. Highbush blueberry culture. British Columbia Dept. Agr. Hort. Publ. *71*, 11.

TOWNSEND, L.R. *et al.* 1968. Chemical composition of rhizomes and associated leaves of the lowbush blueberry. Proc. Am. Soc. Hort. Sci. *93*, 248-53.

TREVETT, M.F. 1955. Some growth habits of lowbush blueberry. Maine Farm Research (Oct).

TREVETT, M.F.   1956.   Observations on the decline and rehabilitation of lowbush blueberry fields.   Me. Agr. Expt. Sta. Misc. Publ. *626*.

TREVETT, M.F.   1959.   Growth studies of lowbush blueberry.   Me. Agr. Expt. Sta. Bull. *581*.

TREVETT, M.F., and HILBORN, M.T.   1956.   Blueberries, soils, and micro-organisms.   Maine Farm Research (Jan).

WEST, G.W.   1969.   Evidence of increased fruit set in lowbush blueberry by using honeybees.   HortScience *4*, 211-12.

WOODRUFF, R.W.*et al.*   1960.   Chemical changes of Jersey and Rubel fruit associated with ripening deterioration.   Proc. Am. Soc. Hort. Sci. *75*, 387-401.

YOUNG, R.S.   1952.   Growth and development of the blueberry fruit.   Proc. Am. Soc. Hort. Sci. *59*, 167-72.

Chapter 6

Cranberries

The cranberry *(Vaccinium macrocarpon)* is a low-growing, trailing, woody, broadleaf semi-evergreen plant. It should not be confused with the berried highbush cranberry *(Viburnum)* which is an ornamental plant and is sometimes used for jelly in the North.

CHARACTERISTICS OF THE CRANBERRY

Cranberry culture is a highly specialized industry, producing an accessory fruit. An accessory fruit is a simple fruit developed from an inferior ovary and so is derived both from the ovary wall and the floral tube, which is composed of the basal parts of the sepals, petals, and stamens. This tube is fused with the ovary wall, becomes fleshy, and ripens with it.

The cranberry is a native of bogs or marshes in northeastern America, and westward across the continent in northern areas. The vines make a mat all over the surface of a cultivated planting. They bloom in spring or early summer. Most of the fruit is harvested in October.

Runners.—The cranberry plant produces trailing woody stems or runners 0.3 to 1.83 m (1 to 6 ft) or more long. The runners lie on the soil surface or on low-growing vegetation and may grow from basal or terminal buds. The runner is vigorous and produces leaves which tend to fold upward, rather than remaining flat and fully exposed to light (Dana and Klingbeil 1966).

Uprights.—Short uprights 5.1 to 7.6 cm (2 to 3 in.) long originate from axillary buds on the runners, have horizontal leaves, and bear the flowers and fruit. An upright grows vertically for 1 to 2 years without support. As it becomes longer, the shoot either is supported by the mass of other uprights or bends over in the basal area, with only the 10.2 to 12.7 cm (4 to 5 in.) tip remaining upright. Each new extension of vegetative growth is compensated for by sagging of the basal part of the stem. Thus, an upright may be several feet long and the tip stand only 15.2 to 30.5 cm (6 to 12 in.) high.

Leaves.—The individual leaves stay on the plant for 2 to 3 years before dropping. The dark glossy green leaves of the growing season change to a dullish red brown in winter and again become green in spring.

Roots.—The root system differs from that of farm crops in that there are no root hairs. The cranberry plant maintains a symbiotic relationship with certain soil microbes. Although an association of a fungus with the roots is called mycorrhiza, the definition of the word must be examined to include the condition that exists in the Ericaceae, for in this family the fungus is not confined to the roots but is coextensive with the growth of the plant, occurring in practically every organ. The roots will not grow under water, but they can live under water for months.

The root system is not extensive—only a few centimeters deep—and is made up entirely of very fine, fibrous roots that develop in the surface layers of the soil. Roots may grow at almost any point on the stem which is beneath moist soil. This ease of root stimulation provides a convenient means for vegetative propagation and also has other important implications in cultural methods.

Nutrients probably must be absorbed by unelongated epidermal cells or must enter these cells through the mycelium with which they are ramified.

Fruit.—The developing fruit changes from a bright green to greenish-white, then pink, and finally red; it may be round, oval, bell-shaped, or pear-shaped, and may contain many small, brown seeds in the 4 open locules. The flesh is firm, crisp, and highly acid. At harvest the outer surface is red, but the inside of over-ripe berries reddens with age.

Marketing.—Cranberries are sold for both fresh and processed use. Berries for processing are usually placed in freezer storage soon after harvest. Berries for the fresh market are stored for shipment at Thanksgiving and Christmas seasons.

INDUSTRY, REGIONS AND DISTRICTS

Practically all the world's commercial cranberry crop is produced in North America. The bogs or marshes are usually located in areas poorly adapted to other agricultural enterprises. Plantings are about as follows: Massachusetts 6070 ha (15,000 acres), Wisconsin 3035 ha (7500 acres), New Jersey 1416 ha (3500 acres), Washington 607 ha (1500 acres), Oregon 202 ha (500 acres). There is a total of about 80 cultivated ha (200 acres) in Minnesota, Iowa, North Carolina, and New England (outside of Massachusetts), and 486 ha (1200 acres) in Canada.

Some 3000 growers cultivate over 10,118 ha (25,000 acres) of cranberries. The total crop of about 15 million barrels has a gross return of about $20,000,000 by areas as follows: Massachusetts $9,000,000; Wisconsin $7,000,000; New Jersey $1,500,000; Washington,$1,000,000; Oregon $50,000.

Massachusetts.—(45.36 million kg, or 21 million bbl of 100 lb) The cranberry industry is the chief feature of the agriculture of the southeastern part of the state. It has given large value to an acreage of peat and muck that previously had little value and produces the state's leading export crop. The industry is largely confined to Plymouth, Middlesex, Bristol, Dukes, and Nantucket counties.

Wisconsin.—(36.3 million kg, or 800,000 bbl) The industry started near the city of Berlin about 1860. About 1890 the center of the industry shifted to the Cranmore area some 24 km (15 mi.) west of Wisconsin Rapids. Later, marshes were developed in the Black River Falls, Warrens, and Tomah areas, and still later a gradual shift northward included marshes near Spooner, Hayward, Manitowish Waters, Eagle River, and other scattered sites in northern Wisconsin.

New Jersey.—(5.7 million kg, or 125,000 bbl) The acreage is mostly in the central Pine Barren region. The chief area is Burlington County, centering at Chatsworth, South Pemberton, Atsion, Upton, Medford, and New Lisbon. Smaller areas are in Ocean, Atlantic, and Cape May counties.

Washington.—(6.1 million kg, or 135,000 bbl) From 1909 to 1915 several hundred acres were planted, chiefly near Ilwaco and Long Beach, with cuttings from Cape Cod. The planting area and production have expanded greatly in recent years.

Oregon.—(3,175,000 kg, or 70,000 bbl) In the north, Counties Coos and Illamock, and in the south Clatsop and Curry are the leaders.

Canada.—British Columbia leads with 4218 kg (9300 lb) from 400 ha (1000 acres) in the Fraser Valley (Tallman and Eaton 1974), followed in order by Nova Scotia 3402 kg (7500 lb), New Brunswick 1134 (2500 lb), and Prince Edward Island 680 kg (1500 lb). There is some production in Quebec near Nicolet and Shawinigan Falls, and in Ontario in the Parry Sound and Muscoka area.

CULTIVARS

The "Big 4" cultivars are Early Black, Howes, Searles Jumbo, and McFarlin, which account for over 90% of the total planting. In earlier days fairly large areas were planted with selections taken from the wild. The "natives" are called Jerseys or late Jerseys in New Jersey; Bell and Cherry, Bell and Bugle, and Berlins in Wisconsin; and Stankavich in Oregon. The natives are disappearing from market outlets.

No flooding area should have more than one cultivar. Planting other cultivars on the same flooding area complicates pest and cultural control.

Ben Lear.—Early, fruit medium to large, slightly oblong, dark crimson. For early market. Does not keep well.

Early Black.—Early, fruit pyriform-shaped, dark red. Produces about 70% of the New Jersey crop, 60% of the Massachusetts crop, and 10% of the coastal area crop. Massachusetts 1857.

Crowley.—Grown in Washington, two weeks ahead of McFarlin. Fruit medium size.

Howes.—Supplies the late market, including Thanksgiving. Fruit attractive, shiny, medium-red when mature, oblong, firm, colors well in storage, excellent quality; excellent for scooping. Produces about 35% of the Massachusetts crop, but only 4% of the Wisconsin crop. Massachusetts 1843.

McFarlin.—Resistant to false blossom. Not well adapted to scooping.

Courtesy of Massachusetts Cranberry Station

FIG. 6.1.   THREE CRANBERRY CULTIVARS: A — EARLY BLACK, B — HOWES, C — McFARLIN

Less attractive in color than some others. Produces 85% of the Washington crop, 20% of the Wisconsin crop, and 4% of the Massachusetts crop. Massachusetts 1874.

Searles Jumbo.—Midseason. Fruit large, oblong, deep red when ripe, without gloss, sometimes mottled, fair keeper. Subject to rot in the East. Produces 80% of the Wisconsin crop, 10% of the Canadian crop, and dominates in Washington state. Wisconsin 1893.

Stevens.—Late midseason. Strong vine. Fruit round, dark red, glossy, keeps well. U.S. Dept. Agr. 1951.

POLLINATION

The flower primordia develop in terminal buds of vigorous uprights in July and August. Flower buds are larger and plumper than vegetative buds.

New shoot growth in spring initiates at the tips of uprights and runners and from some axillary buds on runners and uprights. The flower bud usually begins to swell in early May. The flowering shoot reaches 5.1 to 10.2 cm (2 to 4 in.) long before the lower buds appear; 1 to 7 flowers are borne in the base of the new shoot. Beyond the flowers toward the apex or tip is the new leaf development and shoot growth. Individual flowers are borne on a pedicel attached directly to the main axis of the shoot. The flowers open in midsummer and may remain on the plant for several days (Dana and Klingbeil 1966).

The flowers bend down (forming "hooks"). The anthers do not shed pollen directly into the air like many other plants. Ripe pollen is delivered into long, hollow tubes attached to the anthers. As the flower begins to open, pollen is liberated near the stigma of the pistil, which by then is equal in length to the anther tubes. The stigma is receptive at this stage. Wind-borne pollen is not distributed any great distance, but wind may shake the flowers and cause pollen to fall from the tubes onto the stigma. When insects visit flowers for nectar they mostly aid pollination by jarring the flowers, or by transferring pollen directly from tube to stigma. A peculiarity that aids fruit set is that the pollen is not a single grain, as in most plants, but is a tetrad capable of germinating into four functional pollen tubes. Also, fruits may set with few seeds maturing (Roberts and Struckmeyer 1942).

The bud opens by separation of the petals, which curl back (reflex), exposing the ring of stamens surrounding the pistil. When the petals are first reflexed the stigma is not visible unless the stamens are mechanically separated. The pollen is mature at the time of petal separation but the stigma is not exposed for natural pollination until some time later. The berry matures 75 to 100 days after pollination (Rigby and Dana 1972A).

Seed number and fruit volume are positively correlated. Effective pollination of the maximum number of ovules should result in large berry size and, potentially, in high fruit yield. In Wisconsin, Howes is the last to bloom, and has the least exposure to effective cross-pollination by other cultivars. This may explain, in part, its relatively small size and low yield in that state (Rigby and Dana 1971).

Flower development in Stevens cultivar has been studied on uprights thinned to a single flower. Flowers started opening each hour of the day in the greenhouse. The interval from petal separation to fully open flowers varied from 2 to 12 hr, 80% of the flowers being fully open within 6 hr. Elongation of the style and emergence of the stigma through the anther ring occurred on 94% of the flowers during the 24 to 48 hr period after the petals were fully reflexed. The stigma was pollen-receptive at petal separation. The pollen tube had traversed the style 48 hr after pollination in 37% of the flowers. Removal of the style 72 hr after pollination no longer prevented fruit development. Apparently receptivity of Stevens cultivar is earlier than reported for other cultivars (Rigby and Dana 1972A).

Place beehives in large bogs or marshes, since the native pollinating insects may not be sufficient to set maximum crops. In Wisconsin, growers average 1 colony of bees for every 0.8 ha (2 acres) of vines. A strong colony weighs 1.8 to 2.3 kg (4 to 5 lb), and has 20,000 to 25,000 bees. The bumblebee is the most efficient of the wild insects.

FRUIT-BUD FORMATION, GROWTH AND FRUITING

Normally, uprights do not bloom the first year, but will the second year. Fruit buds are formed terminally on the uprights and differentiate during late summer or fall. Buds that bloom the following spring are generally mixed buds containing flowers, leaves, and a growing point. Terminal fruit buds develop into uprights, the blossoms being placed near the base below the leaves; each upright may, in turn, bear a fruit bud at its tip in autumn. Fruit buds start growth in spring with or slightly after purely vegetative growth.

Searles in Wisconsin seldom produces flowers on more than 50% of the uprights; under favorable conditions at least 35% should bloom. On good, reasonably weed-free soil, upward of 400 uprights could be produced per 0.1 m² (1 ft²); in most years 140 or more are likely to set fruit buds in autumn and to bloom the next year if not killed meanwhile. Uprights often have 3 or 4 flowers when the individual flower buds are not injured; they average 1 to 1½ berries with good pollination. A relation exists between growth made by the uprights and yield. Large yields result from 200 to 300 uprights per 0.1 m² (1 ft²). A proper growth of 6.3 to 7.6 cm (2.5 to 3 in.) is made by the time of bloom. Poor fruiting on the more vegetative uprights in areas of high stands is due to both shading and poor pollination.

In Massachusetts, growth is slow in autumn, ceases in winter, but proceeds rapidly after removal of the winter flood. Late drainage delays resumption of flower-bud growth, but development then proceeds so rapidly that bogs held late are only a few days later than early-drained bogs in reaching full bloom.

In Washington state, buds start to break about May 1 and are in full bloom in late June or early July.

REST PERIOD

Cranberries have a rest period which can be broken by temperatures below 7°C (45°F) for 2500 cumulative hours. "Umbrella bloom" (terminal bloom), which has been considered an indication of frost injury, occurs on cultivars that have not been frosted but have had only 1000 hr exposure below 7°C (45°F). A normal winter in Massachusetts has 3300 to 3500 hr below 45°F. Bogs in Washington state may not accumulate 1500 hr below 7°C (45°F) in some years, and this may explain their prolonged bloom period (Chandler and Demoranville 1958).

Insufficient chilling is a factor limiting cranberry growing in the South.

Long days are necessary for the normal outgrowths of the fruit bud; no flowers are produced under short days. Increased chilling is required to produce bud break when the plants are under short days. Under favorable light conditions, 80% of the buds may grow out after 600 hr below 7°C (45°F). However, production of normal flowers is not ensured by satisfaction of cold requirement but also involves exposure of the buds to temperatures above 7°C (45°F).

Chilling requirements are decreased if the temperature fluctuates during the chilling period. If temperatures are too high there may be devernalization even though a portion of the daily cycle is cold enough to satisfy chilling requirements. Because of the varying effect of the chilling temperature cycles, a threshold temperature, below which either the vegetative or floral chilling requirement can be met, cannot be specified unless the actual treatment conditions are described (Eady and Eaton 1972).

Gibberellic acid may cause 80% or more of the buds to break, regardless of chilling, and may cause faster bud break even after adequate chilling (Rigby and Dana 1972B).

PROPAGATION

Cranberries are propagated by cuttings (pieces of vines). Take these from a planting in good condition, free from pests, and uniform as to cultivar. In securing cuttings, mow the vines, as with a scythe or tractor-mounted sickle bar, in the spring before the terminal bud grows. Keep them moist to avoid loss of vitality. About a barrel of cuttings are obtained per sq rod, or 1468 kg per ha (4 tons per acre). If cuttings have a lot of new growth, much of it dies and further growth is slow for a time. One who buys such vines pays for unnecessary bulk.

LIFE OF BOG (MARSH), YIELD AND COSTS

Life of Bog (Marsh)

A well-constructed bog in Massachusetts (marsh in Wisconsin) should bear for 60 years or more. Cost of replanting and again bringing a bog into bearing is too great to make the practice common. Complete bog renovation is expensive. However, renovation is practiced by some growers. Making over an old bog that is in a good location may call for the destruction of all growth and for grading, sanding, and complete replanting. Sometimes unproductive bogs may be returned to a profitable condition by merely following good management practices.

Yield

Usually 3 to 4 years elapse before a newly-planted bog bears profitable crops. Full-bearing bogs in Massachusetts may yield 40 bbl or more per ha (100 bbl or more per acre). Few bogs, however, average over 26 bbl per ha (65 bbl per acre) year after year. An average crop may be 14 bbl per ha (35 bbl per acre). Growers should study their conditions if yields average less than 12 bbl per ha (30 bbl per acre).

Fully 20% of the crop may be left on the bogs after harvest. Berries that drop are in poor condition and decay quickly. Such berries may be taken from the water as floatage on the after-picking flood, cleaned of trash quickly and while wet, with special screens, and sold to canners.

Yield is high in Wisconsin. In 1965 it was 38 bbl per ha (93.8 bbl per acre).

Costs

Costs of making a cranberry bog or bringing it into bearing depend mainly on the make-up and location of the site. The investment in a large, new bog before it begins to give the owner a possible return on his investment may amount to several thousand dollars per hectare.

His investment includes land development, planting stock, mechanized equipment, warehouse buildings, machinery sheds, water control, and other items.

ESTABLISHMENT OF BOGS (MARSHES)

Requirements

Some points must be considered before undertaking site development. Considerable capital is required. An acid soil (see later) of peat or gray sand, and sand (coarse or screened from gravel) for sanding, resanding, and leveling, are essential. The site must be large enough to be profitable and permit mechanization (generally a minimum of 12 ha (30 acres) of established vines). Ample water is needed for irrigation during droughts, for flood protection against cold injury, and in some cases for harvesting. Not only must a large volume of water be accessible, but both legal and quantity restrictions must be complied with. There must be adequate grade for rapid drainage of cold air away from the site. There should not be a nearby area from which cold air will drain onto the site.

The summers must be moderately cool. The New Jersey, Massachusetts, and Pacific districts are near the coast and have fairly cool summers; the Wisconsin region is farther north. In New Jersey, prevalance of disease necessitates more spraying or dusting than in other

Courtesy of F. J. Franklin, Massachusetts Cranberry Station

FIG. 6.2.   ESTABLISHING A CRANBERRY BOG

commercial areas. Diseases are even more serious farther south, and the high temperatures during and after harvest shorten the life of the berries and increase marketing difficulties.

Soil and Indicator Plants

Soil Reaction.—Bogs or marshes that are suitable for cranberry production usually have a soil reaction of pH 4.0 to 5.0. Some evidence indicates that cranberries persist natively in acid soil because of the inability of competing plants to survive acid conditions.

Types of Swamps.—The types of swamps used for cranberry bogs are: leather leaf, brownbush, or peat, often with accompanying Labrador tea, sphagnum moss, wild cranberries, and mossberries; gray sands (savannahs); pond bottoms.

In Washington state a brown sphagnum peat is better than one of decomposed leaves, grasses, sedges, decaying wood, or of heavy black muck. Vines on some of the more decomposed peats or black mucks tend toward excessive growth, diseases, and low yield.

On most cranberry land in New Jersey, the top layer is an acid peat or muck, varying from 0.3 to 6.1 m (1 to 20 ft) deep. Under this layer there is one of sand which may vary in thickness, and which is underlaid with an impervious hardpan. When the upper or muck layer is thin, it may break up so that the land looks blackish or grayish, and is known in New Jersey as "savannah land" and on Cape Cod as "gray sand bottom."

Classification of Bogs.—Cranberry bogs in Massachusetts are classified as: dry (no water cover); with winter flowage (covered by water in winter); with winter flowage and spring flowage; and with full flowage protection. Water may be flowed on by pumping or by gravity from a reservoir, pond, lake, or stream, or may be supplied by snow and rain. Bogs with winter flowage and 1 or 2 spring flowages receive protection against winterkilling and spring frosts. Spring frosts that cause crop failures often come long before bloom. In Wisconsin a marsh with only 2 flowages would be worthless. Bogs with full flowage protection have sufficient water to overflow the bog in winter and to protect the vines from spring frosts and insects and the berries from fall frosts. It is important to be able to drain away excess water quickly.

Size of Bog.—Cranberry bogs and marshes range from small to over 80 ha (200 acres). Those of about 12 ha (30 acres) are usually more profitable than smaller ones.

Wisconsin marshes are subdivided into sections 0.8 to 1.6 ha (2 to 4 acres) in size, usually rectangular in shape, and placed symmetrically one to another. Sections larger than 1.6 ha (4 acres) may lead to problems in rapid water distribution during first flooding and are hard to drain. Sections of uniform size and shape facilitate the use of equipment for pest control, fertilization, weed control, and harvesting. Very small sections do not lend themselves to modern mechanical operations.

Roadways on a sufficient number of dikes and sections make all parts of the area reasonably accessible.

Location of Bogs and Water-supply Systems.—A water supply for flooding as much as needed at any time adds greatly to the value of a bog. In Wisconsin, an average of 7.3 ha (18 acres) of pond or reservoir supplies water for each 0.4 ha (1 acre) of cranberry marsh. If after use the water is returned to the source by suitable pumping facilities, then the total quantity will be less than that required if the water is lost down the stream after each flooding.

A third of the bog area in Massachusetts is flooded by pumping from ponds, lakes, reservoirs, or streams at lower levels. Water held in reservoirs for flooding is often pumped back into them again. The pumps range in lift from 0.3 to 4.3 m (1 to 14 ft), averaging 1.8 m (6 ft). A pump delivering 38,000 liters per min (10,000 gal. per min) floods 5.7 ha (14 acres) in 10 hr if the bog is not over 0.3 m (1 ft) out of level. Bogs that must be flooded by pumping are generally better drained than those flooded by gravity, are less weedy and therefore cheaper to take care of, and average a higher yield. But Wisconsin growers feel greater security with a gravity-feed system (necessitating a perfectly operating plant). With dependable modern pumps, growers need not shun pumping locations.

Drainage.—Poor drainage favors weeds, pests, and fruit rot, and checks the growth of cranberry roots. Land below the bog should slope rapidly, so that water may be drawn from the ditches at any time.

Cut a ditch 0.9 m (3 ft) wide and 0.6 m (2 ft) deep entirely around the bog. Dig other ditches across the bog, dividing it into sections. The marginal ditch prevents upland growths from working onto the bog, keeps off many crawling insects, and offers some protection from forest fires. Cross ditches hasten the distribution of water over the entire area in flooding. They usually should be 30.5 m (100 ft) or more apart, about 0.6 m (2 ft) wide at the top, 0.3 m (1 ft) wide at the bottom, and 0.46 m (1.5 ft) deep. Run a wider ditch lengthwise of the bog in the path of the direct flow from the water supply to the outlet, to hasten flooding and drainage. Excessive ditches interfere with bog operations. Tile drains may be useful if the bog is hard to drain.

Grading and Leveling.—Non-level beds cannot be flooded evenly. Soil thrown out in ditching may be used in grading. Grade by the water line in the ditches. Where harvesting is done while the bog is flooded, a level site is very important. If the swamp is large and much out of level, it is often best to divide it with dams into separate areas, each nearly level, at different elevations according to the lay of the land. This reduces the water needed for flooding. The deeper the flood the more it harms the vines.

Turfing, Scalping, and Leveling.—After the land has been cleared, ditched, and drained, it is turfed and scalped, e.g., with dragline and/or bulldozer, to remove surface vegetation and provide a clean surface. Cut the turf into squares of handy size, turn these upside down, and allow to dry. Then break up the turf squares and burn all pieces of roots found in them. Remove the soil from the roots of ferns and other plants likely to give trouble later. Complete all work on the land up to sanding late in summer or in autumn.

On brownbush marshes, remove 7.6 to 10.2 cm (3 to 4 in.) of the surface material; in tree-covered marshes it may be necessary to go deeper. If the material removed in scalping is piled at the edge of the section, it forms a dike which can be smoothed at the top to provide a roadway around the section. Land preparation is usually completed the summer before spring planting.

Dams.—The purposes of dams are to hold an adequate supply of water in reservoirs, maintenance of summer and winter floods, irrigation, separation of a large field into smaller sections, and other purposes. Proper management of water is very important. For convenient flooding a section is limited in Wisconsin to 1.6 ha (4 acres) and in New Jersey to 6.1 ha (15 acres). In Massachusetts some sections are 40.5 ha (100 acres), but those of 6 ha (15 acres) or so are relatively more profitable.

Sometimes a dam is made 3.7 m (12 ft) wide at the top (for a roadway) and sloping at 60° to a wider base. In large reservoirs or bogs heavy waves may be kicked up by a swift wind and damage the dam. For protection, drive light piles just above the foot of the slope and pack brush between the piles and slope, or drive rough slabs close together flat against the surface of the dam. Make a spillway to carry off excessive floods when the reservoir is full.

Ditches or Dikes.—These hold water on the sections, and may be made from the scalpings. Ditches are dug inside the dikes and completely surround the sections. They are made about 45.7 cm (1.5 ft) wide and 60.9 to 91.4 cm (2 to 3 ft) deep, with vertical sides, and with a slight drop from inlet to outlet. If the section is more than 30.5 m (100 ft) wide, a single ditch may be provided down the center of a section.

Each section is flooded individually from a main canal at the high end and drained into a common canal at the low end.

Gates or Flumes.—These are used to control the water flow to and from sections. Gates need cut-off walls or sheet piling to keep the water from leaking through the embankments of the sides of the gate and eventually washing it out. On firm ground, the chief head gates should be made of concrete; for other situations treated lumber is satisfactory.

An open flume is well suited to bogs lying across a stream where the gates must accommodate the entire flow of the stream and occasional flood flows. In other types the trunks are constantly submerged and the sills at receiver and outlet ends are higher than the top deck of the trunk. Thus, the buried portion of the trunk remains full of water regardless of the water level in the ditches. The outlet gate must be large enough to quickly carry off water of heavy rains and flowages.

Locate the breaks or checks for irrigation at intervals in ditches with comparatively steep slopes to hold the water back in the upper reaches and reduce the flow. The checks consist of a shallow flume with a short cut-off wall of sheet piling provided with guides for holding boards across the stream.

Sanding, Resanding, and Leveling.—After scalping, level each section; if necessary bring in fill from outside the section. Non-level beds cannot be flooded evenly. They afford poor frost protection and are inconvenient in harvesting.

When a 7.6 cm (3 in.) layer of sand (coarse or screened from gravel) is spread over the peat, the benefits are as follows: it levels the land by filling small depressions left in grading; weeding cost is reduced, especially in the first 2 years after planting, since weeds grow less rapidly on clean sand than on peat; it stimulates rooting; vines bear earlier, often covering the ground and smothering weeds in 2 years; it helps prevent frost damage; it aids in control of certain insects; it provides best drainage and aeration and is least subject to drought.

In Wisconsin the sand is commonly spread in winter on the ice when it can support trucks. Cranberry vines continue vegetative growth each year. The production uprights and best runners are eventually located at the ends of stems that may be several feet long. Normally these stems do not form roots, even though they may be in contact with the soil surface. Vines become more vigorous and productive and are more easily harvested if the stems are stimulated to root. Rooted stems provide a closer tie between the fruiting area and root. Rooting may be stimulated by periodically covering the sections with a 2.5 cm (1 in.) layer of sand (Dana and Klingbeil 1966).

Sand also anchors the horizontal stems, so that machine-harvesting equipment causes less vine damage. Apply sand every third year in winter. When the ice melts, the sand settles onto the marsh surface. Sand absorbs heat during the day and releases heat rapidly at night.

Winter spreading of sand is sometimes done in Cape Cod, but there is not enough ice for it more than 1 year in 3. In Washington, where the sand underlies the swamps and is not readily available elsewhere, growers have pumped it up in the water and sent it through pipes, in some cases over 0.4 km (0.25 mi.).

Massachusetts growers put a 7.6 cm (3 in.) layer of sand 756 m^3 per ha (400 yd^3 per acre) on a bog at the time of construction, apply another layer 8 to 13 mm (1/3 to 1/2 in.) deep after 3 years of growth, and thus encourage the rooting of runners and a heavy stand of uprights. Vines so treated are well anchored and easily scooped.

Cranberry roots form a dense growth in the sand over the peat and become soil-bound. Resanding gives them more soil to grow in and promotes thriftier and more productive vines. Bogs not resanded regularly become covered with moss and fallen cranberry leaves which, being poor conductors of heat, are very subject to frost injury. Every other year or lightly every year, resand bogs where there is little water for reflooding; every 3 to 4 years, resand those that have plenty of water for frost and insect flooding and a moderate vine growth. Put on 6 to 25 mm (¼ to 1 in.) sand at a time. Bogs with ample water supply and heavy vines need not be resanded.

Resanding in early spring may cause some injury; resanding later in the spring causes more injury. Help is generally more plentiful in autumn and better care can be given this work then. Resanding may reduce the following crop. Rake the tops of the vines out of the sand if they are covered too deeply.

In Washington state, resanding stimulates the formation of uprights on young bogs and anchors the runners. However, after a bog has been resanded 3 or 4 times and the sand becomes 12.7 to 15.2 cm (5 to 6 in.) deep, the roots in contact with the peat may die. This leaves the vines growing exclusively in sand. They then require heavy fertilizing to maintain production. The trouble probably is caused by packing of the very fine sand.

PLANTING

Set the cuttings in the spring soon after sanding. They do not start as well if the sand is packed by rain before planting. Cuttings 15.2 to 20.3 cm (6 to 8 in.) long are planted directly in place by hand or machine without rooting. The surface soil is saturated (but not flooded) with water as planting starts.

The vines are spread over the soil surface at the rate of 2241 kg per ha (1 ton per acre) and pushed into contact with the soil by means of a wide-track crawler or disk-type roller, or by hand tampers.

Planting distances in the East are 15.2 to 45.7 cm (6 to 8 in.) each way. The spacing is closer in Wisconsin because of the slower growth due to cooler weather. The closer the vines are set in any region the sooner they cover the ground, the less weeding is needed, and the sooner a paying crop results. Vines that are set close become well-anchored and best resist pulling in harvesting.

For hand-planting with a dibble, set 2 to 5 cuttings at each spot at a spacing of 23 × 23 to 40 × 40 cm (9 × 9 to 16 × 16 in.). Push them into the sand to contact with the peat beneath; most of their roots grow in the sand. Cuttings need not protrude from the sand more than an inch. New runner growth from the cuttings is then close to the ground and roots readily in the sand. Cuttings may be whipped loose by wind, or may dry out, if too much top protrudes. On muck-bottom land, where the wet soil discourages kneeling, one man drops the cuttings and another man presses them in with a long-handled dibble and firms soil around them with his feet.

Cuttings may be made 15.2 cm (6 in.) long, spread broadcast, and covered lightly with sand; but this requires more vines than the former method and they may not become as well anchored. However, some growers plant directly into the peat and put the sand on later.

A machine-planter will scatter cuttings over the sand. Avoid bunching, which keeps the disk from setting them to proper depth. The disk should be heavy enough to press them through the sand until they meet the peat. If not more than 5.1 cm (2 in.) of sand are used, the planter pushes the vines to proper depth without difficulty. Disk over the vines in one direction and again at right angles to anchor them thoroughly. A single, disk-type planter powered with a 2 to 3 horsepower engine plants 0.4 ha (1 acre) in 8 hr. Where 2 or more disks are used, set them 20.3 cm (8 in.) apart. Though it requires more vines to plant by machine, the extra vines help to prevent sand shifting by strong winds, which is often important in newly planted bogs.

Root and top growth of cuttings appear within two weeks after planting. The second year a few runners develop. The third year the ground becomes considerably, though often unevenly, covered with vines. After the third year the plants cover the ground more uniformly and come into bearing. Constant roguing may be necessary the first three years to remove plants infested with false blossom.

USE OF WATER

New Bogs

In Massachusetts, apply water right after planting; hold it near the surface a day or so to wet the vines and pack the soil around them; then drain it to the bottom of the ditches. If the bog is flooded again the first year, do it for only 1 or 2 days, to wet the sand or control insects.

Flood new bogs for winter when the soil begins to freeze, for frost in the soil heaves out new sets. Let off surplus water at times of thaws or heavy rains in winter or early spring; otherwise raising of the ice pulls out the vines. The first three years, let off the winter flowage early in May; earlier removal may promote heaving.

In Wisconsin, during the first summer after planting, keep the soil moist with natural rainfall seepage, or irrigation. Water should not stand on the soil surface. However, because of the very shallow rooting of the vines, try to maintain the moisture level at or near the surface.

Winter Flooding

Vines often winterkill severely if exposed for a week or more to drying winds when the soil around the roots is frozen. This is due to desiccation, since under these conditions the plants cannot replace the water lost by the leaves. It usually occurs before winter, but may occur at any time from December to late March.

Flooding for winter protection is usually done in December in the East (as soon as the top of the sand remains frozen all day), and in late October on new plantings and in late November or early December on old ones in Wisconsin. Hold the water just deep enough to cover the vines. The water freezes to form an ice blanket that prevents drying of vines and minimizes fluctuations in temperature.

In general, flood whenever weather conditions indicate that the water will freeze within a few days and will remain frozen for an extended period. The winter flood is usually applied in successive layers, each layer being allowed to freeze before the new layer is applied. Use enough water to cover the vines and drain the excess from the sections, leaving the vines under the blanket of ice (Dana and Klingbeil 1966).

One hazard of flooding is that the vines may be unable to obtain O_2 from the water and may suffer varying degrees of low O_2 injury. Dormant vines may suffer damage if poor freezing occurs after flooding, during warm periods in winter when the ice melts, or in early spring before the winter flood is removed. As long as the water remains frozen, there is no problem. When the ice thaws, low O_2 may occur during warm, cloudy days, when photosynthesis is low and respiration is high. A convenient colorimetric test will determine the O_2 content of the water.

In flooding, release of heat from the free water warms the air near the tender vines and blossoms. The colder the weather, the deeper should be the flood. On nights of light frost, an inch of water or less on the soil surface may prevent damage, but when the temperature drops to $-6°C$ (20°F), 7.6 to 10.2 cm (3 to 4 in.) of water may be necessary (Dana and Klingbeil 1966).

Although the cranberry plant tolerates submergence for extended periods, frost flooding is only a means to prevent catastrophe. Apply only enough water to provide the necessary protection.

Winter flooding is unnecessary on the Pacific Coast cranberry areas.

Allow the highest parts to protrude a little when the bog is much out of level. These vines are as well protected when frozen into the ice as any other way, though they may heave badly if not well-anchored and if thick ice is lifted by water. Heavy ice may break off the vines where it cracks; this injury appears in spring as though a cleaver had severed the vines and cut into the ground beneath them.

Letting off the winter flood late in March, reflooding 3 to 4 weeks later, and holding this water a few weeks serves all purposes of holding this flood late, airs the vines, and permits work on the bog.

Abnormally warm weather in April and May reduces the crop, probably because of the restriction of respiration of the vines and their roots resulting from occasional O_2 starvation under high temperature with reduced sunlight. Sometimes water injury (O_2 deficiency) causes a poor set of the bloom and a short crop, especially on marshes that are flooded for long periods in April and May. Warm weather in March may indirectly promote water injury. One effect of water injury is poor pollination, which may be partially avoided by increasing the population of pollinating insects.

Spring Flooding

Cranberry winter buds endure $-4°C$ (25°F) until they swell. They usually withstand $-6°C$ (20°F) until late April in Massachusetts. Often $-2°C$ (28°F) is reached in a time of tender growth without injury, if the depression is short. Temperatures above $-1°C$ (29°F) do little harm.

To avoid frost injury in late spring or early fall, water may be let down from the reservoirs to fill the ditches or be brought up around the vines. The protection is due to direct radiation of heat from the water to the air because of the high specific heat of water. It usually takes only 5.1 to 7.6 cm (2 to 3 in.) of water under the vines (they are not covered) for protection. Do not flood during bloom, for this blasts the blossoms and promotes fruit rots.

In Wisconsin there is no truly frost-free period, although the interval from June 15 to August 15 is often considered frost-free. There is no date, even in July, when there has never been a frost in at least one cranberry bog. Before June 15 and after August 15 frost is common in all areas (Dana and Klingbeil 1966).

In Wisconsin the vines must be protected against winter and early spring killing throughout the long, severe cold season. Frosts may occur frequently from May, when growth usually starts, until late in June, when blossoming begins, occasionally in July and August, and with increasing frequency in September.

In September and October danger often necessitates flooding again for protection, but greater chances can be taken than in spring. Water may be held on the marsh from one night to another occasionally, as in spring, if it is necessary. In the greenish-white stage, the berries usually stand $-2°C$ (28°F) without injury, but a prolonged period at $-3°C$ (26°F) may harm them greatly. Freezing begins in ripe Early Black at about $-6°C$ (22°F); softening may not follow even at $-5°C$ (23°F). With ripe Howes and McFarlin berries on the vines, often only a 10% freeze at $-9°C$ (16°F), and a 20% freeze at $-16°C$ (4°F) may cause damage; 25% may soften at $-8°C$ (18°F). Loss is greater with Early Black at these temperatures.

Various weather services offer timely reports on frost.

Sprinkling for Frost Damage

The temperature of water for sprinkling is generally about 7°C (45°F). This water, when sprinkled on the bog, releases heat as it cools to the freezing point. Chief protection comes from release of the latent heat of fusion as the water freezes. Sprinkling may provide protection to the blossoms from cold as low as $-5°C$ (23°F), and to ripe berries as low as $-6°C$ (20°F). Some protection results from the insulating effect of the slush ice (which protects the plants much as snow would), and also because of the high humidity. However, if frost is severe this protection may not prevent injury.

Because the heat required to thaw the ice is taken from the vines as well as the air, a further lowering of temperature may result when the ice is thawing. For this reason, sprinkle until the ice disappears. Start as soon as the temperature drops to 0°C (32°F) and run continuously until frost is over. Light frosts that may cause only 5 to 10% loss may be controlled with intermittent sprinkling.

Sprinkling irrigation is used almost year-round in cranberry bogs and marshes. In spring, growers use their systems 10 to 12 times for frost protection after buds and young fruits begin to grow. Water protects cranberries by raising the bog temperature during cold nights. Damage can be controlled by low-volume applications even when temperature is as low as $-8°$ to $-9°C$ ($15°$ to $18°F$). The critical period between frost warnings and effect on crop protection is shortened to just a few minutes when sprinklers are used.

Sprinkler irrigation has definite advantages over flooding for frost protection. It is a quickly responsive method of water application. Growers can delay application until conditions are actually at hand. The amount of water used is less than with flooding. It is unnecessary to fill ditches and saturate the soil before protection begins. Distribution of disease spores and weed seeds is less as a result of screened intakes and little horizontal movement of water flow on the sections (Dana and Klingbeil 1966).

A grower in Wisconsin who uses sprinklers also needs to flood for winter protection, for harvesting, and for long cold periods in spring and fall.

Sprinkling to prevent scalding of berries and vines by high temperatures is sometimes practiced where cloudy, cool weather with temperatures around $15.6°C$ ($60°F$) occurs during most of the summer. Plants and berries grown under these conditions are tender and scald quickly when exposed to high temperatures and drying winds. Because the humidity is low at such temperatures, evaporation from sprinkled vines lowers the temperature, increases the humidity, and thus prevents injury. The temperature of sprinkled areas may quickly drop $4°$ to $6°C$ ($8°$ to $10°F$). Turn on the sprinklers before the temperature reaches $26°C$ ($80°F$). In autumn, frost may threaten the maturing fruit. Systems may be used 10 to 12 times in September and October before harvest is over and the bogs are flooded for winter. More than 762 km (2.5 million ft) of irrigation pipe have been installed by Massachusetts cranberry growers; this may also be used to apply pecticides and herbicides.

Flooding for Irrigation

The shallow root system produced by the cranberry plant cannot absorb water from a large volume of soil. Cranberry plantings often suffer from drought, especially in August; the fruits are reduced in number or size, are retarded in ripening, and in severe cases the vines die. Occasional light flooding for a few hours at night, followed by complete withdrawal of the water, is sometimes done, but it is usually better to hold the ditches partly full during dry spells.

In New Jersey, best yield occurs when the water is held at least 15.2 cm (6 in.) below the surface. Water at or near the surface decreases the length of uprights. Uprights are fewest where the water is near the surface and largest where it is 15.1 to 30.5 cm (6 to 12 in.) below. The warmer air associated with a lowered water table is the underlying cause of this difference, since growth occurs early. On unsanded bogs, maintain the water table at one point; otherwise when the water is raised to near the surface, the root system is disturbed and rot may occur.

In Massachusetts keep the water table 25.4 to 30.5 cm (10 to 12 in.) below the surface during growth. After heavy rains, empty the ditches for a few days, then refill them to the 25.4 to 30.5 cm (10 to 12 in.) level.

Irrigation in August and September helps to prevent injury to the condition and yield of the crop caused by heat, sun, and drought. Application of water may lower the temperature toward the tops of the vines about $-16°C$ ($4°F$) by evaporation from the soil. In New Jersey, where summer bog temperatures are higher than on Cape Cod, fruit from grassy areas is often in better condition than that grown nearby without such shade.

Flooding for Insect Control

Flooding bogs in Massachusetts in June to check insects may be wise once every three years, but is a dubious annual practice for it carries fungi to the new growth, promotes fireworm infestation, and may drown the flower buds. Put this flood on at night and take it off at night. Flower buds are less likely to be damaged if the weather is clear while the water is on, for light is necessary for the photosynthesis by which the plants give O_2 to the water. Cloudiness with a high water temperature is especially dangerous, for the warmer it is the faster the plants respire and the greater their need for O_2. Do not hold the complete flood over 24 hr unless the weather is clear and cool, and not over 20 hr if the bog has a bad record of injury by June flooding.

Flood the bog for a week soon after harvest to water the disturbed roots and float fallen berries, leaves, and other trash. Provide catch basins around the bog margin; otherwise, rake the trash from the water where the wind drives it ashore. This flood helps control the girdler when girdling is done late in September. No flooding is needed after this until the water is pumped on for winter protection.

FERTILIZER

Fertilizer usually results in greater vine growth and, to some extent, yield. But as the rate of certain fertilizers is increased, the incidence of rot in mature cranberries may increase enough to make the yield of sound fruit greater on unfertilized plants. Marketable yield is increased with fungicide-fertilizer treatments.

Nitrogen (N)

Of the various essential elements, N seems to have the greatest effect on the development of the cranberry plant. It is the most frequently needed fertilizer element, and the most often used.

Form of N.—Adams and Mounce, in 1932, could not detect nitrates in either plant or endophyte at any time. Thus if nitrates are absorbed as such, they probably must be converted into other substances immediately.

The ammonium form of N (NH_4-N) can be used by cranberry plants and may be essential. No trace of an enzyme commonly found in other plants which changes N to ammonium N occurs in cranberries, and so cranberries could not use the N even if it were absorbed. This characteristic of cranberries may originate in the fact that they are native to highly acid, wet soil. Such conditions may provide only small amounts of nitrate N; thus the species may have evolved without the gene for producing a N-reducing enzyme. Ammonium N should be applied in small amounts throughout the growing season (Greidanus *et al.* 1972).

The ways in which yield of cranberries can be increased include: (1) increasing the number of uprights, (2) increasing the percentage of uprights that flower, (3) increasing the number of flowers/buds, (4) increasing the percentage of fruit set, and (5) increasing berry size (Eck 1976).

Foliar Levels.—Desirable tissue level in British Columbia is 1.0 N. Above this level yield, soluble solids and anthocyanins decrease. A foliar level of 0.88% and an annual application of N (16.8 kg per ha, or 15 lb per acre) seems adequate during the establishment of a new bog (Eaton 1971; Eaton and Meehan 1973).

Vine growth may be used in addition to leaf N to ascertain N sufficiency. Flower production is greater on plants treated at a high N rate but the percentage of fruit set is less compared with a low rate.

Excessive vegetative growth may influence N composition in runner leaves, uprights, and runner production by a dilution mechanism.

Narrow Range.—There is a narrow range in N concentration between deficiency, sufficiency, and excessive vegetative stimulation. There may also be a critical N content for flower bud initiation in some very limited concentration range (Torio and Eck 1969).

Some stimulation of vine growth is desirable, particularly when new bogs are being established. Bogs that are rapidly covered with vines have a lower incidence of weeds and bear a commercial crop sooner than bogs sparsely covered with vines. But over-stimulation of vine growth is often inversely related to yield (Eck 1971).

Delay application until the vines have started rooting and shoot growth begins in the first fruiting year. Light applications of fertilizer in July and August encourage vine growth. Use a total of 56 to 168 kg per ha (50 to 150 lb per acre) of N fertilizer each year until fruit production begins. Divide this into several applications of 16.8 to 33.6 kg per ha (15 to 30 lb per acre) every 2 to 3 weeks (Dana and Klingbeil 1966).

Split applications provide readily available N for early-season growth and development, as well as the other nutrients and some additional N after the time of most frequent frost flooding.

Effect on Uprights.—In Wisconsin, cranberry plants reach top productivity when the new growth on uprights is 6.4 to 8.9 cm (2½ to 3½ in.) long. A population of 200 to 300 uprights per 0.1 m² (1 ft²) seems best (Dana and Klingbeil 1966).

Urea and Urea-formaldehyde.—Urea and urea-formaldehyde are slowly available forms of synthetic organic N. As a source of N they may be beneficial in sandy bogs which are subjected to rapid leaching of quickly soluble forms of N. They may also be effective in soils containing 4% organic matter.

Phosphorus (P)

Acid organic soils are low in available P and may be improved by use of this element. P stress causes a general restriction of growth, pinkish red and purplish leaves, and is associated with low tissue P concentration. P concentration for severe deficiency ranges from 0.034 to 0.08%, hidden hunger from 0.09 to 0.11%, and sufficiency from 0.12 to 0.27%. P removed from nutrient solutions is recovered in the plants (Greidanus and Dana 1972).

One recommendation is to add 56 to 112 kg per ha (50 to 100 lb per acre) of available P. Use a soil test to determine initial P level and the required rate.

Potassium (K)

K is seldom a limiting factor with cranberries. Desirable tissue level is 0.34 to 0.40% K. Fruit of the cranberry may serve as a K bank. Fruit K is nearly three times as great as leaf K. Movement of K

from vegetative parts to the fruit may explain in part the low K value
of the leaf (Torio and Eck 1969).

Minor Elements

In British Columbia desirable tissue levels are as follows: Ca 0.60 to
0.70%; Mg 0.27 to 0.31%, and probably higher; Fe, probably below 50
ppm; Mn, below 150 ppm. Since Fe levels above 50 ppm and Mn levels
above 150 ppm are often found in cranberry, luxury consumption of
these levels may be more important in cranberry nutrition than has
previously been supposed. Tissue Ca and Mn are decreased by N and
P applications. N, P, and K tend to decrease tissue Mg (Eaton and
Meehan 1973).

NPK

In bearing bogs, increased tissue N, P, and K results from increased
applications of the respective elements, and these nutrients are positively correlated with one another. Applied N increases yield, yellowness, lightness, and decreases fruit redness. Tissue P is positively
associated with fruit yields, yellowness, and lightness, but negatively
with redness. Effects of both N and P are modified by K application
(Eaton 1971).

PRUNING

After harvest or in early spring, cut off (by hand or machine) runners that have been pulled up during harvesting. This operation thins
out runners and uprights and tends to stimulate growth of vigorous
new shoots.

WEATHER RELATIONS

Important causes of poor condition in Massachusetts as the berries
come from the bogs are as follows:

Putrefactive Fungi.—High temperatures and abundant moisture
in March (when most bogs are completely flooded and there is some
ice on the water early in the month) may cause an early development
of cranberry fungi on nearby uplands. Advancement of cranberry
growth by high spring temperatures, which lengthen the period of
fungi infection of the new growth, may also be a factor.

February sun aids in maintaining O_2 sufficiency in bog waters toward
the end of winter. March sun tends to reduce moisture from rains by
increasing evaporation.

Heat, Sun, and Drought.—On many bogs, retain the winter flood for much of May. The O_2 demand of flooded vines is greater than that earlier because of higher temperatures. Sun contributes to a high O_2 content in the water. On bogs where the winter flood has been withdrawn earlier, sun helps build up reserves for the next year's growth.

More than normal sun in August, September, and November of the year before the crop is related to the accumulation of carbohydrates that help the vines withstand the rigors of winter and provide the necessary supplies for new growth, flowering, and fruiting the next year. Harvesting operations may account for lack of relation between the sun of October and yield. Disturbed vines are exposed to drying weather, the leaves lose their orientation to the sun's rays, and the roots are injured; thus water rather than sun becomes the limiting factor.

Reduced winter sun results in O_2 deficiency in the flood waters, and this in turn affects the vines. Leaf drop and loss of flower buds occur and tend to reduce the crop. Scant sun in February reduces the crop by forcing the vines to draw on their carbohydrate reserves. A large crop in Massachusetts seldom follows a February with less than 150 hr of sun.

In May, when vine growth is active, do not prolong the flood. Flood waters reduce the intensity of sun reaching the vines and restrict the amount of O_2 available for respiration. Similar considerations apply to August, September, and November, when the sun helps build reserves for winter and the following year.

Withdraw the flood during February if heavy snow cover or lack of normal sun reduce the O_2 content of the water. But before doing this consider the possibility of replacing the flood when the snow and ice cover melts, the possible increase in fruitworm infestation, and the probable lessening of the spring frost hazard, since vines exposed to winter cold develop more slowly in spring than vines protected by flood water all winter.

Temperature, Rain, and Yield.—Low temperatures in March, July, September, and October of the crop year favor a good yield. High temperatures in May tend to increase the crop. May temperatures are more directly related to size of crop than are those of March.

Rainfall in October of the year preceding the crop is important to the crop of the following year. Rainfall in July is especially important; too little is favorable to the crop of the next year and too much is unfavorable. Drought in the growing season, May to August inclusive, reduces the current crop.

Sun, Temperature, Rain, and Berry Size.—The more sun in March, April, June, September, and October of the preceding year, the smaller the berries. In January of the crop year most bogs are flooded and the vines are relatively dormant. Reduced sun in January often induces an O_2 deficiency in the winter flood water; the carbohydrate reserves are diminished in the vines and small berries characterize the following crop. Normal sun maintains enough O_2 in the flooded waters and merely preserves the stored carbohydrates with little chance of adding to them.

Low temperatures in June of the year before the crop, high temperatures in March and April, and an early start in the growing season favor development of large berries. In the crop year, rainfall of July and August is the most important in development of large berries.

WEEDS AND THEIR CONTROL

Weed-control methods consist of hand-pulling, mowing, and chemical treatments. Weeds generally are most troublesome during the first 2 to 3 years after planting. The young cranberry plant is a poor competitor against weeds.

Weeds infesting cranberry plantings include mosses, ferns, horsetail, sedges and rushes, grasses (perennial and annual), and broadleafs (herbaceous, perennial, annual, woody). The worst weed in Wisconsin marshes is creeping sedge. It is tolerant of oil and dichlorobenzil and has survived where many other species have been removed. Some commonly used herbicides besides the above are Moncran, Alachlor, iron sulfate, and Stoddard Solvent.

HARVESTING AND MARKETING

Under favorable conditions a bog may produce about half a crop the third year. It should be in full production 4 to 5 years after planting.

FIG. 6.3. A SELF-PROPELLED ROTARY BLADE CLIPPER TO CUT WEEDS ABOVE THE TOPS OF CRANBERRY VINES

Courtesy of M. N. Dana, University of Wisconsin

In Massachusetts, harvesting usually begins soon after Labor Day (in early seasons, late in August; in late seasons, the second week of September). It continues until about October 20. Because the cranberry area in New Jersey is south of the Cape Cod area, it might be thought that harvesting would be earlier in New Jersey. But cranberries are marketed from Cape Cod as early as from any other region. Acreage of early cultivars is larger in Massachusetts than in New Jersey and, in the latter region, the winter flood is held later, thus delaying maturity.

In Wisconsin, harvesting usually begins about September 10 with early cultivars, and continues into October with Howes and McFarlin. The use of mechanical pickers makes it possible for many growers to delay the start of harvest until October 1.

Bogs or marshes producing the first or second crops may be harvested 10 days before older bogs. Harvesting may continue as late as Thanksgiving if labor is scarce or unfavorable weather prevails.

Harvest cranberries, except when water-raked, only when the vines are dry. A frosty night may compel the flooding of unpicked areas, and usually little harvesting can be done the next day.

Hand-picking

This method, or one involving the use of "snaps," is commonly used in young fields where the roots are easily torn up. In established bogs, if 1057 kiloliters (30,000 bu) are to be picked by October 20, or in 40 working days, 26 kiloliters (750 bu) must be picked daily; if the pickers average 82 to 109 kg (3 to 4 bu), 200 to 250 pickers would be needed.

Scooping

A cranberry scoop (commonly made of wood) has teeth so arranged that the operator can comb through the vines with a rocking motion, taking off and catching the berries in a box-like compartment behind the teeth. The Wisconsin rake differs from the eastern scoop in having a long handle. An adult can harvest 163 to 544 kg (6 to 20 bu) a day with a scoop. In Massachusetts a foreman, 25 scoopers, and 3 helpers can harvest a 0.4 ha (1 acre) bog.

Scooping the vines in one direction year after year tends to draw them uniformly, decrease damage, and speed the harvesting. In Massachusetts after harvest, rake the vines hard, in the direction opposite to that in which they were scooped, with hand hay rakes. The raking clears the bog of the loose vines torn up by the scoops and trains the vines for scooping the next year.

Courtesy of M. N. Dana, University of Wisconsin

FIG. 6.4.   SELF-PROPELLED GETSINGER RETRACTO-TOOTH PICKER

Machine-harvesting in the East (Dry)

The Case and Getsinger self-propelled picking machines are used in the East, but not in Wisconsin. In the Getsinger Retracto-tooth picker, a steel drum rotates and the offset teeth comb through the vines, pulling the berries free and dropping them on an inclined elevator belt. In the Case picker, the fixed teeth pull the berries from the vines and the chain-driven paddles pull the free berries onto the conveyor belt.

The suction picker operates like a vacuum cleaner. Air rushing into the nozzle, or 10.2 cm (4 in.) hose, carries berries along with it and drops them into a rubber-lined hopper. This picker disturbs the vines little and leaves few berries on the ground.

Harvesting "On the Flood"

In Wisconsin, a section ready to harvest is covered with 15.2 to 25.4 cm (6 to 10 in.) of water (enough to reach about to the top of the vines). A machine lifts the unharvested berries so they can be removed.

One type of machine has a series of teeth, which catch the berries but allow the vines to pass through. The berries are pulled from the vines and are transferred to containers for transport.

Another type of machine, the eggbeater, knocks the berries from the vines with a rotating reel. The loose berries are then floated to a corner of the flooded section where a portable elevator (conveyor) lifts them into trucks.

Machine-harvested berries are transferred directly into field boxes which hold ⅓ barrel, or into large metal or fiberglass boats which

Courtesy of M. N. Dana, University of Wisconsin

FIG. 6.5.   SELF-PROPELLED CASE PICKER

FIG. 6.6.   HYDRAULICALLY POWERED EQUIPMENT USED TO LIFT THE BOATS
OF HARVESTED BERRIES FROM THE MARSH SECTION FOR TRANSFER TO
THE WAREHOUSE

hold 10 bbl or more. The boats are attached to the picker and are towed to the end of the section. From there they are lifted onto trucks by hydraulic hoists. The filled boxes are either dumped into trucks in the field or hauled to the warehouse and dumped.

STORAGE

Λ considerable part of the cranberry crop is held each year in common or refrigerated storage for the holidays. Cranberries can be held as fresh fruit for 2 to 3 months at 3.3°C (38°F); thereafter the berries may shrivel as a result of water loss, discolor, lose their natural luster, and become soft and rubbery. Cranberries are seldom available in the market 2 months after harvest because of physiological or pathological decay.

The fruit is dried before storing. If it is taken to a warm room (different in humidity), water condenses on the shiny skins. Such fruit keeps poorly.

"On the flood"-harvested berries are wet and often mixed with weeds and vine fragments. Until 1950, stacked crates of fruit were wind-dried. Mechanical drying was then developed in which heated air (29.4° to

FIG. 6.7.   GRAVITY FLOW DRYER FOR REMOVAL OF SURFACE MOISTURE
FROM HARVESTED FRUIT

Small berries are screened as the fruit comes off the dryer.

32.2°C, or 85° to 90°F) is forced through a layer of moving berries, which are fan-cooled and then transferred to a warehouse.

The berries are usually held in common storage with supplementary fans to blow in cool air, or heated to avoid freezing until marketed. Occasional lots of poorly colored fruit may be held at 7.2° to 10°C (45° to 50°F) for a few weeks to permit more rapid coloring than would occur at lower temperatures. After more than four months at 2.2° to 4.4°C (36° to 40°F), end rot causes the berries to shrink owing to loss of water.

Sorting

The fruit is machine-graded by "mills." It enters the top of the mill and falls down over a series of slanted bounce boards. A good berry strikes the board and bounces over a barrier and onto a sorting belt. A soft berry fails to bounce over the barrier and continues down the mill to the "slush" pile. Firm berries move to a sorting table where workers pick out those that are green, badly shaped, or decayed.

Packing

From the sorting table, the fruit moves by conveyor belt to packing machines. Fruit for fresh market is packed in plastic film bags or window boxes holding 0.45 kg (1 lb) or more. Fruit for processing is packed in 22.7 kg (50 lb) paper sacks or in bulk boxes that hold several barrels.

WEATHER INFLUENCE

Three weather elements that influence the size of cranberries in Massachusetts also affect the keeping quality: (1) the amount of sun the year before the crop year—the more sun, the larger the berries but the poorer their keeping quality; (2) the sun and mean temperature of March of the crop year—the more sun and the lower the mean temperature, the smaller and sounder the berries; (3) the amount of rain in July and August of the crop year—the more rain, the larger the berries but the poorer their keeping quality.

Berries picked when they have a temperature of 28°C (82°F) and stored at this temperature keep only half as long as those picked earlier in the day, when their temperature is 18°C (64°F), and stored at this temperature. Decay fungi grow faster at the higher temperature.

With late Howes berries none of the controlled-storage atmospheres (CA), which range from 0 to 10% O_2 and 1 to 20% CO_2, offer commercial possibilities for increasing storage life. Fruit stored in sealed 1.5-mil polyethylene liners decayed more than controls (Anderson *et al.* 1963).

Respiration

Respiratory measurements were made on developing McFarlin fruits harvested at intervals from 3 to 14 weeks after full bloom. Fruit of optimum maturity was harvested 11 weeks after full bloom, and commercially mature fruit at 13 weeks. Respiration rates were followed for 27 days at 20°C (68°F), as well as the rate of breakdown during 25 weeks of storage at 2.2°C (36°F). Respiration rates and percentage breakdown were less on fruits harvested at 11 weeks past full bloom than on fruits harvested at commercial maturity 13 weeks after full bloom. The chief cause of deterioration in storage was physiological breakdown (Doughty *et al.* 1967).

Softening results from endogenous enzymatic degradation of pectic substances in the cell walls, leading to loss of structural integrity and physiological softening (Patterson *et al.* 1967).

Breakdown.—Berries stored for a month or more may undergo physiological breakdown. At temperatures above freezing (especially above 10°C, or 50°F) the fruit may show sterile breakdown, whereas that stored just below freezing (−1° to 0°C, or 30° to 32°F) may show much low-temperature breakdown. Berries with sterile breakdown are soft and withered. Those suffering low-temperature breakdown are rubbery, somewhat light in color, and lack normal luster; pigmentation of the epidermis is diffused into the pulp. Besides control of temperature, control of humidity during storage and provision for adequate ventilation are also important in reducing breakdown.

Occasional lots of poorly colored fruit may be held at 7.2° to 10°C (45° to 50°F) for a few weeks to permit more rapid coloring than would occur at lower temperature. Keeping quality is affected by maturity of the fruit and the cultivar, and may vary from one year to another in crops from the same bog.

Cranberries for long storage in Massachusetts have been held "in the chaff" in the picking crates. Cleaned and sorted berries can be stored at the market in crates or bags or in prepackaged ventilated consumer units for 2 to 3 weeks at 0°C (32°F), but if held longer at that temperature they may break down.

COLOR

A primary factor in the popularity of cranberries is the attractive red color, which is due to the development of anthocyanin pigments in the vacuoles composing the epidermis of the berry. However, the necessity for dark, uniformly colored berries has created problems for both the industry and the grower. In order to circumvent the cost and inconvenience of frost protection, the grower is inclined to harvest his crop at an early date. At the same time is he aware that early-harvested berries seldom reach the desired color standards set by the industry for cocktail-quality fruit or for fresh fruit sold on the market. Color is important to the grower, since a premium is paid for cocktail and fresh fruit-quality berries. About 50% of the cranberry crop is used for production of cocktail juices. To produce high-quality juice cocktail without artificial color it is necessary to use a fully colored raw product.

With Early Black, a short delay in harvest considerably increases the quantity of cocktail-quality fruit for immediate handling when delivered to the processing plant. Cocktail-quality berries contain a minimum of 0.670 mg anthocyanin per gram of fresh fruit. Anthocyanin development proceeds much more rapidly in berries left on the vine than in berries held in common storage for the same period of time (Devlin *et al.* 1969).

Malathion enhances color development in the berries, and is most efficient when applied as a drench so as to affect all the berries. Low-volume surface sprays may color only the upper layer of the fruit. This material, however, may result in phytotoxicity when applied to actively growing cranberry plants.

Ethephon (Ethrel) applied as a spray, 1.1 kg per ha (1 lb per acre) of active material 2 weeks before harvest, increases anthocyanin development (Eck 1972). Ethephon probably does not increase the potential for red color development, but triggers the process prematurely, i.e., treatment of immature berries causes red color development, but treatment of fully red berries does not. Mature, green berries that are deep in the foliage and away from light exposure color in response to Ethephon. The greatest benefit from Ethephon may be the uniform coloring of all the fruit in a field rather than increase of pigment beyond the natural potential of a fruit. Ethephon probably does not result in more rapid breakdown of the berries during storage. Only at very high percentages of Ethephon is berry size reduced (Rigby *et al.* 1972).

Ethylene treatment of field-harvested cranberries may promote red color development in the fruit when treated with ethylene in the light, thus allowing earlier harvest (Craker 1971).

DISEASES

Red leaf spot infections produce red spots 3 mm (⅛ in.) in diameter on the upper side of the leaves. The fungus spores grow on the underside.

Rose bloom-infected plants develop early dormant buds along the stem. These buds develop shoots with rose-colored foliage that is bunched, twisted, and flower-like.

False blossom, caused by a virus, promotes malformed flowers, which point upward instead of the normal downward, and the petals are usually red. There is a witches-broom effect. The disease is spread by the blunt-nosed leafhopper.

The following rots may occur in storage:

End rot is a soft watery type. Accompanying gases may swell the fruits, which may rupture with a popping noise. The berries eventually collapse and shrink or dry; losses may reach 30% or more. End rot is common in the East. It seldom decays fruit in the field in Wisconsin, but may speckle or spot berries. However, berries stored at above 16°C (60°F) will often decay later, due to activity of the fungus.

Black rot is a firm dry rot that causes jet black rotted berries, which shrink to miniature "prunes" and eventually mummify or harden. Spore-producing bumps or pustules may cover much of the berry.

Fruit rot is a sticky rot. The berries are pale tan to yellow mottled, with syrup inside. The syrup may string out an inch or more from freshly cut berries.

Other rots include *hard rot, blotch rot, bitter rot,* and *ripe rot.*

Insects

Black-headed fireworm overwinters as a small, brownish-yellow egg on the underside of the leaf near the base of an upright. The larvae migrate to the tip of uprights, cause the leaves to turn brown, and may make the planting look as though a fire had swept through.

Cranberry fruitworm migrates from the blossom end to the stem end of the berries, where it bores into the seed cavity and consumes developing seeds. Damaged berries turn prematurely red, and have a web-covered entrance hole and an exit hole.

Sparganothis fruitworm larvae (bright yellow head and yellow-green body) feed on terminal growth and developing berries.

Cranberry tipworm—uprights injured by the first brood usually side shoot and may form a normal fruit bud. But tips injured by the second brood do not have time to do so.

Spanworms (loopers or geometers) are leaf feeders. *Root grubs* may destroy irregular patches of vines.

REFERENCES

ANDERSON, R.G. et al. 1963. Controlled-atmosphere tests with late Howes. Proc. Am. Soc. Hort. Sci. 83, 416-22.

BRAMLAGE, W.J. et al. 1972. Effect of preharvest application of ethephon on Early Black. J. Am. Soc. Hort. Sci. 97, 625-28.

CHANDLER, F.B., and DEMORANVILLE, I. 1958. Cranberry varieties in North America. Mass. Agr. Expt. Sta. Bull. 513.

CHIRIBOGA, C., and FRANCIS, F.J. 1970. An anthocyanin recovery system from cranberry pomace. J. Am. Soc. Hort. Sci. 95, 233-36.

CRAKER, L.E. 1971. Postharvest color promotion in cranberry with ethylene. HortScience 6, 137-39.

DANA, M.N., and KLINGBEIL, G.C. 1966. Cranberry growing in Wisconsin. Univ. of Wisc. Coll. Agr. Circ. 654.

DEVLIN, R.M. 1968. Effect of delayed harvest and storage on pigment development in cranberries. Proc. Am. Soc. Hort. Sci. 92, 793-96.

DEVLIN, R.M., and DEMORANVILLE, I.E. 1971. Tolerance of cranberry to alachlor and two fluorinated pyridizinone herbicides. HortScience 6, 245.

DEVLIN, R.M. et al. 1969. Influence of preharvest applications of malathion and indole-3-acetic acid on anthocyanin development of Vaccinium macrocarpon var. Early Black. J. Am. Soc. Hort. Sci. 93, 52.

DOUGHTY, C.C. et al. 1967. Storage longevity of McFarlin cranberry, as influenced by certain growth retardants and stage of maturity. Proc. Am. Soc. Hort. Sci. 91, 192-204.

EADY, F.C., and EATON, G.W. 1972. Effects of chilling during dormancy on development of the terminal bud of the cranberry. Can. J. Plant Sci. 52, 273-79.

EATON, G.W. 1971. Effect of NPK fertilizers on growth and composition of vines in a young cranberry bog. J. Am. Soc. Hort. Sci. 96, 426-29.

EATON, G.W., and MEEHAN, C.N. 1973. Effect of N, P, and K fertilizer on leaf composition, yield, and fruit quality of bearing Ben Lear cranberries. J. Am. Soc. Hort. Sci. 98, 89-93.

EATON, G.W. et al. 1969. Effect of preharvest sprays on cranberry fruit color. J. Am. Soc. Hort. Sci. 94, 590-95.

ECK, P. 1971. Cranberry growth and composition as influenced by nitrogen treatment. HortScience 6, 38-39.

ECK, P. 1972. Cranberry yield and anthocyanin content as influenced by ethephon, SADH, and malathion. J. Am. Soc. Hort. Sci. 97, 213-14.

ECK, P. 1976. Relationship of nitrogen nutrition of Early Black cranberry to vegetative growth, fruit yield, and quality. Am. Soc. Hort. Sci. 101, No. 4, 375-77.

GREIDANUS, T., and DANA, M.N. 1972. Cranberry growth related to tissue concentration and soil test phosphorus. J. Am. Soc. Hort. Sci. 97, 326-28.

GREIDANUS, T. et al. 1972. Essentiality of ammonium for cranberry nutrition. J. Am. Soc. Hort Sci. 97, 272-77.

HALL, I. 1966. Growing cranberries. Canada Dept. Agr. Publ. 1282.

LEES, D.H., and FRANCIS, F.J. 1972A. Effect of gamma radiation on anthocyanin and flavonal pigments in cranberries. J. Am. Soc. Hort. Sci. 97, 128-32.

LEES, D.H., and FRANCIS, F.J. 1972B. Standardization of pigment analyses in cranberries. HortScience 7, 83-84.

LESCHYSON, M.A., and EATON, G.W. 1971. Effect of urea and nitrate nitrogen on growth and composition of cranberry vines. J. Am. Soc. Hort. Sci. *96*, 597-99.

MEDAPPA, K.C., and DANA, M.N. 1970. Influence of pH, Ca, P, and Fe on growth and composition of cranberry plant. Soil Science *109*, 250-53.

PATTERSON, M.E. *et al.* 1967. Effect of bruising on postharvest softening, color changes, and detection of polygalacturonase enzyme in cranberries. Proc. Am. Soc. Hort. Sci. *90*, 590-95.

PETERSON, B.S. 1968. Cranberry industry. Mass. Dept. Agr. Bull. *201*.

RIGBY, B., and DANA, M.N. 1971. Seed number and berry volume in cranberry. HortScience *6*, 495-6.

RIGBY, B., and DANA, M.N. 1972A. Flower opening, pollen shedding, stigma receptivity, and pollen tube growth in the cranberry. HortScience *7*, 84-85.

RIGBY, B., and DANA, M.N. 1972B. Rest period and flower development in cranberry. J. Am. Soc. Hort. Sci. *97*, 145-48.

RIGBY, B. *et al.* 1972. Ethephon sprays and cranberry fruit color. HortScience *7*, 82-83.

ROBERTS, R.H., and STRUCKMEYER, B.E. 1942. Blossom induction of cranberry. Plant Physiol. *18*, 534-36.

SHAWA, A.Y. 1973. Prolonging the life of harvested McFarlin cranberries. J. Am. Soc. Hort. Sci. *98*, 212-14.

SHAWA, A.Y., and INGOLDSBE, D.W. 1968. Anthocyanin enhancement in McFarlin cranberries at optimum maturity. Proc. Am. Soc. Hort. Sci. *93*, 289-92.

SHAWA, A.Y. *et al.* 1966. Effect of fungicides on McFarlin pollen germination and fruit set. Proc. Am. Soc. Hort. Sci. *89*, 498-505.

SHIMANUKI, H. *et al.* 1967. Differential collection of cranberry pollen by honeybees. J. Econ. Ent. 1031-33.

SOMAGYI, L.F. *et al.* 1964. Influence of nitrogen source and soil organic matter on the cranberry. Proc. Am. Soc. Hort. Sci. *84*, 280-88.

TORIO, J.C., and ECK, P. 1969. Nitrogen, phosphorus, and sulfur nutrition on cranberries in sand culture. Proc. Am. Soc. Hort. Sci. *94*, 622-25.

Index

Related AVI Books

BEES, BEEKEEPING, HONEY AND POLLINATION
   Gojmerac
FUNDAMENTALS OF ENTOMOLOGY & PLANT PATHOLOGY
   2nd Edition   *Pyenson*
HANDLING, TRANSPORTATION AND STORAGE OF FRUITS AND
VEGETABLES, VOL. 1
   2nd Edition, Vegetables and Melons   *Ryall and Lipton*
HANDLING, TRANSPORTATION AND STORAGE OF FRUITS AND
VEGETABLES, VOL. 2
   2nd Edition, Fruits and Tree Nuts   *Ryall and Pentzer*
HORTICULTURAL REVIEWS, VOLS. 1–5
   Janick
LAB MANUAL FOR ENTOMOLOGY & PLANT PATHOLOGY, 2nd Edition
   Pyenson and Barke
PLANT DISEASE CONTROL
   Sharvelle
PLANT BREEDING REVIEWS, VOL. 1
   Janick
PLANT HEALTH HANDBOOK
   Pyenson
PLANT PROPAGATION AND CULTIVATION
   Hutchinson
POSTHARVEST: AN INTRODUCTION TO THE PHYSIOLOGY AND
HANDLING OF FRUITS & VEGETABLES
   Wills et al.
SOIL, WATER AND CROP PRODUCTION
   Thorne and Thorne
TREE FRUIT PRODUCTION, 3rd Edition
   Teskey et al.
TREE NUTS, 2nd Edition
   Woodroof
TROPICAL & SUBTROPICAL FRUIT
   Nagy and Shaw
VEGETABLE CROP DISEASE
   Dixon